Changing Church

Changing Church
Stories of Liberating Ministers

JANN ALDREDGE-CLANTON

CASCADE *Books* • Eugene, Oregon

CHANGING CHURCH
Stories of Liberating Ministers

Copyright © 2011 Jann Aldredge-Clanton. All rights reserved. Except for brief quotations in critical publications or reviews, no part of this book may be reproduced in any manner without prior written permission from the publisher. Write: Permissions, Wipf and Stock Publishers, 199 W. 8th Ave., Suite 3, Eugene, OR 97401.

Cascade Books
An Imprint of Wipf and Stock Publishers
199 W. 8th Ave., Suite 3
Eugene, OR 97401

www.wipfandstock.com

ISBN 13: 978-1-61097-451-6

Scripture quotations are taken from the New Revised Standard Version Bible, unless otherwise indicated, copyright 1989, Division of Christian Education of the National Council of the Churches of Christ in the United States of America. Used by permission. All rights reserved.

Scripture quotations identified KJV are taken from the King James Version.

Cataloging-in-Publication data:

Aldredge-Clanton, Jann

  Changing church : stories of liberating ministries / Jann Aldredge-Clanton.

  p. ; 23 cm. —Includes bibliographical references.

  ISBN 13: 978-1-61097-451-6

  1. FEMININTY OF GOD. 2. Women and religion. 3. God—Attributes. 4. Sexism—Religious aspects-Christianity. I. Title.

BT153 M6 A43 2011

Manufactured in the U.S.A.

Contents

Acknowledgments / vii
Introduction / ix

1 Rev. Stacy Boorn, Pastor,
   Ebenezer/herchurch Lutheran, San Francisco, California / 1

2 Rev. Dr. Susan Newman, United Church of Christ Pastor,
   Associate Minister for Congregational Life and Social Justice,
   All Souls Church, Washington, DC / 29

3 Dr. Bridget Mary Meehan, Priest,
   Mary Mother of Jesus Catholic Community, Sarasota, Florida,
   Bishop, Association of Roman Catholic Women Priests / 57

4 Rev. Dr. Isabel Docampo, American Baptist Pastor,
   Associate Professor of Supervised Ministry, Perkins School of
   Theology, Dallas, Texas / 85

5 Rev. Larry E. Schultz, Minister of Music,
   Pullen Memorial Baptist Church, Raleigh, North Carolina / 111

6 Rev. Dr. Monica A. Coleman, African Methodist Episcopal Minister,
   Associate Professor of Constructive Theology and African American
   Religions, Claremont School of Theology,
   Claremont, California / 139

7 Rev. Marcia C. Fleischman, Copastor,
   Broadway Church, Kansas City, Missouri / 167

8 Rev. Virginia Marie Rincon, Priest,
   Hispanic Missioner for the Episcopal Diocese of Maine,
   Founder and Executive Director of TengoVoz, Portland,
   Maine / 193

9 Rev. Paul Smith, Copastor,
   Broadway Church, Kansas City, Missouri / 221

10 Rev. Judith Liro, Priest, St. Hildegard's Community,
   St. George's Episcopal Church, Austin, Texas / 247

11 Rev. Dr. Rebecca L. Kiser, Pastor,
   First Presbyterian Church, West Plains, Missouri / 275

12 Rev. Dr. Nancy Petty, Pastor,
   Pullen Memorial Baptist Church, Raleigh, North Carolina / 303

Conclusion / 331
Notes / 347

Acknowledgments

My deepest gratitude goes to the twelve "liberating ministers" who gave generously of their time and talents in telling me their stories. They blessed and inspired me with their gifts of wisdom, vision, courage, and hope. My appreciation also goes to the faith communities who have supported their ministries, including their participation in this book project.

For the support of my husband, David, through the whole process of writing this book, I am deeply grateful. I especially appreciate his expert work on the photos.

My appreciation also goes to Dr. Christopher Spinks for his outstanding editorial work and encouragement, and to others at Wipf and Stock Publishers: Raydeen Cuffe, Ian Creeger, Nathan Rhoads, Matthew Stock, and James Stock. They have been responsive and talented publishing partners.

Introduction

If there's a book you really want to read but it hasn't been written yet, then you must write it. —Toni Morrison[1]

For more than 20 years I have researched, preached, taught, and written books to persuade people that we need to include biblical Divine Feminine images in worship if we are to have social justice and equality. There are other people who have been advocating for inclusive worship even longer. How much difference has all this researching, preaching, teaching, writing, and advocating made? The book I wanted to read would help answer this question. Since I find stories more compelling than statistics, I wanted to read stories of ministers who have understood the importance of including the Divine Feminine in worship and who have changed the church through this inclusion. This is a book I really wanted to read, and I couldn't find it. Following Nobel Prize–winning author Toni Morrison's wisdom, I then realized that "I must write it."

This book comes from my location within the Christian tradition with the hope that people in other religious traditions will write stories of transformation through inclusion of the Divine Feminine. More specifically, I am an ordained Anglo minister within the Baptist tradition, growing up in Louisiana and working in Texas. I have served mainly in ecumenical and interfaith settings as a chaplain, interfaith conference director, pastoral counselor, teacher, and speaker. The stories of the ministers in this book come from my interviews with them and from my experiences of visiting their churches.

In 1976, when I was teaching English literature at Dallas Baptist University, the call to gender justice came to me through a book my husband, David, gave me, *All We're Meant to Be*, by Letha Dawson Scanzoni and Nancy A. Hardesty.[2] Before then, I had never questioned the traditional biblical interpretations that men were to be leaders in church and families. And I would have been shocked to hear God referred to as "Mother" or "She." As I read *All We're Meant to Be*, I discovered more than enough biblical support for equality of women and men in the home and the church. In addition, this book opened my mind to the notion that God might be more than male. I became an instant convert and enthusiastic evangelist for these new truths of gender equality.

A few years later I discovered *Women and Worship*, by a United Methodist clergy couple, Sharon Neufer Emswiler and Thomas Neufer Emswiler.[3] *Women and Worship* was one of the first books not only to challenge sexist worship language, but also to provide inclusive language resources. This book further convinced me of the importance of inclusive language for divinity, as well as humanity. For many years I didn't notice that the "liberated prayers, affirmations, and responses" in the book include few female divine names. But the authors take that important first step in eliminating exclusively masculine pronoun references to Deity. Then I began to devour other books on inclusive theology and worship, such as Virginia Ramey Mollenkott's *The Divine Feminine: The Biblical Imagery of God as Female*,[4] Jean Shinoda Bolen's *Goddesses in Everywoman: A New Psychology of Women*,[5] Rosemary Radford Ruether's *Sexism and God-Talk: Toward a Feminist Theology*,[6] Elisabeth Schussler Fiorenza's *In Memory of Her: A Feminist Theological Reconstruction of Christian Origins*,[7] and Miriam Therese Winter's *WomanPrayer, WomanSong*.[8] I found compelling biblical, historical, and psychological support for the inclusion of female divine names and images in worship as crucial to social justice. I began to balance male with female by referring to God as "She," by including Sophia with Christ in the designation "Christ-Sophia,"[9] and by including other biblical female metaphors. I saw the truth of Mary Kathleen Speegle Schmitt's words in *Seasons of the Feminine Divine*: "Until the feminine is revalued and women are seen as valuable in the image of the Divine, we are left with an imbalance of understanding of the godhead, and justice for women is still lacking. Neutral names or images for the Divine would be heard as masculine, and women would still be viewed in the image of the Divine in some secondary kind of way."[10]

Changing Church is a book of stories of ministers who include female divine names and images in worship so that females are seen as valuable in the image of the Divine. One of these ministers, Rev. Stacy Boorn, pastor of Ebenezer/herchurch Lutheran in San Francisco, wrote to me: "I continue to be disappointed and amazed at how many people, including women clergy, don't get it." The "it" she refers to is the importance of the Divine Feminine in worship. So I began writing this book with curiosity to know about Christian ministers who do "get it." Rev. Boorn later said to me that she knows the inclusion of the Divine Feminine in worship must be happening in many places, but she's not aware of them. I hope that these stories will increase awareness and help bring these ministers together for encouragement and for the increase of their power to bring change in church and society. I wrote this book because I also wanted increased awareness and encouragement through the stories of these liberating ministers. I wanted to know the people and experiences that influenced them on their journey. Why do they believe language and symbolism are important enough to go to all the effort to change two thousand years of church tradition? How have they tried to bring theology inclusive of the Divine Feminine to the church? In what ways do they think including the Divine Feminine will change the church and the wider culture? What risks have they taken in trying to liberate the language and symbolism of the church? What resistance to the Divine Feminine have they met within the church? Why have they stayed within the church, and have they ever considered leaving? I wanted to read about their struggles, their challenges, and their victories. I was curious about what helps them through the criticism and the setbacks. Where do they get their inspiration and strength in the midst of discouragement? What rewarding experiences have they had?

Just as the Civil Rights Movement needed people within the church, like Martin Luther King Jr., and people outside the church, like Malcolm X, so does the feminist movement. Roman Catholic sister Miriam Therese Winter, Episcopal laywoman Adair Lummis, and United Church of Christ pastor Allison Stokes wrote a book called *Defecting in Place*, exploring the relationship of feminist women to the institutional church and reporting findings from a national survey of thousands of women who have felt alienated in the patriarchal church but who have stayed within it to try to bring change.[11] Working from within to liberate the church can be daunting. Finding the balance between pushing for change and supporting the institution creates tension and conflict. The advantage of working from within may be the credibility that comes from being an "insider," but that status also carries with it the risk of spending more energy trying to sustain the institution than trying to change it. I wrote *Changing Church* because I wanted to read stories of ministers in the midst of this conflict.

For this book I have chosen ordained ministers not because I believe they are more important to the church than laypeople, but because they have the most to lose in advocating for change within the institutional church. In working from within to change the church, ministers risk sanction by denominational authorities, loss of opportunities for promotion to larger congregations or to prestigious denominational jobs, and often even loss of their jobs. In addition, since ordained ministers depend upon the institutional church for their livelihood, their incentive for bringing much change to the church may be small. If they work for revolution on too grand a scale, what form will the church take? Will it still be able to support them? If not, what will they do since they have spent large amounts of time and money on the education necessary to become a minister? Where will they go, and what will they do to live out their call as ministers?

Finding the ministers to interview for this book proved challenging. Even ministers who believe in the importance of including the Divine Feminine in worship may feel that they cannot do so because of strong resistance from their church members and/or censure from denomination officials. Several ministers I approached expressed appreciation and encouragement for the project, but declined to be interviewed for fear of censure or loss of their jobs. One minister I contacted after I read online her powerful liturgy with the image of God as "Mother" responded that she would like to help with the book, but that she feared for her job because her husband had been fired from his pastoral position because of the controversy her liturgy had stirred within their denomination.

So how would I find ministers from a diversity of denominations and cultures who included the Divine Feminine in worship and who were willing to be interviewed? In the beginning this felt like a daunting task. About the time I began this research, I read the book *Grandmothers Counsel the World*, by Carol Schaefer. The Appendix includes the story of Jyoti (Jeneane Prevatt), who initiated the Grandmothers Council, out of which the book developed. Jyoti had a vision of the Council, but felt overwhelmed and uncertain about how to bring it about. "How was she to find the Grandmothers, and how would she know if she had the right ones?" She prayed for direction, and this answer came: "At the seed of all things are relations. Start there and everything else will grow."[12]

This answer also gave me guidance for finding the liberating ministers to include in this book. I would pray for Sophia Wisdom to lead me to the ministers, and I would begin with relationships. Rev. Stacy Boorn and I had become friends at the annual Faith and Feminism/Womanist/Mujerista Conferences, sponsored by the church she pastored, so I started with her. Then I contacted Rev. Dr. Isabel Docampo, who had become a friend through Baptist Women in Ministry and Alliance of Baptists and a colleague through the internship program at Perkins School of Theology. Rev. Larry E. Schultz and I had become friends through our collaboration on a hymnal and a children's musical that included female divine names, and our friendship led me also to the pastor he worked with, Rev. Dr. Nancy Petty. I remembered my connection with Rev. Paul Smith, whose book, *Is It Okay to Call God "Mother"?: Considering the Feminine Face of God*,[13] I had endorsed. In reconnecting with Paul, I found his copastor Rev. Marcia Fleischman, who had also written a book on Mother God.[14] Guidance came also in unexpected ways, as in my reading an article in the *Dallas Morning News* about Bishop Bridget Mary Meehan's leadership with Roman Catholic Women Priests, and then remembering her books on the Feminine Divine that I had on my bookshelf.[15]

Divine Wisdom also led through people who gave helpful assistance in finding a diversity of ministers. Some leaders of mainline denominations sent emails with my statement of purpose to all the ministers on their distribution lists. I received many responses with suggestions of ministers to include. I contacted these ministers and heard from some. Others did not respond or declined my invitation to be included in the book.

In my search I did not try to be exhaustive, but to find representative ministers who are changing the church through inclusion of female divine names and images. You may read these stories and think, "Why didn't she include so and so?" I hope that you do, and that you let me know of more ministers who include the Divine Feminine in their churches so that I or someone else may write their stories. Among my purposes in writing this book are to learn from as many ministers as possible and to spread the stories of these ministers to inspire others to change the church.

In addition, I wrote this book to find hope and inspiration and to give hope and inspiration to others. I wanted to record stories of ministers who are meeting challenges and transforming the church. In this book you will learn what drives these ministers to take risks to change the church through inclusion of the Divine Feminine. You will read about their passion for including female divine names and images in worship coming from their call to work for the ideals of justice, peace, and egalitarian human life, and their understanding that at the foundation of our patriarchal culture is an image of a white male God, sanctioning patterns of dominance and submission. I share their passion and belief that our language and visual symbolism for the Divine carry great power. Language and visual imagery in the majority of churches reveal worship of a white male God. The strongest support imaginable for the dominance of men is the worship of an exclusively masculine Supreme Being. Our sacred symbols reflect and shape our deepest values. Exclusively masculine divine language and symbolism devalue the feminine by ignoring it. Women receive the message that maleness, since it is used for references to the Supreme Being, is worthy of greater respect than femaleness. Divine Feminine symbolism and language are vital to the revaluing of females. Since male and female are in the divine image, as Genesis 1:27 states, then divinity includes the female, and should be spoken of and imaged as female.

Naming the Divine as "Mother," "Sister," "Sophia," "Hokmah,"[16] "Ruah,"[17] "Midwife," "She," and other female designations[18] gives sacred value to women and girls who have for centuries been excluded, ignored, discounted, even cursed and abused. I've come to understand how worship of an exclusively male Deity forms a foundation for demeaning, devaluing, and abuse of women. In the U.S. alone, every fifteen seconds a woman is battered.[19] One in three women in the world experiences some kind of abuse in her lifetime.[20] Worldwide, an estimated four million women and girls each year are bought and sold into prostitution, slavery, or marriage.[21] "More girls have been killed in the last fifty years, precisely because they were girls, than men were killed in all the battles of the twentieth century. More girls are killed in this routine 'gendercide' in any one decade than people were slaughtered in all the genocides of the twentieth century."[22] Two-thirds of the world's poor are women.[23] There are many more alarming statistics on worldwide violence and discrimination against women and girls.

Sister Joan Chittister journals her participation in the 2009 Asia Pacific Breakthrough: The Women, Faith and Development Summit to End Global Poverty, focused on changing these alarming conditions. Sister Joan writes: "While an entire generation of women and men in the United States seem to think that the woman's movement, that feminism, is over, another whole world full of women of all ages know that it is barely started. Otherwise, how to account for the fact that two-thirds of the hungry of the world are women, that two-thirds of the illiterate of the world are women, that two-thirds of the poor of the world are women. Obviously, given the number of development programs and foreign aid programs around the world, money is being given to someone for something. But obviously not to the needs and development of women. 'Breakthrough,' the Asian-Pacific conference of women is setting out to change that."[24] Sister Joan makes the connection between the Divine Feminine and progress for women. She comments on the Parliament of the World's Religions: "Panels on 'Breaking through Patriarchy' and 'The Place of the Divine Feminine' highlighted in a way that I am not accustomed to in my own Western Christian–Catholic tradition the need for religion itself to face the implications of the sin of sexism."[25]

Men as well as women suffer from the sin of sexism that has foundational support through the worship an exclusively masculine Deity. Making the Ultimate Power of the universe male gives divine sanction to the dominance of men, stifling their full emotional and spiritual development. Dehumanization results when dominance leads to violence. From patriarchal worship practices follow patterns of dominance and subordination, resulting in the interlocking oppressions of sexism, racism, heterosexism, classicism, ableism, and rape of the earth.

A little girl's letter to God illustrates the connection between naming the Divine and social justice: "Dear God, are boys better than girls? I know you're one, but try to be fair."[26] This little girl understands that boys being considered better than girls comes from the belief that the Supreme Being is male. One of the questions that led me to write this book is this: Are there children who are now growing up believing that girls and boys have equal value because they see female divine images and hear female divine language included in church?

Another reason I wrote this book is that I wanted to learn about other ministers' visions for the future of the Divine Feminine within the church and to help spread these visions in the world. Also, I wanted my vision to be rejuvenated and enlarged. My vision is for the Divine Feminine to shine forth in all Her glory in multicultural visual imagery and in the language of worship, supporting equal partnership of women and men. My vision is of a church where the Divine Feminine and women ministers don't have to be defended or marginalized, but are fully and equally included throughout every worship service and every activity of the church. My vision is for the Sacred Feminine to be worshipped not only in Christian congregations, but also in every religion all over the world, and for women to share equally in the leadership of every religion. My vision is for girls to believe they are equal to boys because they hear and see the Supreme Being worshipped as "She" as well as "He." The changes that I envision flowing from the worship of the Sacred Feminine will be profound: abuse and violence against women and girls will end because they will be given sacred value; the virtues of peacemaking and cooperation, which have been traditionally labeled feminine, will be valued by all; there will be justice and equal opportunities for all women and girls, for racial minorities, for homosexual people, for disabled people, and for other oppressed people; there will be economic justice so that all people have their needs met and share in the world's resources; all people will experience self-worth and freedom so that we can become all we are created to be in the divine image; the earth, traditionally labeled feminine, will be healed and nurtured. My vision for the future of the Divine Feminine is large, and some may think unrealistic.

But hearing the stories and experiencing the worship leadership of the liberating ministers in this book has enlarged my vision and my faith that the vision is becoming reality. As I experience ministers, surrounded by female and male multicultural sacred symbols, lifting the

Communion chalice and blessing it in the name of Christ-Sophia, my heart soars with hope. When I talk with little girls in these churches who truly believe they are equal to boys, my belief increases that including female divine names and images in worship makes a difference. When I see all the works of justice and peace that flow from these ministers who include the Divine Feminine, my faith increases that this vision is changing the church and the world.

In this book you will read the fascinating stories of Rev. Stacy Boorn, pastor of Ebenezer/herchurch Lutheran in San Francisco; Rev. Dr. Isabel Docampo, American Baptist pastor, Associate Professor of Supervised Ministry at Perkins School of Theology, Dallas, Texas; Dr. Bridget Mary Meehan, priest for Mary Mother of Jesus Catholic Community in Sarasota, Florida, Bishop, Association of Roman Catholic Women Priests; Rev. Dr. Susan Newman, United Church of Christ pastor, Associate Minister for Congregational Life and Social Justice at All Souls Church in Washington, DC; Rev. Larry E. Schultz, Minister of Music at Pullen Memorial Baptist Church in Raleigh, North Carolina; Rev. Marcia Fleischman, copastor of Broadway Church in Kansas City, Missouri; Rev. Dr. Monica Coleman, African Methodist Episcopal pastor and womanist theologian, Associate Professor of Constructive Theology and African American Religions at Claremont School of Theology, Claremont, California; Rev. Judith Liro, priest for St. Hildegard's Community, St. George's Episcopal Church in Austin, Texas; Rev. Paul Smith, copastor of Broadway Church in Kansas City, Missouri; Rev. Virginia Marie Rincon, Episcopal priest, Hispanic Missioner for the Diocese of Maine, founder and executive director of Tengo Voz; Rev. Dr. Rebecca L. Kiser, pastor of First Presbyterian Church in West Plains, Missouri; and Rev. Dr. Nancy Petty, pastor of Pullen Memorial Baptist Church in Raleigh, North Carolina.

The stories of these prophetic ministers have expanded my vision, my faith, and my hope. My prayer is that people of all faiths will also feel empowered and inspired by these stories to bring liberating change to their communities.

1

Rev. Stacy Boorn

*Pastor
Ebenezer/herchurch Lutheran,
San Francisco, California*

Pastor Stacy Boorn smiles up at me as I descend the airport escalator. I immediately recognize her from her picture on the Ebenezer/herchurch Lutheran website. Pastor Boorn bounces up to take my overnight case, as we walk together to the baggage claim area. Stacy's voice is as brisk as her steps; I find I'm having to listen and walk faster beside her. She tells me how delighted she is that I've come to San Francisco to speak at the first annual Faith and Feminism/Womanist/Mujerista Conference. I feel buoyed by her presence and her words. As we pick up my suitcase and walk toward her car, Stacy and I talk about our excitement for the conference.

The road winds up and down, overlooking San Francisco at dusk. The brilliant colors of the sunset through the fog cast a fairyland magic over the city. Interspersed with my exclamations of this beauty are my questions to Stacy about how she became a Lutheran pastor, how the Lutheran "powers that be" respond to her feminist liberationist views, and how she initiated this Conference at Ebenezer Lutheran Church.

"Not all the Lutheran authorities are exactly pleased with me," Stacy says with a playful laugh.

"How do you pull it off, especially being so visible including the Divine Feminine in the church's name and worship services?" I ask.

"It hasn't been easy, as you know. It's hard to find the balance between supporting the church and the prophetic mission."

"What do Lutheran leaders think of this Faith and Feminism/Womanist/Mujerista Conference you've planned?"

"Some have spoken out against it, and others have ignored it. But some Lutheran pastors, a few male, have signed up for the Conference."

Now we're turning into the parking lot of Ebenezer/herchurch Lutheran. The first thing I see is a huge banner across the outside front of the church that reads: "Everyone welcome at the table. Sunday morning worship at 10:30 a.m. God loves all Her children!" I'm thinking that Pastor Stacy leans heavily in the direction of her prophetic mission.

Pastor Stacy whisks around the church, taking care of last-minute Conference details. Then she rounds up several of the church lay leaders and drives us to downtown San Francisco to the famous Scoma's Restaurant on Fisherman's Wharf. On the way I'm transported as I listen to fascinating stories about Ebenezer/herchurch Lutheran and look out at the Bay lights dancing through the fog like angels on the water.

"I'm a lifelong Lutheran. But I've known something was missing; I just didn't know what until Pastor Stacy came," Inge Horton says.

"Yes, and now Ebenezer Lutheran is also called 'herchurch' and we sing Christ-Sophia hymns and we have Divine Feminine pictures in our sanctuary! Stacy is transforming Lutheranism!" Susan Solstice exclaims.

Attending the Sunday morning worship service on November 4, 2007, at the conclusion of the Conference further convinces me that Pastor Stacy Boorn is indeed transforming not only Lutheranism but also Christianity. The sanctuary of Ebenezer/herchurch Lutheran looks like that of a traditional Christian church with vaulted ceiling, pulpit on a raised platform, large cross above the altar, and stained glass windows with images of Jesus and the male disciples. But, in addition to the cross, above the altar reigns a large, bright Divine Feminine painting by artist Shiloh Sophia McCloud.[1] The image in the painting has long, curly hair and dark multicultural features. Surrounding her are white dogwood petals, red roses, and forest green vines. Instead of pews, the sanctuary has movable chairs arranged in semicircles.

It is All Saints' Sunday. Standing down below the platform in the midst of the congregation, Pastor Stacy Boorn's ebullient voice begins the opening litany:

> Pastor: Christ-Sophia, Wisdom and Guide, Servant and Saving Grace, poet and liberator, who gave us a new life and language of hope,
>
> ALL: Stand here beside us.

The litany continues with celebration of saints of the past, including as many women as men: Perpetua, Polycarp, Martin Luther, Margaret of Scots, Francis of Assisi, Elizabeth Fry, Harriet Tubman, Gandhi, Mother Teresa, Dag Hammarskjöld. The congregation then sings "Come, Christ-Sophia, Our Way" to the tune of the traditional hymn "Come, Thou, Almighty King." Still standing in the circle of congregants, not at the high pulpit, Pastor Stacy preaches a powerful sermon from the Gospel text, Luke 6:20–31. With passionate voice and gestures, she inspires us to follow the example of past saints in serving the poor, making peace, acting with love and fairness to everyone, caring for creation. Then she invites us to take white rose petals from a large bowl and spread them around the church in memory of saints in our lives. Pastor Stacy also expands the traditional language of the Communion ritual through inclusion of the "Christ-Sophia" metaphor and a hymn with these words: "Wisdom calls throughout the city, knows our hunger, and in pity gives Her loving invitation to the banquet of salvation."[2]

Stacy Boorn's story begins in upstate New York. She was born in Schenectady to middle-class Lutheran parents. Her father had his own photography business, and her mother worked with her father to make appointments, take orders, and keep the books. "It was obvious to me early on that the business was a partnership," Stacy says. "My dad was the artist, and my mother, the business manager. But all the checks were written to my dad, and he often didn't recognize that this fact often seemed to invalidate my mother's worth. She never seemed to be bothered by it, although I was!"

Stacy grew up with two older brothers, Jim and Carl. When Jim graduated from high school, their parents bought him a car and sent him to college in Oklahoma. Because they had less money available when it came time for Carl to go to college, he went to State University of New York in nearby Albany so that he could live at home and continue his jobs to help pay for his tuition. Stacy's parents didn't have much money left for her college education, and she didn't earn enough in her high school job at McDonald's to cover all her college tuition. Her pastor asked a couple in the church, Dorothy and Henry VanZandt, to help with scholarship money so that Stacy could attend Concordia Lutheran College. The first year they provided $1,000. The next year Dorothy was diagnosed with inoperable cancer, so they decided to contribute $5,000, the amount they had committed to be spread over the next three years. Dorothy wasn't going to live that long, and she wanted to make sure Stacy got all the money.

Stacy's brother Jim became a pilot and aerospace engineer, working in the Air Force and now with Northrop Grumman Corporation. Carl became an accountant with the state of New York, first in the Department of Transportation and now in the Department of Labor. Stacy's parents were proud that she chose a nontraditional vocation for women, because groundbreaking women were part of her family history.

Stacy describes both her grandmothers as "groundbreaking in many ways." Her paternal grandmother, Augusta Nelson Boorn, called "Gussy," grew up in Cape May, New Jersey, with eight siblings. This grandmother, whom Stacy identified with when she was growing up, worked for the *Schenectady Gazette* as a linotypist. When "Gussy" started working at this newspaper, she was the first and only woman working in the printing department. Her family always expressed pride that she broke into a career that hadn't been available for women. Stacy's maternal grandmother grew up on the farm, but determined not to be a farmer's wife. When she was eighteen, she walked down the hill from her farm to the city of Amsterdam, New York, with just a few dollars in her pocket. She got a job and a room, and upset many of her relatives by never going back to the farm.

Stacy describes herself growing up as "an introverted person, quite shy until way after seminary." Her parents took her to Sunday school and worship services at Trinity Lutheran Church in Schenectady, but they stopped going to church when she was about twelve years old. Stacy's interest in church began when she was a little girl. Ever since she can remember, she "really loved being at church, loved being part of the worship service." Trinity Lutheran was a small congregation with fewer than 100 active members; it was part of the Missouri Synod Lutheran denomination, which still does not ordain women. When she was only nine years old, Stacy announced, "I want to be a pastor. God wants me to do this." She now reflects, "My pastor thought this was just a phase I'd outgrow, but I still haven't outgrown it!" It didn't occur to Stacy when she was a child that women were prohibited from being pastors. As she grew older, she observed that there were only male pastors in the congregations in her town and only male Sunday school teachers and male elders in her church, but she still believed somehow that women could share leadership with men.

As a child, Stacy loved going to confirmation classes. Her pastor, Arthur Hawlicheck, asked her parents to buy Stacy her own Bible and hymnbook, even though her two older brothers had these books that weren't used. Stacy was delighted that she had her own books. She especially loved the hymns and would take her red hymnbook with her into the bathtub. "That was the only place in my house where you could close the door and be left alone," she recalls. "I would sit in the bathtub singing hymns. The red on the edges of the pages had all these little speckles from the water drops. I wish I'd kept that hymnbook. That began my personal journey of the love of liturgy and worship."

When Stacy began college, she still hoped to become a Lutheran pastor. Along with just two other women, Stacy declared herself a pre-seminarian at Concordia Bronxville in New York, a Missouri Synod college. The three women did not get the scholarships that the male pre-seminarians were given. But her Lutheran congregation and pastor, even though he had said she would outgrow the phase of wanting to be a pastor, became supportive. When she was still in high school, Pastor Hawlicheck had given her a Greek Bible and taught her a little Greek. Stacy says that he probably thought, "Maybe she'll just become a teacher or something and that will satisfy her." But before Pastor Hawlicheck retired, he gave Stacy one of his old albs.[3] He was a huge man, so it was much too big for Stacy, only 5'2". An older woman in the church, Ella Gromal, remade the alb to fit Stacy. From the time Stacy was confirmed, the pastor had given her the opportunity to read Scripture lessons and assist with Communion, so now she had her own alb to wear in worship services.

After her first year of college, Stacy Boorn came home on break to find that Pastor Hawlicheck had retired and another pastor, Arthur

Downing, had come to her church. Stacy learned that the new pastor had decided to include the council members, who were now elders, in the leadership of the worship service. These elders, all men, were going to read Scripture lessons and help with Communion. She expressed her discouragement that now she would no longer have these roles in worship. Ella Gromal, in her 80s and shorter than Stacy, marched into Pastor Downing's office and said, "Now listen here. Stacy has been a member of our church ever since she was born, and she's been helping with Communion and reading Scripture for a while. She's gone off to school, and she's studying about the church, and you can't take her jobs away from her." The pastor called Stacy and apologized.

Stacy met with Pastor Downing and said, "I'd like to do something more than I have been doing in the worship service." He asked what she meant by "something more." She recalls that she had no idea what she meant by that, but she "just blurted out, 'Well, I could preach the sermon!'" Pastor Downing said he'd have to think about that. A week later he called to tell her she could preach a sermon, and he worked with her on the sermon. Stacy, only nineteen years old, climbed up the steps into the elevated pulpit of that Lutheran church to preach her first sermon to a congregation of about eighty people. Stacy describes Trinity Lutheran as a beautiful little German church with slate floors, wooden pews, and stone walls with buttresses—like a miniature cathedral. When she reached the pulpit, three women raised their bulletins, looked at one another, stood up, stamped their feet, and walked out. Their high heels went "clunkity, clunkity, clunk" on that hard floor. Stacy stood there bewildered, but Pastor Downing said to her, "You just go on; never mind."

Reflecting on this experience of her first sermon, Stacy says, "These women had been taught all their lives that preaching was not something that women do, and they thought they were keepers of the faith; that's how they experienced some kind of authority within the church." Being grounded in Lutheran tradition, Stacy says that the Gospel had become central for her and that if something isn't "Good News," then she has to ask if that is what God intends. After she preached her first sermon, Stacy realized that the opposition to her preaching wasn't what God intended because the Gospel is supposed to be liberating.

Stacy recalls people, in addition to her pastors, who were supportive to a degree, but "they weren't going to do anything about changing the system." They weren't working to change the patriarchal language of worship nor the church's protocol on women in ministry. They might accept just one or two persons as "special," as the "exception" to the rule. Stacy says, "You go along with that because you like to be told you're special, not realizing what you're doing, participating in keeping a system going that doesn't change things." Stacy worked hard in college and seminary to prove she was exceptional. At Concordia Bronxville College, she took a Hebrew class with a group of mostly male pre-seminarians, whom she describes as "very bright." She says she was determined to do better than they "because that's part of being exceptional; if you're one of few women, you can't be average." Her Hebrew professor, Merlin Rehm, praised her work, holding up her exams with 98 or 100 at the top.

In junior high school, high school, college, and the first part of seminary Stacy experienced painful times of depression. "In college I was diagnosed with clinical depression, rooted in a chemical imbalance that may or may not have been connected with genetic heritage and specific circumstances," she says. "During college and my first two years of seminary this condition became more intense and occurred more often, resulting in three hospitalizations." In the summer of 1983, after her second year of seminary, Stacy as the student body president served on the planning team for the deployment of her seminary from St. Louis to three other locations. "I planned to transfer to Lutheran School of Theology in Chicago, but my faculty advisor, Dr. Everett Kalin, informed me that my transfer would not receive the recommendation of the faculty until I worked through the depression and had a psychiatrist's statement that there was significant healing," she recalls. "A period of drug and cognitive therapy, including a near-death antidepression drug overdose, led to recovery." A year later Stacy decided to transfer to the Pacific instead of the Chicago seminary location, and she received the necessary faculty recommendation.

Not until at least ten years later did Stacy begin to understand that the conflict between her spiritual sensitivity and the church's patriarchal practices contributed to her depression. "The situational part of the depression was rooted in the reality that at a very early age the spiritual dimension of my being was very active and focused, while at the same time I was growing up in a male-dominated religion that inadvertently at best made it clear from the readings of the Bible and early church fathers that women were either second-class citizens in God's eyes or even sub-human and not worthy of salvation," she says. "At the same time I was beginning to menstruate, I clearly remember that in the Bible studies of catechism we were taught that women would have pain in childbirth as a curse and punishment for the actions of Eve, who misled Adam and disobeyed God. I was now bleeding from this curse. I remember thinking, 'This isn't fair,' and then hearing the pastor actually teach, 'This isn't really fair, but it is simply the way it is, as God intends it for good.' The exclusive practices of the church I was beginning to love also prohibited women from being fully human and considered their feminine quality less than godly or even demonic, unless used for specific male-supporting roles."

These painful growing-up experiences contributed to Pastor Stacy's current commitment to feminist theologies and the inclusion of the Divine Feminine. She fully understands the pain that patriarchal/domination systems produce.

Feminist theology was not part of Stacy's education either in college or in seminary. Stacy began seminary in St. Louis, at Christ Seminary-Seminex. This seminary, usually called by the abbreviation "Seminex," got its name from breaking away from Concordia Seminary and the Missouri Synod Lutheran tradition and going into "exile."[4] Seminex integrated historical criticism into biblical interpretation and included views considered liberal by Missouri Synod conservatives. "Some of my grounding for being open to hear different ways God works came out of that seminary experience," Stacy says. "That began a little bit of an awakening, a readiness to hear some of the voices within feminist theology. But there was no education in feminist theology in my seminary in the 80s. There was the big second wave of theological feminism going on all around me, but I had no clue because it wasn't introduced into any of our classes. We read only male theologians." Neither were feminist theologians, like Rosemary Radford Ruether[5] or Mary Daly,[6] part of the curriculum at Pacific Lutheran Theological Seminary in Berkeley, California, where Stacy finished her education.

Although Stacy was not conscious of a glass ceiling in the church, in 1987 a slight crack came with her first call to be an associate pastor at Christ Church Lutheran, a small congregation in San Francisco. Stacy says that there wasn't really money available for this position and probably not enough people in the church to merit a second pastor. It was empowering to Stacy that "Pastor David Rohrer, having already served in that position more than twenty years, worked at being a 'co-pastor,' sharing equally all the fun stuff like preaching, pastoral calls, worship leadership, Bible/faith enrichment, and educating leadership." Stacy's call to Christ Church made it possible for her to be ordained, because in Lutheran tradition a congregation must call a pastor before he or she is ordained. On December 20, 1987, Pastor Stacy Boorn was ordained by the Association of Evangelical Lutheran Churches, a "rabble-rousing" breakaway group from the Missouri Synod denomination. This group became part of the Evangelical Lutheran Church in America (ELCA) when it formed in January of 1988.[7]

When Pastor Stacy Boorn came to Christ Church Lutheran, both Pastor David Rohrer and the musician, Robert Kerman, had already begun to recognize the exclusivity of using only masculine pronouns in reference to God. "However, they did not realize that 'God' is a masculine term, and did not include female images, other than give passing acknowledgement that *Ruah*, the Hebrew word for 'Spirit,' is feminine and therefore the Holy Spirit can be referred to as 'She,'" Stacy says. "They were at least leading the way to excise the terms 'man' and 'men' as so-called generic inclusive terms. Together they changed creeds, liturgy, and hymnody to reflect this gospel intention that was grounded in the grace of God as Lutherans understood it. Since then Pastor Rohrer, now retired, has continued to work at reforming the liturgy and proclamation of the church's gospel in ways that are consistent with feminism and liberation theology. He has remained a friend and important part of my collegial support system. Rob, the classical organist, went on to become musician of an Episcopalian congregation that maintains the status quo of the language of the liturgy and dogma of the church."

In June of 1989, Grace Lutheran Church, a small congregation in Richmond, California, called Stacy Boorn as the solo pastor. "The typical situation for women pastors were small congregations past their heyday who couldn't afford the kind of pastors they thought they deserved," she says. "They went first to pastors right out of seminary and then to women so that they could pay the least amount of salary."

At the time Stacy didn't notice this reality because she was "so ready to begin as a clergyperson." When she went to Grace Lutheran, she found a small group of Norwegians just hanging on to the church. Stacy invited a Laotian family, and soon another large Laotian family of several generations came to the church. Some of the Laotians had a Catholic background, and some were animists. Stacy led the church to open the Communion table to people of all religions and to make the liturgy bilingual and culturally inclusive, weaving Laotian dancing and music into the Lutheran liturgy. The Asian members of the congregation didn't quite know what to do with Pastor Stacy. They had great respect for religious leaders, but in their patriarchal culture they had never experienced women religious leaders. Stacy remembers the first Laotian party at the church: "One side of fellowship hall had a long line of tables for women, and the other side had a long line of tables for men. Then I came in, and they didn't know what to do. They put the tables in a U-shape and had me sit in the middle with all the women on one side and all the men on the other! They didn't know what else to do, because usually their religious leaders go with the men."

While pastor of Grace Lutheran Church in Richmond, Stacy began to realize that "not only are we narrow-minded in our cultural descriptions of the Holy Other, but our language is also narrow because it's all masculine." She became aware of exclusively masculine language for God before she started reading feminist theology. In the Lutheran Book of Worship, which she was then using for liturgy, she started counting masculine divine references. In the hymns, Scripture readings, and litanies she found "hundreds and hundreds of masculine references to God in one worship service and nothing that looked gender-neutral and certainly nothing that looked feminine." Stacy introduced "a little bit of Mother God" into the liturgy, thinking at the time that this was a "big move." There was not too much resistance to this language change because cross-cultural challenges had already stretched church members "to think about something new."

At Grace Lutheran Pastor Boorn taught in the education program, which included Laotian children. She remembers a little girl looking at a picture in the Sunday school curriculum and saying, "None of these children look like me." Stacy at first thought the little girl meant that the children surrounding Jesus in the picture were all Caucasian, but then realized that they were all boys. "Not only was

Jesus a male, but all the children around Jesus were all boy children! In the curriculum there were no children of color, very few images of girls, few role models of women of faith, and certainly no feminine images of God. I tried to introduce pictures of God other than masculine, but these kids, ages three and four, told me, 'That's wrong! Jesus was a boy, and God's a boy; that's all there is to it!' The whole society teaches this masculine God."

Before Grace Lutheran members began to look at the connection between divine imagery and sexism, they started looking at race and images of God. Adults and children of the church sponsored an art project, inviting people to image Jesus from their own cultural backgrounds. The Richmond paper ran a front-page article with pictures of some children and adults drawing Jesus as Southeast Asian. This article sparked controversy in other Lutheran churches. Some people in Missouri Synod churches in the area complained, "Well, they're not our kind of Lutheran!" Stacy comments: "And these were all male pictures of Jesus. Can you imagine if we'd had female, Southeast Asian images of Jesus? That would have been wonderful!"

In December of 1998, Pastor Boorn began serving as full-time interim mission-assessor pastor of Ebenezer Lutheran in San Francisco. Her training with the ELCA denomination to be a mission developer led to this call to help church members assess their potential for mission in the future. It was not until Stacy went to Ebenezer Lutheran that she began to read feminist theology. One of the first books she read was Rosemary Radford Ruether's *Sexism and God-Talk*.[8] She remembers thinking, "Oh, my goodness, what have I missed? Why didn't anybody in my seminary experience point this out?" Stacy began wondering how she could integrate feminist theology into the liturgy but found the church "very entrenched in traditional liturgy, making it hard to introduce a new hymn even without inclusive language."

When she had been at Ebenezer Lutheran less than a year, Pastor Boorn, with the parents' permission, baptized a child "in the name of God who is our Mother and our Father and in the name of Jesus, who is the child of God." This baptism stirred controversy in the congregation. Stacy recalls that one woman "really became upset and said that I was 'not naming the God of the ELCA.'" Stacy wondered, "Does she mean that God is the God of the ELCA and every other church has their own God?" This woman, her husband, and a few others were in a small group who controlled the congregation. They felt threatened also by Stacy's questioning the power structure of the congregation. "The reaction to calling God 'Mother' was connected to the overall use of power and control in the congregation for personal needs, patriarchal structure at its worst," Stacy says. "This group in power would not receive anything I said with any kind of validity. When their former male pastor spoke, they never questioned his sources. But every time I said anything, even 'look the sky is blue today,' they would ask, 'What is your source for that?' If I had an opinion about liturgy or a hymn, they'd ask, 'Where's your source for that?' I'd say, 'I can get sources for it, but now I'm telling you that my source is from my experience as a pastor.' They'd say, 'No, that doesn't count.'"

The group in power in the congregation started writing letters to the local and national bishops, calling Stacy a "heretic" because she "didn't use the proper terminology for God." The woman in this group had always wanted to be a pastor and was never permitted, so she felt threatened by Stacy as a woman pastor. She wrote to the bishops to have Stacy removed not only as the interim pastor of Ebenezer Lutheran but from the clergy roster of the denomination because she was "not theologically sound." One of the bishops responded to these allegations by referring to the Gospel. The woman then wrote a letter to the congregation saying, "In this case the bishop chose to use the Gospel instead of law." Pastor Stacy comments: "She had this whole concept of law and Gospel mixed up. Lutherans' pride and joy is the Gospel; the law is simply there to show us we need God, and then the Gospel comes in to give us God. In her mind you can pick and choose when you want to use the two, depending upon what you want to have done. She faulted the bishop for choosing the Gospel instead of the law."

The controversy continued for a few years, until the power in the church changed with new people elected to the council. Three weeks before Christmas, at the last council meeting before the newly elected group began, the president announced one order of business: termination of Stacy's position as interim pastor to be effective on December 31. No one had told Stacy about this order of business before the meeting. The council members knew that if they wanted to terminate Stacy, they had to do so before the end of the year because new members, who would not vote to fire her, were coming on the council. "I tried to answer some of their questions and defend myself," she recalls. "But one of the council members said to me, 'Shut up and sit down.' His words were spoken so violently and intensely that I felt if he had had a pistol in his pocket, I would have been dead. His words were not only to put me in my place but to annihilate who I was. He would never have spoken this way to previous pastors who were male. Now I was a wreck. I went into the bathroom and cried my eyes out. I was shaking in my shoes for 24 hours I'm sure. But then I felt that empowerment, like Mary describes in the Magnificat, the power that can come to those who have been made least and low by someone."

Pastor Boorn turned the situation into a challenge, going back and telling council members they couldn't fire her because she was pastor of the whole congregation, so the decision had to be a congregational decision. They said, "No, we don't have to do it that way," but Stacy didn't back down. "If you try to move forward on this without the congregation's input, I will sue you," she said. "And I believe the bishop's office will support me because they put me here, and the Lutheran women's organization and the women clergy will be very supportive of me." The majority of church members voted for Pastor Stacy to stay, and the bishop supported this congregational decision. When they realized she was not going away, the group of disgruntled people started leaving the church.

Reading more feminist theology led Pastor Boorn to see the connections between patriarchal structures and the language of liturgy. When Ebenezer Lutheran first began using inclusive language for Deity, one member of the church asked, "This language change doesn't really change the essence of God, right?" Stacy replied, "No, not really." Stacy says she would answer the question differently now because she has come to see that language does influence the way we experience the Holy Other.

In 2002, Ebenezer Lutheran added "herchurch" to its name. As church members considered ways to let people know they were exploring feminist theology, a Lutheran pastor who was visiting the church suggested a simple slogan: "God loves all Her children." So the congregation put a large banner across the front of the church with these words: "Everybody welcome at the table. Sunday morning worship at 10:30 a.m. God loves all Her children!" Then church members thought it was time to have a website, and Stacy suggested naming it "herchurch.org" to connect with the banner statement. Soon thereafter the church became Ebenezer/herchurch Lutheran. After the banner was up, people started calling the church to say, "God is not a She!" Stacy recounts one of these conversations:

"I think that sign on your church is an abomination!" the caller ranted.

"Are you a member of our church?" Stacy asked.

"No, I'm not a member of your church."

"Are you Lutheran?"

"No I'm not a Lutheran. I went to a Lutheran church for a while, but I'm Presbyterian now. We have a woman pastor at our church, and some time ago she ended one of her sermons with 'God loves Her children.' Well, she knows not to do that now. She wouldn't still be with us if she continued to do that!"

Pastor Boorn says she has also received emails filled with condemning words: "You're going to hell. How dare you change the nature of God! You're not doing God's will; you're leading your congregation astray."

In February of 2004, Stacy Boorn received the call to serve as pastor of Ebenezer/herchurch Lutheran. The church could have voted on this call sooner, but Stacy thought it best to wait longer after the controversy to keep from putting the church through more stress. "After I became the called pastor, the church made more dramatic changes, integrating the Divine Feminine more fully into the liturgy and the content of the website," Stacy says. "People became liberated to take part in the church in ways they weren't permitted to participate in the past. Introducing Divine Feminine language seemed to boost the self-worth especially of some of the older women in the church."

Pastor Boorn comments on the impact of language for divinity: "Language helps create who we are. Words have so much meaning, especially in the Protestant tradition because we don't have icons. But words can be even stronger than pictures. We can pretend that we don't have a domination structure because we don't have male icons, but our words have become icons because that's all we have in our liturgies. Words for Protestants have become icons. Some people say that all the masculine words in worship don't matter because they don't believe that God is male. How can they believe that God is gender-neutral if they call God only 'He' and refuse to call God 'She'? I'm convinced that you cannot possibly believe that God is neither he nor she if you cannot call God 'She.'" In the children's summer program at the San Francisco church, Stacy referred to God as "She," and had this interchange with a seven-year-old girl:

"You can't call God 'She.' God's a 'He.'" the little girl declared.

"How do you know that?" Stacy asked.

"Everybody knows that."

"How do you feel about that?"

"Well, I don't like it because I'm a girl!"

Stacy says it's sad that this little girl "had already figured out this was the way it was supposed to be, and there was something less about her." But Stacy believes that continuing to hear the Divine referred to as female at Ebenezer/herchurch will make a difference in the self-worth of this little girl and others because it's clear that the pervasive male language for divinity in the culture has had the opposite effect.

Pastor Boorn expresses her strong belief that the role of the pastor is to be prophet and priest at the same time. "The prophetic word is as important as the healing word or the comforting or pastoral word," she says. "The mission of Ebenezer/herchurch Lutheran is to be a prophetic voice within the patriarchal church. Inclusion of the Divine Feminine will change the whole structure of the church. Eventually the clergy structure will be dismantled. The inclusion of the Sacred Feminine empowers women and men to look at alternative structures, to change power structures that leave people out or belittle them or give a person power over others. Exclusively masculine language for Deity supports those structures. Egalitarian language for the Holy Other supports egalitarian communities."

Several years before Stacy became the called pastor, Ebenezer/herchurch Lutheran began using "God/dess" in the liturgy. A group in the church had studied Rosemary Radford Ruether's *Sexism and God-Talk* and seen this designation in the book. The group liked the term "God/dess" because it includes male and female and is not limited to the parenting imagery of "Mother-Father." Stacy decided to include "God/dess" in the liturgy, indicating that people could choose to say "Goddess" or "God." In leading worship, Pastor Stacy began by alternating saying "God" and "Goddess," trying to balance the words evenly. When church members got to "God/dess" in the congregational response, they all read "Goddess." Then for the entire service everybody read "Goddess." Most of the people in the congregation hadn't read Ruether's book, but they went along with this change in liturgy. Stacy says that "in the front pews were these older Swedish ladies, and they just read 'Goddess' to the top of their voices." Stacy thought that they were "really on board with this," but she soon realized that "their practice was to just follow along." When they caught on that they could choose to say "God" or "Goddess," several chose "God." One woman made a point of saying "God" loudly every time she saw "God/dess" in the liturgy. But others, like Dorothy Hult at age 80, had read Ruether's book and understood the importance of the Divine Feminine. One Sunday sounded like a contest with Dorothy saying "Goddess" as loudly as she could and the other woman saying "God" to the top of her voice.

Sometimes Pastor Stacy uses humor to dispel resistance to the Divine Feminine. A 97-year-old Swedish woman, Signe Rianda, stays in Ebenezer/herchurch, although she would never call herself a feminist. She has resisted some of the language and symbolism change. Before Pastor Stacy came to the church, old copies of icons hung behind the altar: a big picture of Jesus on the throne, and three male disciples and Mary the mother of Jesus on individual panels. Later the church placed Shiloh McCloud's "Tree of Life" painting near the pulpit. Signe told Stacy, "I don't like that woman over there." Stacy glanced over to several of the other pictures and said, "I don't like that guy over there." Stacy says that Signe "would then laugh and let it go. She could handle it, because I was truthful in a humorous way, and she was truthful in a humorous way. It was almost her way of owning the Divine Feminine image without having to admit publicly that she did."

Since the two worship books in the Lutheran tradition do not offer inclusive language for Deity, Ebenezer/herchurch prints liturgies, collecting resources from a variety of sources. "Mother-Father," "God/dess," and "Christ-Sophia" are among the wide variety of divine images the church uses. "Christ-Sophia is one way to refer to the Risen One," Pastor Boorn says. "There are many different ways of looking at the Divine Feminine within the same liturgical setting. Darkness is another image for the Divine Feminine, reclaiming Darkness as being as holy as Light." Ebenezer/herchurch includes many other Divine Feminine images, such as "Midwife," "Shekhinah,"[9] and "Shaddai" from the Jewish tradition. "We especially love the name 'Shaddai,' meaning 'mountain,' 'most high,' and 'the breasted one,' because the church is in the shadow of what are called the 'twin peaks' of San Francisco, two peaks on the northeast side of the church that from a distance look like breasts," Stacy explains. "So we look out and say, 'There She is, Shaddai, right over there!' Another image that has been powerful for us is the 'Baker Woman' in one of Jesus' parables.[10] We have people who have been well educated in the biblical tradition but who have never realized that the Baker Woman in the parable is an image of God. They've learned that the male images in the parables, like the Shepherd, are God, but not the female images. When we start using the female images, like Baker Woman, as a God-name, people say, 'Why wasn't I told that was in the Bible? No one ever told me that was God. Who told me I could only read the Bible certain ways?'"

Pastor Boorn relates another story to illustrate the importance of educating people on the Divine Feminine in the Bible and including female divine names and images in worship services. One of her colleagues, Pastor David Rohrer, whom she served with at Christ Church Lutheran when she was first ordained, told her about a conversation with his four-year-old granddaughter and six-year-old grandson. They were driving in downtown San Francisco and saw a huge crane extended high up to the top of a skyscraper.

"I wish I could be the driver of that crane and then I'd see the whole world. That would be like God, up there and in control of the whole world," the little boy said.

"Oh, yeah! I'd like to do that! I'd like to be God up there in control of the whole world," the little girl replied.

"You can't be God. You're a girl!"

"Oh yeah, that's right."

Pastor Rohrer remembered hearing his granddaughter singing a song she had learned in Sunday school: "I want to be like God the Father, I want to be like God the Son, I want to be like God the Spirit, because He. . ." Pastor Rohrer told Stacy: "Even God the Spirit was called 'He.' She's singing that she wants to be like all these 'He's.' My granddaughter already at this young age has the sense that if she is to be like God, she has to be like 'He.' And after my grandson told her she couldn't be God because she's a girl, she just stopped talking about God for a long time." Pastor Rohrer, who had been working on being inclusive, became even more committed to changing the church.

Pastor Stacy Boorn believes that if children continue to be brought up in patriarchal churches, the wider patriarchal culture will not change. "Children grow up in churches and other religious institutions that have created patriarchy or at least are co-opted by it or keep it going," she says. "I don't see how the world is going to change until the religious institutions change because they are so much a part of who the world is. The more we can provide church in a different way, the more we can hope things change."

Among the changes Stacy hopes for is increased focus on care of the earth. "Religious feminism includes direct focus on ecofeminism," she says. "Some younger people, like MonaLisa Wallace with her children, come to our church because of the connection we make between feminism and care of the earth. We see the earth as Sacred Mother or the way the Holy Other is embodied, so that any abuse of the earth would be an abuse of She Who Is. There are groups of people coming into our church who already have a heightened awareness, a social consciousness about care of the earth. They call for a more green environment in our own structure, down to the little details like compost bins throughout the church, using paper goods and other products that can be recycled." At the most recent Faith and Feminism Conference, the church gave everyone a BPA-free[11] plastic, reusable water bottle.

Pastor Boorn celebrates the work feminist scholars are contributing to the reform of Christianity. However, she finds ritual practice missing in their writing. "You can have scholars talking and writing about reform," she says, "but the majority of people who are part of Christian tradition don't go to seminary and don't read books that theologians are writing. Pastors who do read inclusive theology in seminary and try to apply it in their congregations get chewed up and spit out fast because the church hasn't laid any groundwork for liturgical reform. For reform to happen rituals, liturgy, and hymnody that people do on a regular basis in their Christian communities have to change drastically to include the Divine Feminine."

Pastor Boorn believes that "there will never be full equality or justice for woman and girls globally as long as the religions of the world continue to personify the Holy Other (God) exclusively or unevenly as male either metaphorically or literally." This exclusively male image supports various forms of domination. The Ebenezer/herchurch website explains: "It is not the intent or goal of the Sunday liturgy in this place to seek the eradication of masculine metaphors for God from Christendom but rather to speak and seek the holy liberation that is the core of the church and the One to whom the church gives witness. Claiming and celebrating female images of God in the scripture and the continued revelation of the presence of the Divine is an attempt to balance the predominantly androcentric and hierarchical images of God that abound in our biblical tradition. However, we need to also confront the biblical texts, products of their day and cultures, for the blatant patriarchal biases and misogynist attitudes. The use of feminine images and language for the Divine underscores the issue of justice. There is a direct correspondence between the church's attitudes and actions towards women and the abuse of women. God-language is about relationship. None of the individual names, images, symbols, or concepts for God/dess in Christian talk can ever capture who or what God/dess is. But the exclusive use of some will distort and manipulate the presentation of God/dess."

Many people who have felt alienated from the Christian tradition have experienced a "whole new sense of church and communion, coming through and beginning with images of the Divine Feminine," Stacy says. Prior to the 2009 Faith and Feminism/Womanist/Mujerista Conference at Ebenezer/herchurch, volunteers were sitting around the table talking about ways they could help. "I can't believe it," Dionne Kohler, from a Native American heritage, said. "I just can't believe I'm doing this in a Christian church. I just can't believe I'm in a Christian church again. I swore off Christianity forever because of how they treated me and how they treated women and how they treated other minority groups. I just don't believe it! Not only am I coming to a Christian church, but I'm helping to plan a major event of a kind that I thought would never exist here."

Men, as well as women, express the positive difference that inclusion of the Divine Feminine in the church's liturgy has made for them. Men have told Pastor Stacy "they need the Divine Feminine in their lives to provide more balance and stability, to allow them to look at life differently and to be in touch with their feelings." Stacy says that these men are making "conscious choices to live in the world in a non-patriarchal way." Before Communion, the church reads a litany called "Blessing the Bread," by Carter Heyward. Stacy invites people in the congregation to read the various parts. One voice includes the phrase, "we, the sisters," so a woman usually volunteers to read this part. Sometimes one of the men in the church, Collin Howard, raises his hand to read this part, and Stacy tells him that he can change the phrase, "we, the sisters." But he replies, "Oh no, I'm fine with saying, 'we, the sisters'; I honor our sisters." Steve Rausch, minister of music and classical Lutheran organist, volunteered to bake bread every Sunday morning, beginning one summer when the texts focused on the "Bread of Life" in John's Gospel. Steve said, "We should bake our own bread so we can smell it during worship." Steve started the practice of bringing a bread-making machine into the sanctuary each Sunday morning to bake bread. "Steve honors the nature of the Divine One and all people by taking on a task that has historically been assigned just to women, and to be happy doing that," Pastor Stacy comments. "It's something that's important not only for the women, but for him as well. He says he's taken this task not just because he likes to bake."

In November of 2009, Ebenezer/herchurch hosted the third annual Faith and Feminism/Womanist/Mujerista Conference. Pastor Boorn laments some resistance to the Conference among her clergy colleagues: "The first year at least a dozen women clergy attended, but the second year there were hardly any, and this year, only a few." Lutheran clergy in the San Francisco area, at their monthly meeting, had agreed to support the Conference. Instead of having a November meeting, they all agreed to come at least to the first presentation at the Conference. But the dean of the clergy group failed to send a notice out, reminding the pastors that they had chosen as their monthly meeting the Friday morning presentation at the Conference. "Most of these folks didn't even come to this presentation that they had agreed to attend," Stacy says. "Maybe the title of the presentation, 'Dismantling Patriarchal Christianity,' was too threatening."

For a short time early in her ministry, Pastor Boorn was dean of the clergy group in the East Bay region. After a year she chose to resign because she "didn't have patience for the bureaucracy." She refused another opportunity to be dean because she doesn't like going to the male-dominated synod meetings.[12] She says, "Now I might consider being dean because a member of our church reminded me that part of our mission statement is to be a prophetic voice of the Word and Wisdom of the Divine Feminine to other churches."

Pastor Boorn's prophetic voice is not always welcome. Once she wanted to serve on the regional synod council. But, she says, "I learned that I'm not electable to those kinds of things because I'm too out there for some people, pushing for feminism to be heard within the church." Her nomination didn't get past the local level because of resistance to her theology. People have tried to discount her, as they have other feminists, by calling her a "one-issue person." She responds, "I think that one issue is the groundwork for everything else; along with others in the Christian tradition, I've come to understand that feminism and the Gospel are actually the same." Stacy gives an expansive definition of feminism: "Feminism means an egalitarian world where no one is lesser or greater than another, so there would be no racism, sexism, classism, and economic disparities. Feminism means economic justice and good stewardship of the earth." Although the Evangelical Lutheran Church in America did not name the connection between feminism and the August 2009 vote to change the denomination's policy so as to lift the ban on openly lesbian, gay, bisexual, transgendered, and questioning (LGBTQ) clergy in committed relationships, Stacy sees the connection.[13] "The total acceptance of LGBTQ persons in the clergy and in all aspects of the church connects with the feminist vision of an egalitarian world," Stacy says. "But I know of a few primarily LGBTQ pastors and congregations that are pretty traditional in their language, pretty male chauvinist. They don't make the connection between what we do to women and what we do to LGBTQ persons. I believe that the oppression that happens, especially with gay men, comes from their being seen as woman-like. Gay men are demeaned because they act like women, and women are not seen in as high a realm as men." Stacy gives the example of California Governor Arnold Schwarzenegger's using this demeaning of women as he puts down Democratic legislators he doesn't agree with: he calls them "girly-men."

Pastor Stacy believes that her feminist mission is worth giving up power in the denomination. She hears stories from people, within her congregation and outside, whose lives have been scarred by patriarchal Christianity and who have found healing, peace, and inspiration from the ministry of Ebenezer/herchurch. "What is happening here is prophetic and right," Stacy says. Among the many affirming notes she has received is one from a woman named Christine: "I was so inspired and hope-filled to discover your website. I hadn't dreamed I'd see the embrace of feminine images of God in the Lutheran church this 'soon.'" Another note comes from Debbie: "I somehow stumbled upon the Herchurch website and felt I had come home. I was a member of an ELCA congregation, but drifted away while looking for a God in whose image I was created. Thank you for the wonderful website and for the suggested readings. I plan to read through them and to pray the Rosary."

On the website of Ebenezer/herchurch Lutheran is an invitation to order a custom-made God/dess Rosary for praying while remembering the struggles of women everywhere. Also, the website invites people to attend the Wednesday evening community-spoken God/dess Rosary at the church: "You may come and go as you wish, and use the prayer stations at any time. In an attempt to use biblical, century-old images and developing connections with the Holy Other, the God/dess Rosary is grounded in traditions of the Christian church and the proclamation of the Gospel, which is a vision of release from bondage for a new creation. Midweek is a good time for you to re-center your hectic-paced week and allow the sacred to surround and embrace you! Our God/dess Rosary is not a prayer of contrition or act of penance but a celebration and liberation as one enters into holy communion with 'She Who Is' in order to journey inward, journey outward and journey together with people of justice and faith."

A letter accompanying a God/dess Rosary order illustrates something of the power of the ministry of Ebenezer/herchurch Lutheran: "I found your website with its beautiful rosaries, and I would like to ask you to make one for me. I am a woman, 56 years old, mother of four and grandmother of two. I've done many things in my life, including my current occupation of professional writer of science fiction. I was raised Catholic, in a very conservative, right-wing family. I faithfully attended Mass all my life, until the sex scandals in the American church came to light. As I learned more and more about the deep roots of the scandal, I could no longer justify going to Mass and supporting this system with my presence and resources. But I haven't found another way or place to worship either—nor can I easily undo a lifetime of conditioning to Catholic imagery and ways of thinking of God. At the same time, I've rejected the patriarchal assumptions that provided the foundation on which such an oppressive church structure could be built. I have finally come to understand that to call myself a feminist, it is not enough to ask for equality within a system that guarantees that inequality will persist. So, in the last couple of years, I've decisively turned away from the religion, culture and politics that shaped my entire life. I am angry and sad. I used to say the Rosary almost every day, but I have not been able to say it recently, because the words and images hit me on all my sore spots and remind me of the place assigned to people like me—women—and it's not a place I want to be in any more. If you can, make me a Rosary for an angry woman who needs to find peace within herself, for a sad woman who needs to find a way back to happiness, for a powerful artist who needs to find her voice and courage again. I am sure whatever you send me will be beautiful and empowering for my life."

The deep-down assurance that she is doing what she was created to do gives Pastor Stacy courage to face the criticism she often receives for bringing change to the church. "Strength also comes through worship," she says. "I love worship. Within the liturgy I find great encouragement and strength." Clergy colleagues also give her support, taking her concerns seriously and making changes within their churches, and church members encourage her through affirming words about sermons that gave them power and meaning for daily living. In addition, her spirit is nurtured by her creative work of photography and the friends she's made through this work.[14]

Pastor Stacy Boorn has an expansive, hopeful vision for the future of the church. "It would be wonderful if half of all the Christian churches included the Divine Feminine in worship, if this were not an alternative to the norm but the norm," she says. "The whole structure of the church will change. The 'good old boy' network can't possibly continue. Persons who have been kept in their place by the patriarchal structure won't be kept there anymore. Equal partnership at the table will reap good rewards, resulting in just structures. Women and others who have been marginalized within religions will reclaim their identity and connection to the Holy Other, giving a different reality to the church." Stacy's voice rises with enthusiasm as she tells me how encouraged she feels that this vision "could be real because it's happening in many places." She expresses delight about attending a God/dess Rosary service at University Lutheran Chapel in Berkeley: "There's a God/dess Rosary in another Lutheran church happening on a regular basis now!" The University Lutheran Chapel service took the pattern provided by Ebenezer/herchurch and added guitar music and "Shaddai" chants.

As I experience the worship service on November 8, 2009, at the conclusion of the third Faith and Feminism/Womanist/Mujerista Conference, I feel Pastor Stacy Boorn's vision becoming reality. Ebenezer/herchurch Lutheran's building is now purple, another symbol of the vision of equality and justice. The church chose to paint the outside purple "to honor the Divine Feminine, to be in solidarity with empowering women and all persons who are oppressed and denied equal rights, to advocate for marriage rights for all people." Inside the church building, these beliefs find further expression through the liturgy. The congregation sings with enthusiasm the opening hymn, "Hark! Wisdom's Urgent Cry." Church member Lana Dalberg reads her moving poem entitled "Mother God":

God to me
Is my dark-haired mother,
Stroking my forehead
As she lullabies me to sleep.

My Mother is the earth
And all her creatures—
The web that brings us into relationship
With one another.

God to me
Is the Mother
who spills Her essence into the world,
Creating and calling us to create
From the wombs of our being.

God to me
Is the Mother
whose voice was drowned out
For most of history,

And yet,
I find Her in my deepest wisdom.
Alone, I feel Her touch
Upon my brow,

Mothering me still,
Mothering us all.[15]

The biblical texts for the homily include the Gospel of Mark and the non-canonical Gospel of Mary Magdalene. Pastor Boorn places Mary Magdalene with Jesus in the story of the widow's offering,[16] and gives a fresh, powerful interpretation of this Gospel narrative. The widow, in giving everything she had, demonstrates the courage to reject the capitalist system that has oppressed her. The worship service continues with Judith Dancer, minister of embodiment, entering the sanctuary, adorned with colorful mother-bird plumage and dancing on stilts, delighting children and adults. The celebratory, inclusive "Holy Communion Meal" follows, beginning with this blessing:

Pastor: The peace of the risen Christ-Sophia be with you always.

All: And also with you.

The vision of a transformed church continues to become reality throughout this worship service and through all the liberating ministry of Pastor Stacy Boorn and Ebenezer/herchurch Lutheran.

2

Rev. Dr. Susan Newman

United Church of Christ Pastor
Associate Minister for Congregational Life and Social Justice
All Souls Church, Washington, DC

"The Bible teaches that we are made in the image and likeness of God; therefore, I must believe that there is a male and female expression of God," Rev. Dr. Susan Newman writes in her book *Your Inner Eve: Discovering God's Woman Within*.[1] Before I meet the author, I find myself intrigued by this book that reclaims the Eve of Genesis and focuses on "Inner Eve" as a metaphor for the Divine Feminine. "This is what I call your Inner Eve—God's feminine creative power and spiritual presence inside us," Rev. Dr. Newman explains. She also calls this "feminine creative power" the "Goddess Within" and "God's WomanSpirit." She challenges readers to "re-create our lives" so as to affirm the "spark of the divine" within us. "Behave like the goddess you are," Rev. Dr. Newman writes. "The Bible says, 'Greater is He that's in you, than He that's in the world' (1 John 4:4). Well, speaking in inclusive language and honoring the feminine expression of God's Spirit, I want to paraphrase to say, 'Greater is She that is in you.' God's Spirit has often felt like a nurturing mother, and I want to honor God by living like a goddess. Claim your divinity and walk in it every day, because you are fearfully and wonderfully made."[2]

On September 26, 2010, in Washington, DC, at All Souls Church, I experience Rev. Dr. Susan Newman as living these words, claiming her divinity. Her resonant voice, strong presence, wisdom, and wit rise out from the large oak pulpit to enliven the congregation gathered in this imposing sanctuary with domed ceiling, columns, wooden pews in triple rows, and balcony. Wearing a black robe and bright multi-colored stole, she preaches an inspiring sermon on "Friendship and Faith." The central sacred image in her sermon is "Loving Friend," illustrated by men and women from the Bible and from her own experience. The biblical examples are the men who bring their paralyzed friend to be healed by Jesus,[3] and Ruth who stays faithful to her mother-in-law, Naomi.[4] Rev. Dr. Newman gives the personal illustrations of Joye Brown Toor, her "soulmate" from the time they met at George Washington University, and of a friend, whom she connected with when he was caring for his ill mother and she was caring for hers. "One of the most sacred of relationships that we have is friendship," Rev. Newman proclaims. "Friends bring balance to our lives. A true friend is medicine to our souls. Our covenant group ministry here at All Souls offers a sacred gathering, where your life can be transformed because you shared your spiritual journey and helped someone find their feet. It is a place where a soul can find a home,[5] where we can become friends as we share our faith."

Born and raised in Washington, DC, Susan Newman found a safe place in Goodwill Baptist Church when she was a child. Her mother, Lillian Mae Dabney Newman, took Susan to this church, two blocks from their home. With an associate's degree in education, Lillian Newman worked as an educational aide in the DC public schools for 35 years. On Saturdays she also worked as a manicurist in an upscale downtown barbershop. Her father, King Milton Newman, was an electrician. Susan grew up with a sister, Marguerite, called "Connie," three years older. "My father was an abusive alcoholic," Susan recalls. "When he came home, he was either drunk and belligerent, or he was drunk and depressed. He would cry and go down into the basement to play the organ, 'Rock of Ages Cleft for Me,' and just cry and then go to sleep. Or if he were belligerent, sometimes he would fight with my mother or hit me. My sister never got it, because she would always go off and hide somewhere and read. But I would be there trying to help him, so I would get the brunt of his anger. It was to the point that Monday through Friday at 3:00 p.m., when the school bell would ring, my heart would freeze inside of me because I didn't know what to expect when I went home behind the doors of 1838 Belmont Road, whether my father would be there, how he would be. But come Sunday morning, I knew I was going to Goodwill Baptist Church, and I was going to see Ms. Clara Powell."

When Susan was in the sixth grade, Ms. Powell became her Sunday school teacher. "Ms. Powell grew up on a farm in North Carolina," Susan recounts. "Her mother died when she was young, and her father had her come out of school to help him on the farm. She never went beyond fifth grade, and she was a domestic at St. Alban's, the Episcopal private school on Wisconsin Avenue here in DC. She scrubbed the floor on her hands and knees. But on Sunday at Goodwill Baptist Church, she was Deaconess Clara Powell, and she put on her starched white uniform. I sat there in her Sunday school class and looked in the face of this woman and saw the love of God. I loved being around her. I heard her quote Jesus, saying, 'Come unto me, all you who labor and are heavy laden, and I will give you rest,'[6] and 'Suffer little children to come unto me and forbid them not; for of such is the kingdom of heaven.'[7] As time went on, I got confidence in Ms. Powell, and I would share with her. Back then in the 1960s, alcoholism was a family secret. It wasn't an illness; it wasn't treatable. You kept the family secret. But I felt comfortable enough to talk to Ms. Powell."

Ms. Powell also showed kindness to Susan by bringing her small gifts and helping her take part in an Easter play. "My first cloth handkerchief with my name engraved on it came from her," Susan recalls. "She would bring me oranges and apples and different things. One Easter she gave out parts for the Sunday school Easter play, and she gave me a poem that had ten stanzas, 'The Legend of the Dogwood Tree.' And I said, 'Ms. Powell, I can't learn this,' because I stuttered. I had a speech impediment, probably from nervousness from being at home. She said, 'I will work with you.' She would call me at home, and meet me at church on Saturday. I know 'The Legend of the Dogwood Tree' now, at the age of 53, because Clara Powell, my Sunday school teacher, loved it into me when I was twelve. Also from her teaching I learned the word of God; I read it, and loved it."

At the age of twelve, Susan Newman became the superintendent of her Sunday school, because she knew more about the Bible than most of the adults at the church at that time. At a youth revival at Goodwill Baptist Church, when Evangelist Mary Tilghman was preaching, Susan made a profession of faith. "I used to wear my hair in two long braids and bangs," Susan recalls. "Mary said that night when she gave the invitation to discipleship, all she remembered was braids, bangs, and tears coming down the aisle. The Sunday I was baptized, it was so meaningful to me to have Clara Powell as the deaconess who helped me dress for the baptism."

As the youth leader of Goodwill Baptist Church, Susan selected guest youth preachers to come once a month. "Our pastor didn't like preaching, and he was not a good preacher," Susan says. "I told him one Sunday that God had given me a message, and instead of inviting someone, I'd like to be the youth speaker. He said, 'Well, Susan, you've never announced a calling to preach, so just type it out and read it.' And I did. The text was from Matthew, 'Be perfect, as your heavenly Father is perfect.'[8] After I preached and was standing at the door shaking hands with people, the deacons came to me and said, 'Girl, you preach better than the pastor.' And that was my last Sunday at that church."

Susan Newman helped another minister start a church, and was with him about a year until she realized "he was just doing it for selfish monetary reasons." Then she joined Mt. Sinai Baptist Church in DC, where Rev. David Durham was pastor. "Rev. Durham was known citywide as a great preacher," Susan says. "Rev. Durham was also known not to believe in women preachers and not to support women in ministry. He belonged to the DC Baptist Ministers Conference, which is an African American Baptist ministers' conference that wouldn't even allow women to come to the meetings. If any man ordained a woman to the ministry, he was excommunicated from the fellowship and stripped of his standing."

For a while before joining Mt. Sinai, Susan had been singing with the James Cleveland Gospel Music Workshop Choir[9] and going to Evangelist Mary Tilghman's Bible study on Thursday nights. "I'm in Bible study with this Church of God in Christ evangelist, so I'm learning the word of God," Susan says. "I know it like I know my name. And then I joined Mt. Sinai Baptist Church. Rev. Durham would teach

Bible study on Wednesday before prayer meeting. While he was teaching, he would say, 'Somebody get 2 Timothy 3:9 or somebody get 2 Corinthians 2:8–9,' or whatever. And whoever got the passage first would read it while he was teaching. But as soon as he would name it, I would start quoting. I didn't have to look it up in the Bible. I knew the word of God. Ephesians 2:8–9: 'For by grace are you saved through faith; and that not of yourselves: it is the gift of God: not of works, lest any man should boast.'[10] I'm eighteen at this time. And the whole church started calling me the 'Living Bible.'"

After being at Mt. Sinai Baptist Church for a year, Susan began to sing with a small a cappella group in a storefront Holiness church. "My friends all knew that I was wrestling with a call to preach," Susan says. "After we had sung, we were sitting in the church, and the preacher got up and started taking his text, something about redeeming the time wisely, knowing what the will of God is for you.[11] I was sitting there with my Word in my lap ready to be fed. And he said, 'You know, God has called many of us to do things, and we refuse to accept God's calling on our lives.' My friends started leaning down in the pew looking at me. I wouldn't look either way to the left or to the right. I thought to myself, 'Well, he's not talking to me because, God, I know you're not calling me, because I'm eighteen. I'm too young to be a preacher.' As soon as I thought it, he said, 'It doesn't matter how old you are. God can use you no matter how old or how young you are. I was in a revival in Texas, and a seven-year-old boy preached and souls were saved.' So then I started thinking, 'Well, I know you're not talking to me because I'm a woman, and there are no women preachers.' He said, 'If you're a woman, God can use you. The first woman at the tomb was Mary, and Jesus said, "Mary, go tell the brethren."' And that went on the whole sermon. I'd think of something, and he would speak to it. By the time he finished preaching, I was down in my seat under conviction."

Not knowing what to do, Susan decided to consult her mother. Susan thought her mother would save her from the call to preach: "My momma's not going to let her baby girl be out there in the street preaching all hours of the day and night; she doesn't like me to leave the house after 7:00 in the evening." So Susan asked God to let her know when to tell her mother about her call. One night during the week before Easter, Susan was watching a movie about Esther in the Bible. "The movie went on till about 1:00 in the morning," Susan recalls. "And God said, 'Okay, go tell your momma.' I said, 'You're not talking about Lillian Mae Dabney Newman, because my momma goes to bed about 9:00 in the evening, and you do not wake her up.' God said, 'Go, tell your momma.'" Susan went to her mother and shook her awake.

Her mother turned over and asked, "What is it, Baby? What's wrong?"

"Nothing, Momma. I just wanted you to know that God has called me to preach, and I've accepted God's call."

"Baby, that is so good. I'm so happy for you. I'm praying for you."

"But Momma, I have to be out at night."

"The Lord will protect you. If God called you, God will protect you."

That Saturday, even though it was the busy Easter weekend, Susan insisted on talking with her pastor, thinking he would put a stop to her call to preach.

"Rev. Durham, God has called me to preach."

"Is that all? We've been knowing that. The whole church knew that when you walked in here quoting the Bible like you wrote it," he said.

"But I'm a woman! Don't you think I shouldn't preach?"

"Susan, if God has called you, we're going to do a trial sermon, and we'll see the gifts and graces of God on your life."

On September 5, 1976, at the age of nineteen, Susan Newman preached her trial sermon. "When I finished preaching, the whole church was up on their feet," Susan recalls. "They didn't wait to have a church meeting the next week to vote to license me to the ministry. The pastor stood up and said, 'I need a motion.' And the chairman of the deacon board said, 'I so move that we license her to the Gospel ministry.' It was a unanimous vote. Rev. Durham had my license in the pulpit. He had already gotten it at the Baptist bookstore. He had crossed out with a magic marker every 'he' and put 'she,' every 'him' and put 'her,' because all the pronouns were male."

Although Rev. Newman had gotten a standing ovation on her sermon and a unanimous vote by the church to be licensed to ministry, she had few opportunities to preach. "I only preached at the 3:00 a.m. Halloween service," she laughs and says. "There was no way I was going to preach at the 11:00 a.m. service. Women were not allowed in the pulpit unless it was Women's Day." Later she writes in one of her books: "There is a sickness in the Black church, and it is the sometimes subsiding, but never dying, sexism. Women have been told we should be grateful that we are granted a Women's Day, that women are allowed in the pulpit, that the woman preacher can preach from the pulpit rather than from the floor. We should not complain or even speak of any dissatisfaction. This reminds me of white America during segregation, telling us that we should be thankful for what they have afforded us, and that coloreds need to remember their place."[12]

When Susan accepted the call to ministry, she was beginning her junior year at George Washington University. In 1978 she graduated with a double major in journalism and speech communication and a minor in religion. That fall she began Wesley Theological Seminary; she was the only black female at the school. Because her pastor and the male officers of the church discouraged her from completing seminary and being ordained, and because she didn't know of a Baptist church in Washington, DC, that would allow her in the pulpit on Sundays to do the required seminary internship, Susan dropped out after one semester. "Out of 52 Sundays, I could be in the pulpit only on Women's Day," she says. "So I could not do an internship as a seminarian."

In July of 1979, Rev. Newman attended the Progressive National Baptist Eastern Regional Convention[13] on the campus of Princeton University. An older preacher, Rev. Gantt, was the only other woman from Mt. Sinai Baptist Church at the convention. "They called her 'Rev. Sister Gantt,' and they used to call me 'Rev. Sister Newman,'" she says. "None of the men were 'Rev. Brother.' They were just 'Rev. Green,' not 'Rev. Brother Green.'" At the convention, Rev. Newman registered for the Ministers' Seminar, even though Rev. Gantt refused:

"That's not for us."

Rev. Newman replied, "It says 'Ministers' Seminar.'"

"That's for the men; that's not for the women."

"Rev. Gantt, my license calls me a Gospel preacher. I'm a minister. I'm going."

When Rev. Newman walked into the Ministers' Seminar where there were no other women, some of the men loudly said, "Oh, we must be in the wrong room. Is this the missionary circle meeting in here?" But Rev. H. Wesley Wiley,[14] pastor of Covenant Baptist Church in DC, kindly asked her to sit with him and his son, Rev. Dr.

Dennis Wiley. Rev. Dr. Samuel DeWitt Proctor,[15] professor at Rutgers University, and Rev. Dr. Boykin Sanders,[16] professor of New Testament at Andover Newton Theological Seminary, were the two lecturers for the Ministers' Seminar. Dr. Proctor was so impressed by the way Susan answered the questions raised at the lecture that he came to her afterwards and asked her where she was in seminary. When she told him she had dropped out, he said, "But you need to go back. We need someone with your mind in our churches today. Where would you like to go to seminary?" She told him she would love to go to Howard University School of Divinity in DC, but she didn't have the money. Dr. Proctor recommended her to Dr. Lawrence Neale Jones,[17] dean of Howard School of Divinity, who saw that Susan had a journalism degree and hired her as his graduate research assistant. She entered Howard in August of 1979, and after the first semester she also received a $4000 grant each semester from the Princeton Theological Fund for Education, later called the Proctor Fund.

In January of 1980, when her church, Mt. Sinai Baptist, would not allow her to do an internship, Zion Baptist Church in DC hired Rev. Newman as seminary intern. Rev. Carlton Veazey, the pastor, and Rev. James Wright, the assistant minister, did allow her to participate in worship leadership every Sunday, not just on Women's Day. Rev. Wright, the assistant minister directly supervised Susan's internship, and assigned her the part of the worship liturgy she would perform. "I was never asked to preach or do the intercessory prayer, nothing creative out of my spirit," she recalls. "The only thing I did was the responsive reading every Sunday for a semester. I'd say, 'Rev. Veazey, do you want me to wear this robe?' He'd say, 'Oh, that's a nice dress you have on; wear what you have on in the pulpit.' I thought to myself, 'He doesn't want me to look too much like a preacher in the pulpit.'" When Rev. Newman finally got to preach for the first time on youth Sunday, she received a standing ovation.

In April of that year, the World Council of Churches selected Susan as one of three seminarians to represent the United States at the Ecumenical Institute in Geneva, Switzerland.[18] The selection was based on a paper she had written on the ecumenical movement. For a month and a half, she studied Third World theology at the Institute. When she returned, Zion Baptist Church had replaced her with another intern, the granddaughter of a church trustee. That fall Rev. Dr.

A. Knighton Stanley, pastor of Peoples Congregational United Church of Christ, hired Rev. Newman as seminary intern, even though he had told her in the interview when he looked at her resume: "You test everything male in me. I cannot believe you are 23 years old and you've already done all this."

After Susan completed her internship, Peoples Church offered to ordain her and hire her as assistant pastor. Hesitating about the position because she wanted to be with a Baptist church, she consulted Rev. H. Wesley Wiley, who told her: "Susan, God didn't call you to serve the Baptist church. God called you to serve God's people, and wherever a door is open that you can go and use your gifts and graces for ministry, you go. God did not call you to ministry to see how well you can waste your talents sitting in the pew on Sunday."

Susan graduated from Howard University School of Divinity in May of 1982, and accepted the pastoral position at Peoples Church. The church ordained her to ministry in February of 1983. Her ordination was especially meaningful to her because professors and ministers who knew her family participated. When she was a seminarian doing research for Dean Jones, she had discovered a book on outstanding African American preachers that included her grandfather, Rev. Melancy Newman, and six uncles, who were all United Methodist ministers: Bishop Ernest Newman,[19] Rev. Dr. Isaiah DeQuincy Newman,[20] Rev. Dr. Omega Newman,[21] Rev. Dr. Matthew Clifton Newman, Rev. Marion Lewis Newman, and Rev. James Newman. She hadn't known before that she came from a line of preachers because her father, the only child who was not a preacher, didn't talk about them as ministers, and he didn't go to church. "When I was a child, I saw pictures of my uncle the Rev. Dr. Isaiah DeQuincy Newman in *Ebony* and *Jet* magazines with Martin Luther King, but it didn't mean anything to me then—it was just Uncle DeQuincy," Susan recalls. "Later I learned that Rev. Dr. Isaiah DeQuincy Newman, whom they called 'I Deek,' was the first African American senator for the state of South Carolina since Reconstruction." Many seminary professors, including New Testament professors Dr. Cain Hope Felder and Bishop Thomas Hoyt, who took part in her ordination, knew her uncles. "When I was ordained, my uncles could not be there, but Dr. Cain Hope Felder, representing my United Methodist heritage, robed me, and Dean Jones gave me my charge," Susan recalls. "Then I ascended the steps to the pulpit and was the celebrant of Communion for the first time. That was so powerful because our church had never ordained a woman before in 135 years." In 1983 Rev. Susan Newman became the first black woman ordained by a mainline denomination in Washington, DC, and the seventh black woman ordained in the United Church of Christ denomination.

In February of 1984, Rev. Newman resigned as assistant pastor of Peoples Congregational United Church of Christ. "The senior minister, Dr. Stanley, was being difficult at times," Susan explains. "It got to the point that if I were to remain a friend and colleague with him, I had to leave. Rev. Rubin Tendai, the associate pastor, and I both resigned the same day, not knowing of the other's intentions." Rev. Newman and Rev. Stanley remained good friends, and in June of 1984 he was one of the ministers who performed her wedding, along with Rev. David Durham, who had licensed her to ministry at Mt. Sinai Baptist Church, and Rev. Paul Sadler, a friend from seminary. In 1985 Rev. Newman performed Rev. Stanley's wedding to Andrea Young, daughter of Andrew Young,[22] former mayor of Atlanta and United Church of Christ minister. At the wedding Susan was excited not only to meet Andrew Young but also famous actor Eddie Murphy, a friend of Andrea.

After leaving Peoples Church, Rev. Newman became the first African American resident chaplain at Washington Hospital Center, the major trauma hospital in DC. She had been working there a year when she got a phone call from Rev. Henry C. Gregory, pastor of Shiloh Baptist, one of the major churches in Washington, DC. Rev. Gregory also taught preaching at Howard University School of Divinity, and he had been impressed with Susan when she was one of his students. He came to the hospital to talk with Susan.

"Susan, our associate pastor of Christian education is retiring, and we've been looking for someone to replace him. I would like to offer you the job."

"Rev. Gregory, is Shiloh still Baptist?"

He laughed and said, "Yes."

"You don't want a woman, because I remember last year when I was invited to preach for missionary Sunday. And the day before I was to preach, I was told not to come, that the deacons of Shiloh had voted that they did not want a woman preacher in the pulpit, so you got a woman principal of a school."

"Well, we've been dealing with some things, and we're ready."

Rev. Newman accepted the position of associate pastor at Shiloh Baptist Church. "The salary was almost nothing—$11,000 a year—because I was married, and they felt like I had a husband to take care of me," she says. "But I was just so happy to be at the great Shiloh Baptist Church. In black church circles we always say, 'After you leave Shiloh Baptist, there's no where to go but heaven.' I was the first woman on staff at Shiloh Baptist. The Sunday I came to preach before the church voted on me, you could hear a rat piss on cotton, it was so quiet! I wondered, 'What do you think I'm going to do in the pulpit, take my bra off and swing it in the air over the Bible?' All the deaconesses and missionaries were sitting on the front row with their white uniforms on. They told me later that they were just sitting there praying that I would be so good the church would vote for me." Again, Rev. Newman got a standing ovation on her preaching. The church vote was unanimous to call her as associate pastor of Christian education.

The first Sunday Rev. Newman was on staff at Shiloh Baptist, she asked Rev. Ronald Austin, the other associate pastor, about the church's procedure for the Communion ritual. He told her to follow Rev. Gregory and him when they moved away from the pulpit after the sermon. "We were getting ready to prepare for Communion," Rev. Newman recalls. "Rev. Gregory went down the pulpit steps, and Ronald went down the steps, so I went down after them. They went out the side door. I was following after them. Next thing I knew the three of us were in a men's bathroom, standing around a urinal. They went in to use the bathroom, and to wash their hands to then come out and serve Communion. So we were standing with our robes on, and it was just a little one-person bathroom. Our shoulders were touching. And they looked at me and said, 'Oh! We forgot you were with us,' because they had never had a woman minister. I said, 'I'm just going to slip out in the hall right now.' Because of me, they began a new ritual. The church was started by 21 newly freed slaves from Virginia, who had made this the basin they would use to wash their hands for Communion. So the church brought that basin out, and now all the ministers go to a room behind the pulpit; one person pours the water from a pitcher over another's hands held over the basin, while another holds the towel. It's a time of fellowship for the ministers of the church before we go out and serve Communion."

Shiloh Baptist Church could not give Rev. Newman the raise she needed after she had served as minister there for two and a half years, so she accepted the position of interim coordinator for church and college relations for the United Church of Christ Board for Homeland Ministries in New York. She commuted by train from Washington, DC, to New York City.

In 1989, Rev. Newman also began work toward a Doctor of Ministry (DMin) degree at United Theological Seminary, a United Methodist Seminary in Dayton, Ohio. Dr. Henry Mitchell[23] and Dr. Edward Wheeler[24] were the mentors of the group of students Susan was in, called the "Mitchell/Wheeler Fellows." Also in this group were E. K. Bailey,[25] Cynthia Hale,[26] Carolyn Ann Knight,[27] Gregory Ingram,[28] Alvin O'Neal Jackson,[29] and Frank Thomas.[30] "The women preachers knew about E. K. Bailey," Susan says. "E. K. pastored Concord Missionary Baptist Church in Dallas, Texas, and he does national preaching conventions. E. K. was famous for not supporting women preachers. One day after lunch I came back to class with a big bag of M&M's with peanuts. I was sitting there eating my M&M's, and E. K. was sitting beside me. He kind of tapped my hand with his hand out, wanting some of my candy. I said, 'You don't believe in women preachers, so if that be the case, I'm not here. And if I'm not here, my candy's not here.' But I gave him some candy. We got to know each other in our time together. We all would bring a tape of ourselves preaching and critique it. When we were listening to my sermon on the prodigal son, E. K. said, 'Girl, you can preach!' E. K. and I became great friends. He even had me in his church in Dallas." The month that Susan graduated with her DMin degree, May of 1991, she was going through a divorce. E. K. Bailey, Ed Wheeler, and all of those in her DMin group helped her through this difficult time.

In 1992, Dr. Newman accepted the position of religious coordinator for the Children's Defense Fund (CDF), working with Marian Wright Edelman.[31] "I helped to plan the opening worship service, which was called a 'Moral Witness for Our Children,' for the 1992 Democratic National Convention in New York and the Republican National Convention in Texas," Susan says. "I was one of the three clergy on staff who helped plan the Children's Sabbath[32] that CDF does every October." After a few years Dr. Newman's position ended because of lack of funding.

About that time, Rev. Dr. Susan Newman received a letter from First Congregational Church in Atlanta, Georgia, asking her to be a candidate for the position of senior minister. She didn't reply. "After so many years in ministry, I didn't want to be a token so they could just say they interviewed a woman," she says. "A few months later the chair of the search committee called me and asked, 'Dr. Newman, didn't you get our letter?' I said, 'Yes, I got it. But ya'll are not serious.' He said, 'We really are. Dean Jones recommended you. We've had forty candidates, and we've not been moved by any of them.'"

Dr. Newman went to Atlanta for an interview, after which the search committee narrowed the field to her and two other candidates. One of the candidates, Rev. Dwight Andrews, dropped out to continue as full-time music professor at Emory University. That left Dr. Newman and one other candidate, Dr. A. Knighton Stanley, the pastor who hired her as assistant pastor at Peoples Congregation Church. Dr. Stanley's wife, Andrea, wanted to move back to Atlanta to be close to her mother, Jean Childs Young, who was sick. "So Dr. Stanley, called 'Tony,' was a candidate to be the pastor there, and it was between me and my father in pastoral ministry," Susan recalls. "I went down to preach in March of 1994. First Congregational Church is not known to be an emotional church. But again when I finished preaching, there was a standing ovation. That night when they went home, Andrew Young and Jean Childs Young called Tony Stanley and told him, 'Tony, don't even bother. Go on and withdraw your name. She's got this.'"

In June of 1994, Rev. Susan Newman became pastor of First Congregational Church in Atlanta. "All the movers and shakers of the African American community belonged to either Ebenezer Baptist, Dr. King's church, or they belonged to First Congregational, known as 'First Church,'" Susan says. "The editor of the *Atlanta Journal-Constitution* newspaper, Cynthia Tucker, was the head of my Christian Education Board. Andrew Young was one of my assistant ministers. Michael Lomax, who is now the president of the United Negro College Fund, was one of my deacons. Judge Leah Sears, Chief Justice of the Supreme Court of the state of Georgia, who was one of the possible nominees of President Barack Obama for the U.S. Supreme Court, was a member of the church. Mayor of Atlanta, Bill Campbell, came often. They were calling a woman as their pastor for the first time, and I was their youngest pastor. I was thirty-five at the time."

In September of that year, Rev. Newman had her first meeting of the church trustee board. Before the meeting, a woman who had been on the search committee that had recommended Rev. Newman took her shopping. "The members of the search committee were very invested in my succeeding because they're the ones who said to the church that this is who we think you should call," Susan explains. "One of the members of the committee, a deacon, a wonderful woman who was very friendly, took me shopping because she didn't like the way I looked in my clothes, the style of fashion that I wore. Here I'm coming from DC to this very conservative African American elite church. So this deacon took me shopping to Saks Fifth Avenue to buy shoes. I picked out these high heels that were kind of funky. She said, 'We don't like those.' I said, 'We don't?' So she got me a pair of flat Ferragamo black patent leather shoes with a little bow on the toe. She said, 'Now we love these.' I said, 'We do?' Here are these $150 shoes; I'm used to buying shoes for about $30. This was her gift to me. She spent about $1000 buying me shoes and clothes at Saks so I would look like the 'pastor' of First Church."

Half an hour before Rev. Dr. Newman's first church board meeting, one of the trustees, who was an educator with a Doctor of Education degree, came to her office to talk to her.

"Dr. Newman, what kind of doctorate is that anyway? There are some of us who, um, don't care for your preaching and your way of ministry," she said.

"What do you mean?" asked Dr. Newman.

"Well, it's too, um, earthy. And the way you dress, well, it's just different for us."

"There were 136 people who voted for my earthy style of ministry, because the vote was 136 to 63 to call me."

"Well, two more votes and you would not be here."

This was the first time Rev. Newman had heard that it took a two-thirds vote, instead of a majority vote, to call her to the church. "So I found out that two more votes and I would not have been there," Susan recalls, "When she said that, it was like I had gotten stabbed in my heart because I didn't know that. I thought it was a majority vote, but now I'm told it was a two-thirds vote. I had ten minutes before the board meeting to get it together. I closed my door, and sat there and cried. And I called my mother on the phone, and said, 'Momma, they don't like me.' She comforted me. I got off the phone and prayed and went down to do my first trustee board meeting."

One Sunday morning Rev. Newman was teaching the Sunday school class for the officers of the church. She was excited, focused on teaching the lesson from the book of Romans on not conforming to the world but being transformed.[33] Rev. Newman called on a trustee who looked like she wanted to speak.

"Sister, do you have something you want to say?"

"I don't like your lipstick. From where I'm sitting in church on Sunday, it looks like you don't have any lipstick on."

"That's next Sunday's Sunday school lesson," Rev. Newman jokingly replied. "Do you have anything to say about Romans?"

After the worship service one Sunday, a member of the church commented on Dr. Newman's shoes. "I had on a beige suit and beige pumps to go with my suit," she says. "During the service I had on my black robe. After the service, I was standing shaking hands with people. This one woman stood in line for fifteen minutes to wait to get to me. When she did, she said, 'Dr. Newman, we only wear black shoes with our robe in the pulpit.' I said, 'Well, did you hear the sermon?' It was that kind of thing constantly. They felt free to comment on my dress, my style, how I looked. They would never do that with a man."

At the Atlanta church, Dr. Newman also found race relations to be challenging. "There's something about race relations between black people and white people in the South that's different from in the North," she comments. "In the North we find folks who hide their racism. But in the South, they're going to come out and let you know. Race relations in Atlanta just amazed me. It was 11:00 o'clock one Sunday morning, and we were supposed to have some guests, who were the wives of the presidents of Bank of America, Wachovia Bank, and the big realty companies. They were friends of one of the black members of the church, and they weren't there yet." The church member came running up when the worship service was about to begin.

"Dr. Newman, can we wait and do the call to worship about 11:15?"

"That's late!"

"Well, our white friends aren't here yet."

"Well, your white friends are just going to have to get here and sit down when they get here."

When Rev. Dr. Newman had been pastor of the Atlanta church only three months, Jean Childs Young, wife of Andrew Young, died of cancer. Jean had planned her own funeral from her hospital bed, asking Rev. Newman to do the eulogy at her service held at the Atlanta Civic Center. "All women did the funeral," she recalls. "Maya Angelou did the Call to Worship, 'Still I Rise.'[34] Coretta Scott King[35] talked about Jean Young as a civil rights organizer. Jeanne Moutoussamy Ashe[36] talked about Jean as a spiritual friend. Karen Lowery[37] sang 'We Shall Behold Him,' and Bernice Johnson Reagon, of 'Sweet Honey in the Rock,'[38] led us in singing songs from the movement. And I preached the eulogy, 'Who Can Find a Virtuous Woman.' President Clinton sent a hand-written note that I read. The Governor of Georgia, Zell Miller, and the state senators were there."

Rev. Dr. Newman's book *With Heart and Hand: The Black Church Working to Save Black Children*[39] came out in 1994, about the time she went to First Congregation Church in Atlanta. Churches all over the country began to use it to develop ministries for youth and young adults. At First Congregational she tried to implement one of the programs delineated in the book, an adopt-a-school program. "Our church would adopt a sixth grade class of the school down the street," Rev. Newman explains. "The children all lived in public housing; their parents were on welfare, and some were unemployed. We would tutor the children after school one day a week at the church. And as we got to know them, the deacon board could then help their parents with referrals for job training or with whatever they needed. We would follow this sixth grade class through their graduation and help them be prepared for college. I met with the principal of the school, who was excited that First Church wanted to do this. Some of the church members were going to work with me on this, and we were getting together." When Susan was on vacation, she got a phone call that some church members had called a meeting to vote down this ministry project. "Our church is a historical building," they said at the meeting. "We have just renovated it and put in new carpeting and wallpaper. We don't want 'those' children in our church building." So they voted down the adopt-a-school program. "I could not believe it!" Susan says. "And that went on and on. Every time I tried to move an agenda forward it got voted down. The 63 people who had voted against my call to the church were the senior citizens who were the strong givers and who were there every Sunday and at every church meeting. The 136 people who had voted for me were their children and grandchildren who wanted something new and dynamic. But many of them were entrepreneurs and traveled widely, and were not there every Sunday and at church meetings."

After a year at First Church in Atlanta, Rev. Dr. Newman decided that if things hadn't gotten better in another year, she would leave. The next year, 1996, she submitted her resignation to the church. The church had been willing to call a woman, but it had become obvious that parishioners would not follow a woman's leadership.

Because Dr. Newman had become so well known and loved in Atlanta, within only two weeks she was asked to be the executive director of Georgians for Children, a statewide child advocacy organization. Her work with Marian Wright Edelman on the Children's Defense Fund and her book *With Hand and Heart: The Black Church Working to Save Black Children* also led to this position. As executive director of Georgians for Children, Rev. Newman studied, monitored, and advocated for federal and state budgetary and policy issues pertaining to children and families, and served as the official spokesperson for the organization.

In 1999, Rev. Newman moved back to Washington, DC, because her mother began having problems with her health. Several years earlier she had begun an independent consulting company, Sincerely Susan, which continues to the present day. Dr. Newman travels around the country conducting workshops, lectures, and forums on sex education for teenagers and adults, emphasizing parental training for dialogue with youth concerning sexuality and health. She has worked with the DC Campaign to Prevent Teen Pregnancy, Planned Parenthood, the Virginia Department of Health, and the Illinois Department of Health. In connection with her consulting ministry Dr. Newman has also published articles and books, including *Oh God!: A Black Woman's Guide to Sex and Spirituality*[40] and *Your Inner Eve: Discovering God's Woman Within.*[41]

Back in DC, Rev. Dr. Newman held other faith-based and community positions. For two years she served as senior advisor for religious affairs to the district's mayor. In this capacity she advised Mayor

Anthony William on religious and ethical issues, fostered interfaith cooperation, advocated for the concerns of the faith community, and served on the mayor's HIV/AIDS Task Force. Dr. Newman became even more involved in HIV/AIDS education and ministry when she became executive director of The Balm in Gilead, Inc.[42] She mobilized churches to address HIV/AIDS, conducted workshops with clergy and laity to enhance churches' response to the disease, and wrote training manuals and other resource materials for use by churches and public health professionals. Currently she is a consultant with the AIDS Action Foundation, engaging faith leaders and denominations in the drafting and advocacy of a national public policy campaign to address HIV/AIDS. She has also served as the director of public policy for the Religious Coalition for Reproductive Choice,[43] working with religious leaders and legislators to improve the sexual and reproductive health of young people across the country.

During this time when she was serving in faith-based communities, Rev. Newman also interviewed with churches. Although her preaching drew standing ovations and *Ebony* magazine named her one of the Top Black Women Preachers in America, churches did not hire her as pastor. "The churches were not ready for a woman as a senior minister," she says. "It's very difficult as a black woman to get called to a church. There are churches that don't mind your being the assistant, but they're still not ready for you to be senior pastor. It's gotten a little better, but not much. The reality is if I were a man, I would have been a pastor of a major church a long time ago. I've always longed to be in a parish ministry. But I have met people and been a part of ministries that I would never have been a part of if I were relegated to just one congregation. I would never have gone anywhere; every Sunday I would have to be at the same church. I've always been preaching, even if I'm not on staff at a church. I'm preaching and teaching somewhere around the country. I truly believe that all things work together for the good." For one year she also served as interim pastor of Amistad St. Paul United Church of Christ in the DC area, and then as adjunct minister at Peoples United Church of Christ.

In April of 2010, All Souls Church in DC invited Rev. Newman to preach for Neighborhood Justice Sunday. "This was the first white church in Washington, DC, to hire a black pastor, Dr. David Eaton, who was installed there in 1969," she says. "He became a very famous preacher and great social justice activist. This church helped with freed slaves after the Civil War. The pastor at this time, Rev. William Henry Channing, demonstrated his interest in the freed African Americans by organizing the Freedman's Relief Union, of which he served as president.[44] He also helped form the Miner Normal School, which would become a part of Howard University years later. This has always been a social justice church. This is a majority white church, committed to multicultural, multiracial ministry." When she preached at All Souls on April 18, people responded with standing ovations at both the 9:30 a.m. and 11:15 a.m. services. Rev. Rob Hardies told her that in his ten years as pastor of All Souls Church, no one has ever received a standing ovation. "The energy and the connection were so powerful," Susan says. "I felt such love from these people."

A few weeks later, Rev. Hardies left her a voice message. "I heard some urgency in his voice," Susan recalls. "We had just passed the Marriage Equality Law in Washington, DC, that gay and lesbian people could get married legally. Rob Hardies led that campaign, along with Rev. Dr. Christine Wiley and Rev. Dr. Dennis Wiley, copastors of Covenant Baptist Church. I was one of the ministers who also worked on it, so we had that victory together. Rob and I had known each other for about six years. I was thinking that his urgency was from getting a whole lot of requests to do marriages with gay couples, and he needed help to do them. I called him back, and he said, 'Our people loved you so much that we will pay you to be with us in worship on Sundays for a year. Our associate minister left a few months ago, and we're doing a search for an associate.'"

All Souls Church offered Rev. Dr. Newman the position, with a salary a little higher than that of the faith-based job she was in at the time. "I preach one Sunday a month," she says. "I have one Sunday a month off. Monday is my day off, and Friday I don't have to physically be at the church, but I use Friday as writing and reflection time. I have five weeks paid leave. I died and went to heaven! I was just amazed." Also, Rev. Newman appreciates the opportunity to serve at All Souls because of the church's inclusive leadership. "We don't want the pulpit to be all vanilla on any one Sunday," she says. "We make sure our worship leaders are male and female of various races and ages. It's important what people see in the pulpit of our congregations. When they see people who are their race and their gender, that's very empowering.

The images you see—that's what your dreams are made of. When you begin to decide on what you want to do, you have that image. But I had no models of women preachers. I had nobody to look to. I have had young girls tell me that they've never thought about going into ministry or doing anything in religious leadership until they saw me in the pulpit. A young African American woman told me it was very powerful for her when she came to this church to see a black woman in the pulpit. She had an instant sense of identity. That was what drew her to the church."

To keep her standing as a minister in the United Church of Christ denomination, Rev. Dr. Newman also preaches and participates in the ministry team at Covenant Baptist United Church of Christ. "Covenant Baptist, where Dennis and Christine Wiley are copastors, has been in discernment for two years as to becoming affiliated also with the United Church of Christ," Susan explains. "They became a part of the UCC in May of 2010. So Easter Sunday I joined Covenant Baptist United Church of Christ. I see things coming full circle, because when I felt challenged about not having a place to do ministry in the Baptist church, Rev. H. Wesley Wiley, Dennis' father, was the one who encouraged me to leave the Baptists and join the United Church of Christ. Now I'm able to go back and join a Baptist church, and I can help midwife them into the UCC denomination. Rev. Dr. Barbara Brown Zikmund, a church historian, Rev. Sylvia McDonald Kaufmann, and I are teaching UCC ministry, theology, history, and polity. And it's great that Dennis and Christine Wiley and Rob Hardies are friends and that we all worked together on the DC Marriage Equality Law. So the Sunday I'm off from All Souls I worship at Covenant."

Rev. Dr. Newman expresses gratitude for opportunities to be in pastoral ministry at both All Souls Church and Covenant Baptist United Church of Christ. "These churches are social justice churches, intentionally inclusive in worship leadership and language," she says. "The leaders of these churches use inclusive language as a model for laypeople. They hear us say, 'God who is Mother and Father to us all.' So I can be with these two churches that I feel are great models of the 'beloved community'[45] that Dr. King spoke of. It's very wonderful to be closely connected with both churches."

At these two churches Dr. Newman also appreciates the opportunity to mentor young ministers, as she has done before as an adjunct professor at United Theological Seminary and a guest lecturer at Howard University School of Divinity. Now in her pastoral roles at All Souls Church and at Covenant Baptist United Church of Christ, she teaches and models inclusive theology. "In Covenant Baptist Church we have 25 clergy who are in various stages," she says. "Some are recently licensed, some are in seminary, some are ordained, and some are about to be ordained. It gives me hope that we're sending out into the world these 25 ministers who have learned under male-female pastoral leaders, who are open and affirming and welcoming of gay and lesbian people and people of all classes and races."

Consistent with her theology of the Divine within us all, Rev. Dr. Newman often connects the human and Divine feminine when she speaks about inclusive language and imagery. "It's important for women to be in the pulpit," she says. "I think it's important for people to see themselves, that we're all created in the image of God and that God is male and female, and that God is black, brown, yellow. We need to make sure that everybody can see and hear themselves. I think it's important to recognize that some women have suffered negative relationships with their fathers, so God cannot be Father to them, but God could be Mother. There are times that God is nurturing like a mother. That's why I'm intentional about making it clear that the feminine presence of God's Spirit is inside of us. If 'God is Spirit, and they that worship God must worship in spirit and in truth,'[46] then I'm going to address God interchangeably as 'He' and 'She,' 'Father' and 'Mother.'" Dr. Newman also balances female and male references to God in her book *Oh God!: A Black Woman's Guide to Sex and Spirituality*:

> If God did not want us to enjoy sex, She would not have made Barry White. If God did not want us to enjoy sex, He would not have made the Isley Brothers, Stevie Wonder, Smokey, Will Downing, the Dells, Harold Melvin and the Blue Notes with Teddy Pendergrass, Jeffrey Osborne with LTD, Luther, Marvin, D'Angelo, Maxwell, Lenny Kravitz, Prince, and R. Kelly. If God did not want us to enjoy sex, She would not have let us ever hear and slow drag to "Stay in My Corner," "Stairway to Heaven," "The Love We Had Stays on My Mind," "If Only for One Night," "You Really Got a Hold on Me," "You and I," and "When Something Is Wrong With My Baby."[47]

Many people tell Dr. Newman that they had never thought of God as female until they read it or heard her say it. "So I believe that the oughtness of using inclusive language is on me," she says. "I think including female imagery of God is so powerful that even Jesus did it in the parable of the lost coin; God is the Woman sweeping the house. In the parable of the lost sheep, God is the Shepherd going after the sheep, and in the parable of the prodigal son, God is the loving Father. So in that trilogy of parables,[48] God is male and female. I think that was a very powerful thing that Jesus used female divine imagery while teaching even in that time. Words are powerful because our world is shaped by our language. The way we communicate and bring images to people through our language, through the words we choose, and through our images—that is powerful; that is what creates our mindset."

Rev. Newman expresses appreciation that some of the DC churches she has served also include female divine visual images of various races. "Peoples Congregational United Church of Christ has an African American female image of Jesus Christ in one window and a male image of Jesus Christ in the other window," she says. "Dr. David Driskell, the great artist in residence at the University of Maryland and a member of Peoples Church, created the stained glass windows. Covenant Baptist United Church of Christ has images of men and women, black and Latino and white, doctors and lawyers and teachers and preachers, and historical African American people in the stained glass windows. I remember as a little girl at Goodwill Baptist Church we had Sunday school material that always pictured a blonde-haired, blue-eyed Jesus, holding a little lamb. We create God in our own image. The dominant demographic historically of our churches has been white and male. So the pictures of Jesus are white, blonde, blue-eyed, and male."

Although imagery and leadership of churches are more inclusive now than when she was growing up, Rev. Newman asserts that we still have a long way to go. "There's a stained glass ceiling in the faith community, just like there's a glass ceiling in the secular community," she says. "We have to break the ceiling. I want us to get to a time when there's no such thing as a woman's place. A woman's place is wherever her gifts and graces are needed at that time. One time when I experienced sexism, this man telling me he didn't think that women should be in certain roles, I said to him, 'What if you have a heart attack, and the ambulance takes you to the trauma unit of the hospital and the chief cardiologist, the only one available, is a woman? Are you telling me that you don't want her to save your life because of her gender, when she's the most qualified person in the whole hospital? When it comes to saving your spiritual life, then you would want the most qualified person, not based upon gender, but upon ability, gifts, and graces.' A lot of men say that women should not be in ministry. They will license you, but they won't ordain you. They'll tease you. They'll license you so you can preach on Women's Day and Children's Day and Missionaries' Day, one or two Sundays out of 52 of the year. I say, 'If you are not going to ordain me, don't license me. And if you're not going to license me, don't preach the Gospel of Jesus Christ to me, because once you have released the word of God, the Holy Spirit cannot be controlled. You have no control over the Spirit. If you're not going to ordain me, don't baptize me. Don't preach to me.'"

Obstacles and challenges to her pastoral ministry have not stopped Rev. Dr. Newman from prophetic preaching and writing. She has taken every opportunity to confront the sexism and racism that still prevail in the majority of churches. "Most ministers confronted with the issue of sexism will readily point to one or two women on their trustee board, or women licensed and sitting in the pulpit, but the very fact that we can still easily count who we have in what places is painful," she writes. "I applaud the pastors who do treat the male and female clergy of their churches with equality, but these pastors are too few. For some of my own friends I've helped prepare a church budget for the trustee board meeting, or counseled them on how to transition from their secular jobs to become full-time pastors, yet I've never graced their pulpits. These are men who cannot deny the gift of God within their sisters, but they have no confidence in them simply because they are women. . . . when it is obvious that a woman is experienced and capable and she still is not allowed to enter certain areas of pastoral duties, then I would ask for a reality check; more often than not, the diagnosis will still be sexism . . . Women of spirit can preach, teach, pastor, chair the joint boards, serve on the city council, sit in Congress, fly into space, dive to the ocean's floor, climb the mountain's heights, cook, clean, conceive a life in our wombs, nurture it within nine months, and birth into the world a child who may be the Savior of the world—that's powerful! But the gift that men often overlook is that women of spirit desire to be trusted and loved by our brothers, in order that we may do the will of God in this world together."[49]

Inclusive leadership and language empower marginalized people, Rev. Newman believes. "People of color and women have been marginalized by our dominant white male culture," she explains. "I would love to get to the time when we would no more see in people's biographies and in the news the 'first black this,' or 'the first female that.' Whether we were going to vote for Barack Obama or Hillary Clinton was a big thing for black women, because we wanted a woman but we wanted a black person too. It's empowering to lift up a group of people who've been oppressed because they are black or because they are female; it's the right and just thing to do. I make it a point to lift up women in the Bible when I'm preaching throughout the year, not just on Women's Day. When I do prayers, I often say 'the God of Abraham and Sarah, Isaac and Rebecca, Jacob and Rachel.' I always use the male and the female. I will say 'the God of Martin and Coretta, the God of Frederick Douglass and Sojourner Truth,' using historical people of faith. There is room at the table for everyone. Every voice should be heard; no particular voice is greater or more valued because of gender or sexual orientation or race. We are all God's children. Jesus said this ought to be a 'whosoever will' church, not just a church for straight people, not just a church for men, not just a church for white people. The kingdom of God is welcoming, and the gates of heaven are wide open. I often joke that a whole lot of folks are going to be very upset when they find out that God really is a heavy-set black woman in her mid-fifties!"

There was a time when Susan would send out business cards that had her name as "Rev. S. Newman." People would hear about Rev. Newman and ask Rev. Newman to preach. "They didn't know whether that was Stan Newman or Susan Newman," she says. "Then when I showed up, they would say, 'Oh, you're a woman.' And I'd say, 'Yes, for the last fifty years or so.'"

Even though she has experienced resistance and discrimination in the church, Rev. Dr. Newman has never considered leaving the church. "I'm not going to leave the church and stop doing what my heart feels that I ought to be doing because of someone else's ignorance," she says. "There have been times I've gotten discouraged, and what I do is pull back a little bit, but I never leave. I learned that I could change the church by being part of it, not leaving it, that the church needs me. The church needs somebody running around with a sharp pin busting all these sexist and racist and classist balloons that the church has. So that's why I've been with it for 35 years. What I've grown in grace, wisdom, and knowledge about is that God has not called me to a particular denomination or race of people. I've been in an all-black church, I've been in a racially mixed church, and I've been in the white church. It's about faith and people. You cannot tell me that when I get to heaven, there are going to be all these different sections for different denominations and different Communion tables. I think there will be one big welcoming table, and everybody can come sit at it."

For Rev. Newman this inclusive, welcoming table does not need to wait till heaven. It is also her vision for the future of the church in this world. "I hope for a truly ecumenical, interfaith church," she says. "I would love to see us do more things together across lines of country and belief systems. I would love to see more of the experience I had in 1980 at the Ecumenical Institute in Geneva, Switzerland. We were every race and country and culture. When we would sit at meals and sit around and chat, I would imagine how the upper room was on the day of Pentecost, when all were praising God in their own languages and cultures, speaking the same message, and everybody heard it and understood in their own way. I would like to see more and more of every faith honoring interfaith cooperation. We come together when we work on justice issues. We get together and work on the crisis in Haiti or work in Habitat for Humanity[50] or Oxfam[51] or Crop Walks.[52] When we are able to do justice and work to uplift suffering humanity, put aside our differences and find common ground, I feel we're working towards that 'beloved community.'"

Through her prophetic preaching, writing, teaching, and advocacy, Rev. Dr. Susan Newman works to make the dream of that "beloved community" a reality. She is overcoming obstacles, transforming the church into a greater power for liberation in the world. "No change for good comes without struggle," she says.

3

Dr. Bridget Mary Meehan

Priest
Mary Mother of Jesus Catholic Community,
Sarasota, Florida
Bishop, Association of
Roman Catholic Women Priests

On April 17, 2010, Bishop Bridget Mary Meehan stands in a circle at the Eucharistic altar with all those gathered in Mary Mother of Jesus Catholic Community in Sarasota, Florida. Wearing a bright orange-yellow stole flowing over her alb, Bishop Bridget Mary[1] invites all in the circle to raise our hands toward the bread and wine and to speak the words of consecration together, beginning, "And so, Steadfast One, we call upon Your Spirit to come upon this bread and wine to make them holy, that they may become You in us, the body and blood of Christ."[2] Then we formed two lines to receive Communion from female and male servers. After the Eucharist, Bishop Bridget Mary leads the congregation in the traditional "Prayer of Jesus," or "Lord's Prayer," also symbolizing the equality of male and female by changing "Our Father" to "Our Father and Mother" and "kingdom" to "kin-dom."

At the beginning of the liturgy my attention is drawn to the female image with dark face and flaming gold wings on the cover of the large book of the Gospels at the center of the altar. Michael Rigdon, a married priest who wears a multicolored stole over a yellow knit shirt and who asks not to be called "Father," takes this book from the altar and reads from the Gospel of John. Then Bridget Mary begins a dialogue homily with a few moments of silent meditation and a brief reflection on the Scripture, followed by an invitation for anyone in the congregation to speak: "Spirit brings us together to love and to care. With prayer and love, boundaries of space and time disappear. The Spirit is present in all of us to strengthen and challenge us." Interspersed throughout the liturgy are congregational songs accompanied by the mellifluous saxophone music of Bridget Mary's father, Jack.

As a Roman Catholic priest and bishop, Bridget Mary challenges the all-male priesthood, bringing dramatic change to the church. She and others in the Women Priests movement are prophetic also in changing the hierarchical church back to the early church model of a discipleship of equals. "The community is the expression of the Spirit in our midst," Bridget Mary explains to me in an interview in the mobile home she shares with her father. "Women priests call forth the gifts of the people to share those gifts in a circle of equals. The Eucharist belongs to the believing community. Therefore, when we celebrate Eucharist, we call people to join around the altar to pray the Eucharistic prayer. They say the words of consecration together with the presiders because the Body of Christ is the whole people together. We have a dialogue homily that reflects that the Spirit is in the people. At the liturgy of the Word, we need to hear different voices of how the Spirit is living and calling and vibrantly challenging people to live the Word today in their real lives. It's not just one person's take on what it means to live the Word of God in the world, such as the preacher or presider or priest. We trust the Wisdom of the Spirit in the people gathered in the assembly."

For many years Wisdom has been a significant divine image for Bridget Mary. She has been in the Sophia Holy Wisdom region of a religious order, Sisters for Christian Community.[3] "This is not a geographical region but a spiritual focus," she explains. "The region is reflective of the Wisdom of the Sacred Feminine, unfolding the Sophia feminine Wisdom. Our focus is on fostering the Divine Feminine in life, in our relationships, in our spirituality, in being women who reflect Wisdom Sophia and who join Her in working for justice and peace." Sophia has inspired Bridget Mary to write twenty books: "My ministry of book writing comes from Sophia to foster the Sacred

Feminine." The word "sofia" is even in her email address. "I always felt called to be a passionate reflection of the feminine face of God," she says. "That reflection is healing, reconciling, transformative, empowering, and co-creative of community, rejoicing in the celebratory coming together of others to share our spiritual journeys into the Divine and to be who we are called to be in the cosmic dance of creation with our divine partner and partners, inclusive of all."

Born in Ireland, Bridget Mary Meehan was named for St. Brigit of Kildare, bishop and abbess of Ireland, who was named for Mother Goddess, Brigit.[4] With her parents and two younger brothers, Patrick and Sean, Bridget Mary lived in "a lovely little gray cottage" across from the Erkina River in County Laois, Ireland. "It was a rural, rustic, very beautiful countryside with sheep and cows and beautiful gardens and wildlife," she recalls. "Patrick and I fed the lambs in the field adjacent to our cottage. One day a little lamb swallowed the nipple of the bottle. We went to our mom, crying, pouring out the sad tale about our little pet lamb. The lamb survived, and we grew wiser about feeding lambs. As children in rural Ireland, Patrick and I walked through the fields to school, and on the way home, we often stopped at the local 'sweet shop.' We had no money, but I'd tell Vester, the kind shopkeeper, that my daddy would pay for the sweets when he came in."

Bridget Mary describes her family as "very loving and earth-centered." They didn't have much "store-bought" food. "Everything was grown in our garden, and my mom baked bread," she says. "I didn't have many toys, just one rag doll. What I'd do is make mud pies. It rained a lot in Ireland, so I loved feeling the earth and pretending I was baking and making cakes. Today we're returning to this earth-centered consciousness, but I grew up in it."

Her "close-knit" family prayed the Rosary together every night. Her mom, Bridget, called "Bridie," whom Bridget Mary describes as having "mountain-moving faith," always led the Rosary. Her dad, Jack, filled the house with music of saxophone and trumpet. Her maternal grandfather, "Papa Beale," also provided a "very loving, nurturing presence" in the home. Bridget Mary flourished in the spiritual environment of her home. "After the family Rosary each evening, I'd have heart to heart talks with Mary," she recalls. "We grew up in the kind of household in Ireland where you always felt that the saints and angels and Jesus and Mary were like extended family. We had this prayerful atmosphere and this sense that all of life was encompassed by the Holy—the storytelling, the music." In 1955, at the age of seven, Bridget Mary made her first Communion at Church of the Holy Trinity in Rathdowney, where there is a stained-glass window of St. Brigit.[5] "Eucharist always drew me," she says. "I would go to Mass more times than we needed to. I didn't just go once a week with my family. I liked to be there; I always had a sense of God's presence, somehow drawing me into a very deep relationship with God. Even as a child, I had that sense of connecting with the Holy in the Eucharist, that it was a source of power, a source of being loved, and a source of energy."

The Catholic school Bridget Mary attended in Ireland did not give the love and nurturing that her family gave her. "School in Ireland was very, very harsh," Bridget Mary says. "I was only there, thank God, for two years. In my first year the nuns were kind, but the second year they were very mean. If you missed an answer, they would hit you. Child abuse went on in the industrial schools of Ireland; this was a harsh system, brutal to children. It made me nervous and full of fear to go to school."

After the death of Bridget Mary's Grandfather Beale, in whose home the Meehan family lived, her Aunt Molly wrote to invite the family to come to the United States. In 1956 the Meehan family immigrated to the U.S., sponsored by Molly McCarthy, Bridie's sister, and her husband, Fergus McCarthy. Bridget Mary and her family arrived in New York Harbor in June of 1956 and settled in Arlington, Virginia, in the colonial home of Aunt Molly and Uncle Fergus. Aunt Molly had a lovely doll with red braided hair waiting for Bridget Mary when she arrived. Several years later Aunt Molly and Uncle Fergus moved to a home on a nearby street, and the Meehan family continued to live in the colonial home, which Jack Meehan still owns and rents. Jack Meehan worked as an engineering supervisor at Brookings Institution, a think tank in Washington, DC.

In the U.S. Bridget Mary went to Catholic grammar and high schools. She found the nuns in these schools to be kinder than those in her school in Ireland. "The fear factor was not as prevalent as it was in Ireland, although the nuns were strict," she says. But her first year at Saint Thomas More School in Arlington, Virginia, was difficult. "I was a chubby little girl with curly hair," Bridget Mary recalls. "At recess, some of my classmates would tease me about the way I talked.

Some called me 'fatso' and would not let me join in their games. I often cried, couldn't concentrate in school, and felt as if I didn't belong. My schoolwork suffered as a result as well. I did not begin to flourish in my new environment until the fourth grade, when a lovely, gentle nun, Sister Marita Louise, expressed her belief in me. She would stop by my desk and praise my efforts. I could tell from the sparkle in her eye that she liked my Irish brogue. My spirit soared, my grades improved, and I made new friends."[6]

After graduating from Bishop O'Connell High School in 1966, when she was eighteen years old, Bridget Mary entered a convent. "I loved my religious life," she says. "I always felt called to consecrate my life to God. I felt this amazing Love always enveloping me and calling me to be that Love, to be joyful, and to form relationships of love and kindness and service to other people. That has been my call from the beginning." After three years of formation Bridget Mary made her profession of vows to become an Immaculate Heart of Mary (IHM)[7] sister. During these years of formation she also worked toward her undergraduate degree. In 1969 she began teaching in Catholic schools. "When I became a nun, I was not going to be a mean nun like I'd had in Ireland," she says. "I wanted to be a kind, compassionate nun. At that time we were trained really well as sisters to make education creative and holistic and fun."

During her years as an IHM sister, Bridget Mary lived in a number of places. She entered the convent at the motherhouse in Immaculata, Pennsylvania. Professors from the nearby Immaculata University came to the motherhouse to teach the nuns to keep them from mixing with other university students. "They kept us separate because they were afraid that we would become too worldly," Bridget Mary recalls. "We were isolated and formed in Nunhood 101, which did not include socializing with anyone other than nuns!" Bridget Mary earned her BA degree from Immaculata University, with a major in theology and a minor in sociology. She taught fifth grade at St. Rose of Lima in Eddystone, outside of Philadelphia; fourth grade at St. Barnabas in southwest Philadelphia; fourth grade at Sacred Heart, Manoa, another suburb of Philadelphia; and sixth grade at Sts. Peter & Paul in Decatur, a suburb of Atlanta, Georgia.

While living in Atlanta, Bridget Mary became a member of an ecumenical, charismatic prayer group, a major influence on her spiritual journey and her pastoral ministry. "It broke my Catholic mentality and opened me up to see that the power and gifts of the Holy Spirit are present in all of us, that together we journey toward God and service to one another," she says. "I discovered that the community calls forth the gifts and that the Spirit has no limitations in acting in us or in the community." Bridget Mary attended a charismatic conference in Augusta, Georgia, with Christians of all denominations. "It was the most joyful experience I'd ever had, except maybe my profession as a nun," she recalls. "It was awesome. I thought that this was surely what heaven is about, where all are one. Theologically, I knew that in God we're all one. But for the first time at that conference, I experienced the power of what that means when people come together as sisters and brothers with one another in the Spirit, and that this can happen with people from all walks of life, all religions. That has been a major influence in my life, permeating all my writing and everything that I do pastorally. When I work with people to form community, I have such an appreciation that all are called and gifted, because of that charismatic renewal phase of my life."

In 1976, Bridget Mary took a leave of absence from the Immaculate Heart of Mary religious order to care for her mother, who had had back surgery. Living at home in Arlington, Virginia, Bridget Mary taught religion for two years at La Reine High School, a Catholic girls' school in nearby Suitland, Maryland. During this time she also began studying toward her master's degree at Catholic University of America in Washington, DC. Bridget Mary loved teaching religion at La Reine while she took courses in theology. "It was enlightening to discover much about the early church that I didn't know," she says. "It was helpful to study the desert mothers and fathers,[8] to glean more insight into the Catholic tradition." In 1980, she received an MA degree in religious education with a focus on spirituality.

During the years she was caring for her mother, teaching at La Reine High School, and working toward her master's degree, Bridget Mary participated in a weekly prayer meeting with Regina Madonna Oliver. Regina had been in Immaculate Heart of Mary religious community with Bridget Mary, but they had not met there. Like Bridget Mary, Regina had experienced the charismatic renewal movement. "It became clear to us that we were not being called back into our religious community because it was very structured, and we were feeling freer in the Spirit," Bridget Mary recalls. "We needed community but in a different way from what the convent provided. We were being called out, but we didn't know how that was going to take place. So we trusted God, and our image was walking on water." In 1980, Bridget Mary and Regina joined Society of Sisters for the Church (SSC),[9] staying in that religious order for fifteen years. When SSC began considering a more structured canonical status, they left to join Sisters for Christian Community (SFCC), independent of the Catholic Church hierarchy. "This community has the vision of global interconnectedness of all life and of all people," Bridget Mary says. "Sisters for Christian Community work for earth transformation, fostering relationships that support justice, harmony, peace, and equality for all people."

Soon after she received her MA degree in religious education, Bridget Mary attended services at Fort Myer Chapel,[10] in Arlington, Virginia, with her mother and Aunt Molly. The priest, Chaplain John Weyand, who was presiding at the Mass, engaged Bridget Mary in conversation.

"What are you doing now?" he asked her.

"I just got a master's, and I'm open," she replied.

"Well, we would love to have you do some liturgy and some work with us. Would you come to a meeting?"

"Sure, but liturgy I don't know. I do know community building for the charismatic renewal, and I know how to do life in the Spirit. But I don't do that alone. You need to find me a team of people who would be willing partners to do that with me."

Chaplain Weyand did find a team to work with Bridget Mary, and he became a part of her partnership circle. She formed what she called a "Life in the Spirit" team, and started a prayer group. The Fort Myer community responded with such enthusiasm to the prayer group that the head chaplain, Warren Tierney, offered Bridget Mary the position of pastoral associate to serve the Catholic community. Chaplain Tierney asked her to write her own job description, not as the traditional director of religious education in the military, but as a pastoral associate. "They didn't know what that was, but they said I could do it," she explains. "It was so exciting because I got my dream job. I got to put the gifts that God had given me together with the community that had called me. It was a pastoral associate under a GS-9 job description,[11] which fit under religious education specialist, but it was a new specialty in pastoral ministry. I was like a partner with the priest. I did things like adult faith development, the Rite of Christian Initiation of Adults (RCIA), ministry to the sick, Communion services, and marriage preparation. For marriage preparation, since I'm celibate, I formed a team of couples who worked with me; they did the actual work of couple sponsoring and dialogue on marriage. I worked with a team of young parents on baptismal preparation. In ministry to the sick I worked with a team of senior citizens who had had illnesses and who had a heart of compassion for sick people. My idea was to work with the people who are closest to the ministry."

For fifteen years Bridget Mary served as a pastoral associate at Fort Myer Chapel. "It was a wonderful ministerial community," she says. "I was blessed by many experiences and still have many friends from that time of community. One of the things that began in that Fort Myer Chapel community that still exists is an ecumenical retreat. The Catholics and Protestants join together once a year on a retreat together. That was so successful and such a blessing because it broke down differences and brought people together on common faith journeys across religious divisions. Coming together as a Christian community of different denominations did much to heal the prejudices that the people were brought up with. That was very exciting. During that time my consciousness again was raised about other faiths, being one with other traditions, not just Catholic."

While serving at Fort Myer Chapel, Bridget Mary worked toward the Doctor of Ministry degree at Virginia Theological Seminary. In 1987, she was the first woman and the first Roman Catholic at Virginia Theological Seminary to graduate with the DMin degree. There was only one other woman, an Episcopal priest, in the DMin program at that time. "She celebrated the first Mass I attended at the seminary," Bridget Mary recalls. "It was the first time I'd ever experienced a woman priest. I thought the ground would swallow me up; it was absolutely awesome. At the seminary I had once again that great experience of stretching through ecumenical dialogue and sharing theology. Also, I was reading more and more feminist theology by women like Rosemary Radford Ruether, Elizabeth Schüssler Fiorenza, and Elizabeth Johnson."[12]

Then Dr. Bridget Mary Meehan began writing about female imagery for God. "I felt that if we were to grow in partnership as men and women in equality in the church, we needed to restore the feminine dimension of the Divine," she says. Bridget Mary describes a mystical experience she had before writing her first book, *Exploring the Feminine Face of God*.[13] "I prayed about writing that book," she says. "In my prayer I felt Mary, Mother of Jesus, saying to me, 'Yes, you need to do this. Just do it, and it will be blessed.'" So she wrote this meditation book based on female imagery from Scripture, the mystics, the Sophia tradition, and contemporary works. *Exploring the Feminine Face of God* was so successful that as soon as it was published, it immediately sold out. When I recently read an article in the *Dallas Morning News* on Bishop Bridget Mary Meehan, I remembered how impressed I had been by *Exploring the Feminine Face of God* and how often I had used it in worship communities. I immediately wrote Bridget Mary to request an interview.

Exploring the Feminine Face of God is enhanced by the artwork of Sister Marie-Celeste Fadden, a Carmelite sister. One picture is of a woman with strong, contemplative face and flowing hair; she is standing on the earth with folded wings covering her body, like a mother eagle, and is surrounded by trees and flying eagles. On the opposite page is this poem by Bridget Mary:

Who Are You, God?

I am the womb of mystery
I am the birther of new life
I am the breast of unending delight
I am the passionate embrace of woman
I am the emanation of feminine beauty
I am the Mother of Creation
I am the cosmic dance of Sophia Wisdom
I am the sister of courage, justice, and peace
I am the feminine face of God
You have longed to kiss.[14]

Dr. Meehan expresses her belief in the transformative power of these female divine images: "In order to balance our church and to change it from male domination, we need images of the feminine, the integration of the feminine into our consciousness and our spirituality." This strong belief led to her next book, *Delighting in the Feminine Divine*. In the introduction to this book Bridget Mary writes: "If we do not mean that God is male when masculine imagery is used, perhaps we should ask ourselves if there should be a problem speaking of God in female imagery. Praying with feminine images of God introduces us into a wonderful variety of new possibilities for prayer that will enrich our spiritual growth and help us to transform political, social, economic systems that oppress us."[15]

The next year Bridget Mary and her friend Regina Madonna Oliver published a children's book, *Heart Talks with Mother God*. In the introduction to the book is an illustration of the importance of teaching female divine images to children: "Noreen, a young mother, in chatting about God with her four-year-old daughter, Louise, referred to God as 'she.' Louise quickly disagreed with her mother: 'No, Mommy, God is not a woman, he is a man.' Her mother, taken by surprise, replied: 'God can be female and male.' But Louise went over to the bookcase and removed her children's prayer book from the shelf and opened it up to a picture of God: 'See, Mommy, God is a man who lives up on a cloud in the sky!'"[16] The beautiful stories, bright-colored pictures, prayers, songs, and activities in *Heart Talks with Mother God* are intended to inspire girls to believe that they are also created in the divine image, and to introduce both girls and boys to the female divine images in Scripture. "The purpose of the book is to get children early on to integrate that God is Mother God, as well as Father God and Creator," Bridget Mary says. One of the pictures in the book, by artist Susan Sawyer, is of a woman tenderly holding a child close to her face. The mother and child with dark eyes and hair have multicultural, serene visages. On the page opposite this picture is a meditation entitled "God, a Nurturing Mother":

Listen my child as your Mother God describes herself to you. . . .

"I am like a tender mother who cuddles, kisses, and holds you in her arms.
I am like a caring mother who provides for your needs.
I am like a comforting mother who dries your tears when you are sad.
I am like a kind mother who always tells you how special you are.
I am like a wise mother who teaches and guides you.
I am like a happy mother who smiles, sings, plays, and dances with you.
I am like a loving mother who tells you lots of times: 'I love you. . . . I believe in you. . . . Keep on trying. . . . I am proud of you. . . . I will always love you no matter what happens.'"[17]

Also, included in *Heart Talks with Mother God* are meditations and pictures entitled "Mary, Mother of Jesus, Shows Us God's Mothering Love" and "Mary Shows Us the Givingness of God." Bridget Mary comments: "Mary leads the way for the church, especially the Catholic Church, to show us the face of the feminine. Although not God herself, she helps remind us of the feminine energy, the feminine presence. She points to the maternal heart of God. She has played a very visible role; otherwise, Catholicism would be devoid of any kind of feminine presence. For me, Mary is pivotal in changing the church into resembling the discipleship of equals of which she and others were part in the Jesus movement."

Her doctoral studies had led Bridget Mary to reclaiming women in Scripture, including women in the life of Jesus and the early church. She discovered all the stories of women as equal disciples and presiders at the Holy Eucharist. The result of her discovery was *Praying with Women of the Bible*,[18] published by Liguori, which Bridget Mary describes as "one of the most conservative, mainstream Catholic publishers." When Bridget Mary was excommunicated after being ordained, Liguori Publications discontinued five of her books, including *Praying with Women of the Bible* and her first book, *The Healing Power of Prayer*,[19] published in seven languages. "It's so funny, because God, I believe, has a great sense of humor," Bridget Mary laughs. "Being the feminist that I am, somehow the institutional church has published me and supported my ministry. All of my work at this point had feminist spirituality integrated into it, and somehow it got published by mainstream Catholic publishers."[20]

Bishop Bridget Mary says that her work also remains in mainstream Catholicism through a television series on religious education. When she ministered at Fort Myer with families, she began to see the deficiencies of CDD[21] as Catholic religious education for public school children. "I felt that families should be involved, so I used Kathleen Chesto's successful program, Family-Centered Intergenerational Religious Education (FIRE)," she explains. "Wouldn't you know the Catholic bishops invited me to do a television series for them on that program. So it's somewhere buried in their archives at this point."

Also to illustrate God's sense of humor, Bridget Mary tells the story of being invited to appear on Mother Angelica's[22] television program. "Mother Angelica is my total opposite in every way, the most anti-feminist nun around," Bridget Mary says. "Yet she's built an empire on television, and she inspired me. When my first book, *The Healing Power of Prayer*, came out, I got a call from her producer to be a guest on her show. I didn't watch her show because I was a very busy pastoral person. But I said I'd be on the show because I would get to share the book." Bridget Mary flew down to Birmingham, Alabama, for the show. In Mother Angelica's absence, a Jesuit priest hosted the show that evening. "The program went very well," Bridget Mary recalls. "Then there were call-ins because it was 'Mother Angelica Live.' The second call was Larry from Dallas; he began by saying, 'devil woman.' There was a pause, and the host said, 'Well, Larry, I don't think we could hear you. Let's go to the next caller.' The gift of that program for me was that I realized that if I could get through 'Mother Angelica Live,' I would not be intimidated by anything on television."

After Bridget Mary left Fort Myer Chapel, her friend Rea Howard asked about her future ministry.

"Well, Sister Bridget, what are you going to do?"

"I don't know. I'm staying open to the Spirit," Bridget Mary replied.

"I think you should try to have a television show and do what Oprah does on television. You could start a spiritual TV talk show and call it 'Godtalk.'"

"I don't even know how to program a VCR, and I don't watch that much television. But it's an interesting idea. I'll take one step."

Bridget Mary says that she's always willing to try one step, to take a risk. "I felt like I was stepping off a cliff with no help in sight," she recalls. "But a voice within assured me, 'Don't be afraid to jump; I'll catch you.'" So she called the local public access cable station, and learned that a producers' meeting was scheduled for the next Wednesday. She went to the meeting, signed up to produce a TV show, took the required classes, and got producer status in 1996. Bridget Mary launched "Godtalk" in 1997 with a five-part series on "The Healing Power of Prayer." In the next ten years she produced and hosted 140 programs, including a series on courageous women in the Bible and in Christian tradition. "I couldn't believe I became a producer of all these shows that were on about fifteen stations," she says. "The reason I was able to do that was because of the experience I had on 'Mother Angelica Live.' I knew I could do TV. I could look in a camera, and

I would be nonplussed. If anything happened, it was okay because I could deal with it. I'm not a techie, but a group of wonderful volunteers whom I had never met before came into my life to help with the program. Two of these young people, Jay and John, had previous television experience."[23]

In 2005, while in formal preparation for the priesthood, Bridget Mary became the media spokesperson for Roman Catholic Women Priests (RCWP), and continued in that position until 2009. Currently she serves on the RCWP media team. She writes a blog,[24] produces and edits shows for Google Videos and YouTube[25] with the help of Rick Sapp, and represents RCWP with the press. Her ten years of producing and hosting "Godtalk" prepared her for all this work. "That got me ready to be spokesperson for Roman Catholic Women Priests under fire and to create the message," she says. "Now media have transitioned to the Internet, so anyone can put clips up. With our team I made videos on women priests, highlighting the first several years of the movement. They're up on Google Videos, so people can download these shows. I've been equipped to transition into this new media because I had that experience with 'Godtalk.'" Bridget Mary says that this experience has also prepared her to accept calls from CNN and *Democracy Now!*[26] to talk about the Women Priests movement and about the Vatican scandal. "I'm equipped to go in and sit in front of a camera with one cameraperson, who satellites me to New York or wherever," she says. "Because of all this experience of working with the media, I'm confident. I feel that the Spirit prepared me every step of the way."

Bridget Mary also believes that the Spirit prepared her for the priesthood through the many years of her pastoral ministry at Fort Myer Chapel and then through her leadership of small faith communities meeting in her homes in Virginia and Florida. "On one occasion members of our women's community in Florida called me forth to be their priest," she recounts. "When they discovered that I had been invited to attend the ordinations on the St. Lawrence Seaway, the first ordinations of Roman Catholic women priests in North America, the women's response was, 'This is great, but we want you to be our priest!'"[27]

On July 31, 2006, Bridget Mary was among the first eight women in the U.S. to be ordained Roman Catholic priests. That morning after a

CNN interview, Bridget Mary had breakfast with family, close friends, and other ordinands. Then the ordination ceremony took place aboard the riverboat "Majestic" at the confluence of the Ohio, Monongahela, and Allegheny rivers in Pittsburgh. Officiating at the ceremony were Bishop Patricia Fresen, Bishop Gisela Forster, and Bishop Ida Raming, all validly ordained by bishops in full apostolic succession. "I was overjoyed that my dream of serving God as a priest was now being fulfilled, and that so many companions, beginning with my family and friends, were there to share in this profound history-making event," Bridget Mary recalls. "My *Anam Cara*[28] and co-author, Sister Regina Madonna Oliver, presented me for ordination. My friend Peg Bowen, who co-led with me for fifteen years the ecumenical retreat at Fort Myer Community, laid out the rug for my prostration before the altar. My dear dad and my brother Patrick were on the boat. My brother Sean and sister-in-law, Nancy, did not get on the boat because Nancy would have been fired from her job as a Catholic school teacher. But they drove to Pittsburgh to support me, along with my niece and nephew, Katie and Danny, who were Catholic school kids so could not be on the boat either. My image as we were ordained on the boat was of Jesus calling us to get out of the boat and walk on water to a new model of justice and equality for women as disciples and equals. The only way to keep from sinking in the waves and storms that life would bring was to keep our eyes on Christ-Sophia and trust in her wisdom and compassionate care. I felt enveloped in Spirit-Sophia's embrace as I prostrated on the floor offering my life in service to God's people, united to them as their sister in mutual loving service as we built together a renewed, inclusive, welcoming church with the Heart of Love energizing us and guiding us on our water walk!"

At the end of the December following her ordination, Bridget Mary received a telephone call.

"Bridget Mary, my name is Dick Fisher. You were ordained in Pittsburgh, right?"

"Right!"

"Well, when are you going to have Mass?"

"Dick, why don't you come next week? We can start having Mass right around my dining room table."

Dick and Pat Fisher, Helen and Jack Duffy, and several others came the next Saturday evening. "So we started a house church in January 2007, right here in this little mobile home in Sarasota," Bridget Mary says. After *Sarasota Herald-Tribune* reporter Susan J. Rife wrote a story on the church,[29] it grew to about twenty-five people. A little while later, the bishop of the diocese, Frank Dewane, saw the announcement in the Community News section of the Sarasota newspaper about the weekly Mass in the house church. "He took umbrage with this, and his people told the paper to pull that little announcement," Bridget Mary recalls. "The *Herald-Tribune* said they could not pull an announcement because the bishop didn't like it, didn't agree with it. Columnist Tom Lyons wrote a big story about this for the paper. Well, that opened the door for ABC to come and do a television program on the Mass here. Then the church drew triple the number of people, and our house couldn't fit them any more. We moved to a larger home, and soon the church outgrew that space also. We went to Pastor Philip Garrison at St. Andrew United Church of Christ in Sarasota, where we are today. This church was so hospitable, loving, and open. We started renting space from St. Andrew at the end of February 2009. As a result of the bishop's telling the paper not to run the announcement, we grew so much that we needed this larger space. Opposition has always proved a blessing to us."

On April 19, 2009, Bridget Mary was among the first four American Roman Catholic women bishops to be ordained. Leading this ceremony were Bishop Patricia Fresen and Bishop Ida Raming from Germany and Bishop Christine Mayr-Lumetzberger from Austria. Bishops Raming and Mayr-Lumetzberger were among the seven women ordained on the Danube River between Germany and Austria in 2002, beginning the Women Priests movement. Bridget Mary's ordination as a bishop took place somewhere in Santa Barbara. "One of the major reasons for not revealing the place is that we wanted a prayerful, quiet, non-media event," Bridget Mary told the *California Catholic Daily*. "Our focus is not on the bishops' ordinations but on servant leadership to the Catholic community."[30] Another function of women bishops is to ordain other qualified candidates as deacons, priests, and bishops without having to depend on male bishops, who must hide their identities from the Roman Catholic hierarchy. The women ordained as bishops in 2009 served four regions of the United States. Bishop Bridget Mary Meehan served the Southern Region, which became the Association of Roman Catholic Women Priests.

On February 6, 2010, Bishop Bridget Mary participated in the ordination of the first women priests in Florida. Bishop Dewane threatened to excommunicate not only Bishop Bridget Mary and others who officiated, but everyone who attended. "I don't know how many excommunications I've had; I haven't counted them all," she says. "I think they're badges of honor actually, blessings. When the bishop threatened to excommunicate everyone, we held our breath, wondering who would come to the ordination. We had over 200 people come! And the media were all there to chart the story. The paper ran an article the next day saying that the bishop's threat of excommunication obviously didn't hurt; it just drew more people. They were all happy, and they weren't scared of the excommunication at all. When the bishop speaks in opposition to what we're doing for women priests, our numbers increase, and we gain more support. My experience is that opposition can really be the source of growth and blessing."

Although Pope Benedict excommunicated the first seven women ordained in 2002 and excommunicated others ordained since then, the women priests reject the excommunication. "The Catholic Church teaches that a law must be received by the faithful," Bishop Bridget Mary explains. "Seventy percent of Catholics in the U.S. support women's ordination. Therefore, canon 1024, which states that only a baptized male may receive Holy Orders, does not have the force of law because it has not been accepted by the community. In fact, we have a moral obligation to disobey this unjust law. St. Augustine said that an 'unjust law is no law at all.' We also reject the excommunication because we are validly ordained; the male bishop who ordained our first women bishops is in full apostolic succession. Therefore, our orders are valid. We are violating an unjust, man-made canon law that discriminates against women. We are not leaving the church; we are leading the church into a new era of justice and equality for women in our church."

Bishop Bridget Mary points out that Pope Benedict, who is "big on excommunicating women priests," has also canonized women who have been excommunicated in the past. "Shortly after he became pope, he canonized Mother Theodore Guerin,[31] who had been excommunicated in the nineteenth century," Bridget Mary laughs. "He is going to canonize Mother Mary Mackillop[32] from Australia, who was also excommunicated in the nineteenth century. Excommunication is becoming the fast track to sanctification, to canonization in our church. So why should we worry about excommunication, when the present pope who is excommunicating us, is also busy canonizing excommunicated women? Opposition has not hurt us. It keeps spurring us on."

A growing number of Catholics and people of other faith traditions are supporting the Roman Catholic Women Priests movement. "The most wonderful thing is that the people, Catholic people and Christians of other denominations and Jewish people, are more and more supportive as they hear the stories of our call to be like Rosa Parks, refusing to sit in the back of the bus, and to lead the church into a new era of justice for women," Bishop Bridget Mary says. "They become supporters spiritually and by helping us to keep on spreading the word. The media have also been helpful in sharing our stories, and the Internet is major because we write prolifically about this vision. We are no longer willing to sit in the back of the Catholic bus and be subordinated, mainly because Jesus called women to be disciples and equals, and Jesus called women to go and tell. Mary Magdalene was the first witness of the resurrection, and she was called to be an apostle. The word 'apostle' means 'go and tell,' and she did. There is no discrimination in Christianity because we must follow Christ. In Luke 8 we find many women among Jesus' disciples: Mary Magdalene, Joanna, Suzanna, and more. The early church also had women leaders: Deacon Phoebe, Apostle Junia, Prisca, Mary Mother of Mark; they were leaders of house churches, celebrated Eucharist with the communities, were under persecution, were faithful and courageous. With the men they set the pace for the early Christian movement to be one that was loving, forgiving, nonviolent, centered in peace, focused on justice, living love, being Christ. We need to follow the example of Jesus, which was justice and equality for women, and we need to reclaim the early church tradition of women in equal leadership as deacons, priests, and bishops."

With passion in her voice Bishop Bridget Mary speaks about the great need for inclusive, egalitarian faith communities. "So many people are adrift and looking for spiritual resources, for community," she says. "Many have been alienated by the institutional church, including the divorced and separated, gays and lesbians, and women who feel like second-class citizens in their own church. We need to open our hearts, our homes, our churches to provide inclusive, welcoming, loving places of spiritual nurturance and spiritual challenge to live the vision of Jesus, the prophetic Gospel of justice and love and peace in our world, which embraces equality at its heart because all are in the image of God, male and female, Jew and Greek, every race. All of us are one. Ultimately there is one heaven, and ultimately we are all one in the Divine. And that Divine has a feminine face." Bridget Mary tells the story of Marie, who experienced this loving welcome at the Sarasota church. Marie, who had been divorced and remarried, cried when she received Communion at Mary Mother of Jesus Catholic Community. After a hostile encounter with a priest years before, she had felt unworthy to receive the Eucharist in her parish community. Now she says, "I feel like I have come home at last."

Bishop Bridget Mary sees the close connection between inclusion of women as leaders of the church and inclusion of female divine language and imagery in worship. This connection between the gender of the Divine and of ministers is especially pronounced in the Catholic tradition. In fact, Catholic Church officials argue against women priests because there must be a "natural resemblance" between Christ and the person who offers the sacraments. If a woman performed this priestly role, states the Vatican, "it would be difficult to see in the minister the image of Christ, for Christ himself was and remains a man."[33] Although Bridget Mary and other Catholic women priests envision an ideal church without distinctions between clergy and laity, they believe that ordaining women needs to happen now to bring justice for women in the church. "Women priests remind us that women are equal symbols of the Holy," she says. "Women and men are created in God's image, and both may represent Christ as priests. The Divine has a female face because all of us, male and female, are created in the divine image. Until we integrate the Divine Feminine in our religious systems, in our governance, in our structures, and in our whole approach to life, we will be flying on one wing. We will not be whole. We will have the patriarchal domination continuing, and that obviously is leading the world and religion to destruction. We're experiencing the destructiveness of the all-male dominator model in Roman Catholicism with the global sex abuse scandal. The patriarchal model is not working for people. It's not going to work. It's not of the Spirit."

Drawing a bridge in the air with both hands, Bridget Mary illustrates what she believes to be the mission of women priests. "I see us as a bridge," she explains. "Over here you've got the hierarchical, male-dominated, all-boys' club, misogynist church, and over here you have the discipleship of equals which is the feminist vision. Here you have a chasm in between. So there is a call to build a bridge. Some are already in the discipleship of equals." Motioning to the in-between chasm, she continues: "There are a lot of people who are here or not anywhere, but they'd like to take the journey. So the role of women priests is to make a bridge and to try at every venture on the journey to model the discipleship of equals, to model equality and justice, to transform the structure into the renewed model. In order to bring change we have to fit somehow within the structure, to be ordained as priests with apostolic succession, even though the pope and some bishops have cast us out and said 'excommunication, excommunication.' We're perceived as the biggest threat, and they're right on that. They should perceive us as a threat because we are about transforming the hierarchical model. It is what has destroyed the church and caused this corruption. So women priests are trying to make a bridge from this hierarchical model to this discipleship of equals; we're trying to join hands with both so that people may safely cross this chasm. We're beginning to see the movement in communities. People are being freed up and are making the journey with us. As more people experience this, they'll know that it is one way that the Spirit is moving in our time. We don't claim it's the only way. But we do believe that it's one way the Spirit is moving, and it's one way for women in the church to reclaim our rightful role as equal members."

Another way women priests are serving as a bridge between the hierarchical to the egalitarian church model is by partnering with married priests, who had not been serving because of the Vatican's position on a celibate priesthood. In the Sarasota Mary Mother of Jesus Catholic Community, Michael Rigdon and Lee Breyer serve as "priest partners" with Bridget Mary, co-celebrating at each liturgy and assisting with the needs of the entire congregation. "Who would ever think that the women priests would be the catalysts for the married priests and that together we're forming this great leadership circle with the people," Bridget Mary comments. "We have other people in our leadership circle. It's a very dynamic group."

In the leadership structure and in the liturgy, Bridget Mary and other women priests seek to transform the church into a discipleship of equals. "It's about changing the whole model," she explains. "Instead of having top-down power of a magic few and replacing with a woman, it's a change to empower all of us as sisters and brothers on the journey. We are companions on the journey, and all belong in our circle of love. That's what Jesus was about, welcoming all into the circle of love. It's a shift in theology, moving from the male-dominated, power down model to a circular model. The power is within the dynamic of the circle. All of us join together as sisters and brothers to pray together and to celebrate the sacraments together. The Women Priests movement has a profound understanding of sacraments in a feminist spirituality motif with a major emphasis on the relationship building and the growth in love of the Divine that sacraments symbolize."

Catholic women priests celebrate the central sacrament of the Eucharist in this circular model. "Eucharist is our celebration as a believing community together," Bridget Mary says. "The presider is not the celebrator alone. We're all celebrating together because the Eucharist belongs to the community. We are the magic because we are Christ." Also, the community together celebrates the sacraments of ordination, reconciliation, and anointing of the sick. At Bridget Mary's ordination in Pittsburgh, the women priests and ministers of other faiths gathered in circles around a table. "If we could have fit all 250 people who were there around the table with us, that would have been the ideal," Bridget Mary says. The community also experiences the sacrament of reconciliation together, instead of confessing to a priest alone and receiving forgiveness. "We're restoring the community's role as the locus of forgiveness versus the priest alone," Bridget Mary explains. "Our failures diminish and hurt the community, hurt our relationships. Therefore, the community is the instrument of forgiveness and healing. We have the whole community say the words of absolution to restore the relational communitarian understanding of reconciliation. The sacrament of the anointing of the sick also includes the community. We invite the family and other community members to gather around the person who wants to be anointed. Not only the priest, but others can anoint too, or they can extend hands on the person. One of our priest partners, Michael Rigdon, was about to have a medical procedure, and some of our members gathered around him after church to pray for him. We asked Imogene, his wife, to anoint him. And we all said the words and prayed in the Spirit. It's like combining the sacramental and the charismatic dimensions, having the community come together and pray for the healing of the person."

Bishop Bridget Mary also sees the need for inclusion of women priests and the Divine Feminine to reform the wider culture along with the church. She views the ban on contraceptives by the Catholic male hierarchy as an "anti-life" position. "One of the worst examples is the church's not allowing women in Africa who are in monogamous relationships to protect themselves when their husbands are HIV positive," she says. "It's morally reprehensible to put a faithful wife at risk of HIV-AIDS by not allowing the use of condoms. That kind of teaching is hostile to women and hostile to life. The sad part is the institutional church has so much influence on structures and systems throughout the world because of their network of healthcare and outreach in the Third World."

In addition to speaking out against such church policies that they believe are destructive, Bishop Bridget Mary and other women priests together with their church communities take part in a wide variety of social justice ministries. For example, Mary Mother of Jesus Catholic Community in Sarasota has joined with the U.S. Conference of Catholic Bishops in working for justice for immigrants. Before the liturgy I attended, several church members distributed postcards for people to send to senators, calling for meaningful and compassionate immigration reform.[34] The church also works with the United Church of Christ on justice initiatives in the region, such as Sarasota United for Responsibility and Equity (SURE).[35] "We see ourselves as working within the larger community and the interfaith world and the ecumenical world so that we will continue to create partnerships with movements for justice and peace and equality," Bridget Mary says. "We don't see ourselves as isolated, but as an integral part of other communities. We see ourselves as partners with other people who do good in our world, however that's done."

Bishop Bridget Mary and other women priests have also taken on the cause of U.S. nuns who are under investigation by the Vatican. "There are two investigations going," Bridget Mary explains. "One is a general investigation with Mother Mary Clare Millea[36] going around to the convents doing interviews and surveys. She will be sending a report directly to the Vatican. The nuns think it's unfair that they will not see the report, and I say to them, 'Why are you allowing this oppression to come? This is an inquisition.' The second investigation is of the heads of all the women's religious orders. Vatican officials don't believe the nuns have done enough to promote the Catholic Church's teaching against women's ordination, the church's position on homosexuality as a disorder, and the Catholic Church as the true church." If the nuns refuse to follow the Vatican on these issues, they may lose their canonical, pontifical status. Bridget Mary writes in her blog to these women: "Rejoice and be glad. Cast off the fear. Cast off the albatross. Is it going to be peace at any price, or will you say, 'We're going to continue obeying the Spirit. We will not subjugate ourselves to more discrimination, but we'll lead the way toward justice and equality.'" Bridget Mary acknowledges the practical difficulties these nuns face with their financial security, including pensions and healthcare, tied to the institutional church. One of her dreams is to establish a fund to help support women who choose to leave religious orders, until they become connected with local communities who will support them. She encourages nuns to "move forward and be ordained if they are so called by their communities." Current and former nuns comprise a large share of the supporters of the Women Priests movement and of the applicants to the priesthood. "We'd love to ordain them," Bishop Bridget Mary says.

In spite of excommunications and threats of excommunications, Bridget Mary has never considered leaving the Catholic Church. "Catholicism is in my DNA, a mystical, justice-oriented, best of Catholicism," she says. "I stay in the church to reform and renew and transform it. I want to be an agent of change in solidarity with a vast group of sisters and brothers who are reformers and who love the church and want to restore it to its mystical, Christ-centered, justice-doing focus. We want to transform it from its hierarchical, male-dominated, insular view of the world to an open, democratic, participatory, people-empowered model of church, where the community of believers are the ones who bring their wisdom to guide the church into the future. For now the institutional church has strayed. The Vatican is at the heart of global destructiveness. The institution has strayed because of the teaching on homosexuality as a disorder, the teaching on annulment, the ban on artificial birth control, the oppression of women—these are some ways the institutional church has alienated Catholics. The oppression of women has sent them running from the doors of the Catholic Church. There is no place for a well-educated, vibrant woman who is used to being treated as an equal in her job, in her family. That doesn't exist in the church. There are no equal roles for women, because ordination by church law is tied to leadership roles, to decision making. The canon law is set up so that the only ones who make decisions in the Catholic Church are ordained males. Women can have other jobs, but they are not truly decision-making roles. That canon law needs to change. You should not need ordination to have authority and decision-making power in the church."

On a visit to Ireland in July of 2010, Bridget Mary continued to denounce the Vatican. She called on the pope to resign, advised parishioners to stop giving money to the Catholic Church, and likened the Vatican to the mafia, covering up crime and hiding criminals. "It's an abuse of spiritual power and that is really a deadly sin," she said. "Never, ever mess with people's faith." She also denounced the Vatican for placing the ordination of women on the list of grave sins with pedophilia, heresy, apostasy, and schism. "Is it a crime to ordain a woman, or is the real crime the institutional church's discrimination against women?" she asked. She called the Catholic Church a "toxic place" for women.[37]

Bishop Bridget Mary believes that it is time for reform and that Catholic women priests are at the forefront of changing the church. "We are not leaving the church; we are leading the church," Bridget Mary says over and over. "Roman Catholic women priests are prophetic because we are a movement that restores justice for women in the church, rooted in the example of Jesus, who called women and men to be equal disciples, and rooted in the early tradition of the church where women were deacons, priests, and bishops. Women priests in partnership with married priests and others are already positioned to reform the church, to move it from hierarchical and misogynist to egalitarian. There's a new partnership between women and men in grassroots communities, empowering and welcoming to all. People are now more open and ready. Some tell me, 'I can't stand it any longer.' I think there's a tipping point coming in Catholicism. The largest religious group in the U.S. is Catholics, and the second largest is Catholics who've left because they've been turned off or rejected. We can transform the church to an open, people-oriented community of believers."

In her vision for the future, Bishop Bridget Mary sees women priests and the Divine Feminine as closely linked. She expresses hope for the future not only of churches, but also of the world through including women as representatives of the Divine and through including Feminine Divine language and images in worship. "If the symbol system that patriarchy has given us of a male God is changed, our worldview could be radically altered. As we reimagine our divine beginning, we can incorporate a symbol system that reflects the Feminine Divine and the experience of women as images of the Divine Presence."[38]

Because our sacred symbolism has great potential to bring transformation, Bridget Mary believes it is vital that we teach children that the Divine includes female and male. "The God language and images we hand down to our children and grandchildren have the potential to transform everything—the way we see ourselves, the way we relate to God and to one another, our economic, political, social structures—indeed, to create a new paradigm where all human beings live in mutuality, justice, equality, and love."[39] Bridget Mary tells of teaching her niece and nephew to include female divine images. "When my niece, Katie, was four, and her brother, Danny, was two, I played a Mother God game with them. We would run around the yard and pretend to be Mother Eagle, who carries her eaglets on her wing and then launches them on their first flights. So Mother God carries us as Her beloved children and helps our spirits to soar! With my niece and nephew I tried to integrate female images of God with fun activities like playing with Mother God."

To instill the values of mutuality, justice, and equality in children and adults Bishop Bridget Mary rewrites traditional prayers. For example, one of her books includes this version of the "Prayer of Jesus":

> Divine Parent, you are everywhere; sacred is your presence.
> May your family grow in oneness and closeness to you,
> as we forgive ourselves, others, and you for the hurts that wound us.
> Show us how to love as you love. Help us to embrace one another as family. Empower us to meet every challenge. Deliver us from all that divides us, for you are our Mother/Father, the Giver of Life forever and ever. Amen.[40]

Bishop Bridget Mary believes that this is a historic moment in the Catholic Church, which in turn has far-reaching influence in the world. "Women priests believe that in order to do justice, women need to be ordained now in a renewed priestly ministry," she says. "Where that will wind up in the future, we have no clue. We're walking on water. We have to keep an open spirit and a loose grasp, trusting that the Spirit is leading and will unveil the vision as we move towards it. We believe it's to a Jesus vision. Where Jesus had the most opposition was with the religious leaders of the time who told him he was a rule-breaker and was associating with all the wrong people. Women priests are getting some of this criticism because we're open. We don't have rules that keep people out; there's no second-class citizenship with us."

Criticism does not dampen Bridget Mary's spirits nor deter her from her prophetic ministry. She continues to affirm her belief that opposition can be a blessing. One of the reasons her blog has become well known is that most of her blog followers write in opposition to the Women Priests movement, Bridget Mary says. "They're constantly putting down the movement, constantly arguing, propelling the blog to be major because there's so much action on the blog."

The Women Priests movement is growing mainly because of the positive response of grassroots Catholics. "What's going to change the church is the people, when they experience what it means to live in an open, empowered, partnership kind of church that honors the Spirit within them," Bishop Bridget Mary explains. "They share their experience with everyone, and they want to have more of the same everywhere they go because it's so authentic, and it's so right. They know it in their spirits, and they spread that around to their friends. Then more and more people come and are touched. One of our members went up to Bishop Dewane and said, 'I'm so happy we have a woman priest in this diocese!' Recently a woman from another area of the country, who was aware of the Florida ordinations, called a parish in southwestern Florida and asked, 'Where are the women priests?' The answer from the parish put her in contact with Judy Lee, a Roman Catholic woman priest, who ministers to the homeless in the Fort Myers community. Can you imagine the local pastor when he found out about this inquiry, scratching his head and wondering if the next caller will be asking, 'What time does the woman priest preside at Mass?' The message is women priests are here to serve the people, especially the millions of Catholics who feel rejected and alienated by their church. Now people are getting the message."[41]

With radiant face and passionate voice, Bishop Bridget Mary expresses deep faith that her vision of change is happening. Bridget Mary preaches, teaches, writes, and lives this vision. Her book *Delighting in the Feminine Divine* includes a prayer for this transformation to become reality:

> *Womb of Creation,*
> *Shekinah, She-Who-Dwells Within*
> *God, the breasted One*
> *Woman Mentor*
> *Sophia, Holy Wisdom,*
> *Help women to delight in their identity as imago Dei (images of God).*
>
> *Angry Woman Preacher*
> *Liberator of the Oppressed*
> *Welcoming Hostess*
> *Washerwoman God*
> *Seamstress Elegant*
> *Transform patriarchal structures and sexist attitudes that prevent us from acknowledging women as imago Dei.*
>
> *Jesus-Sophia, the Crucified One*
> *Mother Jesus, birthing the world*
> *Merciful Mother Jesus,*
> *Jesus-Sophia, Healer of our Stress*
> *Jesus, Mirror of Sophia*
> *Reveal your saving power through women, imago Dei.*[42]

4

Rev. Dr. Isabel Docampo

American Baptist Pastor
Associate Professor of Supervised Ministry
Perkins School of Theology, Dallas, Texas

"It's probably the same sermon I've been preaching all my life," Rev. Dr. Isabel Docampo says about her first sermon, delivered in her seminary preaching class. It was a "justice sermon," inviting "people to look at the Scripture from a different perspective, not the dominant one, but the perspective of people who are hurting."

Years later at Grace United Methodist Church in Dallas, Texas, Rev. Docampo preaches a powerful justice sermon entitled "The Essence of the Divine Is Shalom/Peace." She urges us "to overcome the subtle ways that the ugly manifestations of homophobia, ageism, sexism, racism, and classism arise," and to express "outrage and stop politely tiptoeing around the elephant of injustice in a world where little girls are killed by their father in a Dallas loft apartment or where the immigrants we serve in our clinics are denied civil rights because they lack legal immigration status, where gay/lesbian sisters and brothers are victims of hate crimes and are denied access to the church as full members." She preaches about the difference including the Divine Feminine in worship makes to justice and peace, quoting Scripture and fourteenth-century Christian mystic Julian of Norwich: "As truly as God is our Father, so truly is God our Mother."

Rev. Docampo stresses the difference language makes in our relationships with others, in our relationship with the Divine, and in our self-worth. "We cannot deny that how we address one another in human relationships dictates how we relate to and approach each other. The same is true for the names which we use to address the Divine in prayer and song, Sunday after Sunday. They affect not only our relationship with the Divine, but also our relationship with all of humanity, and how we see and understand ourselves. Women who never hear God as female unconsciously integrate that they are not totally created in God's image, limiting their sense of worth and power. Men who never hear God as female unconsciously integrate that they have greater knowledge and worth because they always hear their male gender equated with ultimate power and wisdom. The Divine Other in its different manifestations claims no one nature greater than another. They are perfectly united in love."

In her sermon Rev. Docampo also gives strong support to the importance of the Divine Feminine from her own story. "Words make a lot of difference. The first time I heard God described as female Creating, Loving, Powerful, Forgiving, tears streamed down my face. It was like my soul had been touched in a new and powerful way. I felt in that sacred place that I was being affirmed for the first time as truly created in the image of the great Divine. I had already felt very certain of God's calling me to give my life to serve the Christian church. But for the very first time, I felt truly created in the image of God with the full blessing of the Divine. Three years later when I was being told that my gender made me inherently sinful because of my connection as a woman to Eve's role in the Garden of Eden, and therefore, could not serve as an ordained clergy teaching men, but only in other prescribed roles, I found strength and courage as I remembered that Sophia-God created the earth, sent Jesus to redeem us, and had placed Her hand upon me. I didn't give away my God as Father, but now I had Sophia-God as my Friend and Soul Guide as well. You see, God as Father was unapproachable for me at that time as I was facing so many Christian men who used 'God the Father' to try to silence me. I knew the God they were proclaiming was not the God I knew. It was easier for me to address the feminine God, and She gave me strength. I could approach Her in prayer. It was profoundly important. And I can tell you many stories from my ministry with very devout Christian women, victims of domestic violence, whose only reference to God was a male, giving males more power and dominance in their eyes and keeping them at risk for their lives. How we address the Divine makes a big difference."

On that Sunday morning at Grace United Methodist Church, Rev. Docampo joins others from the New Wineskins Community to lead worship.[1] After her sermon she invites the congregation to the Communion table, blessing the bread and wine in the name of Christ-Sophia. As people come forward to receive Holy Communion from Rev. Docampo, "The 23rd Psalm" by Bobby McFerrin plays in the background, beginning with these lines: "The Lord is my Shepherd, I have all I need./ She makes me lie down in green meadows, beside the still water She will lead."[2]

Isabel Docampo's story reveals that she has indeed been preaching a "justice sermon" all her life through her actions as well as her words. Her parents were first-generation immigrants from Cuba. When they came to the United States in 1955, her mother was four months pregnant with Isabel. Born in New Orleans, Louisiana, Isabel was baptized Roman Catholic. Isabel's family joined *Primera Iglesia Bautista Hispano-Americana*, a mission of Coliseum Baptist Church, after Cuban Pastor Garay visited them. Growing up in church, Isabel listened to *testimonios* of Latino/a immigrants from Panama, Honduras, Nicaragua, Ecuador, Puerto Rico, and Guatemala, as well as from Cuba. These stories wove together deep gratitude to God for the United States and heartbreak over family left behind and injustices still endured. As she grew up, Isabel says she began "to lose that naïveté of how wonderful this place is and started to understand the institutional racism, classism, and other injustices." But Isabel says that the shattering of her childhood view didn't make her cynical. "What it did was make me believe that my patriotic and Christian duty was to help America be the best it can be. My work to change injustice comes from my understanding of what God is calling me to do, of what God is calling all of us to do. I'm grateful to be in a place that still preserves freedom of religion. That freedom to exercise my faith is what I move into. Therefore, when I'm working for justice issues, I feel that I'm working for my country to preserve freedom. Freedom of religion spills over into all the other freedoms for everyone. We have to hold onto that freedom to live fully, freedom from being a racist society, freedom from sexism, gender inequality. Because I have freedom in my religion, I feel that I need to use it for the greater good."

Most of the families in the church where Isabel grew up were lower-income day laborers and domestic laborers. Even though poor, "they were trying to send money back or to get their family members to the United States," Isabel says. Her parents, like most others in the church, struggled to make a living. They had left Cuba because they couldn't make a living under Batista,[3] even though they worked hard. They saw America as a place where they could give their children a future. Isabel says that the "struggles of the underclass" became part of who she is, along with a sense of gratitude for being in America.

Like other children in her church, Isabel navigated two cultures, translating for her parents. She also learned to live cross-culturally with other Latinos/as, because Cubans were a small minority in her church. "Since I was a child, I've not only been navigating the Cuban and American cultures, but also within this church, navigating these other cultures," Isabel says. "We learned about customs. I could never address Guatemalan adults with the familiar *tu*; I always had to address them with *usted*.[4] To the Hondurans, Panamanians, Puerto Ricans, I could say *tu*. We learned social etiquette and cultural taboos that have informed me in my adult years."

As a little girl, Isabel loved Sunday school. "We had Sunday school books in Spanish," she recalls. "I loved my Sunday school book, and I loved reading. It was not until I was in seventh grade that my school had a library. We were living in a working-class neighborhood, so our schools didn't have everything. In seventh grade I devoured everything in the library. When I was in first grade, my mother taught me to read in Spanish, using the Bible. My brothers and sister and I all memorized Psalm 121 in Spanish. I had a great Sunday school teacher, named Juvelina. She was a single woman, and I thought she was beautiful and sophisticated, dressed well, had a good job, knew how to speak English as well as Spanish. I accepted Christ in this class when I was nine years old. She sent me to the pastor, Donald Levy, a Cuban even though he had an English name. That gives you an idea about the mixing of the cultures. I went through classes with Pastor Levy, and he baptized me. I felt so close to God that day. After the service, everyone who had been baptized stood at the front of the church so people could welcome us, and someone gave each baptized person a Bible. My mother was the one who came forward and handed me my Bible; it was very special to me to have my mother give me that Bible. It was a big fat Spanish Bible, the whole Bible, hardback with a bright green cover. I don't have it anymore because it fell apart, but I had it all the way up until I went to college. I had bound it, pasted and duct-taped and covered it. I loved that Bible."

Isabel's mother became her first Latina heroine. She and other strong women in her church would never claim to be feminists, but their strength in facing challenges and their debunking of "ridiculous stereotypes" influenced Isabel. Her mother was one of the first two women deacons ordained in the church. The Puerto Rican pastor at that time, Eliud Camacho, asked the congregation, "Shouldn't we have women deacons?" And the church said, "Yes." It seemed natural because the church already had a family ministry deacon model. Isabel describes her mother as a contradiction, not embracing feminism but being subversive in the way she has dismantled patriarchy to do whatever she wanted to in the way she wanted to do it. Isabel has tried to raise her mother's awareness of the prevalence of sexism: "Look at all these novelas that you're watching on Univision.[5] Look at the picture they're giving of women. This is horrible!" In recent years her mother has acknowledged the need to address sexism. Another of Isabel's Latina heroines is Doris Diaz, from Guatemala. Ms. Diaz, the head of the Spanish Baptist Woman's Missionary Union for many years, helped Isabel's mother "become this subversive person in her own turf."

When Isabel was ten, her father, a merchant marine, was injured. Isabel says that her family was "plunged into destitution." Her mother had to work long hours, from about 6:00 a.m. till 6:30 p.m. Isabel and her two older brothers, Pedro and Eduardo, called "Eddie," ages fourteen and thirteen, took on many family responsibilities. She started dinner every evening, cared for her dad who was disabled, and watched her younger brother, Francisco, "Paco," and younger sister, Alida, "Lila." Isabel says that when things got really scary for her, she would go to her room and read her Bible, especially Psalm 121. "And I would know that God was with me and was going to take care of our family; then I wouldn't worry. That was the way I got through those years."

Isabel's church considered young people to be like adults at age sixteen. Already active in her youth group, Isabel became a leader in *Primera Iglesia Bautista Hispano-Americana* when she was sixteen and served on church committees. Her older brother Eddie and Isabel were leaders in Training Union[6] and organized all the youth activities. Because Isabel was bilingual, she became secretary of the church, ordering the entire curriculum and helping Sunday school teachers. She started a church newsletter, organizing youth and young adults older than she to help, and she became editor of this newsletter called "Agape." Also, Isabel served as church pianist for a while.

At age seventeen Isabel began studying at University of New Orleans. That fall, when she turned eighteen, her father was diagnosed with cancer, and she had to take a lighter load of classes so that she could help her mother in caring for him. Isabel took him for chemotherapy treatments. She describes how agonizing it was to see him go through chemotherapy treatments, because at that time there were no medications to help with nausea. "All he did was vomit. He would get chemotherapy on Friday, start vomiting on Saturday, vomit till Wednesday night, and feel good on Thursday. Then we'd start the cycle all over again. That was a very difficult time for me. I was angry with God over my dad's illness. But I watched his faith, and it helped me as a young person to deal with all those questions. Mainly it helped me realize those were the wrong questions, that the most important thing was that God's presence was with us and that was palpable in my father's life as he was dying and in the way my mother handled it." Isabel's father died when she was eighteen, ten months after his diagnosis of cancer.

The next year Isabel's mother lost her job. After attending University of New Orleans only one year, Isabel had to drop out and go to work full-time at Pan American Life Insurance Company to help support the family. While she was working at this company, Isabel realized that she was called to be a minister. "It was a quiet experience, like a light bulb, 'Oh, I belong in the church,'" Isabel says. "I felt that my favorite place to be was in church. Everything I liked to do was in my church, working with the youth, planning Bible studies, working with Vacation Bible School, organizing the adults. I built the youth group from about four or five to about thirty. I found I had a knack for going out and talking to kids and bringing them in. I wasn't afraid of going to the housing projects." Isabel's older brother Eddie had made the decision to be a minister two years earlier. At that time Isabel says that it never crossed her mind that she would be a minister. "I didn't have a woman to show me the way," Isabel explains. So she didn't know how to articulate her call and what it meant.

When Isabel was teaching a January Bible study at *Primera Iglesia Bautista Hispano-Americana* to about fifty young people, Dr. Byrd, a professor of religious education at Louisiana College, brought a group of students to visit her class. Dr. Byrd took an interest in Isabel, and they had a conversation about her ministry.

"Have you ever thought about ministry as a calling?" Dr. Byrd asked her.

"Well, I love being in church. I just don't know how to do that. I don't want to get married to anyone," Isabel replied.

"You don't have to get married to anyone. You can be a religious education director," he said.

Isabel's church had only one paid minister, a male pastor. Isabel saw his wife also ministering to people, but she knew she didn't want to be a pastor's wife. The only other women ministers Isabel saw were foreign missionaries. Isabel says that she loved missions and had been active in Girls' Auxiliary.[7] "I got all my badges, and made it all the way to Queen Regent," Isabel recalls. "I learned about missions far, far away." But when Isabel went to the altar to tell the congregation about her call, she stated that she did not want to be a foreign missionary. "The mission field is here, and I want to work in the church here. The people are here. I love working with people in need. This is what I feel God is calling me to do." Her conversation with Dr. Byrd had helped Isabel see that she could become a religious education director, perhaps serving in her church in New Orleans, if she could go back to college.

When Isabel was twenty-one, she enrolled in Louisiana College, a private institution affiliated with the Louisiana Baptist Convention. "For me to get to Louisiana College was huge, because it cost a ton of money," Isabel explains. "My mother finally got her job back, so instead of giving money to her, I could save for college." Also, Isabel's church contributed to her education, and her brother Eddie, who had joined the army for benefits to go to college, transferred to New Orleans to help with the family finances. When it came time to go to Louisiana College, four hours north of New Orleans in Pineville, Louisiana, Isabel says it felt "like the end of the world." She was scared to go by herself into a different culture, so she worked hard to get a scholarship for a friend from her church, Anna Maria Gonzalez.

At Louisiana College Isabel poured herself into social ministries. With other students Isabel organized programs for Abraham Mission in an urban housing project. "For the first time I met women who had all these children who were druggies and who were drug addicts themselves, and their girls were being pimped out," Isabel says. "I saw abandoned children. I just saw everything. It prepared me for domestic violence work I did later." Isabel and some good friends she made at Louisiana College reflected together on their calls to ministry. Isabel began to realize that she might be a minister beyond the church, perhaps working in a place like the housing project. "It helped to open up possibilities for me," she explains. "But still I had no women as models." Isabel did, however, have men who supported her. At Louisiana College Dr. Fred Downing, Dr. John Heard, Dr. John Rast, and Dr. James Young, head of the Department of Religion, encouraged her to go to seminary and to think about ordination. In 1979, Isabel graduated from Louisiana College with a Bachelor of Religious Education degree.

When Isabel visited Southwestern and Southern Baptist Theological Seminaries to decide which to attend, she found admission officers at both schools to be patronizing. They questioned whether Isabel understood that she had marked the Master of Divinity degree and not the Master of Religious Education degree.

"Yes, I understand what I'm doing," Isabel told them. "I have a bachelor's degree in religious education. Now I need to learn theology. I need to sink my teeth into theology and philosophy and Bible study, so if I'm going to teach anything in church, I'll know what I'm doing. And I want to write curriculum."

"Uh, we don't think you're going to do that," they responded. "Are you sure?"

Isabel says she found the admissions officers' questions "so insulting." She chose to go to Southern Seminary, because "at least Southern had a women-in-theology group, and Southwestern didn't."

At Southern Baptist Theological Seminary in Louisville, Kentucky, Isabel met PhD student Claude Mariotini, a Brazilian who had started a mission church, ministering to Latino Fort Knox soldiers, mainly from Puerto Rico. Claude asked Isabel to help, and together they developed Hispanic Mission of Stithton Baptist Church, which lived on after they both graduated through the ministries of other students. At the mission church Isabel led the women's and children's ministry, learning much about ministering to women who are victims of domestic violence. She learned how to remove children from violent homes and to find resources. Parenting classes, counseling women and their husbands, Sunday school for children, Bible study for women, and playing the piano were also part of her ministry at this church. Claude encouraged her preaching, and Isabel was slowly feeling more comfortable in the pulpit.

Isabel says that she used a lot of "he" language for God when she began seminary. A teaching assistant in her systematic theology class was the first person to question Isabel's use of these masculine pronouns. "She had been a Baptist and had just become an Episcopal priest," Isabel recalls. "She wrote in the margins of my paper, asking if I could identify with a male God and what would be some detriments of that. She opened for me the idea that language for God is metaphor and asked if I could use another metaphor for God beyond the male. She asked in a way that I was able to receive it, and she didn't grade me down." The women-in-theology group also raised Isabel's consciousness of the importance of inclusiveness in worship. "The seminary used to love to sing 'Rise Up, O Men of God,'" Isabel says. "The women-in-theology group had a campaign to quit using that hymn or to change it to include women because there were so many women in seminary. That made a lot of sense to me. I went to women-in-theology group meetings a couple of times; I stopped going because the women were so angry. But when they would do these campaigns about chapel services, I thought that made sense. I realized that there's a good use of anger. While I wasn't comfortable with their anger, I realized that we need people who are angry to move us along." Isabel also appreciated the women-in-theology group's fight for women to receive the annual preaching award that had always been given to men. The group questioned, "Are you saying that women who make A's in preaching class are not ready to preach in chapel?" Before Isabel finished seminary, a woman won the award and preached in chapel.

As the only woman in her preaching class, Isabel says that she "got terrible, terrible hits" from the students. One man in her class said, "She got up there, and she looked like Miss America with her long, flowing hair, and she started talking civil religion." This comment, of course, upset Isabel, but she was grateful that her preaching professor reprimanded the student for calling her "Miss America" and for saying she was preaching civil religion. "You obviously didn't read her manuscript, which is the furthest from civil religion," the professor said. "She's critiquing civil religion. This is a justice sermon." In her sermon Isabel quoted Martin Luther King, Jr., who had been her hero for many years. For one of her seminary class assignments, Isabel wrote a long paper on Dr. King, after reading all his sermons and many books about him. "Years later I find out about all his womanizing which was disheartening for me," Isabel says. "That speaks to sexism in the church; it was right there even in someone who was so wonderful. I think if he were still alive today, he would be held accountable for that, and he would either have to ask forgiveness or lose his standing as a hero. I could forgive him, because he did some really important things for the poor and racial minorities, and he needs credit for that."

For her field education at Southern Seminary, Isabel chose to go to Chester, Pennsylvania, near Philadelphia, to start a mission church for poverty-stricken Puerto Ricans. She worked with Rev. Juan Kovalchuk, pastor of Ukrainian Baptist Church, who had been brought up in Argentina so was fluent in Spanish, and who had begun a Bible study with a small group of Puerto Ricans. Isabel soon learned that Chester was a broken-down, drug-ridden city. Knocking on doors to invite people to the "safe place" of church, Isabel often discovered that she was walking into crack houses. Her fiancé, Steven, a Southern Seminary student doing field education in a nearby town, came to accompany Isabel as she walked around Chester. In addition to bringing Puerto Ricans to church, Isabel delivered water to them, engaged the older Ukrainian women in the church to cook a meal for them every Wednesday, and translated and advocated for them to access Catholic Charities. Isabel felt, like Esther, that she was in this position "for such a time as this."[8] She says, "I couldn't change the world for them, but I did as much as I could." The Pennsylvania Baptist Convention Missions Director was impressed with Isabel's ministry that resulted in the growth of the Puerto Rican church, and Rev. Kovalchuk wanted her to stay as pastor. When Isabel and Steven went for the interview, the missions director offered her husband-to-be the position.

He said to Isabel: "We all know that you will really be doing the work, and your husband will get another job. But on paper we have to do it this way because of the Southern Baptist Convention resolution.[9] I can't hire you as a pastor. I have to hire him as pastor of a new church plant."

"That's unacceptable," Isabel replied. "I need you to advocate for me. You have lots of years here. I need you to use your influence and say, 'This is the person we need. She happens to be female. Her husband is a very good support, and he can do other things because he's also seminary trained. But we need to put her name as pastor.'"

"It will never pass," he said.

"I don't care if it ever passes. I just need you to do that. I can't take the position unless you do it that way." Isabel didn't get the position as pastor.

When Isabel married Steven Austin, who was very supportive of her and other women ministers, she didn't change her last name at first. But because her name had been an issue during an interview for a ministry position in Baton Rouge, Louisiana, she had changed it by the time she graduated from Southern Seminary in 1982. On her Master of Divinity diploma, her name is "Isabel N. Docampo Austin." In Baton Rouge, Isabel at first went by Isabel Docampo-Austin. When she started signing her name and introducing herself as Isabel D. Austin, Isabel noticed that people became friendlier. "It was a miracle," she laughs. "When I started using Steve's name, all of a sudden we got all these invitations to people's homes to have dinner with them. Both of our families were also delighted that I was now Mrs. Austin and not Ms. Docampo-Austin!"

The semester before Isabel and Steve graduated from Southern Seminary, one of the people they spoke to about ministry positions was Rev. Rafael Melian, a Cuban Baptist pastor and good friend of Isabel's. He was a refugee who had settled in New Orleans and studied at New Orleans Baptist Theological Seminary, even though he had a degree from the Baptist seminary in Cuba. His wife, Miriam, was also in ministry; she had studied at the seminary in Cuba, and was a very strong role model for Isabel. At the time Isabel and Steve graduated from seminary Rev. Melian was the Language Ministries Director for the Louisiana Baptist Convention, and he recommended Steve and Isabel for a position in Baton Rouge. For a year they shared this position of minister to merchant marines through Seaman's Center, supported by the Louisiana Baptist Convention and Judson Baptist Association. The chairperson of the association's Seaman's Ministries Committee had trouble with a woman in ministry and with the concept of coleadership. Isabel recounts this conversation with him:

"Someone has to lead," he said.

"Why? Why does someone have to lead?" Isabel asked.

"Because you just do. What if I have a question? Who do I go to?"

"Pick one. If I'm here, you can ask me."

"Well, who's going to lead?"

"I will at that moment. You can go to Steve at other times, and he will lead. When we need to, we'll meet and make decisions together."

"Well, I need someone to give me the bottom line. Who's going to give me the final answer?"

"One of us will," Isabel said. "Just call one of us."

The next year Isabel took the position of Director of Christian Social Ministries for Judson Baptist Association, while Steven continued as minister to seamen. Isabel's ministry included working with women and children who experienced domestic violence, starting the Greater Baton Rouge Food Bank and serving as the first board president of the Food Bank, teaching English literacy classes to Muslim women, and giving pastoral care to her elderly volunteers. Isabel says that one of the high points was her ecumenical work in overseeing the fast-growing Food Bank. She especially appreciated collaborating with Jim Colvin, a Baptist layman and head of the United Way of Baton Rouge; Fred Griggs, retired director of St. Vincent de Paul; and more than one hundred volunteers. Another highlight was Bruce Springsteen's concert in Baton Rouge in connection with America's Second Harvest.[10] Springsteen made generous contributions to the Baton Rouge Food Bank.

As a certified Laubach English as a Second Language (ESL) trainer, Isabel further expanded her multicultural skills. "I'm twenty-six, sitting in a room with all these women from Iran covered in their burkas; I can't see their faces," Isabel recalls. "On the other side of the room are women dressed like me except for their little scarves. Then I had one woman right beside me dressed just like me with no scarf; she had a PhD and was a professor in Cairo. She had come to Baton Rouge with her husband, who was a visiting professor at Louisiana State University. That was my introduction to Islam and its variations and the cultural differences between Iran, Iraq, and Egypt. I made good friends with some of these women. One of them became my nanny when my son, Benjamin, was born. Working with these Muslim women was my impetus for starting an interfaith dialogue group in Dallas after 9/11." Isabel also began a literacy ministry for native English speakers, Caucasians and African Americans who were functionally illiterate. She trained her volunteers to preserve the dignity of these people who were smart enough to have made it this far, keeping their illiteracy a secret even from their families.

While in Baton Rouge, Isabel and Steven also joined Bienville House for Peace and Justice, a community founded by Quakers and Mennonites. With that community Isabel and Steven joined the SANE/FREEZE nuclear disarmament movement, doing advocacy and education and participating in marches in Washington, DC. They took part in the protest against the United States' funding of the El Salvadoran government because of the thousands of people being massacred.[11] "When I went to El Salvador in 2000 and saw where people were massacred, there was no doubt that being part of this protest movement had been the right thing to do," Isabel says.

On February 10, 1985, Isabel was ordained by Broadmoor Baptist Church in Baton Rouge. University Baptist Church joined to support her ordination. Dr. Walter "Buddy" Shurden, who had encouraged her ordination when she was at Southern Seminary, preached the ordination sermon; John W. Goodwin, pastor of Broadmoor, and George Haile, pastor of University Baptist, participated in the service. Isabel was the first woman ordained at Broadmoor who stayed there in Baton Rouge to minister. "And that's what set everything on fire," Isabel says. "All hell broke loose. Several months later two pastors marched into the associational office and demanded that I rescind my ordination because it was unbiblical." Rev. Docampo engaged them in a theological conversation.

"Let's just look at what the Scripture says; let's look at the Scripture in context." Isabel had all her biblical and theological support together and presented it to them.

Flustered, one of the pastors said, "I didn't go to Southern Baptist Theological Seminary where they give you all that context nonsense; I just know what the Scripture says."

"Well, you do have the power to terminate my employment with Judson Baptist Association," Isabel told the irate pastors. "But let me tell you what you don't have the power to do. You do not have the power to take away the call that I have from God. I know that the God who has called me into ministry will provide another place of service for me if you end this one. But I also know that the God who has called me into ministry has called me to ministry here. And if you do terminate me, it's premature, and it's not God's will."

Rev. Docampo comments on this meeting with the protesting pastors: "It was unexpected, but I felt very calm. Those words just came out of me. I had spent that entire morning at the courthouse with a battered woman from Nicaragua and two of her five children, getting a restraining order on her husband who had beaten her so that she had to go to the emergency room. Her children, two and four years old, were in my office eating crackers while I was having this conversation with the pastors." After they left, Isabel's supervisor, Koy Lee Haywood, said to her: "That was great! You were so calm. What you said to them was just perfect. They're going to make a mess, but we'll be fine."

The protestors did make a mess. "I had to go through a whole year of that mess," Isabel recalls. "Koy Lee had to put together a committee of men, all these pastors to hear my story. I took them to all my ministries, including the food pantries and ESL classes. I had them all over the town so they could learn about my job. I had them talking to all my volunteers." At a meeting of Judson Baptist Association, delegates voted on two questions: whether to fire Rev. Docampo and whether women should be ordained to ministry. "The meeting was packed," Isabel recalls. "This had been the talk of the town. It had been in the state and associational Baptist newspapers." When the vote was taken, only the two pastors who had come to the association office to protest voted to fire Isabel. But the vote went against the ordination of women.

Support for Rev. Docampo's position came from a partnership between Judson Baptist Association, the Louisiana Baptist Convention, and the Southern Baptist Home Mission Board. Although the association had voted by an overwhelming majority for Isabel to keep her job, several months later she learned that the Home Mission Board had withdrawn support because she was ordained. The Home Mission Board, in the midst of the surging fundamentalist movement, opposed not only the ordination of women but also social ministries. "I was a means to an end," Isabel says. "They saw me as their chance to eliminate the program."

The year-long controversy began tension between Isabel and Steven that later contributed to the end of their marriage. "Steven got a lot of hate mail about how he wasn't the man of the house," Isabel recalls. "So Steve left the church. He said he would never be held hostage by bad religion. He was going to leave the ministry, and even though he didn't pressure me to leave ministry out right, I felt such a great divide between us that it frightened me. He didn't want to go to church, and I just had to go to church. We were having tension because he was ready to walk out on faith, and I wasn't. Now after many years he has come back to faith and joined a Presbyterian church. That year of the controversy I was pretty depressed. I had to go to all these meetings with these men. I tried to keep a happy face, but it was hard because I had to prove my innocence, prove my worthiness. It was very demeaning. Then we were getting all this hate mail from crazy people. One person wrote that I was a very sinful woman, that I had the devil inside me, that before I became ordained I was on the right path and then when I was ordained, I became the daughter of the devil."

During this time Isabel was pregnant. Relma Hargus, a laywoman in Baton Rouge, and Paul Chapman, an American Baptist pastor, helped to keep her grounded through the controversy. "Relma was always there, encouraging me and being angry along with me," Isabel recalls. "She was my 'older sister' in the Christian faith through this ordeal. Her smile always gave me hope. She also gently pushed me to stand firm, and I appreciated that a great deal." And Paul Chapman encouraged Isabel when he said to her, "Think about how wonderful it is that God gave you this pregnancy to remind you that God is always about creating new life, while evil people are always about killing things and bringing death." Isabel says that this image gave her hope. "Every time I'd get a bad letter or people would say nasty things or I'd read some mischaracterization of me in the *Baptist Message*,[12] I'd pat my stomach and think about my baby and say, 'God's about creating new life. There's new life beyond this.'" Isabel's and Steven's son, Benjamin, was born a month after the packed association meeting where delegates voted for Isabel to keep her job.

After the Home Mission Board's elimination of the Christian social ministries program in Baton Rouge, Rev. Docampo worked two more months without pay because she felt such a deep call to this thriving ministry. Steven accepted an offer from the Presbyterians to serve as minister to the seafarers in the port of New Orleans. He commuted back and forth from New Orleans to Baton Rouge for several months, and then Isabel took a job in New Orleans as a legal secretary to help support the family. As a secretary in an immigration attorney's office and then in an oil and gas law firm, Rev. Docampo felt her call to ministry affirmed. In the immigration law office she worked with Latino/a clients, translating for them and hearing their stories. In the oil and gas firm she became such an effective counselor to secretaries, who had been abused by boyfriends or spouses, that the personnel director offered her a full-time job as an in-house counselor. After struggling with this offer, Isabel decided not to take it. "This is not my place to be," she thought. "This offer is for me to understand that I belong in ministry; this is an affirmation of my call."

When Steven received offers to pursue graduate work in cultural anthropology from University of Florida and American University in Washington, DC, Isabel was clear that she couldn't go to Florida. "I'm not going to Florida," she said. "I've got to go East, where I can become an American Baptist like Paul Chapman suggested. I need to go where women can be ministers, where I can leave Southern Baptists behind, and I can be what I need to be. My calling is not to fight the denomination but to serve people in need." Steve took the American University offer, and they moved to DC.

In Washington, DC, Rev. Docampo first had to build networks with Baptists before she could get a ministry position. To pay the bills, she worked a year for the Smithsonian as an administrative assistant executive to the president of a small organization with the National Academy of Sciences. During this year she visited Baptist churches and reconnected with Ester Gonzalez, with whom Isabel had worked when she served as a summer missionary from Louisiana College. Ester worked full-time at Geico Insurance Company, but she lived out her pastoral vocation by starting Bible studies. Isabel describes Ester as an "amazing woman from Ecuador, only 4'11" tall, full of fire, full of excitement, full of joy." Returning to DC ten years after working with Ester, Isabel found that the Bible study groups Ester had begun were now full-fledged churches but that Ester was not serving in any of these churches. "The churches had pastors from Central and South America, and they didn't believe in women in ministry," Isabel explains. "The pastors weren't seminary trained, but they booted her out. Here's this woman whom I watched preach. Ester was the one who raised these churches, who made them viable enough to bring a pastor. And then these pastors were not allowing her to take part in leading those congregations." Isabel visited those churches, but the pastors didn't welcome her leadership either.

Carol Ripley-Moffitt, an ordained American Baptist pastor, introduced Isabel to Elaine Tiller, head of the community outreach program for Baptist Senior Adult Ministries in Washington, DC. Elaine hired Isabel to serve in this outreach program, working closely with all the DC Baptist Convention churches to help them strengthen or begin ministry to seniors. "Because of the way Elaine set up the program, it was never going to be a patronizing ministry," Isabel says. "It was to elevate seniors and to give them agency over their own future. Seniors had their own council. We spent time helping them find resources to improve their lives. We did caregivers' support groups and advocacy groups with the National Coalition on Aging, based right there in Washington, DC, to get laws changed and to help seniors with all kinds of health care issues and ageist issues in the work place." In addition, Isabel and Elaine led intergenerational ministries in churches and seminars for pastors to help them give attention to seniors' concerns. Isabel took a special interest in the African American churches in the DC Baptist Convention. "Many senior adults in those churches were raising their grandchildren," Isabel explains. "That was a brand new issue at the time. I went to seminars with AARP and other organizations trying to get kinship laws recognized because these grandparents had no rights, and yet they were raising these children."

In 1989, while in Washington, DC, Rev. Docampo had her ordination transferred from Southern Baptist to American Baptist. She became active in Calvary Baptist Church, affiliated with American Baptist Churches USA, giving leadership in Christian education. In the education program of the church Isabel worked mainly with children, choosing curriculum with female, male, and non-gender metaphors for the Divine. In neighborhood small groups, she and her friend Rick Goodman led studies of books on justice and peace, such as Elsa Tamez's *Bible of the Oppressed*.[13] In the Deja-Vu adult class she participated in book studies such as *Saying Yes and Saying No*, by Robert McAfee Brown.[14]

At Calvary Baptist, Rev. Docampo also worked with the children on play-acting biblical stories and writing liturgy for "big church." The pastor used this liturgy in worship services without editing it because his children had helped write it. "The liturgy written by the children was full of inclusive metaphors for God," Isabel says. "The children's liturgy led the way. Some church members would have never accepted this liturgy if I had written it. But when they saw that it was written by the sixth grade class or the fifth grade class or the third grade class, they would recite it."

When Isabel introduced the Bible story about Mary and her sister Martha to the second grade class, a little boy said, "The guys are left out in this story."

"You're right," Isabel responded. "Where do you think the guys would be? What can a guy learn from this story? You make a good point that this day we didn't talk about boys. We talked about girls."

One of the little girls then said, "Well, now you know how we always feel."

"That's true," Isabel said. "Most of the stories we hear in the Bible are about boys, and girls feel left out. It never feels good to be left out. God doesn't leave anyone out."

Isabel also found inclusive worship in DC at Potter's House and Seekers Church, communities within the Church of the Savior.[15] They used diverse metaphors for the Divine and had women preachers. She says that it was helpful for her to hear a woman preacher every so often in worship services at Potter's House and Seekers Church. Isabel also appreciated the focus on the poor at Potter's House, meeting her theological understanding of what church is all about.

In 1992, Ken Sehested, executive director of the Baptist Peace Fellowship of North America,[16] asked Isabel to represent the Fellowship in witnessing the first Baptist woman ordained in Nicaragua. At the ordination Isabel met a woman from Chicago, named Rosemary, who wanted to know all about Isabel and to go with her to a Nicaraguan

Baptist Convention mission with the poor in a rural village. "I spent the whole day with her," Isabel recalls. "She was asking challenging theological questions, and I shared with her what I had been thinking about women in ministry, about how God is conceived, and about how woman need to take agency. I told her what I was learning from Nicaraguan women about claiming power. We were having this wonderful conversation."

Rosemary said, "I want you to meet me another day and go to this Jesuit bookstore with me; I have a couple of books I want to give you."

"Great!" Isabel said. "I want to read more about Nicaragua and about this theology we're talking about. I love this conversation."

Rosemary wrote her name and contact information on a card. The name on the card, "Rosemary Ruether," looked familiar to Isabel, but it didn't dawn on her who this "Rosemary" was until the next day at the Jesuit bookstore.

"There's this theologian named Rosemary Radford Ruether, who wrote the book *Sexism and God-Talk*," Isabel said. "Would you be any . . . ?" Rosemary smiled broadly, and Isabel said, "Oh! Now I don't know what to say; I'm so embarrassed."

"I didn't want this to happen," Rosemary said. "I loved just talking to you."

After Isabel got over her embarrassment, they had an even better conversation about God and sexism. Because Isabel, at this time a single parent, had little money, she couldn't pay for the books Rosemary pointed out at the Jesuit bookstore. Rosemary bought the books for her, but Isabel insisted on paying her back later. "I loved that she allowed me to pay her back because that was also a way of staying connected to her," Isabel says. "Dr. Rosemary Radford Ruether is a very genuine human being. I was in awe of her, but I experienced her as a very humble person."

In November of 1996, Rev. Docampo went to Cuba with the Alliance of Baptists to participate in the annual meeting of *La Fraternidad de Bautistas*.[17] This first trip to Cuba was important to Isabel because of her origin, the opportunity to see family members still there, and the connection with Cuban Baptists. "This trip helped me feel my identity," Isabel says. She was also delighted to hear about ordained women in Cuba.

In August of 1997, Rev. Docampo joined the faculty of Perkins School of Theology in Dallas, Texas, where she now serves as the associate director of the intern program. She describes herself as a "theological field educator," placing students in a ministry setting during their year of internship and supervising them throughout the year. In 2003, Isabel earned her Doctor of Ministry degree from Perkins. Her DMin project was the integration of the Hartford Institute for Religion's Congregational Studies method into the internship curriculum.[18] Rev. Dr. Docampo's ministry has extended into the Dallas community through her cochairing of the Workers' Rights Board with another Perkins professor, Dr. Joerg Rieger, and through her activity on the board of the Dallas Peace Center and on the advisory council of the Dallas Women's Foundation's Faith, Feminism, and Philanthropy project.

When she went to Perkins, Rev. Docampo had been serving on the board of the Baptist Peace Fellowship of North America, and she continued to serve for a few years. She says that during this time the Fellowship took a "very open stance on homosexuality" and received much criticism. She also appreciates the Fellowship's commitment to racial diversity.

A month before her fiftieth birthday, Isabel married Scott Somers, a United Methodist pastor. "He was a wonderful surprise, my gift," she says. "Scott is very supportive of my Christian vocation."

For many years Rev. Dr. Docampo has been changing church and society through her preaching, social justice ministries, and mentoring of students. In the internship program at Perkins School of Theology, she has influenced hundreds of churches not only through the students she supervises but also through her work with the lay committees and mentor pastors. Because Perkins is an "open-minded, progressive seminary," Isabel says that students study feminist and other liberation theologies. Students read Sallie McFague's *Metaphorical Theology*[19] in the introduction to theology course and learn about "Sophia" and other feminine divine metaphors from biblical studies professors. Isabel challenges her students to find creative ways to apply this inclusive theology in the church as they lead Bible study and worship.

Rev. Docampo says she has found it hard to raise awareness of sexism with some of the women students when they claimed that they were not "feeling any pain." Isabel often had to wait until incidents came up in their ministry and then help the women compare experiences with their male colleagues so that they could see the gender discrimination. Isabel now finds students in the women's studies certificate program, recently introduced at Perkins, or who come to seminary with women's studies backgrounds to be more aware of gender issues and to understand feminist theory. Over the years Rev. Docampo has been at Perkins, many of her students have discounted the importance of inclusive language by calling it "just political correctness," and by saying that church members ask if political correctness belongs in the church. She invites students to go deeper to discover that language forms our identity, affecting our self-worth and our relationships with the Divine and with others.

"If we're constantly hearing male metaphors for God and not hearing female metaphors, our identity is affected," Rev. Docampo says. "Women second-guess themselves all the time. I do, and I know better. Men can be completely wrong, but they don't second-guess themselves because all this male God-language they've been hearing makes them feel in their subconscious that they're blessed. Of course, that is not true for all men. I know incredibly thoughtful feminist men, and I appreciate their witness enormously."

Rev. Docampo gives an illustration of her belief in the power of language to form identity. Recently she and her mother watched Don Francisco interview children, ages three to eleven, on the Univision program *Sábado Gigante*.[20]

"Who's the boss at your house, your mom or your dad?" Don Francisco asked the children. "Who should be the boss, your mom or your dad?"

"It has to be the dad," a little girl answered.

"Why?" he questioned. "We've all been talking about how mothers have the babies and how mothers are smart and run the house."

"Because men are better," she said.

Disheartened, Isabel said to her mother: "Now where did she get that idea that men are better? It's everywhere. But it's definitely in the Divine. We go to church and hear, 'God the Father knows best,' and never hear 'God the Mother.'"

In her mentoring of students one-on-one and in small groups, Dr. Docampo challenges students to see the connection between gender issues and other social justice issues. She encourages them to grapple with the hard questions about the underlying structures that create injustices and guides them to see the difference between social charity and social action. She is honest with them about the risks of social justice ministry. "We talk about the institution of the church, that if we really want to help people engage with these tough issues, the risks we take sometimes involve even the denominations we serve," she says. "There's risk when you follow Jesus. Ministry is risk taking; it's not a comfortable job. If you do it with a sense of integrity, you're going to bump heads. Sometimes you bump heads with the highest people who can squash you down and take you out of ministry. I find joy in my work through seeing many of my students exercise courageous leadership during their internships as they take risks in their commitments to social justice."

On the faculty of Perkins, Rev. Dr. Docampo has chaired the Committee on Gender, Racial, and Ethnicity Concerns. "I'm proud of our school," Isabel says. "We have good faculty representation in gender and race, but we need to do better." Isabel and her committee use resources from the Association of Theological Schools on helping seminaries take diversity to the next level. This goes beyond tokenism, she explains, to "leveraging diversity to influence and frame teaching differently, constructing theology differently, and relating differently."

Dr. Docampo has also worked for change at Perkins School of Theology by serving on the task force that led to the Center for the Study of Latino/a Christianity and Religions and by being one of the chairs of the Urban Ministry Committee. She feels gratified by the accomplishments of both these groups. The Urban Ministry Committee has sent students to the Central Dallas Urban Ministries prayer breakfast, to a big convocation in Chicago sponsored by SCUPE (Seminary Consortium for Urban Pastoral Education),[21] and to community organizing training events sponsored by IAF (Industrial Areas Foundation).[22] "I've had several students who went through this training who are now very active in the community as a result, and it gives me pleasure to see them involved in community and urban issues," Isabel says. "One of my former students was on TV recently; he had taken a group of immigrants to the big demonstration in Washington, DC."

To increase students' experiences of women in authority, Rev. Dr. Docampo has challenged herself and her colleagues in the intern program to recruit more female mentor pastors to work with interns. "We have a much better balance of women mentor pastors now than when I first got here, but we still have to keep at it," she says. "Last year we ended up with only two women as mentor pastors, and the power dynamics were all askew." In meetings with mentor pastors, Isabel has given presentations on "Race, Gender, and Power in the Supervisory Relationship" and brought in the video series called "A Sacred Trust,"[23] developed by the FaithTrust Institute, dealing with relationships in the parish, including discussions on sexism.

Rev. Docampo has also participated in the annual Women's Week at Perkins and on occasion has been invited by students to help them lead chapel services. She supported students who led a chapel service focused on "Christ-Sophia" and other balanced male and female divine images. On a panel with several other women faculty members, Isabel took part in a chapel service led by Pam Oliver-Lyons, a Perkins Master of Divinity student. Rev. Docampo told a Japanese fairy tale entitled "The Handless Woman," from *Waking the World: Classic Tales of Women and The Heroic Feminine*,[24] about a girl whose hands were cut off by her husband. Her baby was taken away from her and thrown in the river. Although the girl had no hands, she found her power and went into the river to save the baby. "I told that story, and then talked about how women in the church and in society are cut off," Isabel says. "Our hands are taken away from us. In some countries, it's not metaphorical; the hands are really cut off, but in our country it's metaphorical. We have to stand by the river and say, 'What am I going to do? Am I going to just weep, or am I going to jump in?' In the story, the girl saved everyone, not just herself and the baby, but her husband and the others in the story. Her husband and the others had been trapped by evil, but she brought wholeness."

Rev. Docampo begins to articulate her vision for the future. "My vision is that women would no longer be expendable and disposable anywhere on this planet. That's my biggest sadness, that I'm fifty-four years old, and beginning with the religious institutions, women can still be expendable and disposable. They can wait. They can be in the back seat. And even if they're in the front, even if they're the pastor or the bishop, their gifts and their needs have to be conforming. Women are still not free to change things. Women have gotten to be in these positions, and then we've conformed. We have not transformed. We have not engaged our brothers to really liberate them and us so that we could create something new."

After September 11, 2001, Rev. Docampo, along with four other women, began the Dallas Women's Interfaith Dialogue group and co-led it for five years. For her work with this group of Muslim, Jewish, and Christian women, Isabel received the Dallas Peace Center award. "That's been hard work, because we do not see eye to eye on the justice issues," Isabel says. "But the most magnificent thing is to sit in a room, to be in relationship, to hear each other's stories. I ended meetings saying, 'The Divine Feminine has been with us tonight,' and they would all agree. These were Muslim, Christian, and Jewish women from conservative to liberal; they were all over the place theologically. But at the end of those meetings when we really listened, when we heard each other's pain, when someone's story really touched us and we realized that we were all women and that God was working through us and in our lives in ways that we could not even fully articulate, I could say, 'The Divine Feminine has been with us tonight in the most special way,' and everyone would receive that. We were going to walk out of that room changed women, much more open to each other now." With deep passion in her voice, Rev. Docampo elaborates on this kind of dialogue group as her vision for the future of the Divine Feminine, changing the church and the world. "If we could be unafraid to truly be in relationship with the Great Other and with the 'other,' whoever that may be—women, poor people, different races—and stay connected and do that kind of work where you really listen, the church will become less of an institution that has to have programs but becomes a place where there's healing because the stories are told and received, and every person is transformed."

All her life Rev. Isabel Docampo has indeed been preaching and practicing the same sermon—one of justice, of peace, and of transformation.

5

Rev. Larry E. Schultz

Minister of Music
Pullen Memorial Baptist Church,
Raleigh, North Carolina

On Pentecost Sunday, May 15, 2005, Rev. Larry Schultz leads the choirs, orchestra, and congregation of Pullen Memorial Baptist Church in the opening "Song of Adoration," "She's/He's Got the Whole World":

> *She's got the whole world in Her hands . . .*
> *She's got the whole world in Her hands.*
> *He's got the little tiny baby in His hands . . .*
> *He's got the whole world in His hands.*
> *She's got everybody here in Her hands . . .*
> *She's got the whole world in Her hands.*
> *He's got the wind and the rain in His hands . . .*
> *He's got the whole world in His hands.*
> *She's got the whole world in Her hands . . .*
> *She's got the whole world in Her hands.*

Rev. Schultz has changed the words of this traditional song because of his deep belief in the importance of worship language. He and the pastor, Rev. Nancy Petty, wrote a statement on inclusive language for a card on "Worship at Pullen" that takes its place beside the hymnals in the pew racks of the church:

> With the understanding that all language for God is metaphorical, and that language instills truths of equality and justice in human relationships, we intentionally use inclusive language in our worship. This includes changing scripture to gender-neutral language or using a variety of feminine, masculine, and non-gender images in referring to God and humanity. Hymns, litanies, prayers, choral offerings, and other worship elements are also chosen, altered, or created to express this inclusive and expansive view of God and God's people.

With the exuberance of a revival minister and the artistry of a symphony conductor, Larry directs "She's/He's Got the Whole World" and other spirituals on this day of Pentecost, celebrating the Spirit's coming with a sound like the rush of a mighty wind and tongues as of fire[1] to empower the beginning of the church. Near the end of the service we sing "Sister Spirit, Brother Spirit," a hymn celebrating the equal partnership of women and men and imaging the Spirit as both Sister and Brother. For this hymn Larry composed a vibrant, flowing tune, "Spirit Dance," that enhances the meaning of the words.[2] He brings congregation, choir, organ, orchestra, and hand bells together for a stirring rendition of the hymn. Larry holds a baton, but he conducts with his whole being, alive with the music.

The day before, I sat mesmerized as I watched Larry direct a choir of eighty children in the musical *Imagine God!*[3] I had come to Raleigh for this premiere performance of the musical sponsored by the Eastern North Carolina chapter of Choristers Guild, held at Hayes Barton Baptist Church. Children from seven churches of various denominations had spent months learning the musical, and had now come together for the first time to sing it under the direction of the composer. For two and a half hours of rehearsal and a one-hour performance Larry held all those children's attention and inspired them to sing like a professional choir. To calm the children in the rehearsal, he began with the gentle, expressive song, "Tenderly Comes Our Shepherd God." He moved on to the lively "Mother Eagle, Teach Us to Fly" and "Listen, Wisdom Is Calling." The performance also included an intergenerational circle dance to "Our God Is a Mother and a Father," children's accompanying "Like Rock and Light and Wind" with Orff instruments,[4] and children's placing on the altar various symbols they had made to represent the divine images in the songs.[5]

It was fascinating to see Larry work with these children to create this multisensory feast.

Larry Schultz's story begins quite literally in church. He was born on a Sunday night when his three sisters—Linda, Louella, and Laraine—were attending the worship service at their church, Phoenix Avenue Baptist in Tulsa, Oklahoma. "My mother and father were at the hospital," Larry says. "My sisters tell the story that right as the service was coming to an end, the phone rang. Everyone in the church could hear the phone ring, because it was in the pastor's study, which was behind the sanctuary off the foyer. The pastor asked the person who prayed the longest closing prayers to pray so that he could run back to the phone during the benediction. My sisters knew that call had to be from the hospital, so they were anxiously sitting there, and the man was praying and praying his lengthy prayer. As soon as he said, 'Amen,' from the back of the church the pastor yelled out, 'It's a boy!'" Larry laughs and says, "And I've been in the church ever since."

Larry grew up in what he describes as a "conservative" but not "legalistic" Southern Baptist family with a "very loving" mother and father and three older sisters. His youngest sister, Laraine, is eleven years older than he. "I was from the earliest age taken care of by my mother and sisters, because they were so much older," Larry says. "It was like having four mothers." His father, Edmond R. Schultz, a World War II veteran, worked as a stationary engineer in maintenance and mechanical jobs in various buildings in downtown Tulsa and then for American Airlines. When Larry was young, his father worked a second janitorial job in an insurance agency office. Larry remembers going with his father when he gave his time doing handyman jobs in people's homes. Although a deacon in their Baptist church, his father worked more behind the scenes than up front. Larry describes him as a "very hard-working, gentle, patient person." Larry saw his mother, Opal Lee Yarbrough, as a "leader, a very organized, up front person." She did not work to support the family financially, but she led church and civic organizations as a volunteer. She served as director of Vacation Bible School, head of a community committee that helped to save the high school from closing, president of the PTA, and as a leader in Woman's Missionary Union (WMU) and in many church and community organizations. "Before the days of childcare, I would go with her to those meetings," Larry says. "So all along I witnessed her as a leader with good organizational skills. I did not grow up in a church that had a woman on the staff as a minister. My mother is probably the first woman I saw in the pulpit, because she was the director of the Vacation Bible School for years and years. My mother is a very strong woman." These experiences of his mother and father influence the way Larry images God: "Now as we think about creating hymn texts that speak of God in male terms as very gentle and in female terms as very strong, I have this picture in my home."

Because of their common sense approach to life, Larry says that his parents were "open for their context." They welcomed people of various races into their home. "I remember a biracial couple who were welcomed into our home at a time when that probably was not the thing to do in our part of the country," Larry recalls. "At holiday times we would have all sorts of folk around our table, anyone who needed a place to be. Our best friends were a Cherokee family, who had come to be part of our church. Margaret Adair, the mother of that family, became my mother's best friend and another mother to me. She and her husband, John, had three girls, Donetta, Sharon, and Kathy, and we would call each other 'brother' and 'sister.' I learned from my parents' actions. They didn't talk much about openness or inclusion, but I saw these values in their actions. They probably don't realize how much I gleaned from them, from their openness. I often credit them that I'm open and inclusive."

Larry cites his multicultural experience in elementary, junior high, and high school as another major influence. He lived in an area of Tulsa that had a mixture of races and socio-economic classes. "My friends growing up included African American, Hispanic, Vietnamese, and a biracial boy, along with my three Cherokee 'sisters,'" Larry says. "I think that experience has influenced a very natural openness to people. I also seemed to be drawn to persons who are out of the ordinary or even the more downtrodden. I think that comes from the emphasis on reaching out that was so instilled in us through the strong missions education in my church."

As a child in Phoenix Avenue Baptist Church, Larry saw women doing most of the work, but not as paid ministers. In this traditional, medium-sized church, a few blocks from his home, the teachers of the Sunday school and missions organizations were mostly women. "My mother bemoaned the fact that you couldn't find any men to lead the Royal Ambassadors[6] group," Larry recalls. "Most of my experience was with a woman leading this group for boys. I knew that the pastor was a person of honor and leadership, because he would preach each Sunday. But I had a good idea that the women of the church were doing the hard work, with the exception of my father, who worked very hard to keep the church yard and building in order. I think it was formative for me as a child to experience the detailed work that the women would do. At home and at church I saw my mother organizing mission offerings and projects and leading groups. My oldest sister, Linda, was also highly involved in WMU, and continues to be. She now lives in Little Rock, Arkansas, where she worked for many years as a member of the Missions Support Team of the Arkansas Baptist Convention. When I was a child, I saw all the basic positions of leadership in the church held by women, even though they probably didn't think about the possibility of being paid ministers. For all practical purposes my mother did the work of what we would now call the 'minister of Christian education,' but not for pay. She told me that her mother was also highly involved in church."

When he was five years old, Larry made a profession of faith. According to Southern Baptist tradition, he walked the aisle on a Sunday morning. "The two people who met me to pray and counsel with me were my Sunday school teacher, Mrs. Wiley, and my mother," Larry recalls. "Growing up I viewed women as the spiritual leadership in my life."

In the mid-1970s, during a peak in the charismatic movement, Phoenix Avenue Baptist hired a pastor who brought in more than one hundred Oral Roberts University students to the church every Sunday and put them in leadership positions.[7] "They brought charismatic worship to our traditional Baptist church," Larry recalls. "Ted Haggard[8] was one of these students who came in and took a teaching position. He became the youth minister of the church. My parents were very traditional Southern Baptists in worship and ministry. So this major change in the church was upsetting to them, and they knew it was very confusing for me. They had attended Phoenix Avenue for thirty years, since their marriage. But we made a move."

When Larry was going into the seventh grade, he and his family moved their membership to Red Fork Baptist Church in Tulsa. During a revival service at Red Fork, at the age of thirteen, Larry decided that music ministry would be his calling. "I walked the aisle during the revival and made a commitment to church music ministry, but I remember that it was just a simple decision," Larry says. "It was no earth-shattering calling. For me it was a very logical decision, realizing what my gifts and interests are, and then realizing that could be a calling. I discovered this call by using my mind that God gave me and what I feel that I can do well. Early in my life I was involved in music making in church. My sisters involved me in music experiences, like piano lessons. So it was a natural thing then for me to see music as my calling. My churches did a good job of developing the gifts of those who expressed a sense of calling. The minister of music at Red Fork, Lex Blankenship, immediately invited me to follow him during the week to see what music ministry is like, and he gave me many ministry experiences. And my church invited me to help lead a youth revival. At thirteen, I did my first revival! Then in the summers that followed, I was a revival leader for various churches throughout Oklahoma, making a little money. My first paying job had been cleaning chairs in our church sanctuary when it was being remodeled."

A theme in Larry's story is that he has always been ahead of his time and advanced for his age. At the end of his eleventh grade year, Phoenix Avenue Baptist Church hired a new pastor, Tom Branch, a graduate of Southwestern Theological Baptist Seminary. By this time the Oral Roberts University students, including Ted Haggard, had left Phoenix Avenue, and the church had dwindled in size. Tom Branch asked Larry to come to Phoenix Avenue to help lead music while the church looked for a minister of music. Then the church asked him to be interim and then part-time minister of music. Having begun kindergarten when he was four and having skipped third grade, Larry was just turning sixteen when he began his senior year in high school and became a minister of music. "That was a really good experience to be part-time minister of music at my original church, Phoenix Avenue, for a little over a year before going to college," Larry recalls. "The church was getting back to what it once was, although it never came back in numbers. Some of the strong women I saw growing up were still there. Some of these members and the young pastor brought to me the idea of ordination. I didn't really know what ordination meant, so I went to the Baptist bookstore and bought the *Baptist Church Manual*,[9] but didn't find much there. I came to understand that ordination was the congregation's affirmation and blessing of me as a minister. Most ministers experience ordination after they've finished education and done some work in the church, but I was ordained before going to college by persons who had witnessed my life from birth and were convinced of my gifts. My summers had been spent leading revivals and getting every Baptist Sunday School Board study course diploma in church music I could. I was very focused. I knew from an early age that church music ministry was what I was to do."

When he was just sixteen years old, on June 20, 1982, Larry Schultz was ordained to ministry at Phoenix Avenue Baptist Church. His father was chair of the Ordination Council,[10] and his grandfather was also on the Council. When I was in Larry's office interviewing him, he proudly showed me his ordination certificate with his father's name, Edmond R. Schultz, at the top. On down in the list of Council members is his maternal grandfather's name, Lawrence Yarbrough. "The committee was all male," Larry says. "But there at the reception, putting the cake out, was that Sunday school teacher, Mrs. Wiley, who had prayed with me as a five-year-old when I made a profession of faith. That was very meaningful to have the strong women still there."

Also while Larry was part-time minister of music at Phoenix Avenue, he won a composition contest, sponsored by the Baptist General Convention of Oklahoma. Mary June Tabor, from the Convention's Church Music Department, called to tell Larry that his choral anthem had won in the high school division. "I had no instruction in composition, but had taken piano all my life and had music experience in the church and at school," Larry says. "The contest winners went to a festival at Oklahoma Baptist University (OBU), where I was getting ready to go to school. This was the spring before the fall that I was to begin OBU. I was planning to be a voice or piano major at OBU, because I had taken piano all my life and sung in church, and I thought that's what a minister of music majors in. But when I was there for the festival, hearing the winning compositions sung by a youth choir and preparing to enroll for my classes the next fall, Mary June Tabor said to me, 'Have you considered majoring in music theory and composition?' Even though I had won the contest, I don't think that possibility had crossed my mind."

That fall of 1982, Larry began OBU in Shawnee, Oklahoma, as a music theory and composition major with the goal of using his gift in composition in his music ministry. "It was rather unique, not being a voice or piano major, but to use music composition in ministry," Larry says. "I look back at that point and realize how instrumental Mary June Tabor was in the direction of my life. I had known and respected her for a while. She was the woman in the Church Music Department who did all the work for every festival. She was also the long-time secretary of the Southern Baptist Church Music Conference, an organization for ministers of music. So people all over the country knew her." Larry tells about another providential role Mary June Tabor played later in his life, perhaps influencing the publication by Choristers Guild of *Imagine God!: A Children's Musical Exploring and Expressing Images of God*. "When I was at Southern Seminary, she connected Jeff Reeves and me. Jeff was a couple of years behind me in OBU, and we only knew of each other there. Mary June wanted to help Jeff get established at Southern, because it was a little unusual for an OBU student not to go to Southwestern Seminary. Jeff had attended my senior composition recital at OBU and knew of my interest and abilities in music composition. Later, when he became an editor at Choristers Guild, he asked me to compose a musical. Mary June's connection helped all of that come to be."

Larry talks about other strong women who have influenced his openness to women as pastors and to the Divine Feminine. At OBU his major professor, Dr. Nancy Cobb, and his first music theory teacher, Dr. Kathryne Timberlake, had a significant influence on him. "They were very powerful women in my college experience," Larry recalls. "Also, when I got to OBU, I joined First Baptist Church in Shawnee, and on staff there was Charlotte Weedman. She was the first woman I knew who was called a 'minister' in a church. She was the minister to college students. She would lead worship very creatively, reading from a variety of translations and paraphrases. Up to that point, I had used only the King James, NAS, TLB, and the NIV.[11] Along with expanding my experience with Scripture a bit, she was also the first woman I saw in worship leadership. At OBU Dr. Rowena Strickland taught biblical courses, and was an honored professor. I did not have her, but realized she was a pioneer as a strong woman in the religion department."

A major influence on Larry as he developed as a composer and conductor was Dr. Warren Angell, who had already retired as dean of the College of Fine Arts at OBU when Larry went there. Dr. Angell conducted the choir at Falls Creek Baptist Youth Camp,[12] and Larry sang in this choir for five summers before going to college. "I had to sneak in the choir that first year, because I was a little young for the requirements," Larry recalls. "But I just blended in with the three to five hundred singers. Dean Angell was full of energy and life; he had an infectious enthusiasm. He was such an inspiring figure. Experiencing him made me want that same charisma so that I could inspire people to sing as he did. He instilled in me the desire to be inspirational in my music ministry. He also taught me in those summers that music is the vehicle for the text, that the music could find its best expression as it interpreted the meaning of the text. Especially in his later years, he also focused on the soft and beautiful expression of music. In Oklahoma, with its gospel choirs and quartets and evangelistic groups, music was often boisterous and rousing. But he helped us experience God in the soft and the beautiful, leading me to experience God more as Mystery. Continuing on this path certainly led me to an acceptance of expressing God in multiple ways, including feminine. Dean Angell had a theology of beauty, that God is beautiful. That was an expansive thing for me to think about God in those ways. I wrote the piano accompaniment for 'Tenderly Comes Our Shepherd God'[13] in his style, which was very expressive and tender."

After experiencing Dean Angell in those summers at Falls Creek Camp, Larry knew that he wanted to attend the Warren M. Angell School of Fine Arts at OBU. When Larry began OBU, Dr. Angell still lived in town and stayed connected to the Bison Glee Club, which he founded, and in which Larry sang. "I latched onto him at every opportunity to continue to learn from him," Larry recalls. "Dean Angell was organist for a time at Norman Vincent Peale's church,[14] and told of hearing Peale say that we were all sparks off the Great Mind. That comment was a stretching moment and affirmed what I had been feeling about using my God-given mind in figuring out a calling and interpreting Scripture."

Several other experiences at OBU stretched Larry's theology. When Larry was a freshman, on the first day of his required Bible class, the professor gave all the students a Southern Baptist Convention journal article on why all the language of the Bible is not literal.[15] "That was one of those light bulb moments," Larry recalls. "The teachers at that time taught this openness as we studied the Bible. And my English professor, Dr. Laura Crouch, in a team-taught Western civilization course, said that Bold Mission Thrust[16] was very egotistical on the part of Southern Baptists to want to save the world all by themselves, disregarding the help of other faith groups. Her brave statement started me down the road of ecumenism and now 'interfaithism.'"

Directing music at a Methodist church during his OBU years also expanded Larry's ecumenical experience. Larry played in the OBU band, and the band director, Ron Howell, was also director of music at Wesley United Methodist Church in Shawnee. "All four years when I was at OBU, I was his fill-in director when he was away," Larry says. "That was my first experience leading anyone but Baptists. The music director in that church wore a robe instead of a suit, and I had never seen a minister or music director in a robe. I remember calling home to talk with my mother about wearing the robe!"

After graduating from OBU in 1986, Larry enrolled in Southern Baptist Theological Seminary in Louisville, Kentucky. His major professors at OBU and Warren Angell had encouraged him to go to Southern instead of Southwestern Seminary in Fort Worth, Texas, closer to Larry's home, because the church music school at Southern was less evangelistic and more worship oriented. "I'm glad I listened to them as that was most likely an important fork in the road," Larry says. "When I got to Southern, I chose to take Dr. Molly Marshall for the formations course, required for all persons entering the seminary, because I had heard that her courses were really great. It was a course where we thought about calling and tried to flesh out why we were at seminary. Later, because of that experience, Cindy and I chose her to be the minister for our wedding there at seminary. That showed some progression from my upbringing as far as experiencing women in ministry. I think what formed me most at Southern Seminary was the fundamentalist takeover of the Southern Baptist Convention.[17] It forced me to really study Baptist life and polity and issues. The women-in-ministry issue was the one that stood out for me. The Bible was being used as a weapon to hurt others, and those I saw being hurt were women professors, like Dr. Molly Marshall.[18] Here were people I knew from our student-teacher relationships who were being treated so harshly. That's what solidified for me that women in ministry and as professors at seminaries should be valued, not because I'd had a revelation from Scripture, but because I had experienced these people who were now being fired. My support of women in ministry connected also with my upbringing in my family, knowing that women were strong leaders in the church. I think that would eventually connect with my supporting worship of the Divine Feminine."

Another formative experience for Larry at Southern Seminary was studying the distinction between the Jesus of history and the Christ of faith. "We studied Albert Schweitzer's book *The Quest of the Historical Jesus*,"[19] Larry recalls. "My Christology began to change at that point. Most of the hymns I sang growing up would equate Jesus to God. Now I've come to the place where I say the 'God in Jesus.' It's helpful to me when we want to sing of God as 'She' or as 'Ruah' or with other female names, that Christian worship doesn't have to be tied up in the male Jesus of history, but the God in Jesus, which is the God in us, expressed in so many ways."

A Southern Seminary conducting professor, Dr. John Dickson, impressed upon Larry the importance of the musical text by changing the word "brotherly" to "sisterly" in the anthem "Gracious Spirit, Dwell with Me." Larry was singing in the chapel choir when Dr. Dickson made that alteration. "That's a very simple, but wonderful change," Larry says. "Since the women sang that line alone, it made complete sense for them to sing of their actions being 'sisterly' instead of 'brotherly.' That was the first time I recall a choral conductor asking a choir to make a change related to gender issues or any other theological issue. Dr. Dickson placed a high priority on the text of a musical work, and had an impact on my thinking."

At Southern Seminary Larry met his future wife, Cindy. "We became best of friends and shared virtually every experience," Larry says. "Through all that Southern Baptist takeover, before and after marriage and continuing to this day, we have been figuring out our theology together. She has been the most pivotal in bringing me to where I am today. Conversations with Cindy helped to form my theology. She grew up in a fairly progressive church, First Baptist, Morganton, North Carolina, that had women deacons. Cindy's mother was a music director in several churches in her growing-up years. So she witnessed women in leadership roles, and that played into our conversations. By that time I was valuing women in ministry. Of course, I was in awe of Cindy for many reasons, especially for her gifts. We worked together part-time at Yorktown Baptist Church in Louisville before we were even engaged. From that point forward we have shared a partnership in ministry and in life. We married in 1989, and both graduated that year from the church music school at Southern; I graduated in May, and Cindy in December. Finding that kind of partner for life and knowing that kind of intimacy and love, for me connects with God. So I could easily love a Divine Feminine God, loving Cindy as I do. And then later when I came to understand parenthood, I could see God as Parent. And the image of God as Friend comes to life for me, because Cindy and I were best friends and have always focused on that friendship. Cindy and my children, Ryan and Kelly, instill in me the importance of a balance of masculine and feminine divine images." Larry's belief in this balanced divine imagery comes through in his dedication on the front page of *Imagine God!: A Children's Musical Exploring and Expressing Images of God*:

> *To Cindy, Ryan and Kelly—*
> *magnificent images of God.*
> *L.E.S.*

Larry emphasizes that his experiences, even more than his academic and biblical discoveries, have expanded his divine imagery. "As I think of the persons who have influenced me the most, certainly that would be Cindy, Ryan, and Kelly, and then my family growing up," Larry says. "My experiences of loving them helps me think of God as Parent or Lover or Partner. You can have an academic idea of what these images of God mean, but you have to experience them first to understand the fullness. I think my openness to the Divine Feminine was due to my natural experiences from childhood through marriage. The Divine Feminine seemed the most natural thing in the world to me because of all these experiences. Then discovering that the Bible actually contains Divine Feminine images was icing on the cake. That was a wonderful discovery, to see these lesser known, but just as powerful, images in the Bible."

After Cindy and Larry were married, Cindy still had one more semester at Southern Seminary. During that time Larry held the only secular job he ever had; he worked as an office clerk for Miller Pipe Organ Company in Louisville. But he says that even this job felt like an extension of his church music training as he learned more about the pipe organ and the role of the technicians. "At that company we worked with churches, and I sat around with my fellow workers there, singing hymns all day," he recalls.

During that semester when Cindy was finishing her degree at Southern Seminary, Larry had what he describes as an "epiphany." Dr. Paul Richardson and Dr. Hugh McElrath, hymnology professors at Southern, brought Dr. Brian Wren to the seminary. "I was excited that he was coming to campus, knowing that he was one of the leading figures in what was called the 'hymn explosion' in Great Britain that had come across to America, this new wave of hymn writers using contemporary language," Larry says. "Cindy and I went to the hymn festival Brian Wren led. That was the first experience I had in singing to God in anything but male language. We sang his hymn 'Bring Many Names,'[20] which includes a variety of feminine and masculine images of God, old and young. The hymn speaks of 'strong mother God' who works 'night and day, planning all the wonders of creation, setting each equation, genius at play.' I remember thinking, 'Wow! I've just sung to God as Mother.' Perhaps I was subconsciously thinking of growing up seeing all those very strong women doing all the hard, detailed work of the church. I felt that almost everything to that point in my life came full circle, especially singing to God with feminine imagery. Even though I had left revival days, it felt like one of those 'mountain-top' high, emotional revival evenings because of the feminine imagery. Growing up I had always sung to God as Father, and that was meaningful for me because I have a wonderful father. And I had grown up with all the other usual masculine names: 'Lord,' 'Jesus,' 'God,' 'Christ.' It gave me great joy to sing to God as Mother and so many other varied ways."

After the hymn festival, Larry and Cindy went to a reception for Brian Wren. At the reception Dr. Hugh McElrath congratulated Larry that his hymn text, "O God, We Ask for Strength," had been accepted for publication in *The Baptist Hymnal* of 1991. "I had not heard about it," Larry says. "Cindy and I were already thrilled with the evening, and then to get this good news! It was a dream come true to have a hymn published. I wrote the hymn in the midst of the Baptist battle. I saw so many fundamentalists using the Bible to treat others harshly that I wanted to try to make a difference." Larry's hymn is a prayer asking for strength to live in "peace and love" and "to never speak a hurtful word." The hymn also prays "for minds to think before we say or do," and "for grace to hear when others disagree." Larry says that he is surprised this hymn, calling for open-mindedness, got in the hymnal during the fundamentalist takeover of the Southern Baptist Convention. "It tries to give room for all viewpoints, even though it doesn't touch specifically on the Divine Feminine or other images of God," Larry comments. "It certainly opens the door for an open mind to take those in. At the reception I shared with Brian Wren that my hymn had been accepted, and he was also thrilled. I had bought his book *What Language Shall I Borrow? God-Talk in Worship: A Male Response to Feminist Theology*,[21] and he signed it to me: 'on a night of good news.' That book formed my initial strong theology about how divine imagery and how words we sing form us and reveal our beliefs. Then I realized it takes more than just an understanding, that I had to be willing to put that theology into practice in the trenches of the real world and the real church."

As his story continues to unfold in the three full-time churches he has served as minister of music, Rev. Larry Schultz progresses in putting this theology into practice. Many ministers of music are even more resistant to inclusive language than pastors because of the difficult tasks of finding inclusive anthems and hymns, of changing existing exclusive words, and of creating new hymn texts. Also, ministers of music often face copyright issues when trying to change words in more recent music as well as the resistance of choir members and congregations to singing new words. "You have to be brave enough and to find ways to bring inclusive music to worship," Larry comments.

In 1990, Rev. Schultz began his first full-time ministry position at First Baptist Church, Walterboro, South Carolina. Larry describes this church as having a "high view of worship," a "fairly progressive" staff, and a "fairly conservative" congregation. The pastor, Rev. Posey Belcher, spoke out against the fundamentalist takeover of the Southern Baptist Convention, and became involved with the Cooperative Baptist Fellowship (CBF).[22] Larry and Cindy also became active in CBF while they were at the Walterboro church. Larry continued to read the work of Brian Wren and to ponder how to put it into practice. "At Walterboro, just out of seminary, I was still working through how my understandings could play out in the life of the church," Larry says. "We didn't reprint many hymns, so we mainly used what was in the hymnal. But I began to highlight with the congregation the few feminine images in the hymnal and to select hymns with gender-neutral language."

Moving on to First Baptist Church of Greenwood, South Carolina, in 1996, Larry found a more "progressive" congregation. Here, as in the Walterboro church, Cindy became the church organist. They were delighted to serve together in both churches. The pastor, Rev. Bill Harris, like the pastor of the Walterboro church, became a mentor to Larry. "I witnessed both Bill Harris and Posey Belcher taking many brave stands," Larry recalls. "Posey would get up at every convention and speak out against any form of the Baptist takeover. Bill would do so in his preaching, saying things that may not be popular on racial issues and acceptance of all. The faith communities in which I've worked have had an influence on what I have done in my ministries around the Divine Feminine and other theological issues. At the Greenwood church I incorporated more slight alterations in hymn texts and used 'Bring Many Names' from time to time and other hymns that incorporated some feminine imagery. I remember one woman commented to me that she understood the word 'brotherhood' or 'brother' to mean all of 'mankind'! I also got comments like, 'You're just trying to be politically correct.' Some people didn't understand that my emphasis on language in hymns was for reasons of theology and a more expansive worship."

While minister of music at the Greenwood church, Rev. Schultz became more active in Cooperative Baptist Fellowship. He served as president of the South Carolina CBF Church Musicians, and then on the national coordinating council of the Fellowship. But when the chief executive officer and others in the top leadership brought to the national meeting a recommendation that CBF be "welcoming," but not "affirming" to homosexual people, Larry left CBF. "I felt sickened that we were going to be excluding a group of people," Larry says. "I remember being almost physically sick because that's how the Southern Baptist Convention had been treating people. That's the first time I had seen any form of exclusion in the CBF. Up to that point it had been inclusive of women in ministry and all sorts of churches. But now the recommendation was to defund students getting scholarships to institutions, like Wake Forest Divinity School, who were accepting of homosexual folks, and students known to be homosexual would not receive scholarships. At the end of that meeting in Atlanta, Donna

Forrester, moderator of CBF at that time, asked any of us who would to offer a brief word or Scripture. I stood up and recited off the top of my head the passage that in Christ there is 'neither male nor female, Jew nor Greek, slave nor free.'[23] I ended with 'in Christ there's neither heterosexual nor homosexual, for we are all one in Christ Jesus.' That was basically my exit from the CBF. I think I would have felt that way no matter what the exclusion had been. It's interesting that it was this issue shortly before I came to Pullen."

When Larry was at the church in Walterboro, he had read about the stand Pullen Memorial Baptist Church took in 1992 to endorse unqualified acceptance of homosexual Christians and their full participation in the life and work of the church. Within the year, Pullen was excluded from the Raleigh Baptist Association, the Baptist State Convention of North Carolina, and the Southern Baptist Convention. "I remember thinking, 'what a brave, autonomous church; I'd like to be a part of a church like that some day,'" Larry says. In 2001, Rev. Schultz became the first full-time minister of music at Pullen.

Shortly before going to Pullen, Larry and Cindy attended an Alliance of Baptists Convocation in Decatur, Georgia, where I gave one of the covenant addresses on the importance of balancing female and male divine names and images in worship,[24] and where the congregation sang two of my hymns, "Sister Spirit, Brother Spirit" and "O Spirit of Power."[25] Larry describes this as another of his "pivotal, epiphany" experiences. "Cindy and I were thrilled because it took us from the foundational understanding we got from Brian Wren to the next step of using it in worship, to be bolder and more proactive about it." Larry says.

Larry and Cindy and I didn't meet that evening of my covenant address nor in the days of the Alliance Convocation to follow. Several months later I received an email from Larry, expressing appreciation for my address and asking permission for Pullen Memorial Baptist Church to use my hymns that were sung at the Convocation. I wrote back that I'd be delighted and honored. A few weeks later came another email from Larry, asking if I had any texts without music. Up to this time, I'd been writing hymn texts to familiar hymn tunes, with one exception. I had recently written a hymn trying to express theodicy struggles. Can God be all good and all-powerful with so much suffering and evil in the world? The hymn text came to me in the form of a child's questions.

On the morning of September 11, 2001, Larry opened my email in which I'd sent the hymn text, "Are You Good and Are You Strong?"[26] He later told me of the cathartic experience it was for him, after the horrors of 9/11, to take these words and compose a children's anthem and a hymn tune.

At Pullen Larry experiences more freedom than in his two previous church positions. "I'm grateful that we're here because I feel that we are able to be as open-minded as we would like to be," Larry says. "At Pullen we're open to a variety of expressions for God. We use the Divine Feminine in spoken word, song, and visual art. In the mid-1980s, when Mahan Siler was pastor, Pullen voted to use inclusive language in worship. I think in the beginning Pullen's idea of 'inclusive' was what I was doing in Walterboro, which was gender-neutral language. But we've been able to move progressively into balancing female and male names for God and into non-gender terminology."

When Rev. Schultz came to Pullen in 2001, Rev. Jack McKinney had been senior pastor for about a year. In 2002, the church voted for Rev. Nancy Petty, who had been associate pastor, to serve with him as copastor. "I've had the joy of working with copastors," Larry says. "Talking about a balance of male and female imagery—there it was in the people preaching up in front!" In late 2009, Rev. McKinney resigned, and the church voted in 2010 for Rev. Petty to be senior pastor. "Cindy and I think it's high time for Pullen of all places to have a solo female pastor," Larry says. "Currently I'm the only male minister. But it's interesting as I look back on my life how everything has been preparing me for this time, growing up with sisters and nieces and then having all those strong women professors."

These personal experiences, along with his discoveries of the ethical and biblical reasons for including female divine images in worship, have paved the way for Rev. Schultz to venture where few ministers of music will go. He alters the words of some well-loved familiar hymns that are not under copyright. For example, Larry modified "Wonderful Words of Life," to include Sophia (Wisdom) language:

> *Wisdom graciously gives to all wonderful words of life;*
> *listen now to Her loving call, wonderful words of life.*
> *All so freely given, moving us to heaven;*
> *beautiful words, wonderful words, wonderful words of life.*

> *Sweetly echo Sophia's call, wonderful words of life;*
> *offer justice and peace to all, wonderful words of life.*
> *Wisdom-Guide and Savior—sanctify forever;*
> *beautiful words, wonderful words, wonderful words of life.*

Rev. Schultz even changed the "Gloria Patri"[27] to the "Gloria Matri" and references to God as "He" to "She" in an anthem with regal images. "Many churches will just substitute 'God' for the word 'He' in an anthem or hymn," Larry comments. "I've found that you end up singing such a guttural word, 'God, God, God,' back to back, and it's just not pleasing poetry. And the word 'God' has male connotations. So a wonderful thing we've done, out of a sense of balance, is not to change 'He' to 'God,' but to change 'He' to 'She.' In this entire anthem we sang recently I changed every 'He' to 'She.' It was an anthem that used psalm-like words: 'worship God in majesty,' and 'worship God who rides on the wings of the wind.' Immediately, I thought, 'That's Mother Eagle who rides on the wings of the wind.' So it made utmost sense to sing 'She': 'She rides on the wings of the wind'; 'She reigns in glory and in majesty.' We ended with the 'Gloria Matri': 'Glory be to the Mother and to the Christ and to the Holy Spirit; As it was in the beginning, is now and ever shall be, world without end.'"

When copyright issues are involved, it takes even more commitment for ministers to change words in worship. Because of his strong belief that "what we sing in worship shapes us," Rev. Larry Schultz works hard to use gender-balanced imagery. When Rev. Nancy Petty was installed as copastor with Rev. Jack McKinney, Larry wanted to use the anthem "And the Father Will Dance" to go with the congregational hymn "Sister Spirit, Brother Spirit," that also has dance imagery. But he was determined to include "the Mother" in the anthem, so he persisted in getting copyright permission to change the words. "I thought the perfect choral piece to go with 'Sister Spirit, Brother Spirit' was 'And the Father Will Dance,'" Larry says. "So I called the publisher to say that our congregation sings to God in feminine ways as well as masculine and that I wanted to use the piece with our copastor model. I think the publisher was surprised at the question, very much, and then hesitated about giving me permission. It took a few phone calls to finally get permission to make changes. I created the anthem to include both 'Father' and 'Mother,' so there are points in the anthem where the male voices sing the Father imagery and the female voices added Mother imagery. There are times these phrases come close together: 'and the Father will,' 'and the Mother will.' So it almost sounds like 'Father-Mother.' Our copies of the anthem from that installation service have the title 'And the Father-Mother Will Dance.'"

When people object to the alteration of words in hymns and anthems, Larry cites the example of Isaac Watts, called the "father of English hymnody,"[28] who wrote hymns in which he paraphrased Psalms and included references to Christ. "Watts is known for Christianizing the Psalms, writing hymns that are metrical psalms, connecting Jesus with the Psalms," Larry comments. "When I get resistance, I have used that example in teaching congregations about hymnody and about altering of texts. Isaac Watts is a good example because he Christianized the book of Psalms, the hymnal of the Bible. Now we're altering texts to meet the needs of those who want to sing with more expansive images, like with the Divine Feminine."

If Larry cannot find appropriate music with inclusive language or cannot get copyright permission to alter words, he creates new music. "Every time I get a packet of music from a publisher, it's all exclusively 'he,' 'Lord,' 'Christ,' 'God,' 'Father,'" Larry says. "Publishers are publishing what they can sell to make money to keep afloat. As a composer and text writer, I don't have a desire to contribute to the already vast supply of male-dominated theistic images such as 'Lord' or 'King.' The word 'Lord' is a much harder one to get away from in church life, because so much has been written with that word in it. But Brian Wren's book *Praying Twice*[29] made me start thinking about the word 'Lord' being not only male domination but also in the English system this 'overlording.' As Americans, we don't realize the full connotation of 'Lord.' But I grew up using 'Lord, Lord, Lord, Lord.' When I say the word 'Lord,' I really don't have any picture in my mind, and it also has a guttural sound. Probably growing up I envisioned a male image when I said, 'God.' But 'Christ,' 'God,' and 'Lord' have been so overused that they are not very descriptive. Now it's so wonderful to sing descriptive images, like 'Mother Eagle' and 'Friend.'"

Rev. Schultz finds fulfillment in creating music for Pullen and for a wider audience through his publications. "My purpose has always been music ministry, and composing has given me even more meaning in my work," Larry says. "It's fulfilling to spread the good word, to bring the Divine Feminine and other expansive imagery to adults and children. Singing together uses multiple parts of our brains. The lyrics are locked in and encoded in us. We remember words we sing more easily than words we hear or speak. That's one reason I've gravitated toward writing for children."

An experience with his own children reinforced Larry's determination to provide children female and male divine images to sing. Larry, Kelly, and Ryan were riding in the car, listening to a musical setting of *Old Turtle*,[30] in which various animals and elements of nature argue about who God is.

"She is a great tree!" sang the willow tree.

"That's my part!" Kelly, three years old at the time, joyfully exclaimed.

Ryan, who was seven, responded to the description of God as a growling male bear.

"When she was only three, my daughter had identified with a feminine image of God, and it made her exuberant," Larry says. "This experience with my daughter and son affirmed that children delight in the realization that God is like them and that they are made in the divine image. This understanding gives each child a deep sense of self-worth. Kelly and Ryan related to images of God whose gender matched their own, while learning that the divine image was also in others different from them."

About a year later, Larry jumped at the opportunity to write a children's musical that included female and male divine images. "*Imagine God!* has been one of the most fulfilling creations to get out there, and Choristers Guild is such a highly respected publisher," Larry says. He recounts a conversation with editor Jeff Reeves about possibilities for the musical.

"Do you have any ideas for subjects?" Jeff asked.

"What about a musical to help children think about God in a variety of ways? I wonder about writing a musical that includes masculine and feminine images for God, biblically based," Larry said.

Larry recalls that Jeff didn't balk at this suggestion, but sounded excited. "He had to take this idea to the board of Choristers Guild; he had the job of trying to sell that to them," Larry says. "This is the mystical part, as I look back on it. Choristers Guild was transitioning between directors, and the editors were doing most of the work. So Jeff went right to the board and sold it. I had thought of asking Carl

Daw, Molly Marshall, and Michael Hawn[31] to write endorsements for the musical. Jeff said that the board thought it would be a great idea to have these well-respected musicians and theologians put their stamp of approval on the musical."

Not everyone has approved of *Imagine God!* Two groups pulled out of the premiere performance Larry led in Raleigh. "One was the big United Methodist church downtown whose minister of music was very much in favor of the musical, but a children's choir leader was up in arms against it when she found out the content," Larry recalls. "Another large Methodist church in Dallas had planned to do the musical. I saw it advertised in their brochure for the choir year, and I was thrilled. It did get into some large churches like that. I emailed the person whose name I saw on the brochure to thank her and to ask her to let me know how it went. She wrote back that she was very sorry that they could not do the musical. She was in charge of the children's choir, but the interim minister of music found out about it and told her she could not do it." Russell Moore, dean of the School of Theology at the now fundamentalist-controlled Southern Baptist Theological Seminary, denounced *Imagine God!* in an article entitled "Mother God Goes to Children's Church." Moore objects to the lyrics that speak of God as "Mother Eagle" and that use female pronouns to refer to Deity. He calls the musical "dangerous" because it is easier to transform the imaginations of children than of adults. "Children are less bound to masculine images of God as Father, Lord, and King at an early age than they will be after years of teaching from the church,"[32] Moore writes.

Although *Imagine God!* has had detractors, Larry finds it rewarding to learn about children singing the musical in numerous churches around the country. "When Cindy and I drove to several states to introduce *Imagine God!* to church musician conferences, folks came up in tears to thank us," Larry says. "So there are those persons out there; it may not be the masses, but it's meaningful when they come and say, 'Thank you for this musical. There's nothing like it.' We heard of some churches doing Bible studies related to the images in the musical. That's wonderful that it inspired them to study these images." Larry talks about how rewarding it has been to hear responses from children who have experienced the musical. A nine-year-old boy commented:

It was a great feeling. My favorite songs are "Listen, Wisdom Is Calling," because the rhythm is great, and "Mother Eagle," because the words are very creative. I loved doing the art. It was great to make paintings of different images of God and make the eagle's nest. I learned new images of God like Mother Eagle, Rock, Light. The music camp was fun, outstanding, phenomenal!

An eleven-year-old girl said that her favorite song in the musical was "Listen, Wisdom Is Calling," that includes the biblical "She" references to "Wisdom," because this song made her "feel strong."

One of Larry's anthems, "Whoever Welcomes You Welcomes Me,"[33] also teaches children that the Divine lives in them. Larry wrote the words and tune for this Advent anthem. "I used the word 'Christ,' but it was an effort to unpack what that means," Larry comments. "I've found in my journey that questioning is important, so this anthem asks questions: Where do we find you? What will you look like? How will you be dressed? Will you be visiting prisoners or children or the hungry? And I used what Scripture reveals Jesus said, 'Whoever welcomes you welcomes me.'[34] Then I jumped off theologically with the way I feel that would play out: 'Advent is when you discover I AM in you!' I used 'I AM'[35] in capital letters as a code for the Divine in us. I wanted to help children think about how the I AM in Jesus is the I AM inside of them. Another line in the anthem I'm sure was influenced by my Divine Feminine experiences: 'Whatever you look like, I will look like too.' So that's boy, girl, male, female. This expansiveness in imagery certainly influenced me to put in that phrase. And I believe it's important not just for adults to include the Divine Feminine and other expansive imagery, but that we bless our children with it, instill in them at the earliest ages. Then it becomes a natural and meaningful expression for them. One of the reasons for our *Sing and Dance and Play with Joy!: Inclusive Songs for Young Children*[36] is that I've not found any other music resources for that age group with the Divine Feminine and other open, inclusive theologies. *Sing and Dance* is a full curriculum of resources for teaching and experiencing, and that's even more rare."

Sometimes Larry feels the conflict between his commitment to writing music with imagery that balances female and male divine imagery and the realities of the publishing world. "If you want to get something published in the wider world out there with the mainline publishers, it's a little tricky," Larry says. "Sometimes I go back to more gender-neutral imagery, and I want to do more than that. But some publishers would close the door immediately. There's a sense of having to get my name out there for publishers to look at me, so I feel I need to do enough that's going to be sort of pleasing to them and that they're going to publish; so then they'll have some confidence to take my music with more expansive imagery."

A strong sense of calling and the growth in his understanding of that calling have kept Rev. Schultz in the church. "I was raised with such an emphasis on finding a calling and developing my gifts," Larry says. "My parents instilled in me that sense of calling and purpose in life through all that we did in church. That sense of calling has kept me connected to church and church work. I've found, however, that calling changes and grows. My original thought was that music ministry was mostly for evangelistic purposes, because that's the context of the churches of my childhood. When my world was turned upside down and I learned that life in the church was not all about evangelism, I saw my calling morph into worship as the priority. Then I asked, 'Who is the God I'm worshiping and how do I name and image that God?' The Divine Feminine opened up a whole new world, and I realized that God is more than just a grandfatherly figure rocking up there in the clouds somewhere. Now that continues to play out as I think, 'Who is the God we worship in Her/His fullness?' I've stuck with my initial calling to music ministry, but I've had to keep finding new expressions of it to have it be authentic. I keep discovering these new paths, and the Divine Feminine has been a very big part of that."

Larry's calling includes leading music that reflects and expands a congregation's theology. Some congregations pride themselves on the inclusive, progressive theology they hear from the pulpit, but they don't see the need to change the exclusively masculine language of hymns. "Because I view singing as sustained speech, I don't look at hymns or anthems any differently from a prayer or a proclamation or a word of praise," Larry says. "A congregation should not sing anything in worship they wouldn't proclaim in spoken word. In the selection of hymns and choral music, nostalgia should not be considered in the planning of authentic worship. Often persons express a like or dislike related to a hymn's tune and their ability or disability to sing it well, instead of considering the hymn text's theology and liturgical function. Singing a hymn with a nostalgic tune from childhood that expresses inappropriate theology doesn't make sense, and for all practical purposes, halts the worship service for a mere 'sing-a-long.' Congregational hymns and choral anthems are expressions of praise, prayer, or proclamation, and should be selected and placed in a service with care. Worship through singing moves toward being an authentic expression for that particular worshiping group when it connects with the group's theological identity."

Rev. Schultz describes his big vision for inclusive theology to spread throughout the church and the world. "One of my passions is that expansive theology spreads and grows because of the benefits," Larry says. "It gives me purpose and meaning to have discovered the Divine Feminine and other theologies of inclusion. This is the Good News message for me now, a liberating message. Jack McKinney, the former pastor of Pullen, in one of my annual reviews, called me 'Pullen's evangelist' because of my publications and getting out in the world and leading conferences. I hadn't used the word 'evangelism' since doing those revivals, and it's another kind of evangelism now. I've had to rediscover in my ministry and calling what that Good News is. Originally in my childhood and youth, the Good News was 'salvation.' Then that lost its meaning, as I came to understand 'salvation' from a more universal view, that everybody's going to be all right. My focus shifted to worship, and then discovering the Divine Feminine gave me this Good News aspect of 'Oh, this is wonderful,' and an excitement to share it. For me now the Gospel to share is the Divine Feminine and expanding imagery and theology because of all the benefits for women and men and children. For a long time I've known about abuse of women and girls. My mother has been very involved throughout her mission work with a battered women's shelter in Tulsa, and I've heard her talking about that. I want to provide music resources that include female and male divine images so that both girls and boys grow up to know they're valued."

To advance this vision, Larry would like to sponsor a hymn or an anthem contest with guidelines for inclusive language. "My vision for the future is to encourage others to create music with the Divine Feminine and other expansive images, so that there would be more resources available out there," Larry says. At youth, adult, and children's festivals, which involve many choirs from various denominations,

Larry advocates for the selection of music with expansive divine images. "We buy from mainline publishers, and there's nothing much out there," Larry says. "Because of my speaking up, an adult festival at least incorporated a Mother image in one of the hymns. And one festival included an anthem with nature imagery, 'Sing a Festive Song!'[37] for which I wrote the words and tune. As a church musician, I want to expand our theology, to point to Mystery. There is no language that can fully express the Mystery, so we use metaphors that point to what something is like, but also what something is not like. God is a Rock, but is not a Rock. The Divine Feminine opens up so much more in our imaging Mystery. There are ways of singing about the Divine that we haven't explored, like with transgendered images. And what are the divine images on other planets? I'm sure there's life out there. What are their expressions of Mystery? Perhaps there's a third gender out there, or four or five genders. It's very important for me now to balance images, to help interpret the feminine that was lost when patriarchy took over. And now string theory,[38] the concept of all the particles of life being vibrating strings, opens new possibilities for music ministry. If we discovered what it means for us all to be musical beings, vibrating sound waves, how would that connect us with the universe?"

The powerful possibilities of music come alive through Larry's prophetic creative works and through the artistry and passion with which he conducts choirs and congregations. One of his recent compositions uses musical metaphors for the Divine. "Music is so mysterious," Larry comments. "It touches the spirit as well as the mind, but we feel it. People use it for healing." For the eighty-fifth birthday of Kathryne Timberlake, his college music theory teacher, Larry wrote the words and tune for "Composer of All the Music We Hear":

> *Composer of all the music we hear,*
> *of harmonies rich and melodies clear,*
> *of rhythm that pulses with tempo and beat,*
> *your music enlivens our voices and feet.*
>
> *Conductor of all the music we sing,*
> *your gestures inspire each offering we bring*
> *of instruments gathered with voices in song.*
> *Your music enfolds us; to you we belong.*

*Conveyer of all the music we feel,
with power to comfort, strengthen and heal,
in modes that express deep emotion, we find
your music engages both spirit and mind.*

*Musician Divine, the gift of your art
enriches the mind and body and heart,
enlightens our journey through life with its sound.
We praise you for music, your gift most profound.*[39]

6

Rev. Dr. Monica A. Coleman

African Methodist Episcopal Minister
Associate Professor of Constructive Theology
and African American Religions,
Claremont School of Theology,
Claremont, California

"Womanist theologies of salvation state that Jesus Christ can be seen as a black woman," Rev. Dr. Monica A. Coleman writes in *Making a Way Out of No Way*. "Postmodern womanist theology argues that a black woman is often Christ. The Savior may be a teenager, a person living with a disability, a lesbian woman."[1] Before I meet the author, I am impressed by this book's scholarly delineation of postmodern womanist theology and by the illustrations of Saviors. In the womanist tradition of engaging black women's literature, one illustration comes from *Parable of the Sower*, a science fiction novel by Octavia E. Butler.[2] Lauren Oya Olamina, the African American teenage protagonist of the novel, walks north from a fictional suburb of Los Angeles when in 2024 her neighborhood enclave and family are destroyed. Other refugees join her journey, and she teaches them her "God-Is-Change" theology, which she calls "Earthseed." Rev. Dr. Coleman comments: "Lauren emerges as a Savior because she courageously uses her abilities to creatively transform. We know a Savior by what she does . . . Lauren survives the destruction of her walled neighborhood and leads a group of people into community and a viable future. Nevertheless, Lauren is an unlikely Savior. Because Lauren is young, black, and female, her leadership is questioned by the larger world."[3] *Making a Way Out of No Way* gives another example of a Savior: Rev. Dr. Kathi Elaine Martin, founder of God, Self, and Neighbor (GSN) Ministries in Atlanta, Georgia, offering religious community to people who experience racism and heterosexism in both Christian communities and the wider society. "As an openly black lesbian woman with mental health challenges and multiple sclerosis, Martin does not appear to have the characteristics of a Savior," Rev. Dr. Coleman writes. "Yet as a theologian, teacher, preacher, and activist, Martin proves to be a worthy Savior. . . . Like postmodern womanist theology, GSN understands the Savior as one who puts forth a theology of love and justice while generating greater awareness and health in the community."[4]

In third-wave postmodern womanist theology "no one is left out, and no one is left behind," Rev. Dr. Monica Coleman proclaims at the fourth annual Faith and Feminism/Womanist/Mujerista Conference at Ebenezer/herchurch Lutheran in San Francisco on November 13, 2010. Radiant and strong, she stands at the pulpit in the church sanctuary with Divine Feminine pictures from various cultures in the background. She elaborates on the "open hands" of third-wave womanist theology, which engages black women's religious experiences as it draws from Christian and other religious traditions as well as from black women's literature. The goals are "justice, survival, quality of life, equality, acceptance, and inclusion."

Monica Coleman grew up in Ann Arbor, Michigan, as the only child of Pauline A. Bigby, a public school administrator, and Allen M. Coleman, a General Motors executive. Active in Ann Arbor's Bethel African Methodist Episcopal (AME) Church, Monica also spent much time at Shiloh Baptist Church in Washington, DC, when she visited her grandparents on Christmas and summer vacations. "We were always at church," she says. "Going to church was like brushing your teeth. It's just something that you do. It was not optional. My parents grew up together in Shiloh Baptist Church. So when I was in DC, I'd see both sides of my family at church." Monica spent more time with her mother's side of the family because there were more cousins for her to play with on that side. Her maternal grandmother had an especially strong influence on Monica. "My grandmother was a deaconess," Monica recalls. "The deaconesses would prepare the Communion in these little cups and prepare little crackers. That was the coolest, holiest thing to me. I'd be sitting there looking at my grandmother, and she would sneak me a cracker. They used Matzo crackers, and they would crush them with their hands with white gloves on; everything was very pristine. That was the early 80s, and was the most fun thing to me. My first cousins and I would be there with my grandmother all day Saturday, and then all day Sunday. When I got to the age when I was not allowed to fall asleep anymore, we'd play tic-tac-toe and other games to stay awake in these very long services. They're really long when you're a kid!" Monica remembers this exchange with her mother:

"Oh, Grandma's going to work!"

"Where do you think Grandma works?" her mother asked, because at this time her grandmother was retired.

"At church, of course!"

Monica explains that she went to church with her grandmother not only on Saturdays and Sundays, but on other days of the week for Bible study, prayer meeting, small circle group meetings, deaconess meetings. When Shiloh Baptist built a Family Life Center, she was delighted because it included a restaurant where they could eat. "That was exciting for us as kids because now we didn't have to be hungry all day at church," she says.

When she was home in Michigan, Monica didn't spend all day at church, but she went often. "That was what you did," she says. "I had three kinds of clothes—church clothes, school clothes, and play clothes. For church I had patent leather buckle shoes, white for summer and black for winter. We were always active in Sunday school and other church activities. That's the culture I grew up in. It would never have occurred to me not to go to church, even when I was in college and I partied all night. I would stay awake and go to 8:00 a.m. service and then sleep. That was just how things were. So it wasn't that I questioned if I believed this. That really wasn't something I would think about. When my high school Sunday school teacher asked if we were saved, I thought, 'Well, what does that mean?' I'd been going to church since I was born. Was I supposed to declare something? I thought, 'Well, yeah, I guess so.' My parents decided when it was time for me to join the church. They said, 'Okay, you're ten, it's time,' and

I said, 'Okay.' This was partly a more Catholic understanding. I went to a Catholic elementary school, St. Francis of Assisi. I don't think I'd thought about not being Christian."

Monica grew up with messages about the importance of education as well as church. Her maternal grandmother, one of nine children, finished high school and college, and then went on to earn a graduate degree. She was the one her family chose for higher education. She had twins, one of whom was Monica's mother. Monica describes the twins as the "chosen ones of the chosen one," both earning master's degrees. When Monica was two years old, her mother went back to school and became the first woman in her family to earn a PhD. "I went to classes with her, and learned how to read by the time I was three," Monica says. An article in the *News & Record* of Greensboro, North Carolina, where she taught at Bennett College, comments on her precocious independence as a child: "It's easy to imagine her as a barely-out-of diapers, high-energy youngster who sometimes put her clothes on backward—reveling in her independence. 'I said, "She's being willful, she's being disobedient," recalled her mother, Pauline Bigby, an educational consultant and retired educator. 'Her grandmother would say, "No, she's being who she is. Let her be."'"[5]

When Monica was thirteen, this maternal grandmother died. "I was very unhappy with God," Monica recalls. "I felt that God had taken my grandmother away from me. My other grandmother had a pretty uncool theology, saying, 'God promised everyone to live threescore and ten years; everyone should live to seventy years old.' And my maternal grandmother had died when she was sixty-nine. My paternal grandmother said, 'She must have done something wrong.' That was a horrible thing to say to a kid, especially since my grandmother had actually lived with breast cancer for over twenty-five years, which was a long time back then. She was diagnosed when my mom was a teenager. So it really was a miracle that my grandmother lived so long. But that wasn't explained well to me. Everyone was just so sad that she died, and I was sad because I was very close to her. I was like, 'God has taken away the person I love and want to be around, and who really understands me. So forget you, God.' But it wasn't like I told the church. It wasn't that I didn't go to church. I just stopped praying to God. I prayed to my grandmother. I said, 'Grandma, you tell God I said this.'" Monica's current perspective as a postmodern womanist theologian draws from traditional African religions as well as from Christianity to include veneration of ancestors. She comments that her childhood prayers to her grandmother were like "an ancestral thing," although she didn't think of them that way at the time. "But I figured Grandma could hear me, so I would talk to Grandma. If she wanted God to know, she could tell God, but I wasn't going to pray to God right now."

Several years later, as Monica finished high school, her parents divorced. "My faith became very renewed, interestingly enough, when my parents divorced because I felt like their marriage was a hopeless situation," she says. "I really wanted them to get divorced, but no one asked me. So when they did, I thought, 'There is a God! Maybe I do like God again.'"

Monica describes herself as a "church girl" when she was growing up. "I grew up in church—church hats, church dresses, gloves, and the whole nine!" she says. "There were many education and community programs that took place in my church. When I was in high school, I even earned my Girl Scout Gold Award at my church.[6] For my Gold Award I developed a program for middle school students to help them be successful in high school. I did this program, called 'Getting the Most Out of High School,' at my church. I got funding from the NAACP and from my church, Bethel AME in Ann Arbor. I ran the whole program on about $200, just enough for pizza." When she was fifteen years old, Monica started questioning what preachers said. "I wondered, 'Why should I trust you to tell me what to believe?'" she recalls. "My parents didn't like my questioning at church, but I was a born theologian."

When she was only seventeen, Monica entered Harvard University. "When I went to college, I was still a church girl," she says. "I still went to church, and I became active in Campus Crusade for Christ." Monica remembers Campus Crusade as a meaningful experience for her because she learned about developing a personal relationship with God. "I had never heard of things like discipleship, *Lectio Divina*[7]—all these kinds of things that one can do to develop a spiritual life. I became a leader of a Bible study group, and we were all really close. We also had a lot of fun—good clean fun. I'm a church girl, right?" Monica left Campus Crusade when she saw a lack of connection in the organization between evangelism and social justice.

"Their emphasis became overseas evangelical missionary work, and I never connected with that," she says. "I always felt like, 'Shouldn't we be doing something for people right here?'"

While she was at Harvard, Monica became active in the campus ministry, called College Fellowship, of St. Paul AME Church in Cambridge. When she went home in the summers, she also worked with young adults, teaching workshops on prayer and spiritual life. "But I wasn't thinking at all about being a minister," she says. "That was nowhere on my radar. It just never occurred to me. I was going to be an academic, and I was just active in church."

Before she went to college, Monica had never seen women ministers or young ministers. "I never saw a pastor under sixty-five until I went to college," she says. "And it wasn't till I went to college that I actually saw women clergy. I thought, 'Oh, that's cool!' I didn't think about being a minister, but now women clergy seemed more normal. One of my best friends, who was in my Bible study group in Campus Crusade, was experiencing a call to ministry, and I thought it was great. I totally encouraged her. I could see how difficult it was, because she was from the South. She was a fifth-generation minister, but she was the first woman, and was getting a lot of flak from her high school boyfriend and family who said that women shouldn't preach. And I thought that was just horrible. In hindsight now I believe that God had put me in a place where I could accept the call because not only did I see women ministers in my church, but also I met seminarians." At the Black Women in the Academy Conference in 1990 at MIT, Monica couldn't get into a packed room where she wanted to hear Toni Morrison and Henry Louis Gates Jr. speak. Standing outside in the cold, she met a student from Andover Newton Theological School. He invited her to go with him to visit a friend at Harvard Divinity School. "So I met him and all their friends," Monica recalls. "They became my big brothers in ministry. They were first-year divinity students, and I was a junior in college. That's when I saw that ministers were like regular people." She began to think about going to divinity school, but only for intellectual exploration of some of her theological questions and only after she completed her PhD.

Then Monica felt a call to ministry. "I knew it clearly when it happened," she says. "It wasn't a dream; it was like a vision that I had. I knew exactly what it meant. I was like, 'No, no thank you, God. I don't want to do this.' I told my friend, the one from Campus Crusade who was going into ministry, about the vision. I didn't say, 'What do you think?' I didn't say what I thought. I just told her what happened. She knew, and I knew. But I didn't want to think about ministry. I didn't think it was me. I didn't like public speaking, and I didn't want to preach. So I was like, 'No.'"

Not long after, Monica was in Atlanta attending a National Black Women's Health Project Conference,[8] where Angela Davis[9] and Renita Weems[10] were speaking. Monica met Angela and told her about her thesis that looked at religion and nineteenth-century women slave narratives. Angela said to Monica, "You need to meet Renita Weems." While listening to Rev. Dr. Weems preach, Monica started thinking again about her call to ministry. She remembered that things went more smoothly when she did what she knew God wanted her to do. "I'm going to do this," she thought. "Okay, I'm going to be a preacher." Monica then met Renita and for the first time said out loud, "I'm going to preach." Renita responded, "Well, good for you!" Monica told her mom, who also responded with excitement. "She thought I should now dress like a nun or something, start wearing long skirts," Monica says. "I had pretty much that attitude at the time. But I felt I was just a Christian trying to do what God wanted me to do before, and I was still a Christian trying to do what God wanted me to do. I wasn't super holy or Puritanical just because this was what God wanted me to do. I never felt pressure to be extraordinary or anything other than a regular person. Later that summer my friend preached her first sermon, and she was a great preacher. She grew up in a preacher culture, and I didn't. I didn't know how to preach. This was not something in my family, so it took me a long time to find myself in ministry and not to imitate what other people were doing. Then I said, 'Okay, just do me, and it should be okay.' It took me years to figure that out."

In 1995, Monica Coleman graduated magna cum laude with honors from Harvard University with a degree in African American studies. "I had a great experience at Harvard, really amazing teachers and mentors, like Evelyn Brooks Higginbotham,[11] great African American religious historian; Henry Louis Gates Jr.,[12] great literary critic and cultural critic; J. Lorand Matory,[13] noted anthropology professor," she recalls. "They were great influences on me. They were really tough, but also believed I could learn what they assigned.

That's how I model my teaching." Monica tells the story of a prior family connection with Evelyn Brooks Higginbotham. "She was doing her master's degree in the Washington, DC area," Monica recounts. "She grew up in Shiloh Baptist Church. She's a bit older than my mom, and they didn't know each other growing up. My maternal grandmother was a lay historian and had collected all these records of Shiloh, compiling them into this archival history, which she called 'Days and Deeds of Shiloh.' It was a very very big deal. We all flew in for Grandma's big ceremony. I got a new dress. My mom and my aunt, identical twins, got new coordinated outfits, same outfit, different colors; this was how they dressed most of the time they were together when I was growing up. It was a very big deal for Grandma. I have a picture of Grandma giving her archival record to this young historian, Evelyn Brooks, who used it to work on her master's thesis. And I'm in the background of the picture; I'm like ten years old. So many years later, here I am at Harvard, and Dr. Higginbotham is my tough thesis adviser. Finally, at my graduation dinner she said to me, 'Your grandmother would be so proud of you.' I felt like, 'Oh! Wow!' because I missed my grandmother so much."

After she had accepted the call to ministry, Monica applied to three divinity schools: Boston University, Union, and Vanderbilt. She considered Union Theological Seminary in New York because James Cone[14] and Delores Williams[15] were professors there. "I was teaching *Sisters in the Wilderness* to my students last week, and I found the note Delores Williams had sent me with the book," Monica says. "It was dated 1994 and sent to my Harvard address. The note read, 'Hope you come to Union.' Also, I had some friends from Harvard who had gone to Union. I applied to Vanderbilt only because Renita Weems was at Vanderbilt. Otherwise, I would have never looked below the Mason-Dixon Line." When Monica prayed for guidance as to where she should go, she felt God leading her to Vanderbilt Divinity School. "I wrote in the application letter that I wanted to go to a school where I could be a Christian intellectual and an intellectual Christian," Monica recalls. "I thought that Vanderbilt was that kind of place, and it really was for me. I loved it. I had the best mentors: Renita Weems, Victor Anderson,[16] Sallie McFague,[17] Howard Harrod[18]—these people who had marched with Martin Luther King. They were very progressive. Sallie McFague was my advisor most of my time there. And I took everything Renita taught, in addition to required courses. I had New Testament with Fernando Segovia.[19] At Harvard I had learned historical-critical methods of studying the Bible. At Vanderbilt I learned ideological critiques of the Bible. I learned to ask, 'Who has the power? Where is the empire?' This was before anyone used the word 'postcolonial,' and that was how Fernando Segovia taught Bible. Renita Weems used the same method. She would always look for the women, for the voiceless, for the powerless. I had these amazing professors with so much passion in what they did. They had really great feminist and social justice approaches to religion."

Monica had better experiences in the academic world, in both college and divinity school, than in the church. "The AME denomination in Michigan wasn't used to women clergy, and they weren't used to young clergy," she says. "At that time the AME denomination did not have a requirement that ministers get MDiv degrees, so there wasn't necessary an educated clergy. The pastor I had grown up with in my home church had died, and we had a new pastor. We knew each other because he was there when I came home from college and led workshops. But he was not very supportive. This was my home church; I grew up there, so all the laity always had my back and really pushed for me. But it was a very difficult process. I was under some women-hating bishops, who would make women cover their heads in church. And this was the 90s! This was not in my home church, but in the other conferences of the AME church. Some people would make fun of my going to Harvard, because I didn't go to a historically black college. I thought, 'What's up with this?' I felt like there was a lot of anti-intellectualism. When we were in high school, they wanted us to grow up and go to college. And then we go, and they did this hateration thing. It was really difficult because I needed mentorship, and it wasn't happening."

Because Monica was getting an MDiv degree, her denomination did not ask her to go through many of the standard ordination requirements. But she had challenging experiences when she met with ordination committees several times a year. "They would ask me these totally sexist questions like, 'What if you marry a Baptist?'" Monica recalls. "I said, 'I'm nineteen. I'm not thinking about marriage.' I know they weren't asking guys that. I had this radical idea about equity, and people could see that." Monica recounts a conversation she had with one pastor:

"Are you going to change clothes?" he asked her.

"Why would I change clothes?"

"You're wearing pants."

"Well, you're wearing pants."

"I told you that you need to wear a suit."

"This is a suit. It's a pantsuit."

"Well, you can't take your purse in the pulpit."

"Why not? Are you taking your wallet to the pulpit? I'm not going to leave my purse out here."

Monica's experiences with a woman mentor were not much better. "I had a chance with a woman minister when I was in Nashville, and that didn't go well, not because she was a woman, but she wanted to tell me how I should dress and wear my hair and makeup," Monica says. "I had my hair natural, not straightened. I didn't wear make-up, and she thought I should. I said, 'I'm grown. Don't tell me how to dress.' I was with few ministers I could respect as I was going through the ordination process. Some of the difficulty came from the Southern culture vis-à-vis my very Northern sensibilities. I talk fast, and just didn't fit in culturally. I wasn't used to black people being on one side of the tracks and white people being on the other. I didn't think it was still like that. I somehow didn't realize I was going South. I knew I was going to Vanderbilt, but I really didn't think about where Nashville was. I was unhappy in Nashville for a long time, even though I loved being at Vanderbilt."

Another challenge to finding a pastoral mentor came from a traumatic experience Monica had in 1996. "It was almost three years after accepting my call to the ministry and nearly one year into my studies in divinity school," Monica writes. "My commitment to both God and the church had just recently transformed from that of an active church member to that of a professional. I was still trying to figure out what that meant. In the middle of this process, I was raped by a man who was also a seminarian, and also clergy. And I didn't have much of anything to say to God. I had talked to God throughout the rape, pleading for intervention. Pleading that somehow, some way, God would stop this thing from happening. After the rape, there was no more pleading and no more praying. Honestly, I was absolutely disgusted that the same God to whom I prayed and whom I worshipped was the same God to whom my rapist would pray and worship. It was too much for me to handle."[20] In her book *The Dinah Project: A Handbook for Congregational Response to Sexual Violence*, Monica also recounts her discouraging experience of trying to find a pastor who could hear her pain. "When I told the pastor of the church where I served, he listened to me while watching a sports event on a television above my head," she recalls. Another pastor asked, "Well, what was he (the man who raped you) doing in your apartment anyway?" Another pastor told her that her depression was the "tool of the enemy." Making the struggle even harder for Monica was that her plan of study in divinity school required that she contract with a church to serve as minister for a year. "If I had not been a minister, if I had not been compelled to find a place for studying ministry, I fear I might have left the church altogether,"[21] she writes.

Six months after the rape and after visiting five churches, Monica finally found a church with a pastor who responded appropriately to her painful experience. "I adored the pastor, Ed Sanders, who became a second father to me," she recalls. "It was an interdenominational church that was inclusive of everyone, Metropolitan Interdenominational Church. The theme of the church was 'whosoever.' The church had openly transgendered, queer, homeless, some Jewish and white people, kind of everybody. The worship was definitely in the black church tradition. At that time Metropolitan Interdenominational had the oldest AIDS ministry in a black church in the Southeast. About half the staff members of the church were women, and all of us had gone to Vanderbilt or were still at Vanderbilt. The church really understood social justice and had a clear theological approach, which was that everyone was welcome. I did my internship at this church, and that's where I grew in ministry. I really needed a pastor to mentor me and teach me how to do ministry. I got that with my pastor there; he encouraged and supported me. That was huge for me, because I was able to find my voice and do the ministry that I felt called to do."

After her traumatic experience, Monica developed a creative project to help churches respond to sexual violence in compassionate and healing ways. At Metropolitan Interdenominational Church, Monica started the Dinah Project. Monica had found psychological, medical, and legal resources. "But there was something missing," she writes. "I still struggled in my personal relationship with God. I didn't quite know how to pray anymore. I didn't know how to worship God anymore."[22] Because she wanted to include God in her healing process, Monica created a ritual that became the first Dinah Project worship service on June 1, 1997, at Metropolitan Interdenominational Church. This project gets its name from the rape of Dinah, Jacob's daughter.[23] "When we read Genesis 34, we hear about all the incidents that followed the rape of Dinah," Monica writes. "We read about the response of her rapist, Shechem. We find out about the response of her father, Jacob. We learn about the reactions of her brothers, Simeon and Levi. But we never hear Dinah's voice. We never find out about what really happens with Dinah. She disappears from our scriptural heritage just as silently as she entered it. . . . So it seems appropriate to name a church response after Dinah because she is so silent and so overlooked, and yet she is one of us. We are silent about the crisis of sexual violence. We overlook the pain of the victims and victimizers in our midst. We respond with silence, anger, violence, and bargaining, but we don't stop and notice our own Dinahs."[24]

The Dinah Project grew to a comprehensive ministry program to assist churches with healing responses to sexual violence through worship, community education, and counseling. The program spread beyond Metropolitan Interdenominational Church to churches all over the country. In her book Monica Coleman details methods for planning and implementing this program in local churches, and she gives pragmatic resources for organizing this ministry. "The Dinah Project was the toughest thing I've ever done," Monica says. "It was emotionally painful, and we had no money. People talked about me all the time, saying I was the girl who always talks about rape. People told this guy I dated, 'Oh, don't date Monica, because she'll say you raped her.' That was hurtful, really hurtful. But there was nothing I did that was more rewarding than the Dinah Project. There were even moments when one or two people had an amazing breakthrough and I thought, 'I can die now, and it'll be okay.' These moments came when I was ready to give up. I would get so discouraged, and then something would happen. Somebody would call, somebody would say how helpful the program was, or the counseling group would go really well. Then I thought I could keep doing this. I believed God had given me this affirmation to keep going. For me it was Dinah, Dinah, everything was Dinah, week after week. It was hard. But it was also really good, the work we did in the community, the people who came to group. I knew that this was what God had called me to do and that God would give me what I needed to do it. Even after I had graduated from divinity school, I was still doing this work and had other jobs to support doing Dinah Project."

In 1998, Monica graduated from Vanderbilt Divinity School with a Master of Divinity degree. In August of 1999, while still living in Nashville, she was ordained as an elder in the African Methodist Episcopal Church. "I had chosen the AME church," Monica says. "I knew the history of the AME church, which had a great social justice history. But I had also had this great experience at an interdenominational church, and I felt that I wasn't a very denominational person. It was not like a bishop called me and said, 'Monica, do you want to be a minister?' I felt that God called me, so my loyalty is to God. I never said I don't have loyalty to the AME church, but it probably just came out of my pores. Since I've never tied my financial well-being to the church, I never had the same need for the church as some ministers have. I think the fact that I never had that level of loyalty made my ordination process challenging, and because I didn't want to be treated any differently than men, and I was direct in saying so. When it came time for my ordination examination, one of the ministers on the ordination council completely redirected the conversation. He asked the presiding bishop if he had seen my article in the *AME Journal* on clergy sexual misconduct and my article in *Essence* about the work I was doing in the area of sexual violence. So we spent the whole time talking about that." Then the bishop and Monica had this exchange:

"Well, what do you want to do?" he asked.

"I want to be a professor," she replied.

"Good. Go be one of the church's great scholars."

So Monica received approval and was ordained. Her mom said, "I knew the Holy Spirit would intervene."

To pursue a PhD Rev. Coleman moved to California and began coursework at Claremont Graduate University. "Deciding to do the doctorate was difficult because I'd be leaving full-time ministry with the Dinah Project," she says. "It was also hard to go from community activism to reading about one thousand pages of philosophy a week. It was, of course, intellectually hard, but it was also hard on my soul.

California was really far from my family. But I knew I wanted to be a professor, to teach college students in ministry. And you have to get a PhD to get there. I also knew that I wanted to learn more theologically and to become better at understanding process theology[25] because that was really powerful to me in working with survivors of violence. I loved what I learned, but did not like my educational experience. I had great professors, but found few classmates I related to. Also, the churches were really conservative. I was like, 'Oh, this sucks,' and I got sick. So I decided to leave."

After completing course work, Rev. Coleman moved to Atlanta, Georgia, where she joined Circle of Grace Community Church. "I had gone often to Atlanta before when I lived in Nashville because it wasn't that far, about four hours," she says. "There I joined Circle of Grace,[26] a feminist church, and loved it. It's my real church home now. It's a small church, a house church. Sometimes we meet in buildings. I remember the sermon that the pastor, Connie Tuttle, preached the first Sunday I was there visiting the church with students I was teaching at Emory University. She preached on Lot's wife, and I had never heard a sermon on Lot's wife. You always hear about Lot's wife disobeying; she looked back and got punished by being turned to a pillar of salt. Rev. Tuttle's sermon was not that at all. She is a military brat, so she moved around a lot. And I was moving a lot during that part of my life. She talked about what it means to leave your home, and what Lot's wife had probably experienced there, having children and family and community. What kind of God would punish you for looking back on that? Rev. Tuttle also said that salt was sacred and rare in that culture and that God was honoring the fact that we have to look back. That was a beautiful sermon. I was like, 'Wow! I have to come here.' I had very few mentors in ministry, Ed Sanders in Nashville and then Connie Tuttle at this feminist church in Atlanta. She is one of my very very dear friends. I look up to her. She often says, 'No, no, we're like peers or colleagues.'"

Because she felt called to teach, Monica continued working on her PhD degree at Claremont Graduate University while living in Atlanta. In 2004, she received her Doctorate in Philosophy of Religion and Theology. That fall Dr. Coleman became Assistant Professor of Religion and the founding director of Womanist Religious Studies at Bennett College for Women in Greensboro, North Carolina, the first undergraduate religious studies program to focus on the spiritual experiences of women of African descent. When she was officiating at a friend's wedding on a cruise ship, Dr. Coleman had met the president of Bennett College, Dr. Johnnetta Cole, who recognized Monica's innovative intelligence and initiated the process of hiring her to the faculty. "Dr. Monica Coleman is among a group of young clergy who think, write and act positively outside of many of the traditional ways of the thought and practice of organized religion,"[27] Dr. Cole said. In her first year as director of the program, Monica developed four new courses in religion and two lecture series, including such topics as African American biblical interpretations and the love-hate relationship between Christianity and hip-hop culture.[28] "I loved teaching at a women's college," she says. "It was hard work, but it's so neat to have all women around you. The president is a woman; the provost is a woman; the dean is a woman; the students are women. The faculty members are mostly women, and they have doctorates. Bennett is a historically black women's college. It's so nice that the young women can see what they want to be. It wasn't till my MDiv program that I saw what I wanted to be. Renita Weems is the first black woman professor I ever had for a teacher. At Harvard I worked with Evelyn Brooks Higgenbotham, but she was never my teacher, because she came my last year. It makes a big difference when you can see what you want to be." In 2005, the interdenominational preaching magazine *The African American Pulpit* named Dr. Coleman one of the "Top 20 to Watch—The New Generation of Leading Clergy: Preachers under 40."

Rev. Dr. Coleman feels called especially to teach ministers. "I had such a great MDiv experience, being introduced to theology and religious scholarship, that I like being able to provide that for others," she says. From July of 2006 to June of 2008, she served as Assistant Professor of Systematic Theology at Lutheran School of Theology in Chicago. In the fall of 2008, she became Associate Professor of Constructive Theology and African American Religions at Claremont School of Theology and Co-Director of the Center for Process Studies. "There are not many black faculty at Claremont," she says. "When I first got to Claremont, the black students were so happy I was there. In my first class my first year, one young woman, a very bright student, came right up to me and hugged me. She said, 'Now I have a black woman teacher.' I am the only black woman on the faculty. There's a black man who's been there a little longer than I have. He teaches preaching and New Testament; black religion isn't part of what he teaches. I can see what a difference my teaching makes for the students, and that feels really good."

Diverse leadership and symbolism in church, as well as in academia, make a difference, according to Rev. Dr. Coleman. "It was so important for me to see women clergy," she says. "Those who identify as feminists are especially helpful because they preach differently. Some preachers are women, but there's nothing different about how they look at things. Feminists look for the underside of the texts. That approach speaks to me and feeds me. People who are committed to a feminist or ideological critique of the Bible look for who doesn't have power, and look at texts besides the Bible. I also find that exciting and rich. Racially diverse images in worship are so important too. I think you should be able to see yourself. When I teach Christology to my divinity school students, I use diverse images of Jesus in Asian art. I have many Korean students now, and they are blown away. They have never seen these images, and they are excited about them. It makes a difference to see yourself in your religion! When I was in Nashville, I wandered into the gift shop of an Eastern Orthodox Church and saw brown icons of the saints and Ethiopian Coptic images of biblical figures. I saw brown icons of Moses and of Mary. And I went, 'Wow!' I think it's important at the self-esteem level to see yourself, but also to understand that God doesn't have one way of looking."

African traditional religions have also influenced Rev. Dr. Coleman's divine images. "My images of the Divine being female came more from my work with African traditional religions than from womanist theology," she says. "I took this course at Harvard on West African religions and the way they manifested in the Americas, taught by Randy Matory. That's when I learned about Yoruba, Ifa, Santeria, Candomble, Haitian Vodun, and other African religions. They had female deities that I guess you could call 'goddesses,' but that's not really the right language; they called them *orisa*. I learned about Yemoja, the Mother, Oshun, and Oya. I thought, 'That's kind of cool.' In the class, we saw statuettes of them. I learned the *orisa* by heart. When I lived in Nashville, I took West African dance and was close to the Ifa community there. It didn't take long to know the community well, because I was an activist and community organizer. I spent time with the Ifa community, which many women led. Women taught dance, and we sang religious and cultural songs as we danced. When I got to California, I found an Ifa temple in Los Angeles in an area called Leimert Park. I wandered into the temple and went up these stairs to a room where there were floor-to-ceiling altars to the *orisa*. They were beautiful, the male and the female *orisa*. I had never seen that kind of honoring for the *orisa*. Each one took a whole corner—floor to ceiling. The colors and everything were beautiful. I was like, 'Wow!' This is where I wanted to be. I felt like that was who I was as well."

Rev. Dr. Coleman also believes in the power of inclusive divine images in church and has worked to bring them into worship. "The interdenominational church I went to in Nashville had a commitment to inclusive language, and this was rare in Nashville, Tennessee," she says. "They would check with me to see if they were doing it right because they said, 'Monica's a theologian.' I would keep them on inclusive language tasks. It has gotten to a point where I have become offended by male language. It's like nails on a chalkboard; it just grates me when I hear it in churches. I think Mary Daly's so right: 'If God is male, then male is God.' God is not male. It's that simple. The Christian God doesn't have genitalia. God is a Spirit. We need either a plethora of images or gender-neutral ones. I was reading Sallie McFague's *Models of God*, and it made sense to me to have female language for God. I think it's important because of the prevalence of patriarchy. And the fact that people rail so much against female language for God shows how important it is. Some people are okay with a male God. I don't know that womanist theology in general is outspoken about female divine images, but in some ways womanist theology does it very well. I can have a theoretical argument, or just show you images of women, which is what I tried to do in *Making a Way Out of No Way*. We can say, 'Oh, Christ can be a black woman,' or 'Let me show you Saviors, who happen to be black women.' That's what I wanted to do in the book, like here's a teenage girl who is a crack baby, or here's this overtly queer woman who got kicked out of her whole denomination and lives with a disability, and she's a Savior. I can say, 'Women are like God,' or 'Look at who's doing this great stuff.' Not that men aren't doing it, but if you can see it in a black girl or a disabled black woman, then you can get it."

When Rev. Dr. Coleman meets resistance to female divine images in worship, she urges churches to use gender-neutral language. "It's a little easier to pull off gender-neutral than female images in black churches," she says. "But trying to get inclusive language into a black church is like pulling teeth. I try to work on the pastors, because they're the ones with the power. Metropolitan Interdenominational Church in Nashville was already using inclusive language, except in the music, when I got there. I was always fussing at them about the music. They'd say, 'That's the way it was written.' I'd say, 'So what? You can do better!' The pastor of one of my churches says he uses inclusive language, but he doesn't. I guess if it doesn't occur to you till you're fifty, it's harder to unlearn traditional male language. I can't get him to change the liturgy to save his life. I say, 'Come on. Get with the program.' He's pretty progressive in other ways. It's always amazing to me how much resistance there is to inclusive language. The pastor's wife, who is also a minister, and the other women on the staff of the church are committed to it. But they say, 'Oh, people don't want it.' I say, 'Don't ask them; just do it. You're in charge. If you're going to have a hierarchical structure, then use the hierarchy to your advantage. You don't have to say, "She," but at least say "God."' It's just amazing to me how much people are attached to God's being a man. There's resistance to inclusive language in white churches also. But I think there are more conservative black churches, even though there are some progressive ones. When I officiate at weddings, I use very inclusive language. You have to be the person in charge in a black church, because it's such a top-down structure."

In teaching theology students, Dr. Coleman finds receptivity to expansive divine imagery. "That's why I like training ministers, because I get to expose them to liberation and feminist and womanist theologies," she comments. "It's exciting to teach this new information to people who are preparing to be ministers and leaders. I bring my activism into teaching by books I choose and by how I teach. When I teach *Imago Dei*,[29] I use the example of transgendered children. I could teach *Imago Dei* many ways, but that's how I do it. My students say, 'Wow! We didn't even know that there was such a thing as queer theology.' When we work on language for God, my students don't always dig this female language. So I have them rewrite the twenty-third Psalm, using images I give them, like 'God is my Mother' or 'God is my Counselor,' instead of 'the Lord is my Shepherd.' I say, 'What do we know about sheep? We live in L.A.! What do we know about shepherds?' I also encourage them to use non-personal language for the Divine, like 'God is my Rock.' I give them many different images. My students rise to the occasion and write the most wonderful, creative psalms. They have to follow the imagery all the way through the psalm, and they get it. I ask them what they learn from doing this. They say, 'Oh, it's a really different way of thinking of God, but you understand different parts of God, depending on the language you choose for God.'"

Some of the schools where Dr. Coleman has taught have had inclusive language policies. "Bennett College didn't have an inclusive language policy, which was horrible because it's a women's college, so you would think it would!" she says. "But other places I've taught did have this policy, and I would take off points if students didn't use inclusive language for humanity and God. When students say, 'What? I lose points?' I say, 'We have an inclusive language policy, and that's non-negotiable.'" Some students also want to present exclusive views on homosexuality and Christianity. She responds: "In my class, we are going to take the 'radical stance' that women, people of color, and queer people are full human beings and that's really not something I want to argue."

Although Rev. Dr. Coleman has received some criticism for her ideas about third-wave womanist theology, she has also had support from people in the academy and in the church. "People in the church tend to do okay with womanist theology," she says. "People want to know more about this theology, because it draws from the experiences of black women and there are mainly black women in church. With the Dinah Project you're already halfway there or more. We did this project at my church, Christ Our Redeemer AME Church, in Irvine, California. It went over really well, and the pastor said, 'This is good; we have to do this every year.' I also encouraged him to do a session for men. We did a radio show afterwards about notions of masculinity, about how social constructions of masculinity keep men as well from being their full healthy selves. This was a really important thing to talk about because masculinity inadvertently gets to issues around violence and power and control. This might not be called 'womanist,' but to me it's a very womanist thing to do because it relates to health and wholeness in black churches."

When Monica led the Dinah Project in Nashville, part of the program was working with clergy. "Even though I was young and female, I was also clergy," she says. "Black people still respect the clergy more, so it makes a big difference if something comes from clergy, even if a layperson knows just as much. Being a Reverend, or a Reverend Doctor, makes it holy." Monica recounts the preventive education she did with pastors, telling them what not to say to people who have experienced sexual violence:

"Don't say, 'This happened to you for a reason,' or 'What did you do to . . . ?'"

"Why shouldn't I say that?" some ministers asked.

"Well, think about it. It's mean."

Churches of all races and theological perspectives use the resources in *The Dinah Project* in response to sexual violence, and professors in colleges and seminaries teach the book. "There's nothing black about the Dinah Project," Rev. Dr. Coleman says. "It's not a black church project. But because I'm black, people in black churches think it is. But people who aren't in black churches don't. I've taken it into black and white churches. People who are process theologians think there's process theology in it. People who are evangelical see themselves in it. I love this because I want it to be for all churches, not to say you have to believe this way, but here are things we share in common. A church can do the project on a $50,000 annual budget, or with only $10 a church can do something to make a difference. I wrote *The Dinah Project* because I wanted this book that I couldn't find. I have friends who teach the book to college students. One friend in South Dakota teaches *The Dinah Project* to college students in a course on suffering and evil, and people teach it in pastoral theology and Christian education courses in seminaries. They say it works better than any other academic book. I would never have guessed because I wrote it for church people."

A precocious activist as well as minister and scholar, Rev. Dr. Coleman has been changing the church and the wider culture since she was a teenager. Beginning with her high school Girl Scout project to help middle school students succeed, she has engaged in social activism ever since. When she was only eighteen, a student at Harvard, she traveled with The Martin Luther King Jr. Center for Nonviolent Social Change to sign up voters for the election that would give South Africa its first black president. In addition to developing the comprehensive ministry program on responses to sexual violence, Rev. Dr. Coleman has also worked with Ujima House, Inc. to advocate against domestic violence, and she has served as a community organizer with low-income neighborhoods. She helped to found the Nashville chapter of the National Black Women's Health Imperative. Having received training at the Woodhull Institute for Ethical Leadership,[30] she has also served on the advisory board of Civic Frame, a nonprofit organization that encourages civic dialogue about pressing social issues.[31] Monica calls herself as a "greenie," sharing the commitments of the Green Party.

Including women pastors and the Divine Feminine in church also changes the wider culture, Rev. Dr. Coleman believes. "When children take this inclusivity as normative, it changes how they go out into the world," she says. "My pastor's daughter in Nashville grew up in this inclusive church, and then she went off to college. For the first time she heard the Doxology with male language, and she thought there was something wrong with it. I said, 'Yes!' She's now finishing her PhD in women's studies. At Bennett College I taught a course on women in ministry and justice. I used a book of stories of women preachers, about how hard it was to be a minister. My students just didn't understand. In one way I thought, 'This is too bad; they don't know their history.' But then I thought, 'How amazing that they don't think this is abnormal or hard because they've always seen women chaplains and preachers; this is what we wanted.' When I was growing up, being a minister wasn't an option. People would say to any guy who liked church, 'Oh, you be a minister.' But no one said that to girls. Now my students think that's actually possible, and it's not abnormal or hard or crazy or revolutionary. That's a big deal."

Rev. Dr. Coleman sees inclusive leadership, language, and theology in the church as inseparable from social justice. "In many ways this inclusiveness is part of the social justice movement within the church," she comments. "It's an important step towards gender equity. But some in the leadership of the church are actually happy with gender inequity, even if they're not saying women can't preach anymore, which of course some churches do say. Many churches have women preachers, but then they don't treat them the same. There's so much sexual harassment that goes on and that's tolerated and covered up. And then women, even if they have more education than men, get smaller churches that don't sustain them financially. All that still happens. So to take any steps toward gender equity within the church—that's a social justice movement within the church. I don't think it's possible to do that and not do social justice outside the church, though it is possible to do social justice outside the church and not do gender or racial equality in the church. Unfortunately, not everyone connects those. I think they're connected, because I think those are part of the movement. If you're able to see injustices in the church, then you're usually able to see injustices in other places too and understand that part of the divine calling is to resist injustice wherever it's found. But sometimes that happens, and sometimes it doesn't. Like some churches can see race all day long and not see gender, and vice versa, which I just don't get. Or they can see gender and race but not sexuality; it's all the same stuff!"

Although she has met many challenges in the church, especially during her ordination process, Rev. Dr. Coleman has never considered leaving the church. "Where else are you going to go?" she asks. "I remember hearing Louis Farrakhan give this lecture at an NAACP meeting, when I was working with the Religious Affairs office of the NAACP. He said, 'When you work with people, your love level has to be greater than your hate level.' If you work for the church, if you work with people, your love level has to be greater than your hate level. And ministers know more about the church than the average person, so you know enough to hate it. But you love it more. You love the church. You don't just love God, because plenty of people love God. But you love *church*. You think that you can't be spiritual without being religious. You don't hate denominations. They have flaws in them, but you don't hate them. You think it matters to get together in community. I think most people who are ministers had a good experience in church somewhere, and it's so important to them. So even when I hate it, I still want to go. It's still part of who I am. Even if I leave one church, I go somewhere else. I don't leave church; I just leave that church. Most times I go to two churches or go to church and then to an Ifa community, because I want it all. I'm pretty sure I'm not going to find it all in one place. That's okay. I can church all day; remember I grew up that way! And that feels comfortable to me. As long as I get fed somewhere in there, I'm good."

When she has faced criticism of her prophetic ministry, Rev. Dr. Coleman has found strength from her supportive family and from hearing about the difference she makes in people's lives. "In the ordination process, which was so tough, my mom was really supportive, and my dad came to be supportive after I preached my first sermon," she says. "During my ordination process in Michigan, I was doing this great ministry of the Dinah Project in Nashville. So that would balance it out. For me the strength comes from the ministry. In the Dinah Project we'd do programs on different themes: awareness, forgiveness, and healing. At a program with the theme of healing one woman gave a testimony, saying what a difference the Dinah groups had made. I knew her journey, and had seen her going from being very scared and conflicted and lost with God about it to being very strong and able to talk about it. She was very committed to becoming a child psychiatrist, which she is now, several years later. Also, I've had people read *Making a Way Out of No Way*, and say, 'This is the first time I ever saw myself.' A student said to me, 'I never saw anyone else combine African religion and Christianity, and that makes sense to me.' A comment like that's enough for that teacher heart part of me. That's all it takes. This is why I'm doing this, going to endless, countless meetings, and all the other stuff that's no fun. I guess that's how ministry works; because most of what I feel called to do I don't always enjoy doing. It's hard. It's just hard. I love doing the Dinah Project, but it's also emotionally draining. Now God has also called me to talk about mental health challenges. And that is so hard. But it's rewarding when someone says my blog[32] makes a difference."

Rev. Dr. Monica Coleman has a clear vision for the future of the Divine Feminine and womanist theology within the church. "A feminist church is my vision for the Divine Feminine within the church," she says. "It looks like Ebenezer/herchurch in San Francisco. It looks like Circle of Grace in Atlanta. Of course, woman images of the Divine are in inclusive churches. They're not dogmatic, but very welcoming to people of all faiths. I think of these as churches for the exiled in many ways, for people who've been kicked out or left out or have walked away, but who want church. They need a really inclusive place, an affirming place. They need a community where they can see themselves in worship. I think everyone should get that. One vision I have is that feminist churches know of each other. I would love to see a national organization of people doing feminist church so they can find each other, and a website so you could type in, 'What's the closest feminist church in my zip code?' Then people know where these churches are and could get to them, because I think they're hard to find. My vision for the future of womanist theology is that it would be as expansive and diverse as black women are in all ways. It would be this open discipline that would be willing to learn and grow from whatever is helpful, talking about how we are who we are. I see womanist theology growing in the church as the leaders learn it and teach it. Those are some of my particular hopes for a short-term future, not a hundred years future, but maybe ten or twenty years."

In November of 2009, when James Cone received the Martin Marty Award for the Public Understanding of Religion from the American Academy of Religion, Monica, who cochairs the Black Theology Group of the Academy, heard him speak at a session on black theology and black power. He said, "I was just this guy who was mad, writing. Who would have thought that anyone would be reading this forty years later?" Monica envisions womanist theology as also continuing and growing in different directions. "For a field you love, you want to see it grow," she says. "When I was connecting African religions with process theology and all these white professors didn't know what I was doing, David Griffin,[33] this well-known philosopher of religion, said to me: 'When you're a professor, you're finite; you can't do everything, and you're not meant to do everything. But it's so exciting when you see your students do things that you'd like to see done, even if it's something you'd never do.' That's what I would like to see with womanist theology. I try to do new stuff, but I want my students to do even newer stuff, based on their interests and their experiences and their knowledge base. I want womanist theology to grow. And I want it to grow in ways that make the circle wider, so more people can see themselves in it and see their experiences represented, and that it wouldn't be so Christian and so straight and so descriptive. I'd like to see womanist theology be so much bolder about normative claims. I think that's still hard for all women. I think it's easier, not just for womanists, but for all women to critique what's been done than to assert our own authority. When you get ordained in my denomination, the bishops put their hands on your head and say, 'Take thou authority.' I want to say, 'Take thou authority to assert your voice, not to just say, "This is what I believe," but to say, "Everyone should believe this too; here I stand, and I recommend you do too, because something different happens when you stand here."'"

In her preaching, teaching, activism, and writing, Rev. Dr. Monica Coleman asserts her prophetic voice. "Postmodern womanist theology is a metaphysical and metaphorical proposal that describes salvation as 'making a way out of no way,'" she writes. "Salvation is found as we participate in teaching and healing communities that promote the social transformation of the world. . . . Postmodern womanist theology is an activity. It is a verb, a gerund. Health and wholeness come through teaching, healing, remembering, honoring, possessing, adopting, conforming, and creatively transforming. Saving. It is making a way. We are being saved over and over again, feeling God's continual calling toward survival, justice, and quality of life, using each opportunity to become in higher and more intense forms than we did in the last occasion. . . . Saviors use their perceived vulnerabilities and differences to create, strengthen, and creatively transform community. A Savior is known by what she does. A Savior creatively transforms and draws upon the guidance of the ancestors. She leads a community that makes a way out of no way."[34]

7

Rev. Marcia C. Fleischman

Copastor
Broadway Church, Kansas City, Missouri

Wild Woman Theology: In the Arms of Loving Mother God, by Rev. Marcia C. Fleischman, arrives several weeks before I meet the author. On the cover of the book is an image of Mother God, a robust African American woman, holding the world in her hands and wearing a lime green t-shirt with infinity signs on it. Rev. Fleischman created this image for her book and gives this additional description of Mother God: "The infinity designs speak of her infinite essence. Her face is only partially revealed to express the fact that God is always somewhat hidden. She wears a string of pearls around her neck since she is the Mother of Pearls. Her charm bracelet includes the symbols of major religions of the world. All these symbolize her loving creative energy from which all things are born. The sun and the moon rise over her shoulders."[1]

Fascinated, I turn a few pages and see the picture repeated along with the first poem in the book that celebrates "Holy Mama" as "knowing all, loving all, seeing all, all in all." Holy Mama's love knows "no bounds" and "no punishment," only "lessons." The book continues with forty-five vibrant pictures and rhyming stories of women from the Hebrew and Christian Scriptures, told from a feminist viewpoint in a whimsical style. They include the stories of Lot's wife, "A Pillar of Tears"; of Deborah, "The Judge Is In"; and of Mary "Don't Mess with Me" Magdalene. The book ends with a letter from Mother God, asking questions, such as why women are abused and rejected, why the Feminine is repressed, why equality is refused, where the men are who will work for equality. The letter concludes with these lines:

> *Where are the bold ones who will play my song,*
> *Which from the beginning I wanted all along?*
> *Male and female dancing together,*
> *Joined by love, respect and not a tether.*
> *A grand symphony of musical light*
> *Playing, displaying throughout the night.*
> *The love of the creation with which I flow,*
> *To join the chorus of joyous glow.*
> *Who are the people who will hear my song?*
> *With Mother God you always belong.*
> *Within the Feminine you can't go wrong.*
> *The balance so divinely choreographed,*
> *The steps, the swaying—Glory at last!*
> *Love always and forever,*
> *Mom*
> P.S. *I lovingly await your response.*[2]

On a snowy Sunday morning in February of 2010, Rev. Marcia Fleischman stands before the congregation of Broadway Church to deliver a sermon entitled "Energy." The Broadway sanctuary resembles that of traditional Christian churches with wooden pews in triple rows separated by aisles, piano on one side and pipe organ on the other, Communion table with lighted candles, vaulted ceiling, balcony, and stained glass windows. But there are no pulpit chairs, and a small lectern takes the place of a pulpit. The service opens with the sound of a meditation gong. Along with the piano, drums and guitar accompany the hymns. Broadway Church, a white stone edifice built in 1903, stands on a corner across the street from Our Lady of Good Counsel Roman Catholic Church and Westport United Methodist Church in midtown Kansas City. On window stickers sold by the church is this slogan: "Broadway Church: An Old Church with New Ideas!"

Rev. Marcia Fleischman begins her "Energy" sermon, the second in a series entitled "Winter Survival Kit: Lessons from the Predni 'Zone.'" As part of her treatment after a double-lung transplant in 2003, Marcia has taken prednisone.[3] From experience she speaks of struggles that lead to transformation, of learning to see better through the rough winters. The energy to survive, she says, comes from praying and connecting with the Spirit, "the presence that vibrates." Energy also comes from connecting with others, through "osmosis, soaking up someone's energy." Since arriving in Kansas City the day before, I have been soaking up Marcia's creative, radiant energy. Now I am experiencing her glowing presence in this worship service, already energized with the congregation's singing of "In the Garden" with references to Jesus as "She" as well as "He," "Abba Father, Amma Mother,"[4] and other songs with balanced female and male divine names. Huge bright images to go with the songs and sermon are projected on the front wall of the sanctuary. Singing "Welcome Our Sister-Brother Creator," we see Sister Creator with long swirls of purple and deep blue flowing from her brown face, breathing the world into existence and holding it in her outstretched hands, and Brother Creator pictured as a robed monk inside a clear globe, held by a large hand and surrounded by a glowing sunrise. When we sing "In the Garden," we see lush scenes of green gardens filled with red roses. Marcia's own creations of female and male divine images shine down on us during her sermon. The service also includes a song Marcia wrote, meant for each one singing to affirm these words about herself or himself:

> *I am Spirit, I am love,*
> *I am light divine.*
> *I am Father, I am Mother,*
> *Both and all combined.*
>
> *I am One, I am three,*
> *Blessed Trinity.*
> *I in Thee, Thee in Me,*
> *We are One, we are One,*
> *All are One.*

That afternoon, Rev. Marcia Fleischman begins telling me her story by showing pictures she's created for a new book she's working on called *What Does God Look Like?* She's writing this book because of her strong belief that our essence flows from our image of God. "If we have a judgmental, punishing God, we become judgmental and punishing," she says. "If we have a kind and loving God, it's easier for us to be kind and loving." The first picture is of Mother God with her head on a cloud like a pillow and her feet on the earth. Ursa Major, the Great Bear constellation, is pulling a blanket of stars over her as she dreams the solar system into existence. Her toenails and fingernails are painted bright red. Other pictures are images Jesus talked about: the loving Father watching the prodigal son coming home; the Mother Hen with chicks; the Woman finding the lost coin. Marcia shows me her pictures of people worshiping, of the homeless in a soup kitchen, of a new-born baby, of nature experienced by a man out fishing, of a grandfather reading to his grandchild, of a loving mother holding her child, of the burning bush, of a woman looking in a mirror, of the infinite universe—all images of the Divine. She holds up another picture that she says is inspired by Paul Ingold, a member of Broadway, who told of waiting at a bus stop with his mom; she folded him in her coat to keep him warm, and he said he felt that this was God sheltering him. In another picture Marcia depicts her friend Rick Bowman, holding his brother Mike, who has severe autism and Down syndrome. Rick says, "It's like having an angel" on his lap because Mike exudes joy and trust, so Marcia calls this picture "God on My Lap."

Marcia Fleischman says that she has been looking for God all her life. She grew up in Lexington, Missouri, and went to First Presbyterian Church, a small church that her family had gone to for generations. She remembers sitting in the pews when she was in elementary school and wondering, "What is this all about?" She would stare at the nativity scene in her dining room at home, pondering the meaning. In preparation for joining First Presbyterian when she was twelve years old, Marcia attended communicants' class that met every Saturday for a year. In the class each student had the opportunity to teach a lesson. As Marcia taught about a hymn she liked, "Sweet Hour of Prayer," she felt an energy flowing through her. Afterward, the minister said to her, "That was really inspired." At that time Marcia had no idea what he meant, but looking back on that experience, she says, "I think the presence of the Spirit was in what I was saying."

Her Presbyterian church, Marcia says, "didn't emphasize anything like being born again or being saved; there was just an acceptance that God loved us, and we were all in." She was glad to feel this acceptance, but she kept looking for more. "I got a sense that something was missing," she recalls. "I couldn't find what it was, but I knew there had to be something else. The minister gave me three books to read, but I couldn't get anything out of the books. I visited various churches with my friend who was a Methodist; we were on that same kind of quest."

Marcia describes her dad, a surgeon, as a "quiet, intense, driven person." Her dad became so angry with Baptists that he stopped going to church after William Jewell, a small Baptist college where he received his undergraduate education, fired his science teacher for teaching evolution. Her mother continued to take Marcia and her sisters to church. Marcia says her mother was "very independent" with a "freedom in herself" and a "sense of duty to the community," expressed through serving as a Girl Scout leader for forty-five years and on the leadership board of First Presbyterian Church.

Growing up, Marcia was interested in science. She told her dad about her desire to be a doctor, and he said, "I'd never send a woman to med school, because she'll just get married and have babies." In that one sentence, Marcia says that she heard "that women couldn't go to med school and do something important because they were just going to do something unimportant like get married and have babies." She said that she struggled with her dad's statement because she, like him, is a "driven person," who likes "working and studying and accomplishing things." But at that time Marcia says that our culture gave her the message that "women could only be teachers, secretaries, or nurses." Her dad had also voiced a demeaning saying about teachers: "Those who can, do, and those who can't, teach."

Marcia says that her two older sisters, Lucia and Shelly, are feminists who have supported her nontraditional vocation and books. But growing up, Marcia was wounded by their teasing. A powerful leader in high school, Marcia was the first girl elected student body president. Her sisters had laughed and said, "You're such a big frog in a little pond now, but when you go to college, you'll just be this little frog in a big pond." Marcia says that statement had "worked like a curse." When she went to college, she didn't volunteer or get involved in anything. She became depressed and had self-doubts that took a long time to overcome.

After studying for two years at DePauw University in Greencastle, Indiana, Marcia studied French at the Université de Strasbourg her junior year. "While I was in France, my best friend and my boyfriend wrote me that they had found Jesus," Marcia recalls. "I thought, 'Oh, there're nuts.' When I came back home, my boyfriend shared the 'Four Spiritual Laws' from Campus Crusade for Christ,[5] and asked me to pray the prayer for salvation. It was clear to me that if I didn't pray that prayer, I would lose a boyfriend. At that point, I didn't want to lose him, so I prayed the prayer. A couple of months later we went to a Campus Crusade retreat, and I heard some young women on staff talking about God like they knew God. The only other time I had heard anyone talk like this was when an older African American woman had taught my fifth-grade Vacation Bible School class. Here were these young women talking the same way. Something in me knew I was on the path that would take me to the place where I would know God as they did. I was awakened to this incredible love, and it was overwhelming. Later I realized that the Spirit was working in me at this time."

Marcia's boyfriend was in training to work for Campus Crusade for Christ. One day when they were together, Marcia suggested that they pray. He said, "I'm the head of the relationship, and I'm the one who says when we pray, not you." Marcia was beginning to see that Campus Crusade held the strong belief that "women were second-class, and men were the heads of relationships." Marcia struggled with weight problems at that time, and her boyfriend also said to her, "When we get married, I'll be able to tell you what to eat and what not to eat because you'll have to obey me." She thought, "What a load of crap!" But she felt conflicted because the people in Campus Crusade seemed to experience God so powerfully and yet had this belief that women were second-class and had to obey men. At first she thought she had to buy these rules "because these were the people who had Jesus." When it became clear that leading Bible studies was more important to her boyfriend than she was, Marcia broke up with him.

After she graduated from DePauw University, Marcia immediately went to graduate school at the University of Missouri-Columbia and received a Masters of Education degree in guidance counseling. She worked in the Campus Crusade organization and considered joining the staff. Instead, she got a job teaching French and working as a guidance counselor in Bell City, a small town in southeast Missouri. Here Marcia experienced gender-related job discrimination for the first time. She learned that a man, who did not have a master's degree nor the experience of living in France as she did, had been offered the same job at the Bell City school for higher pay. When she confronted the school superintendent, he said that the man was offered a higher salary because he had a wife and child to support.

Rev. Marcia C. Fleischman

There were three churches in Bell City: Methodist, Baptist, and Assembly of God. The same day that Marcia asked God to direct her to one of these churches, the Methodist minister showed up at her door. She took that as a sign and went to the Methodist church. In the springtime a gifted evangelist came to the church. "When he spoke, it was almost as if I could see the Holy Spirit like a mist flowing over the congregation," she says. "He invited people who wanted more of God to come forward for prayer. I remember going and kneeling at the altar and experiencing the joy of God. I began laughing in the power of the Spirit."

While working in Bell City, Marcia dated Ken Fleischman, who lived in Kansas City. At a Bible church in north Kansas City, Ken heard that Rev. Paul Smith, pastor of Broadway Baptist Church,[6] was a wonderful teacher. Ken started going to Broadway, and when Marcia visited him in Kansas City, they attended Broadway. Marcia says, "Paul talked about the love of God like no one I had heard in my life; it was amazing." After two years of teaching in Bell City, Marcia moved to Kansas City and married Ken. They left Broadway to attend a charismatic church for a few months, and then returned to Broadway.

Marcia and Ken became active in Broadway Baptist Church, which at the time had many small groups meeting in homes. At one meeting Marcia was sitting next to Paul Smith in the prayer circle and heard him speaking in his prayer language.[7] Marcia says she felt her "spirit open up in a new dimension." A few weeks later in church, her two-year-old daughter, Sarah, was sitting on her lap. Marcia was afraid her worship experience would be disturbed by Sarah's wiggling, but she closed her eyes, and a picture popped in her mind. "Jesus was in the center of thirty children," she recalls. "The children were all pushing and shoving and yelling and screaming and running and having a wild time. Jesus was laughing and laughing with all the children around him. I knew the message to me was to relax and enjoy this wiggle-worm on my lap. I felt God speaking to me in this picture in my mind. This was the first vision I had." Marcia began the spiritual practice of journaling, writing answers to questions she asked God, a practice she continued for twenty-five years.

After many years of only men in leadership, Broadway Baptist Church hired a young woman, Alicia Crafts, as youth minister. Marcia called Paul Smith and the other copastor at the time, Randy Horn, to ask them to treat Alicia as an equal. Marcia told them that if women weren't treated as equals, she couldn't go to church at Broadway anymore. Paul had started talking about equality, but Marcia felt that she had to push for Alicia to be treated equally. At the time Marcia also worked to overcome racial discrimination. In Advance, Missouri, where she lived when she taught at Bell City from 1972 to 1974, Marcia had witnessed appalling discrimination against African Americans through "sundown rules."[8] In Kansas City she joined the Panel of American Women, a community group working to overcome racial and religious prejudice. She became codirector of the Panel and spoke out on justice issues.

Marcia had also been staying at home with her daughters, Lucia and Sarah, and volunteering as a children's worker at the church. After the church hired the youth minister, the volunteer children's workers advocated for a minister to take care of the growing number of children in the church. The men in leadership asked the volunteers, "Are any of you interested?" Marcia expressed her interest, and they hired her as children's minister. Before long she questioned them: "What is this I'm hearing that you guys get because you're ordained? You get housing allowance, and it's a big tax break. Women deserve the same thing."

Marcia was ordained in June of 1986, a year after she was hired. She had pushed for equality and was ordained, even though at the time she didn't have seminary education. "I realized it was hard for me to think that my ordination was bona fide just because the church voted on it," she says. "In the Presbyterian Church ministers have to go through seminary and many examinations before they get ordained. It was hard for me to believe in my ordination as the affirmation that it was, that the church saw me as part of the pastoral staff." Also, at that time the church was beginning to downplay the separation between clergy and laity, so there was no ceremony to recognize Marcia's ordination, as is the tradition in Baptist and many other Christian denominations. The church voted on her ordination[9] and announced it in the church bulletin. "It was hard enough for me to own my position as it was, struggling for equality as a woman minister," she says. "It would have been empowering to have had a ceremony, and we didn't have it. It felt like I was just kind of a minister. It took a long time for me to own who I am as a minister."

In 1988, Rev. Fleischman went to Broadway's annual church camp in Estes Park, Colorado. One evening during the camp worship service, Marcia received the message that the Spirit had anointed her to preach the Gospel. The next week in staff meeting, Rev. Paul Smith asked, "Does anybody here feel that they want to preach some time?" He had never given that invitation before. Marcia raised her hand and said, "I think I'm supposed to," and she told them what she had heard from the Spirit. The first opportunity she had to preach was at a monthly Sunday night healing service. Her sermon on joy in the Spirit came from the text: "My brothers and sisters, whenever you face trials of any kind, consider it nothing but joy."[10]

Soon Rev. Fleischman discovered that she also had the spiritual gifts of healing and prophecy. "When I prayed for people in the healing services and in staff meetings, I would see pictures for them in my mind," she recalls. "When I first started getting the pictures, I didn't tell people what I was seeing. Finally the Spirit spoke to me: 'I'm not giving you these pictures for your own entertainment; they are for the people, so you have to share them.' It was embarrassing to get past that barrier of putting the pictures out there; it's kind of scary. But then people would be touched by them and say they had personal meaning for them." At that time Broadway Baptist had prophecy times on Sunday mornings. The worship leader would invite people to tell anything they heard from the Spirit for the church. "Sometimes it was as if I were lifted out of my seat and carried to the microphone," Marcia says. "I realized that the things I was hearing from the Spirit weren't for me because they didn't have any personal meaning. So I would say what I was hearing to the church. People would come to me after the service and tell me that the message was for them."

When Marcia started teaching the spiritual gifts class at the church, she felt unsure of herself. Paul Smith, who had created the class, encouraged her, saying, "It's okay, Marcia, just be yourself." Through teaching this class, Marcia discovered more about who she was while helping others discover their gifts. She found that women especially had trouble claiming their gifts. Some would say that they had a gift like administration, but it wasn't exactly that, and they didn't know what it was. But as women and men began to share leadership as equals in the community, women started recognizing their gifts of leadership. Marcia says, "I have understood over the years how powerful it is to have a community that accepts women as equals, because we go out in the world, and we're not equal."

One of the copastors of Broadway Baptist, Randy Horn, had difficulty accepting women as equals in the church. Paul Smith, the other copastor, didn't teach gender justice for a while because they had decided to be in consensus on what they taught. Even though Randy didn't want Paul to teach on equality, Paul finally did. Some men and even women in the church didn't think equality was important. One of the male church leaders railed at Paul and Marcia: "I'll never want women to be in charge of anything!" Marcia was astounded by this attitude, and felt grateful to have gotten away from the boyfriend who believed that she should be second-class and that he should be the head of the relationship. When Marcia married Ken, her older sister, Lucia, asked him how he felt about equality in marriage, and he said, "We're equals. That's the way it has to be. I know Marcia is really smart. Why wouldn't I want her input on things? I see us as equal partners." Marcia acknowledges that Ken's support of everything she wanted to do helped her heal from the wounds of that boyfriend's prejudice.

Also healing for Marcia was her mystical experience of the Divine Feminine. Paul Smith's teaching about the equality of women led to his research, writing, and teaching on female images of God. When Broadway Baptist Church was exploring female divine images, Marcia was still healing from the abuse she had suffered from her boyfriend's and her dad's messages about the second-class status of women. She challenged God, saying, "I have to know if I'm made in your image." Marcia's older daughter, Lucia, looks like both Marcia and Ken. When their younger daughter, Sarah, came along, people said, "She doesn't look like either of you; she just looks like herself." But one night when Marcia was tucking Sarah in bed, the bedside lamplight fell on Sarah's face in a way that made her look like Marcia when she was a child. "I could see that Sarah looked just like me," Marcia says. "I heard God say, 'Just as your daughter looks like you, you look like me.' That was the answer I needed. It was one of those mystical moments."

After that experience, Rev. Fleischman couldn't understand why people had such a difficult time accepting the Divine Feminine. The church went through a period of controversy, and some people left the church. During this time in a Sunday worship service, people spontaneously began to change the words of one of the songs, replacing "He" with "She." With tears in her eyes Marcia continues: "You could hear it across the whole congregation. They were singing about God as 'She.' It was a moment of joy. It was wonderful because it had been painful to go through that change. Now we could call God 'She' in worship services and be more open to embrace female images of God." The church dance team also included a female divine image in a performance to the hymn "Near to the Heart of God." A woman in a white dress with a gold sash and a man in a white tunic with a gold sash symbolized the balance of female and male divine images. "I loved that dance!" Marcia says. "They were God, male and female working together."

After hearing the call to preach at church camp, Marcia thought, "I better go learn how," so she enrolled in Midwestern Baptist Theological Seminary in 1988. While continuing to serve as children's minister for Broadway Baptist Church, she went to seminary part-time and graduated in 1993. Marcia also went through a time of loss while she was in seminary. During those five years, her parents and her husband Ken's parents all died.

The professors at Midwestern Baptist Theological Seminary were supportive of women in ministry, but many of the male students were not. In Marcia's preaching class, students gave verbal and written evaluations to one another. Marcia was one of only three women in the class. Marcia received positive verbal feedback on her sermon from all her classmates, but got a written note from a man who told her that she should wear a jacket when she preached. "This meant he was having trouble because he was looking at my breasts," Marcia says. "Apparently he thought it was my problem and that I needed to cover up. I was horrified! A year later the preaching professor heard about this comment, and he came to me to see if it were true. He was very upset and told me he wished I had said something to him about it at the time." In one of the first classes all students were required to take at the seminary, the instructors gave the Myers Briggs personality test. "They asked, 'Who's an ENFJ?'[11] This is the ideal personality for a minister,'" Marcia recalls. "In the class of thirty-five people, I was the only one with this personality type. The women in the class were overjoyed that the only one who had the right personality to be a minister was a woman!"

While Marcia was in seminary, a friend she had met there, Jo Ellen Witt, and her husband came to visit Broadway Baptist Church on a Sunday Marcia was preaching. When Marcia introduced herself to Jo Ellen's husband, he asked, "What do you think about the verse in 1 Timothy that says women should be silent in the church? Don't you think that's the thing to do?" Marcia says she felt stunned by his questions: "I didn't know he was in opposition. I had thought he was as supportive of Jo Ellen's ministry as Ken was of mine. I didn't know how to argue with him. But Paul Smith went toe to toe with him and took him to task, giving him all the biblical arguments in favor of women's preaching."

The Kansas City Baptist Association threatened to oust Broadway Baptist Church for ordaining women. The Association met at First Baptist Church in Raytown, a suburb of Kansas City, to vote on whether or not Broadway would have to leave. The pastor of the Raytown church had been in Marcia's practicum class at seminary. He had asked the only other woman in the class about her ministry goals. She told him she wanted to be a missionary nurse, and he told her that was fine because she wouldn't need to be ordained. Also, he told her that he "just loved that cute little outfit she had on and that nail polish, that she looked so good." Marcia said she felt like vomiting. "It was just awful. He didn't even ask me what my ministry goals were because he knew I was from Broadway." At the Association meeting at the Raytown church, Rev. Fleishman sat on the front row with two other women ministers from Broadway. "It felt horrible to be sitting there like in a witch trial," she recalls. "We were being told we were less than because we were ordained and we were women." The vote was taken, and Broadway stayed in the Association by four votes.

Not long after, Broadway Baptist Church began discussing the homosexuality issue. Rev. Fleishman had been counseling with a gay man who was going through Second Chance Ministry, which tries to change homosexual people. Marcia met with the director of Second Chance, Pat Smith, to learn about the process. Pat explained, "We meet together, read Bible verses, and pray. After a period of time, people change and give up being gay. They're healed." Marcia thought, "This doesn't feel right. If they don't change, what are you doing to them and their faith? What are you saying?" One day as she was praying, Marcia had a vision of Jesus at a party with gays and lesbians.

"There was a line in the sand, and I was on the other side of the line, watching this party," she says. "I knew it was my choice. I could go and join the party, or I could stay over here where I was. At this point it felt to me that I could lose my salvation for making this decision. But I decided I wanted to join the party. So I stepped over the line and joined the party because that's where Jesus was. I never looked back." Later the man whom Marcia had been counseling told her, "I've quit Second Chance Ministry; I just can't change." Marcia said to him, "I've changed my mind. I don't think there's anything wrong with being gay. It's part of who God created you to be, and I want to bless it."

Soon Paul Smith told Marcia that he had changed his mind about the gay issue, and that he now believed that Broadway Baptist Church should become gay affirming. Marcia replied that she had already changed her mind: "It's the right thing to do to be gay affirming. This is just another part of God's diversity, and we've been doing the wrong thing." Although Marcia and Paul agreed on the issue, some of the others on the church staff did not. The church became more and more divided over the issue. Randy Horn, who had been copastor with Paul for many years, left the church, as did some other members.

Because Broadway affirmed all sexual orientations and performed gay unions, the church was voted out of the Southern Baptist Convention in 2004. Soon after, the church took "Baptist" out of its name; now it was "Broadway Church." Rev. Fleischman tells a story about the church sign that shows God's working "in mysterious ways." On both sides of this solid stone sign were the words "Broadway Baptist Church." There was no way to remove the word "Baptist" because, along with the other words, it was carved in large letters. At that time the church didn't have funds to replace the sign. One evening a drunk driver was in a high-speed chase with a police officer. The drunk driver ran off the road into the stone church sign and smashed it to pieces. The insurance money collected by the church paid for a new sign. The new sign looks somewhat like traditional church signs with changeable letters to convey various messages and announcements. The Broadway Church sign carries messages such as "Would we recognize God if we saw Her?" and "You are the Light of the World."

During the time the church was debating the homosexuality issue, Rev. Fleischman began to experience shortness of breath. At church camp in 1997, she had to leave by midweek because she had such difficulty breathing in the high altitude of Colorado. Marcia had been taking Fen-Phen, the diet medication. Marcia now sees body image as another feminist issue. When she was young, her dad harped on her and her two sisters, saying, "Don't get fat, don't get fat!" When Marcia looks back at pictures of herself in high school, she thinks, "I wasn't fat. Why was he talking like that?" Her dad even gave her a diet medication, which turned out to be a controlled substance and made her high. "My dad was such a driven person; he was hard on himself, and hard on us," Marcia recalls. "We would go out to dinner and order dessert, but it was all spoiled because he'd make some ugly remark about being fat. I had body distortion images because I was always taught I was fat. And that boyfriend had said he would control my eating. My husband, Ken, also made remarks about my gaining weight. I finally told Ken he had to stop talking about it. I went to Weight Watchers the first year we were married, and got to within a few pounds of my goal. I kept dieting on and off for many years, struggling with feeling fat. When I heard about Fen-Phen, I went to a diet clinic and started taking it."

After she got home from the Colorado church camp, Marcia went to a few physicians to talk about her worsening shortness of breath. They listened to her heart and lungs, and said she was fine. Next she went to her gynecologist, who referred her to the best pulmonologist in Johnson County, Dr. Rodney Hill. After Marcia went through all the pulmonary function tests, Dr. Hill also pronounced her fine. She asked him why she was short of breath, and he said he didn't know. He did say, however, that there was another test, but it was too expensive. Later Marcia thought, "If I were a man, they would have fought tooth and nail to see why I was short of breath. But I present myself as a cheerful woman, and they think it's no big deal." Marcia told Dr. Hill that she was worried because she had taken Fen-Phen, and she persuaded him to give her the expensive test. She went to a cardiologist for this sonogram of the heart on a Friday. "When I called Dr. Hill for the results on Monday, the nurse sounded nervous and told me that Dr. Hill was talking with the doctor who did the test," Marcia recalls. "Finally Dr. Hill came on the phone and told me I had advanced primary pulmonary hypertension (PPH). I called Ken and asked him to come home. He came home and just held me, because I knew it was over. When I went to the cardiologist for the report, he was so depressed that I had to comfort him. He just said, 'You're going to die. You have to get your affairs in order. There's nothing we can do for you.'"

But Rev. Fleischman drew hope from church members, friends, and a physician at Kansas University Medical Center in Kansas City, Dr. Steven Stites. He told her, "Yes, PPH is a fatal disease, but there is a treatment. We can put you on this medication, called Flolan, that goes directly into your heart through a central line. It should help. Then we will sign you up for a double lung transplant. You have to work your way up to the top of the waiting list, and then you can get the transplant." Marcia told Dr. Stites how upset she had been by the cardiologist's telling her that she was going to die. Dr. Stites said, "Well, that's not necessarily so." The first step in the treatment process, a right heart catheterization to measure the pulmonary artery pressure, was delayed because Marcia had recently changed insurance companies. Marcia and Ken had to keep pushing the new company to approve the treatment. After a miserable experience of coming out from under the anesthesia during the painful heart catheterization, Marcia asked some church members to come pray for her. "When they prayed, I had a vision of flowers and trees starting to grow," she recalls. "I could smell fresh air and hear birds singing. I've never had such a vivid vision, but I didn't know what it meant. Later I told a friend about the vision, and she said, 'Marcia, it certainly wasn't a picture of death, was it?'"

Marcia soon learned that many people who have taken Fen-Phen develop heart valve problems. At first the pharmaceutical company didn't know about this heart valve side effect, but knew Fen-Phen could cause primary pulmonary hypertension and put the drug on the market anyway. The large majority of people who have taken Fen-Phen are women. Marcia says that the company knew it could market Fen-Phen to women and that the drug could kill them.

Marcia was diagnosed on October 13, 1997, and Broadway Baptist split over the homosexuality issue in February of 1998. "Sally and Joe Burgess were on the pastoral staff, and they liked to discuss the issue," Marcia says. "But they sided with the group who didn't want to take action to become gay affirming for fear of losing church members. I remember going to comfort Sally after her cousins had been killed in a car wreck, and she whispered in my ear: 'I just don't want anything to happen to you.' I wondered why she was whispering this. I didn't realize that the church was gathering forces against Paul and me. We had an arbitrator come in and lead staff meetings. At one meeting Joe said to me, 'I've checked with my medical experts, and I now know about your disease, that you're going to die, so I don't have to fix my relationship with you.' I couldn't believe that nobody said anything to Joe about this hurtful statement. Later we were asked to tell the whole church our side of the story. I expected the church to be appalled by Joe's words to me, but nobody said anything." The group against the church's becoming gay affirming recommended that Marcia and Paul be fired. The church voted by a narrow margin to keep them as pastors, and the people who lost the vote left to start a new church. Later someone from this group told Marcia, "All those people who left believe you're dying." These words felt especially painful to Marcia because the only thing she had asked the church to do for her during her illness was to believe she would be healed.

The people who remained at Broadway Church were loving to and supportive of Rev. Fleischman. When she was in St. Louis waiting for her transplant, she stayed connected to the church. Several times on Sunday mornings, Rev. Paul Smith arranged for her to speak to the congregation and pray for them over the phone. Church members supported her through prayers, visits to St. Louis, and gifts. For example, Charlie and Carol Ramirez, who have been at Broadway for more than thirty-five years and who oversee the Chit-Chat Café, cooking and serving lunch after church every Sunday morning, gave her a subscription to the *St. Louis Dispatch*. When I visited Broadway, I relished the delicious food in the Chit-Chat Café and the warm hospitality of church members. On the Saturday night before, Marcia had taken me to dinner with some of the women in a group who had been especially supportive of her: Dr. Sheryl Guth Stewart, Donna Blackwell, Thressa Newell, Christy Bowen, Carolyn Thompson, and Ronnie Hruby. Getting to know these women, I understood why they had been so powerful to Marcia during her treatment. Ronnie, a former Catholic nun, had come to St. Louis one day to see Marcia. When she got off the train, Marcia asked her if she had brought a message from God. Ronnie replied that a phrase had been going over and over in her head since she left the station in Kansas City: "You are at the end of your trail of tears." The next morning at breakfast, Marcia received the call that lungs had arrived for her transplant.

On February 20, 2003, Marcia had the double lung transplant and remained in an induced coma for five days. Her daughters later told her that she was left open for two days, wrapped in what looked like Saran Wrap; they could see her heart beating, and it was the size of a basketball. With the new lungs, the surgeon told them, it would become uncongested and return to normal size. When Marcia woke up from the coma, she became furious when she saw several nurses flirting and working on the computer instead of paying attention to her needs. When the surgeon came in with her daughters and husband, she told them about the neglect of these nurses. She started swearing and couldn't stop. "It finally got to be kind of funny that I couldn't stop swearing," Marcia says. "I just kept going until I was done. It was the release I needed. For years I couldn't express my anger, and I woke up from surgery livid!" Her daughters said to her, "Mom, we've never heard you talk like this!" When she came back to Kansas City, Marcia told Dr. Stites, "I was hoping that when I woke up, it would be a holy moment, and here I was swearing like a sailor." He said, "Marcia, it was a holy moment." Her friend Ronnie also affirmed her: "Marcia, all these years of your trying to stand up for yourself, and you come out of a coma standing up for yourself. Think about it." Marcia appreciated their words that gave her "peace about this new way of being."

During her three months in the rehabilitation hospital in St. Louis, Marcia came to know Yvonne Sledge, a nurse and an artist. Yvonne encouraged Marcia to begin painting with the art group in rehabilitation. Marcia attributes all the artwork she's done to Yvonne's encouragement. Marcia's husband, Ken, stayed with her in St. Louis for seven weeks after surgery. Although she was progressing well through the remaining weeks of rehabilitation, Marcia didn't know if she would be able to go to their daughter Sarah's graduation from Marquette University in Milwaukee, Wisconsin. Their older daughter, Lucia, told her not to worry because she and her roommate would go to make sure it was a good celebration. Marcia was discharged from the rehabilitation hospital on a Thursday and drove herself back to Kansas City. The next day she and Ken left for Sarah's graduation.

Back at Broadway Church in Kansas City, people continued to give Rev. Fleischman wonderful support. And she wanted to help support a church project of remodeling the kitchen. She decided to paint angels to raise money for the project, although she didn't think she knew how to draw. She looked at some Picasso posters for help, even though she thought Picasso's art was misogynist. Her friend Yvonne Sledge, from the St. Louis hospital, had told her to paint in acrylics, because oils would be hard on her lungs. Marcia discovered that she liked acrylics also because they dried fast. "I started getting these visions of angels and drawing them and then painting them," she recalls. "Then I had an exhibit and sold the paintings and raised $5000 for the kitchen remodeling fund. I painted from 5:30 in the morning till midnight. I was high on prednisone and so energized."

Some of Rev. Fleischman's angel paintings remain on exhibit at the church. Before the Sunday morning worship service I attended, Marcia took me into the foyer of the church to show me these paintings. Amazed, I looked up at the magnificent angel paintings, ranging from six to twelve feet tall, in vibrant colors of purple, emerald, scarlet, violet, teal, gold, blue, and pink. The angel images represent diversity in race and gender, and have titles such as "Cloud of Witnesses," "The Message is Love," "Faith," and "Hope." Marcia created the pictures and text in her colorful storybook for children, entitled *Angels Everywhere*. These angels also vary in gender, race, and size. The book closes with these lines:

> *The thing that angels do the best*
> *is love you, and they never rest.*
> *Angels fill you with light and lots of joy,*
> *no matter if you are a girl or boy.*
> *With angels there is nothing you have to do;*
> *just play and have fun and be the best you!*[12]

For the past seven years since her transplant, Marcia has had to return to St. Louis only twice for treatments. Both times she took her acrylics and painted angels to give away. In one week she did twenty angel paintings, giving them to the transporter who pushed her wheelchair, to the head of housekeeping, to others on staff, and to patients. When she was in St. Louis, she reconnected with her friend Yvonne Sledge. Yvonne now holds a special position as coordinator of art for cystic fibrosis patients. "I started painting angels for Yvonne," Marcia recalls. "She told me that people saw the angels at the nurses' station and asked, 'Is she here, the angel woman?' It brought them a sense of peace to know that I was there, especially after several of the long-term lung patients died. She said to me, 'There's much more to your being here than just for treatment.' I told her about the picture I had created for the cover of *Wild Woman Theology: In the Arms of Loving Mother God*. Yvonne is African American, and has a granddaughter and a grandson, so she asked me to paint her a picture of God as a black grandmother. I painted her one of God as a grandmother standing at the sink with a little girl holding onto her apron, and another one of a grandmother rocking her grandchildren and looking out the window."

After Marcia returned from her lung transplant, she had to raise the issue of equal pay at the church. Marcia says, "It seems that even when people have equality as their value, women still have to push because there is lack of awareness." Several years before, in 2001, the church had voted for Marcia to be copastor with Paul Smith, but she had to ask to be paid equally. David Hunker, chair of the Finance Coordinating Team, supported Marcia's request and took it to the team to see how to make it possible in the church budget. Paul also supported equal pay for Marcia, even if it meant lowering his salary. When Marcia first joined the staff as children's minister, she also had to raise the issue of equitable salary. She had had to push for equality for women through ordination, and then found she had to push for equal pay. "It should have been obvious," she says.

Rev. Fleischman asks this question: "If the church is not going to confront sexism, who is?" She sees equality for women and the Divine Feminine in the church as contributing to social justice and healing in the world. "I think the Divine Feminine would help eliminate abuse," Marcia says. "If people saw God as feminine, could they abuse women? I think the whole dynamic would change. The beginning of Genesis says that male and female are created in the divine image. To me, that's just basic. The Divine Feminine is very healing, especially powerful for women. I'm an intelligent, well-educated person, and I struggle with self-esteem and equality issues. I think of the women who aren't as blessed as I am or as encouraged as I am and the women who are abused and beaten and have such a horrible time. To see that they are made in God's image is healing and empowering. Like in *The Secret Life of Bees*,[13] the women find such a deep connection with the Black Madonna whom they worship."

The Divine Feminine for Marcia is a deeply spiritual issue, as well as a social justice issue. "The first time the church sang 'In the Garden' with 'She' references, the Spirit touched me," Marcia says. "When we sang 'She,' I was bowled over, I started crying, and I couldn't stop. That image of 'She' being in the garden with me reminded me of my mother, who loved raising roses. My father was a distant person. I think one of the problems with the male image for God is that many fathers are distant. People also may have trouble with female images of God because of their mother issues. I believe that female images will help people raise those issues and find healing. The Divine Feminine has healing and empowering possibilities for women and for men. For our church the Divine Feminine has been a doorway opening us up to a larger vision, to seeing things in a larger way. She's a doorway." When Marcia has gone to the Catholic church across the street from Broadway, she has noticed that most of the lighted candles are in front of the statue of Mary instead of the other statues. She believes that many people connect in a very deep way to Mary, that Mary satisfies "an incredible hunger" for the Divine Feminine.

For many years Marcia says she has been "fascinated with images of God and how they need to change." The book *Good Goats: Healing Our Image of God* influenced her thinking.[14] This book makes the case that people naturally conform to whom they worship. If they worship an angry, judgmental God, they become angry and judgmental people. If they worship a loving, caring, forgiving God, they become loving, caring, and forgiving people. "Incorporating feminine divine images helps people get in touch with the nurturing essence of God and the nurturing parts of themselves," Marcia adds. "If we could increase the image of Mother God, people could experience healing." About Mother God in her book *Wild Woman Theology*, Marcia comments, "She's coming up with a system that won't punish people anymore for things they do wrong. She will help them learn. There will never be any punishment anymore, because it's all about learning."

Rev. Fleischman believes that this Mother God image can be healing and empowering for men, as well as for women. Paul Ingold told Marcia that her picture of God as the mother sheltering the little boy in her coat affected him on a "feeling level" because he was close to his mom. David Hunker, who grew up in Taiwan as the son of Baptist missionaries and who is now one of Broadway's worship ministers, talks about the meaning he finds in feminine divine images. "My appreciation for feminine images of God resulted from the gradual realization that my God was too small," he says. "Over the years, because of Marcia's and Paul's teaching and my own experiences, my understanding of God went through a sea change. I realized that God was far greater and more mysterious than I had ever imagined. I also came to believe that God was in each one of us and that we are all becoming 'Christ.' It began to make sense that God not only inhabited each of us in our feminine and masculine forms but also exceeded our finite human categories. I saw that recognizing and internalizing God as Mother, as the creative, nurturing feminine, was a crucial step in expanding my concept of God. I also began to see that using only masculine images of God kept people in bondage to a patriarchal system, however unconsciously. I felt evangelistic about encouraging feminine images and language. I saw how important language is in shaping our thinking. Song lyrics are important vehicles for raising consciousness." As I listened to David Hunker talk about his experience of Divine Feminine images, I recalled the feeling with which David and Ivan Fenwick, another worship minister, had led the Sunday morning congregation at Broadway Church in singing, "And She walks with me, and She talks with me, and She tells me I am Her own."

Experiences of a loving Mother God and of working for equality for women in ministry have given Rev. Fleischman courage to work for the equality of all. When she took a stand for LGBT equality, she almost lost her job. Then when Broadway became a welcoming and affirming church, Marcia initiated a church service to celebrate Gay Pride Week. With pro-gay ministers in the area Marcia organized this first Gay Pride worship service, which became a tradition. When the Gay Pride parade went by Broadway on a Sunday morning, Marcia took her Sunday school class down to applaud and cheer. Marcia performed the first public gay wedding ceremony at Broadway, and news of this event was on television. This prophetic act inspired Adam Hamilton, pastor of the 12,000-member United Methodist Church of the Resurrection in Kansas City, to lead this church in a discussion of LGBT rights. Rev. Hamilton began the conversation in a sermon, showing the TV clip of Marcia's performing the gay wedding. Not all ministers in the area have been so inspired by Marcia and Broadway

Church. Fred Phelps,[15] notorious anti-gay founder of Westboro Baptist Church in Topeka, Kansas, has often brought protesters to picket Broadway. "Seeing their hateful signs has been hard," she says.

When she was still children's minister, Rev. Fleischman was sitting at her desk one day, and a speech about "life, liberty, and the pursuit of happiness" kept running through her mind. She wondered what on earth this was about. Two weeks later in staff meeting, Paul Smith said, "They're trying to repeal the sodomy laws in the Missouri legislature, and they want someone from the church to come talk. Does anyone want to go?" Marcia volunteered, and drove down to Jefferson City for the committee hearing. She was the third person to speak for the repeal of the sodomy laws.

"I'm Rev. Marcia Fleischman, and I'm an ordained Southern Baptist pastor." The room went dead silent. "I'm here to ask that you repeal the sodomy laws. These people are part of our country. They're protected under the constitution for life, liberty, and the pursuit of happiness." Now Marcia understood the speech that had come to her mind several weeks earlier. "I don't want anyone hiding under my bed looking at what I'm doing. It's none of our business; it's between consenting adults."

A man on the second row of committee members asked, "Are you sure you're in a Southern Baptist church?" Marcia could feel the anger flowing over him.

"Yes, I am," Marcia replied.

Another legislator, the son of Marcia's friend Jo Ellen, spoke up: "I'm acquainted with Rev. Fleischman. My mother and she went to seminary together."

When Marcia stopped to get a coke on the way home from Jefferson City, two women came up and asked, "Aren't you the woman who just spoke at the legislature? We just want to thank you for what you said." Marcia learned that they were lawyers and lesbians. Not everyone was so affirming of Marcia's stand. A week later a Baptist newspaper ran a story that expressed outrage over her speech and denied that she was a Southern Baptist minister.

Although Rev. Fleischman has experienced rebuffs from people in churches for taking stands on equality and social justice, she stills believes in the church as the best place to know God. She especially finds strength in the community of believers at Broadway Church.

Only one time did Marcia ever consider leaving Broadway: "At one point I decided that if Broadway wasn't going to treat women equally, then I couldn't stay. I told Paul this, and he agreed that we needed to do that very thing." Now she experiences equality as a minister in the church, and she finds nourishment through the worship services, through meeting with women friends, and through opportunities to encourage others to develop their gifts.

A mystical feminist, Rev. Fleischman talks freely about hearing from the Spirit and seeing visions. Her vision for the future of the Divine Feminine reaches from the church to encompass the whole world. Marcia envisions a Black Madonna, surrounded by rays of light, embracing the earth: "She is affecting all these different situations for women around the world. I see the images of all the abused girls being empowered. You can already see it happening through this whole thing called 'The Girl Effect.'[16] And it's happening through the Central Asia Institute, founded by Greg Mortensen, author of *Three Cups of Tea.*"[17] Marcia tells about hearing Mortensen speak at Lincoln, Nebraska, and giving him a picture she had painted of little brown angel girls lined up in a classroom. She said to him, "I've had a double lung transplant, and I paint angels. I know this one is for you." Mortensen appreciated her painting because he's building schools for girls in Pakistan. Marcia donates a percentage of the profits from her book *Wild Woman Theology: In the Arms of Loving Mother God* to the building of these schools for girls. "What Mortensen sees is that women who are educated give back to their communities," she explains. "People are beginning to see how important it is to deal with women's issues."

Marcia's vision of the Black Madonna holding the earth recalls the picture on the cover of *Wild Woman Theology: In the Arms of Loving Mother God*. In Her love letter at the end of the book, Mother God calls people to "create a co-operative global community." At the beginning of the book "Mama God" proclaims the vision:

> *No longer will my child live in defeat,*
> *But always victorious*
> *Always glorious*
> *Coming always closer*
> *To hear my heart beat.*

Throbbing with life
And happiness always,
I will dry their tears,
Erase their fears,
For I am always near,
A loving mother,
A holy other,
A Holy Mama,
We know each other,
One another.[18]

8

Rev. Virginia Marie Rincon

Episcopal Priest
Hispanic Missioner for the Diocese of Maine
Founder and Executive Director of TengoVoz,[1]
Portland, Maine

In the group of women gathered for TengoVoz/I Have Voice meetings, the Rev. Virginia Marie Rincon begins the liturgy with a poem, often one that she has written. The women continue the liturgy by reflecting on the poem. In her strong, lyrical voice she reads her poem entitled "I Am a Chicana," written at the time she was trying to discern whether she should enter the ordination process.

> I am a Chicana
> I dance and chant my prayer.
> My roots call me to a simple
> but deep and compassionate
> faith.
>
> I love the prayer that comes via my culture,
> bright colors, images of Nuestra Virgen de Guadalupe
> and the smell of tamales and tortillas on the stove.
>
> I am a Chicana
> and
> I believe I have much to offer.
> I love to dance and chant my prayers.

> *These visions are not just mine they are*
> *also yours—*
> *come, dance and chant my prayer.*

Around her neck Rev. Rincon wears a gold medal with two Divine Feminine images, one on each side. She shows me the medal and explains the deep meaning it has for her. "This is my grandmother's," she says. "When she passed, it was given to my mother with the understanding that when she passed, it would be given to me. It's the *Virgen de Guadalupe*[2] and the *Virgen de San Juan*.[3] The *Virgen de San Juan* has a shrine in Texas; she is very strong for me because my grandmother used to go there every year and pray for me that I would fulfill my call. She would tell me, 'You're supposed to do something special. You need to remember that.' And the *Virgen de Guadalupe* is so important to me because I've always seen her first as a feminist, but then later when I was able to articulate that I was a *mujerista*,[4] I realized that she's a *mujerista* I can really relate to with all her different complexities, her fusion of Aztec culture and Catholicism." Rev. Rincon tells me how this image of Guadalupe has also been empowering for the women in TengoVoz groups. "They're looking at the *Virgen de Guadalupe* in a different way, not as the submissive *Virgen*," she says. "Most Roman Catholics will put her up there in this little nice space, but the women of TengoVoz are seeing her as a very different strong woman of action. They're seeing that she was persistent in talking to Juan Diego. They use that story for their own image of themselves, and they're like, 'Wow! Women in the church could create change.' And the *Virgen de Guadalupe* is a combination like them, because most of them are from one country and living in another. They have their feet in both worlds, and so did the *Virgen de Guadalupe*. These are the stories I tell them. And I say, 'Look at the power she has had for centuries, and she still impacts people by her image in their homes.'"

Virginia Marie was born in the small town of Lafollette, Tennessee. Her mother had gone from Houston, Texas, to Tennessee to look for Virginia Marie's biological father. "They were separated at the time," she says. "And for most of the pregnancy he didn't communicate with her. She was due any time, but my mother was determined to go see if he was going to stay in the marriage or not. So she went to Tennessee and found him living with another woman. She got so upset that she went into labor and birthed me there in Tennessee. Three days later my aunt Virginia, whom I was named after, went to Tennessee to bring my mother and me home. She tells me the story that as she was getting off the train, people would stare at her and ask, 'Are you here looking for that Mexican baby that was just born?' And she said, 'Yes.' So they directed her to the hospital. By then the Baptist church and the Pentecostal church were involved, because Mother didn't have money for diapers or formula or anything. So people knew about the little Mexican baby who had been born. When I was forty, I finally met my biological father, Lawrence Prado, who told me that I was in the newspaper. He said, 'I used to carry that piece of paper with me for a long time. It said, "First Mexican baby born in Lafollette, Tennessee."' A year ago I went to Lafollette to see where I was born. It's a beautiful little town nestled around mountains. My birth certificate doesn't say what hospital I was born in. So I went to the two hospitals there, and I did ceremony at both and gave thanks for my birth."

When she was three days old, Virginia Marie went by train with her mother and aunt to Houston, Texas, where she lived with her grandmother and grandfather. "I was mostly raised by my grandmother until I was seven years old," Virginia Marie says. "My grandmother was a shaman, a *curandera*.[5] Now I look back and realize that there are some similarities in how she gathered and approached people and how I do. It wasn't unusual for me to wake up in the morning and my grandmother would have all these women sitting at her table drinking coffee, talking, praying, doing healing ritual, chanting, singing. When I was a little girl, my grandmother would always say that I was special, that I had the gift of healing. And she would teach me things, like to listen. As a kid of five or six years old, I didn't know what I was listening for, but now I know. And when I'd have a bad day at school, she would always know what to heal me with, like hot chocolate or making a tortilla that was just special for me. Or she would use the ritual of the egg. In *curandismo*,[6] you pull an egg out of the refrigerator and let it sit for thirty minutes so it can warm up to room temperature. Then you take the egg and rub it on the person, and you can feel the vibration of where there is pain or something that needs to move in them. Because they say that I was a mischievous child, I was always needing healing. So the ritual of the egg was a big part of my life."

Later Virginia Marie realized that what she really needed healing from in her childhood was the racism she experienced. "At the time I didn't know what I was experiencing, but it was racism," she says. "The healing ritual I remember most was after I went to kindergarten the first time. We were seated in a circle. There were two or three Mexican American children in the circle, but mostly white children. The little boy next to me, who was Anglo, had an accident in his pants. It seeped onto the beautiful little dress I had on. And the teacher, rather than to blame the little boy, blamed me. So I got paddled the first day of school, even though I said, 'I didn't do it; he did it.' I remember coming home and crying and telling my grandmother that I didn't want to go back to that school. And she must have understood. She took the egg and cleansed me. Then she took me to the Goodwill—makes me emotional because we didn't have a lot of money— and she bought me a special coat. And she said, 'When you put this coat on, nothing can harm you.' So every morning from then on she would put that coat on me and tell me, 'Remember, nothing can harm you.' She was very much in touch in her own way with what was out in the world for a Mexican child, and was teaching me a lot about healing and the reality of our lives as Latinos. She sang to me so many songs in Spanish and told me the story of her grandmother and great-grandmother; what she was doing was giving me the richness of our people. My grandmother had crossed the Rio Grande as a child in 1917 during the revolution, when Pancho Villa[7] was recruiting young men and women. Her mother didn't want her children involved in the revolution, so she decided to take the family into Texas."

Virginia Marie grew up in the public schools in Houston, except for a brief time in a Catholic parochial school. When people ask her when she first knew she had a call to ministry, she tells an experience in the Catholic school. "I was about seven years old," she says. "I had done something wrong. I don't remember what I did wrong, but the nun decided that I needed to pray the Rosary. So she took me to the Communion rail and had me pray the Rosary with other kids who had done something wrong. I remember thinking, 'I want to go see what the priests do back there.' So I jumped the Communion rail, and I opened the closet. And I put the vestments on. Then I came out and said something like, 'The peace of Christ be with you.' Of course, all the kids started laughing. The nun came in and was very upset. She had a conversation with my grandmother, and I was sent back to public school. So I didn't last in parochial school very long. But I've always been drawn to the altar and the sacrament. I loved to get my cousins together and play ritual. It wasn't always like the priest did it. We'd dance and do other things that weren't in church, but that was church to me."

When Virginia Marie was eight, her mother remarried. "She decided that she wanted me and my baby sister, Frances, to live with her and her new husband," Virginia Marie recalls. "It was a very painful time in my life, to leave my grandmother and go live with my mother. Her husband, Carlos Rincon, adopted us. He was a good man—very spiritual, very religious, went to church every morning at six o'clock till the day he died. My mother was an alcoholic, so there was a lot of chaos. When my mother took my sister and me to live with her, I would run away. I would jump out of the window and walk over to the train that was about a block away from my mother's home. The train would always slow down in our neighborhood, so I would jump on the train. And sometimes it would take me close enough to my grandmother so that I could go stay with her for the night. Other times I would jump the train because I wanted to see how white people lived on the other side of the tracks. It would take me all the way across town to where Rice University is now."

Two other siblings, Alfred and Gloria, grew up with Virginia Marie and Frances in the Magnolia neighborhood on the east side of Houston. "When Carlos retired from the merchant marines, he did the best he could for us," Virginia Marie says. "He bought a home. Alfred, Gloria, Frances and I were raised under the same roof, so we never said 'stepbrother and stepsister,' just 'brother and sister.' We're very close. Carlos had a child, Carlos Jr., from a previous marriage. Carlos Jr. didn't live with us, but he would come and visit. There were quite a few of us in a little shotgun house. We grew up in one of the most drug-infested neighborhoods of Houston. One time when I was a teenager, I opened the front door and this guy who had been stabbed just fell into our living room. It was a really rough neighborhood."

In high school Virginia Marie decided that she wanted to be a nurse and went to the counselor who told her, "You could never be a registered nurse (RN), but you could probably be a licensed vocational nurse (LVN)." As a member of the National Honor Society with straight A's, Virginia Marie could have gotten scholarships and easily completed the RN requirements. Although Virginia Marie can now see the racism in the counselor's advice, at the time she accepted it. "Back then, that's the way it was," she says. "And I didn't have the support of a loving mother to encourage me. So I went ahead and did the LVN course at Houston Community College, and started my career in 1972. I loved nursing; it was great. It gave me so many experiences. I've done all kinds of nursing. For about a year, I did hospital nursing on the cancer unit."

When Virginia Marie was twenty, she married Robert Nuncio. "I married at a very young age to a very young man," she says. "I was twenty, and he was eighteen. We eloped because his mother didn't want him to marry into our family because of my mother's alcoholism. I stayed married to Robert for thirteen years. We have a beautiful daughter, Marissa Michelle Nuncio. The doctors think I have probably been dealing with lupus ever since my pregnancy and premature labor. Marissa weighed five pounds, four ounces. I call her my 'miracle baby,' because it took everything I had to be able to carry the pregnancy. She's just wonderful, wonderful—my only child. Now she's a lawyer in Los Angeles."

After she married, Virginia Marie took a job with the health department so that she could spend weekends at home. "As a public health nurse, I did family planning, well child, and maternity," she recalls. "That's when things started moving for me in terms of looking at healing and spirituality, especially in the maternity and well child clinics. The women would come and ask me for prayer. I was young, only twenty-three, twenty-four." Virginia Marie recounts this exchange with some of the other nurses:

"Why do you take so long with the women?" the nurses asked.

"I don't know. They're always asking me to do certain things, like pray."

"But you're a nurse. You're not a priest or a *curandera* or anything."

"I know, but I always get asked to do that."

When Virginia Marie moved from Houston to Austin, Texas, with her husband, who was a draftsman with the BJ Hughes Company, she continued to broaden her nursing experience. "I worked at the Austin Diagnostic Clinic as a gastroenterology (GI) nurse," she says. "Then I was a charge nurse at a Montopolis Health Clinic for a brief time, and then did different kinds of nursing in the Montopolis neighborhood, a very poor area in Austin. I would go out to the homes and do assessments of the children, including the Denver Developmental Screening Test.[8] Again the women would see something in me, and they would ask me to pray. And I would have to say, 'I'm sorry; I can't do that because I'm a nurse.' At the same time all that was going on, I was starting to question. I was asking what my call was, where I really felt I could give."

Active in the Roman Catholic Church at this time, Virginia Marie helped lead *Cursillos de Cristiandad*,[9] both in English and Spanish. "I was very connected to Monsignor Lonnie Reyes, who was involved in civil rights in Austin," she recalls. "He talked to me a lot about my call to ordination. He said to me, 'I see something in you that I think you should pursue. And as a Roman Catholic priest, I could never have imagined that I would say this, but I'm going to say it to you. I think you should go to the Episcopal Church to see women do liturgy.'"

Continuing to question her call, Virginia Marie went to a discovery weekend at the Seminary of the Southwest in 1986.[10] "I was exploring, feeling God calling me to something, and I wasn't sure what it was," she says. "I'd been a nurse. I'd felt a call, and I was trying to decide if this call was about ordination or a call to a different career." At the seminary discovery weekend she met Rev. Judith Sessions, who said to her: "There is this wonderful woman priest at St. George's Episcopal Church, Rev. Judith Liro; I think you should go and see her do the liturgy because it seems like you and she would connect." Virginia Marie went to St. George's and for the first time saw a woman at the altar. "I was so moved to see a woman at the altar," she recalls. "I was so emotional, and shed some tears. I got to know Judith Liro. Then I decided I should start having conversations with Judith and the other priest there, David Hoster, about whether the priesthood was something to think about."

In the meantime Virginia Marie and Robert had divorced. "When Marissa was about eight years old, I decided it was time to get divorced," she says. "I came out as a lesbian. I finally figured out that I needed to leave a marriage where he was unhappy and I was unhappy."

Virginia Marie also realized she needed to get a bachelor's degree, so she enrolled at St. Edwards University in Austin. "I started working on a social work degree, because I thought maybe the call was about becoming a social worker so I could do a little bit more with the soul," she says. "By then I had been received into the Episcopal Church, and

Judith Liro was my spiritual director. There were realities if I chose to go through the process to be a priest, whether that was even feasible in Austin because the diocese is so conservative. I didn't need for somebody to know that I was a lesbian right away, but I didn't want to have the stress of going through seminary and being pulled out of the ordination process because they found out. Judith and a group of people put some money together for me to go to a discovery weekend at Episcopal Divinity School (EDS) in Cambridge, Massachusetts, to see if I liked that seminary. I went to EDS and stayed about two weeks to audit some classes. And I fell in love with the seminary. I felt that this was what I wanted to do. I was hearing conversations on liberation theology, feminist perspectives, what the story of Jesus Christ is in relation to the poor and the oppressed, the whole question of sexuality being deconstructed. I was like, 'Wow! These people are talking about homosexuality; they're using the words "gay" and "lesbian" together with "salvation" and "Christ."' I knew I wanted to go to seminary, but I didn't know whether I would be chosen to go through that process."

In 1993, Virginia Marie graduated with a Bachelor of Liberal Studies (BLS) degree with a major in social work, and that same year she enrolled in Episcopal Divinity School. "It was a whole different world," she says. "I remember not seeing myself at all in the seminary; I mean I was the only Latina on campus. It seemed like people knew that they were going to specialize in this or that, and I just wanted to absorb it all. I walked into a class on feminist perspectives of the Bible with Rev. Alison Cheek.[11] It was my first day of class, and I realized that I was sitting with all these white women who had studied the Bible maybe back and forth. It was my first real critical analysis of the Bible class. I left the class and went to my apartment, and I cried my eyes out because I thought, 'I can't keep up with them. There is no way that I could ever do this.'" Virginia Marie went to see Rev. Cheek the next morning and had this conversation with her:

"I'm going to have to drop your class."

"Why are you dropping my class?"

"Because I was not able to hear my voice in it. I felt like I didn't understand what these women were talking about. They never talked about the poor. They never talked about the oppressed. They never talked about suffering. And I just don't think I fit in that class."

In her Australian accent, Rev. Cheek replied, "Virginia Marie, yours is the voice that we need in that class. And if you can hang in there for two or three more classes, I think you're going to find your voice."

Rev. Alison Cheek also encouraged her to stay in the feminist perspectives class by offering her a job. "Once a week I would go to Alison's office to help organize her papers, and we would talk," Virginia Marie recalls. "That's where I started figuring out that there was a theology that women needed to talk about. And there was this word 'feminist' that I could resonate with, but I couldn't. I loved listening to her talk about her struggle to get ordained, and some of the stories of being rejected, and what it meant to be a woman at the altar. It was all fascinating to me. Eventually she made me her assistant in the feminist liberation program. So I organized all the luncheons with speakers, and was part of one of the big anniversaries for the first women's ordinations. Here you had Carter Heyward, Alla Bozarth, Merrill Bittner, and others,[12] the first women to be ordained in the Episcopal Church—all these women had come together. It was so exciting for me. And yet seminary was so hard. I was listening to all this language I hadn't heard about hermeneutics, exegesis, proclamation, liberation—and just trying to take it all in."

A flare-up of lupus made seminary even more challenging for Virginia Marie. "The lupus hit me really hard my first semester because of the stress," she recalls. "I ended up in the infirmary. All my medical records had been lost from Austin to Cambridge, so the doctors were doing all the tests again. I was wondering, 'Now how am I going to do classes with this horrible disease living in me at the same time?' Once they stabilized me and put me on all this prednisone, I just swelled up."

When she returned to her New Testament class, her professor, Dr. Joanna Dewey,[13] recommended that she drop the class because she was so far behind. But Virginia Marie was determined to complete the course. "I was so hungry for the information," she says. "And I was trying to make sense of everything. Here I was this Chicana in what felt like a foreign country to me, coming from the hood, and here I was in Cambridge. So I couldn't imagine letting something like that go. I asked Dr. Dewey to let me try to catch up, and she said, 'All right, if you want to try.' I did, and I passed the course."

As she continued to meet the challenges of the illness and of being the only Latina on campus, Virginia Marie found a course on spirituality and the arts to be especially affirming. "This wonderful professor, Kwok Pui-lan,[14] taught the course," Virginia Marie recalls. "Her course included our blessing each other. We'd bless the third eye.[15] We did all these different rituals. And she had us do art or poetry, and I was like, 'Oh, I can relate to this!' She had about six books for the course. One homework assignment was to look at the books and see where we could find ourselves, our story. One of the books was Gustavo Gutiérrez's *A Theology of Liberation*,[16] and some were on Eastern religion and philosophies. In class we each had to say what we experienced looking through these books. People went on and on and on. When it was my turn, I got up there and said, 'None of this speaks to my experience. I don't feel that I'm resonating with any of this. Liberation theology a little bit, but there's something there that doesn't fit. Maybe it's because I'm a little bit of this and a little bit of that and I mix it all up and something different comes out. The best way that I can explain this to you—because I don't even have the words to articulate it—is to drum.' So I sat there and drummed and chanted whatever came through. Dr. Pui-lan was very supportive. She also encouraged me to write my poems and to use art and color. And she would say things to me like, 'Remember you're in a white world, and sometimes you have to say things for the white man to get where you need to go, but I understand what you're saying.'"

As she worked toward her Master of Divinity degree at Episcopal Divinity School, Virginia Marie took some courses at the nearby Harvard Divinity School. "I was able to go to Harvard Divinity for course work," she recalls. "And for me that was like, 'Wow! I can't believe I'm sitting in Harvard Divinity.' I took this great course with Harvey Cox[17] on feminist perspectives of Christ. He used media to teach the course—poetry, art, music. I was in hog heaven! For our final project, I videotaped women of color at Episcopal Divinity School, telling me what their perspective was from the feminist viewpoint. That was an awesome experience, and I was proud of my A in the course!"

While she was in seminary, Virginia Marie also began the ordination process in the Massachusetts diocese. "From 1994 until 1996 I was very active in getting into the ordination process," she says. "I started noticing that some of how I viewed myself in the world was difficult for church officials to understand. How could I bring my understanding of *curandismo*, of healing, to the Episcopal Church? Where do I fit in there? I would get upset when I heard people preach that we need to help the poor and oppressed, or those who are marginalized, to come forward to become priests, and yet they would be looking right at me and couldn't comprehend me. What they wanted, which was a struggle for me, was for me to become like them. I was already to some degree angry with myself because I had assimilated so much. Bishop Tom Shaw[18] asked me one time, 'If you become a priest, what are you going to do for a broken world?' I said, 'Tell the truth. Tell the truth—why people are dealing with racism, why people are suffering in Mexico, how NAFTA[19] affected the people in Mexico, why they come to the United States, why they sacrifice themselves in the desert to come here. Look at what we're doing to them—tell the truth. You can't always paint a pretty picture. I think we forget that there is an enormous amount of suffering in this world, and we just go around with blinders on. That has to be preached from the pulpit too.' So I was pegged a maverick. I was pegged a militant."

During her struggle with the ordination process Virginia Marie found support from women at Greenfire Retreat Center.[20] "The women of Greenfire were very important to me," Virginia Marie says with tears in her eyes. "The women there helped me so much. They would do women's church, women's circle. We had a ritual where they ordained me. And even though my later official ordinations as deacon and as priest were very important, that ordination to me was so symbolic of women ordaining each other to use our voices. It helped me to be able to start doing the work without waiting for a bishop to say, 'Okay, now you can do it.' I was doing it anyway. And I was understanding the whole thing about how we're all ordained because of our baptism. At Greenfire I met this other Latina, Rev. Maria Aris-Paul, a Guatemalan woman who was ordained in the Episcopal Church, and after two years, she took her collar off and refused to wear it again. Racism has been too much for her. Maria and I would sit and talk for a long time. She and Rev. Alison Cheek, one of the founders of Greenfire who invited me to the Center, were like my mothers there. Some other founders, Rev. Connie Chandler Ward and Rev. Rosanna Kazanjian—they're all Episcopal priests—would help me write my petitioning letters for ordination, and they would always say, 'Remember it's a white man's world.'"

When Rev. Judith Liro was in the process of forming St. Hildegard's Community in Austin, Texas, she went to visit Virginia Marie, who connected Judith with the women at Greenfire Retreat Center. Virginia Marie talks about how important Judith and St. Hildegard's have been to her. "Whenever I went back to Austin, I was always able to go to St. Hildegard's," she says. "The best way I can explain St. Hildegard's is that it's a feeling of an explosion of divinity that we can't capture. St. Hildegard's to me opened up the possibilities. So Greenfire, St. Hildegard's, *curandismo*—all just opened possibilities."

Around this time Virginia Marie wrote a lyrical piece as she was sitting in her apartment in Cambridge looking out a window at the ocean. "I was sitting there wondering where people are in their thinking," she comments. "Isn't it about making progress?" She calls this piece "The Window":

> I open my eyes to see and I realize, I am waking to that which I don't always understand. Beauty, radiance, chaos and turmoil combined in the making. I move and I stand in an endless silent motion of self. I am looking into the window and it is. I am not the picture but the endless wave of illusions speaking to a soul of years passed. And suddenly, I see the plates spinning in my head and the picture is taken and I am for that moment a piece of the greater vision. A moment reflects back to me what I once dreamed would come true; that the beauty is in the perspective and the lens and the window and the wish and the love and in the chaos of our lives. I take the picture from this window and it is beautiful and no one would know that it is not what it seems but I do. It is the endless seam of life that pulls us all into the oneness of that which we are. I take the picture, through the window of my life and suddenly you are there. Awesome, glorious and standing still; a mountain, a river, a tree, and maybe even your smile greets me on the other side. But understand, we are the picture, we are the focus and simply said we are the window of the distant spirit, earth, stars, and our compassionate eyes. I am and you are and so it is that we pause, reflect and take the picture and smile into ourselves to know that the void is always full of love, peace, tranquility and so many pictures of our lives.

Virginia Marie tells one of the most painful experiences she had while she was in seminary. "A maintenance guy on campus who was very white, liked to joke with me," she says. "One day I was in the cafeteria in line getting my food, and he was outside. The door was open, and he could see me in line. He yelled at me from afar, 'Hey, wetback!' I thought, 'Surely, he isn't calling me or anybody else a "wetback."' I looked around, and there were only Anglo people standing in line. And they became whiter than white. So I tried to ignore him, and he yelled out again, 'Hey, wetback!' And he started laughing. So I turned around and said, 'Are you calling me a "wetback"?' He said, 'Yeah.' I remember holding the tray, thinking, 'I want to throw this tray at him. I want to take the tray and just bang the living daylights out of him.' But I took the tray of food, and I left. I didn't eat lunch. I went back to my apartment, and within five minutes the whole campus knew what had happened. The dean of the seminary at the time, Rev. Bill Rankin, called me and said, 'Are you okay? What are you thinking?' I said, 'This is horrible that this is happening on this campus.' I didn't go back on campus for two weeks. Finally an African American student, Janice Yancy, came to my apartment and said, 'You have to reclaim your turf. You need to come out. You can't be missing all these classes. I know you're hurt. I know you're thinking of leaving. I know it's too much, but that's our reality.' So we went out, and she held my hand, and we walked the campus. I remember saying, 'I belong here. I have every right to be here, and I'm going to stay here.'"

Soon after this incident Virginia Marie invited people of color at the seminary to her apartment, and they organized a protest. "There were people from Africa, India, Korea, the African American woman, Janice Yancy, who had walked around campus with me," she recounts. "We sat in my apartment, and they asked me, 'How many times a day do you face racism on this campus?' We stayed to one o'clock in the morning talking about our experiences. Then we decided to organize a protest. We each wrote a sign such as, 'I come from poverty,' 'I come from the oppressed,' 'I am this or this, or whatever.' We decided that giving voice to the voiceless would be our contribution to the Thursday liturgy. So the word got around that we were going to do it. I remember Carter Heyward[21] and Joanna Dewey calling me and saying, 'Virginia Marie, this may be something that will keep you from getting ordained. You need to think about what you're doing.' I said,

'I know. We're going to do it anyway.' So we had the Eucharist, and we were getting ready to receive Communion. At the point where we were to receive Communion, we all pulled out our signs and walked out. And we put our signs in front of the chapel. It was a very powerful statement. A couple of months later I was called to be on a task force. Out of that task force, the position of pastoral counselor to people of color was created, and I was one of the first to get that position."

Years later, in 2009, as part of a project called "Reading, Writing and the Engaged Community," sponsored by the NAACP in Portland, Maine, Virginia Marie wrote about her painful experience in the seminary cafeteria. A writing exercise in this project was in response to Martin Luther King's "A Letter from a Birmingham Jail."[22] Here is an excerpt from what Virginia Marie wrote:

> What do you mean Mexicans go to the back? Aw, I now have the degree . . .Why do you call me a wetback standing here in this Ivy League Seminary in Cambridge, Massachusetts? Aw, call me Reverend and understand I came through the back doors of Texas . . . hot tamales, corn tortillas, beans and rice. . . . Now pour me some hot tea and talk to me of liberation theology. . . . I pause and weep beyond the years that are to come. . . . Martin Luther King Jr., I hear your words, my "feets are tired," and I not only echo the pain of that journey but I cry out in the night, that my master is greater than that white man that shut that door at my favorite burger stand in Houston, Texas. . . . My heart debates, my brain negates, I go in between two worlds, Chicana, Mexican American, assimilated, where do I belong in this great historical debate—oppression and racism . . . Is there a change, is there a new prophetic pulpit for my people . . . better yet the people of the Universe. . . . Give me the verse of reciprocity, give me the freedom to let go of my bruised soul's voiceless pain. What do you mean Mexicans go to the back. . . . Give me prophetic justice. . . . Those unjust laws I see them grinning in my face, you paint your faces with my pain. . . . Hand it to me, my freedom . . . Hand it to me, my voice, the peace, the compassion and the truths. . . . And then my color is the beauty, and then my color is the mixture and the blends that do not hide but shine the light of a full humanity.

Overcoming obstacles of racism and illness and working to put herself and her daughter through school, Virginia Marie graduated from Episcopal Divinity School in 1997. "Throughout seminary I'd get sick, ending up in the hospital off and on, trying different medications to stabilize me," she recounts. "If it wasn't my kidneys, it was my lungs. Sometimes I couldn't walk because the inflammation would get so bad in my joints. It took me four years to finish seminary because of the constant struggle with the lupus and needing to work at the same time. My daughter was attending Mount Holyoke College[23] in western Massachusetts, so there was that responsibility."

Soon after Virginia Marie graduated from seminary, Rev. Butch Gamarra offered her the position of lay pastoral associate at St. Stephen's Episcopal Church. "The church is in the south end of Boston in what is called Villa Victoria, and is mostly Puerto Rican," she says. "Rev. Gamarra is Panamanian, Chinese, and Native American. He was known for being radical, very much involved in community organizing. He was always hitting up against the institution. He did his services bilingually, which I thought was awesome. Because he had been fighting the system for a long time, he was tired. Two months after I was hired, he informed me that he was going on sabbatical and that he wanted me to take charge of the church. I said, 'I'm not a priest.' He said, 'I don't care. We'll organize the calendar so that a priest can come in and do the Eucharist, and you can do everything else.' His six-month sabbatical lasted almost a year."

During that year Virginia Marie initiated summer camp and renewed the acolyte and after-school programs, as well as performing all the pastoral and administrative duties at St. Stephens. When Rev. Gamarra returned from sabbatical, he informed Virginia Marie that he didn't want to be with the diocese of Massachusetts any longer and that he was looking for a job in Los Angeles. "At the time I was a postulant[24] in the ordination process," she recalls. "The bishop called me in and said, 'You're doing a great job at the church. I don't see any problem with you continuing. You're getting good experience.' And then what seemed like one day to the next, a young Harvard Divinity white male showed up, and I'm told that he's taking over the church. The day he showed up he walked me around the community and asked me to introduce him to all the people and tell him what I was doing. The next day he said to me, 'There's not room for two priests in this church, so the bishop has authorized me to tell you that you need to resign.' I immediately jumped up and called the people I knew from the vestry[25] and people I knew in the church who were supportive of the ministry I was doing. There was a meeting that same night. The people rallied, and he couldn't get rid of me. For about a year he kept trying to figure out a way to get rid of me."

After serving as lay pastoral associate from 1997 to mid-1999, Virginia Marie left St. Stephens Episcopal Church. Still in the ordination process in Massachusetts, she stayed in Boston, but went back and forth to Portland, Maine, to visit her friend Rev. Martha Ann Englert, who gave professional and personal support to Virginia Marie. "I was very upset with the bishop because he put another hold on my ordination," she says. "He told me I had to wait for another year. I kept trying to decide what I was going to do. At one point I went to the bishop and said, 'I've decided I want to pull out. So what has to happen for me to not be in the ordination process? Do I just say I'm not in the ordination process or do you?' He said, 'No, I decide that.' His canon to the ordinary[26] said to me, 'Just take the time and go on retreat and discern.' I said, 'How much more time do I need? I'm tired.' But I did two weeks of retreat. When I came back, the bishop told me to continue on the process. I decided not to stop the process for myself, but at the same time I decided I was going to Maine. That was the place I needed to be for healing, whether it interrupted the process or stopped the process. I didn't care anymore."

Crossing the border from Massachusetts to Maine, Virginia Marie saw the sign: "Maine, the way life should be." As she was driving that night, she saw another "sign" that had meaning for her. "I saw this beautiful blue strip of light that went across the sky; it was either a big shooting star or one of those little cosmic things that happen," she recalls. "I had been thinking, 'Now what? Where am I going? What am I doing? Please, God, what am I going to do with my life? I believe in you. I have faith, but I don't know what I'm doing. I don't know where you're sending me or what you want from me.' So I took that blue light as a sign that I was going in the right direction. I got to Portland and lived in one room in what they called the 'Old Monastery,' and tried to figure out my life. I would walk the streets of Portland, and I would see the Latinos. And I'd say, 'Wow! There're Latinos here.' Then one day my friend Martha Ann Englert said to me, 'They're starting a little mission in the Bayside area of Portland. Would you like to go and read the Gospels in Spanish? Would you like to go see what they're doing?' I said, 'Sure. Why not?' I got together with these people who were visioning this little mission." As Virginia Marie and Father Sam Henderson, one of the priests in charge of organizing the mission, were driving to lunch, they saw four Latinos who looked lost. She asked him to pull over, and she spoke to the men in Spanish. She tells me this conversation in English:

"Good afternoon. Are ya'll lost?"

"Yeah. We don't know where we are? We slept in the park last night. We were hired to pick blueberries, and we've been working for a couple of months. The boss man put us in the van, and said he was taking us to another place to work, but he just dropped us off here in this park. He didn't pay us. We don't have any money. We don't know where to go."

"Okay, there's a shelter near this mission that's going to start."

Virginia Marie told the men how to get to the shelter and made arrangements to meet them the next day. They asked her to pray for them that they could somehow get back home to Texas. "The next day Father Sam and I and people who were part of the visioning of the mission set up a piece of plywood on two paint cans and did Eucharist for them," she says. "And we passed the hat around there, and were able to collect enough money so they could all go home on the bus. That's where it started for me to do ministry in Portland, because they told the families at the shelter that there was a Latina Reverend in Portland. People started looking for me. I'd meet them on the streets, and I'd pray with them. I was called into their homes to do liturgy. Before the first Sunday that St. Elizabeth's Mission was ready to go, all shiny and painted and the altar set, I went to the soup kitchen at the shelter and had breakfast with the Latinos. I invited them to come, and they came."

While working at the mission, Virginia Marie supported herself with social work and interpreting jobs, and then with a small salary from TengoVoz. "It came to me that the women needed a place," she says. "So I organized the first gathering of women in a basement of a Unitarian Universalist church. I read some poems, and the women began to talk about their struggle. I encouraged them to think about God in their lives. We would meet every two weeks. I encouraged them to create the sacred space. I would bring four or five pieces, like a candle or a bell or a book or a flower, and then let them set the table. I encouraged them to bring their children because I'm a believer that we need to let children help us create sacred space. So it was okay for a child to run around or sit at a mother's feet; they would eventually get it that something sacred was going on. A friend of mine, Rev. Wells Staley-Mays, who's an activist for Peace Action Maine, told me that I needed to organize the women's group, to create a non-profit, so that I could get paid. When he asked what I wanted to call it, I said, 'TengoVoz, because the women need a voice; I need a voice.' TengoVoz is about giving voice to the voiceless."[27] A lawyer friend of Rev. Staley-Mays filed the articles of incorporation for TengoVoz, and the Maine Council of Churches became the fiscal agent. "We needed a fiscal agent because I was looking at grants," Virginia Marie explains. "The seed money that we'd gotten has always been very minimal, enough to pay me a little—$800, sometimes $1000 a month."

This small salary did not decrease Virginia Marie's passion for TengoVoz. Later in an article entitled "TengoVoz: The Power of Voice," published in the *Maine Women's Journal*, she expresses her purpose in founding this organization:

> I was the first in my family for many things: first to graduate from high school, first to receive a college degree and later a Master of Divinity. My struggle to succeed required a determined voice, one which could be heard. I believe that all individuals should be able to give voice to their desires, dreams and any injustices that keep them from achieving their true destiny. TengoVoz/I Have Voice was founded on this premise. The mission of this newly formed non-profit is to empower Latina women and their children through the arts, spirituality and education. I have held this vision for a long time; I just had no idea that it would be here in Portland. A day of helping people to use their voice takes me many places. I have women, and sometimes men, calling me to take them to the Department of Human Services to see if they qualify for food stamps. A medical appointment is no longer an impossible challenge when you have an interpreter and someone who understands your culture at your side. . . . Finding a job can be a challenge for someone who has limited English skills and it isn't unusual for me to help that process along for some of my brothers and sisters. Unfortunately, domestic violence is also part of my work. I help women find their voice and allow them to make decisions about their future.[28]

In 2001, Virginia Marie was ordained a deacon in the Massachusetts diocese. "My ordination to the diaconate was very powerful because I had struggled for so long to get there and it was a woman, Bishop Barbara Harris,[29] who performed the ceremony," Rev. Virginia Marie recalls. "I remember after she laid hands on me, she cupped my face with her hand, and she lifted my face up and said, 'Baby, you've only just begun. But you are a deacon in the Episcopal Church.' She was the first woman bishop in the Episcopal Church and an African American, so she knew what she was talking about. My ordination was a great day. Two of the women from Greenfire Retreat Center, Rev. Constance Chandler Ward and Rev. Rosanna Kazanjian, preached at my ordination to the diaconate. Rev. Judith Liro and other friends and family came."

By this time TengoVoz was growing bigger and bigger as Rev. Rincon received more and more requests for various kinds of ministry. "TengoVoz was flourishing in terms of women's groups and women needing help with domestic violence issues, and I was doing educational pieces at some of the universities," she says. "I had an office for a while; people would come to consult with me. At times I got called to help deliver babies because the women were afraid to go to the hospital. I organized a rally because immigration came in and started busting down doors and intimidating people. And they were taking people who had papers. I was getting the calls, so we brought NAACP, the Maine People's Alliance, and other organizations together to organize the march. I went to the governor's office and asked if he would see us. We were able to get him to sign an executive order that state agencies could not ask for documents. All the time, in my opinion, I was doing the liturgy in the streets, doing the liturgy by way of action in the chaos of people's lives." One day when Rev. Rincon was wearing a collar, a woman approached her on the street, and they had this exchange:

"Are you a nun?" the woman asked.

"No, I'm a deacon."

"I don't have any money. My kids are burning up with fever, and I think I'm getting sick too. I've heard of you, heard people talk about you, that you help people. Do you think you could help me get some cough syrup for the kids?"

"Absolutely."

Rev. Virginia Marie took the woman to the pharmacy to get the cough syrup and then gave her a ride back to her apartment. "There were ten families living in this one-bedroom apartment," she recalls. "Each one had a little corner or space with a sheet that divided it from the others. I can still feel that moment, just wanting to cry that my people were so oppressed and scared. I did an assessment of all the kids, checking their temperatures, telling the mothers what to do or where to go, how to be safe when they went into the hospitals to get care. All the nursing and social work—everything just kicked in. But the one thing I felt compelled to do was to get them all to kneel down and pray that it had to change, that they couldn't continue to live like this. And they were very open to this. We broke bread and prayed. We had the sacrament of love, the sacrament of compassion, the sacrament of just being a human being, because I think they had lost that—they were struggling so hard that they had lost it. I could only do this ministry because I knew how they felt. So I knew that I had to keep going through the ordination process, that I couldn't give up, that I was called to minister to those who would never make it into the church, who didn't know what corporate worship was, who didn't know what liturgy was, but who did know God and did have faith."

Although Rev. Rincon had been ordained as a deacon, her path toward ordination as a priest continued to be long and arduous. Committees of the diocese of Massachusetts kept telling her that she didn't have a ministry in Massachusetts, that her ministry was in Maine. So she tried to get them to release her to the diocese of Maine. "But they didn't want to release me," she says. "Bishop Chilton Knudsen[30] of Maine kept fighting for me. She said to me, 'I think you have a call, Virginia Marie. I've always believed you had a call. Let's see what we can do.' Finally she was able to get me released." On September 18, 2005, in a ceremony performed by Bishop Knudsen at Christ Episcopal Church in Biddeford, Maine, Virginia Marie became the first woman of color to be ordained to the priesthood in the diocese of Maine. "The beautiful thing is that Bishop Chilton did a bilingual service," Rev. Virginia Marie recalls. "She had asked me what I wanted to happen that day, and I said, 'I want the community where I minister to feel that they're part of this. I don't think they've ever seen a Latina being ordained.' Bishop Chilton said, 'Okay. Then we're going to have a bilingual service, and I will lay my hands on you and call you forth into priesthood in Spanish.' That was a beautiful moment. A lot of Latinos came. My family came—my daughter and my brother and my sisters and my nephews. And Rev. Alison Cheek preached at my ordination." Shortly after her ordination, an article entitled "Rev. Virginia Marie Rincon Looks to Foster Latino Connection" came out in the *Biddeford Journal Tribune*. The article begins with her groundbreaking accomplishments: "She is the first woman of color to be ordained in Maine. Since 2000, Rincon has worked to empower Latina women and their families through her ministry in Portland. She uses spirituality, education and the arts to connect with Latinos and meets with them on the street or at their workplaces."[31]

After serving from 2001 to 2005 as assistant for the priest in charge at Christ Episcopal Church in Biddeford, Rev. Rincon became the Hispanic Missioner/Priest for the Episcopal Diocese of Maine. Among her responsibilities has been the planting and development of Mission San Lucas in Portland and the performing of all liturgical, educational, and pastoral duties. In addition, she has planned and implemented ideas for the growth of Hispanic Ministry in the Diocese of Maine, and organized community and state interfaith educational activities regarding Episcopal Migration Ministry[32] and immigration issues.

One of the first rituals that Rev. Virginia Marie led after the opening of Mission San Lucas was a mass to celebrate the annual feast of the Virgin of Guadalupe. She shows me an article in the *Portland Press Herald* that includes a picture of children playing the parts of the Virgin and Juan Diego, who had the miraculous encounter with her near Mexico City. "This liturgy had never been celebrated here," Virginia Marie explains. "We did drumming and sang to the *Virgen de Guadalupe*. I played some pieces from 'Guadalupe: Virgen de los Indios'[33] with background singing in the Nahuatl[34] language during the procession and recession, and played the music called 'Native Angels'[35] during Communion. At the service were people from Peru, Guatemala, El Salvador, Dominican Republic, and other places. Some had never heard the story of the *Virgen de Guadalupe*. The women were encouraged to share statues they had of Mary or other women they had in their lives as they grew up. I asked them, 'What was at your altar when you were growing up? Did you have a grandmother?' That day they were encouraged to bring those saints to the altar." The article in the newspaper includes further commentary on this creative celebration: "About thirty people gathered in the chapel at St. Luke's, which was adorned with paintings and other pictures of the Virgin, as well as flags from Latin American countries. The Rev. Virginia Marie Rincon, who led the service in Spanish and English, said the Virgin of Guadalupe unites people and is responsible for bringing peace to various cultures. Rincon said the feast helps immigrants from Latin America stay connected to their faith and to their native countries."[36]

Rev. Rincon tells a personal story of how the Virgin of Guadalupe gives her strength to use her voice as a Latina woman. "Once when I was getting ready to begin worship in the chapel at St. Luke's Cathedral, I was approached by a woman who stated she had the use of the chapel from 6:00 to 9:00 p.m. and that I had to leave. For over two years, we had been using the chapel from 5:00 to 7:00 p.m. She asked if I was there to set up the chapel for her concert. I said, 'No, I am setting up for my worship service; I am the Rev. Virginia Marie Rincon. Who are you?' She demanded that I leave. By then, my parishioners were arriving. I told her that we could be out of the chapel by at least 6:30 if I shortened the sermon. She refused, and the incident escalated. A vestry member was called to ask me to leave. I said to this person, 'Give me a minute.' I went to the sacristy and cried and prayed very hard before I returned. I kept refusing to leave, and then one of my parishioners noticed that there was something going on. As a priest I was challenged to do the right thing, whether to leave the worship space, or possibly upset the parishioners by creating a bigger scene. By then the woman was so red in the face and screaming at me that I felt it was in our best interest to leave. Later when I talked to the dean about the incident, he said that I was known for being snippety and difficult to work with. On another occasion, the vestry member who had asked me to leave the worship space asked if I was behaving better these days. I answered, 'Absolutely not, can't change things if I behave.' A few months later in this small chapel where we were asked to leave, I hung this beautiful seven-foot painting of the *Virgen de Guadalupe* that one of my parishioners had created."

In her preaching at the Mission San Lucas, Rev. Virginia Marie has approached biblical interpretation from the perspective of race and class, inviting the congregation to a mutual discussion of the texts. "That was one way of creating a space of reciprocity, of free thinking," she explains. "People may be questioning for the first time. Most of the people at the Mission San Lucas have come out of a Roman Catholic background. And it is very good, very powerful to hear people say what they think or don't think or don't believe. The Mission San Lucas and the women of TengoVoz started melding together. Women empower themselves through TengoVoz; then they start coming to church. And we have these people who have never been to TengoVoz group meetings, and they're hearing these women talk about the *Virgen de Guadalupe* or Mary Magdalene, and feeling comfortable with movement, music, and their children being a part of the liturgy. I would call the children up to the altar at the time of the breaking of the bread, and they would stand behind me and just feel like they could do that. For me liturgy is in the doing. It's in the giving voice to people I can relate to in their joy, sadness, suffering, the complexity of living in two worlds. Some of these people did not really come to this country by choice, but because they had to. I was helping them to light that spirituality within themselves. It was never for me about being the priest up there breaking the bread; it's always been about creating a circle. I remember Father Sam saying to me one time, 'Why don't you wear your collar all the time?' I said, 'I don't need to always wear the collar.' He said, 'You're a priest; you have to separate yourself.' But I never believed that."

Instead of separating herself Rev. Rincon believes in working in solidarity with people suffering from injustice. She will put on her priest collar when it helps in her justice work. "Putting the collar on gives you power to some people," she says. "And I want to make a difference. I stay in the church because of some of the underground work that needs to be done. I'm using my priesthood; it makes a difference in the power people give me." For example, she wore her priest collar when she helped lead a rally, getting Selvin Arevalo released from custody and advocating to keep him from being deported to Guatemala. Arevalo, who had come to the U.S. illegally when he was fourteen to earn enough money to support his mother and siblings, had been detained by federal immigration officials after he left the scene of a minor accident involving his work van because he did not have a driver's license. The *Portland Press Herald* cites Rev. Rincon's important part in this rally: "For community leaders like the Rev. Virginia Marie Rincon, Arevalo's brush with the law is not as important as what he has given to his community. 'Selvin is not a criminal. We must make every effort to stay the deportation of this young man, who believed in the American dream,' Rincon said. 'He left his family to pursue his dream.'"[37]

In a powerful sermon preached at Allen Avenue Unitarian Universalist Church in Portland and included on the Church World Service Immigration and Refugee Program blog, Rev. Rincon relates stories that also show how she uses her position as priest to make a difference. She tells of helping to find fifteen-year-old Sandra (not her real name), whom immigration authorities had arrested at the border and put in a detention center. Sandra's parents sought Rev. Rincon's help because she is a priest, and her clergy connections helped to locate Sandra: "One day, we found Sandra. The stories of how she was treated were horrible . . . no water for hours in the hot sun, and left in a cell alone without understanding what was going on . . . and so on and so on. Because she was a minor they released her to me and her parents." Another story is of a call Rev. Rincon received one Saturday afternoon as she was preparing for a baptism: "I received a call from the child's mother. The police had stopped her husband, and they called immigration. 'He has papers,' she shouted on the phone. 'He has legal status. Why would they do this?' She told me that her husband had gone to the local store to buy the food for the baptism celebration of their child. I hurried to the jail to ask the questions. 'What are the charges?' I asked, and they said, 'No charges, just checking his immigration status.' I showed them his papers, and the officer said, 'Oh, he has to stay here until immigration comes by on Monday.' I explained that I was getting ready to baptize his child and that it seemed unjust that a man who had documents and no other charges was being held all weekend until immigration could come by. It took less than ten minutes on Monday morning to get him released. And people ask me if there is racial profiling in Maine."[38]

Rev. Rincon expresses pride that her daughter, a lawyer in Los Angeles, also engages in justice work for Latinos/as. "During the protests in Arizona around SB 1070,[39] Marissa and ten other activists tied themselves together and lay in the middle of Wilshire Boulevard in L.A., and shut down traffic for three hours," Rev. Rincon relates. "As a result the Los Angeles prosecutor wants them to do jail time for civil disobedience. I was a wreck that day when she called me and said,

'Mom, don't worry, but we're going to protest. I'm not going to give you all the details, but I'm going to be fine.' I was worrying about her. But afterwards when they arrested the protestors, and I saw her on the news, I felt proud. I felt like she really understands that she has a responsibility for her people. She understands her roots, her heritage. So all of this that I've done, she gets it."

In her vision for the future of the church Rev. Rincon includes a gathering of Latina clergywomen. "I want to get the Latina clergywomen together and just talk," she says. "I believe it's important for the healing to begin before we do big picture work: the whole immigration thing, what's going on politically, how we fit in with the perspective that we have. But we can't share it if we're exhausted from pushing up against the system, all the resistance that we get. I feel that if we can make this gathering of women happen, then we'll be in positions of power in different places where we can impact change. We'll be stronger, renewed. We'll feel the Holy Spirit working in us with more intensity, a cataclysmic explosion of spreading the real Good News. It's unfortunate that the Latina women priests don't have the resources that other women clergy have because most of us are in Hispanic ministry where there isn't a lot of funding. And it's a critical time because of the political climate, because of the immigration issue, because of all the hatred that's going back and forth. I think it's going to take coming together and asking what we have to offer out of our experiences as Latina clergy, what we have to offer this chaos that we're in. But in order to get to that conversation, there has to be a time of healing, a time of renewal, a time of sharing our stories. The real Good News is that we still have hope, that we are called to a bigger purpose than just pushing against the institution. The hope is in the creativity that's starting to move in some of us. The church is not going to work any longer the way it's being done. We've got to think about who's coming if we just stand in the pulpit in a nice comfortable church. We've got to go wherever the people are and listen to what the people are experiencing in their lives. We've got to change."

To Rev. Rincon the Divine Feminine is also vital to changing the church. "These images need to constantly be put in front of people's faces," she says. "Not just women clergy, but divine images, like the *Virgen de Guadalupe*. As clergywomen we walk into a meeting, and here we sit with mostly men who are running the meeting. So I believe it's important to put those Divine Feminine images in front of them in our liturgies and in our meetings. Men dominate the Hispanic ministry. And they're not talking about the different shapes the *Virgen de Guadalupe* can take, like the Guadalupe with the big breasts and the big hips. Some women clergy I know have incorporated some of these different images, not only the pretty *Virgen de Guadalupe* with all the stars around her. Rev. Mary Moreno Richardson developed the Guadalupe Art Program, which encourages children to draw images of Guadalupe.[40] And when I was in seminary there was a white woman student, an artist and activist, who put a beautiful picture of the *Virgen de Guadalupe* on the wall of the administration building in the middle of the night. One morning I was going in to the main administration office, and I saw this beautiful picture. It was a very different image of the *Virgen de Guadalupe* holding her breasts. I walked into the administrative office, and Dean Frederica Harris Thompsett said to me, 'When did you do that?' I said, 'Isn't she beautiful? But I didn't do that.' Everybody on campus thought I had done that because I am a *Virgen de Guadalupe* admirer in every way. She is always at the forefront of immigration marches and other justice actions."

Through her work with TengoVoz and as Hispanic Missioner, Rev. Virginia Marie Rincon has been at the forefront of justice ministry. Her prophetic liturgy, advocacy, poetry, *curandismo*, and preaching continue to transform church and society. One of her poetic prayers concludes with these lines:

> I bow my head to the natural process of life. I bow down my head to be anointed in the rainstorms of life. And then raise up my head to your love, raise up my head to your blessing and lastly raise up my arms to receive your love in that way that only you can understand. I am in your complexity and in your Simplicity and in your Glorious Mystery. I am, dear God, ready for the transformative work.

9

Rev. Paul Smith

Copastor
Broadway Church, Kansas City, Missouri

As Rev. Paul Smith gives me a tour of Broadway Church's "Faces of Jesus" collection, he sparkles with enthusiasm. For 40 years he has been collecting these images. In 1997, he added a wide variety of images, framed them, and gave them to Broadway Church. In 2007, he added another 60 pictures, and now all 240 are permanently installed in hallway galleries in the spacious church building. Not only the scope, but also the diversity of this collection impresses me. Here Jesus looks out at me from faces of various races and cultures. The collection includes images of Jesus as female and androgynous, as well as male. First to catch my attention is a painting by Lucy Synk titled "Evolution." Here an androgynous Spirit reaches out toward male and female figures with brown skin and straight black hair, standing arm in arm atop a pyramid of creation that rises from seashells to monkeys. Paul comments: "The Spirit not only originates creation, but also continues to mold and shape humankind through the sacred process of evolution. There is no conflict between the scientific path and the spiritual path."

Paul and I walk up the stairs to the third floor of the church, where I see the Lucy Synk painting that shone gloriously on the front wall of the sanctuary as we sang "Welcome Our Sister-Brother Creator" in the service that Sunday morning. Synk titles this picture "Ruach" and comments: "This was inspired by my discovery that the

Hebrew word 'Ruach' ('spirit,' 'breath') is feminine in gender, and that throughout the Old Testament, Hebrew terms that are feminine in gender are used to speak of the Spirit of God." Paul gives further explanation: "In this image the Spirit, or breath of God, issues from a strikingly feminine image of the Divine. I understand this to be, in New Testament terms, Christ Sophia, present at creation and the instrument of all creation. 'For by Christ all things in heaven and earth were created' (Colossians 1:16)." Close by "Ruach" is Robert Lentz's "Christ Sophia," with this inscription: "In this portrayal Christ Sophia is placed in an egg-shaped mandala to connote her fertility. She holds the ancient Cro-Magnon statue Venus of Willendorf, a pre-historic figure of the Divine as female. The Greek letters in her halo stand for 'I am who I am,' the divine name given Moses at the burning bush. She points to herself as if to say, 'I am She; know me now more fully.'" Another Lentz painting, "Dance of Creation," portrays the connection between "Hagia Sophia, Holy Wisdom, and Logos, Pattern of all Creation, incarnate in the Cosmic Christ."

Winding up and down stairs, Paul becomes more animated as he points to one picture and caption after another. I don't see an empty space on the walls in the long hallways and stairways of the three-storied Broadway Church. "Jesus in the Soup Line," by Fritz Ichenberg, shows the Risen Cosmic Christ continuing "to identify with all the marginalized and oppressed." In "Compassion Mandala," by Robert Lentz, we see "the androgynous Cosmic Christ holding the world in loving arms." Bohdan Piasecki's "The Last Supper" was commissioned by a group of Catholics who advocate opening the priesthood to women. Paul comments: "In order to counter Leonardo da Vinci's powerful men-only image of the Last Supper, here is another setting of the Last Supper as a Jewish Passover meal with women and children present. An argument used against women priests is that there were no women at the Last Supper. Certainly women and children would be present at the Passover meal." Then we come to Janet McKenzie's "Jesus of the People," winner of the 1997 *National Catholic Reporter* contest for the best contemporary image of Jesus. McKenzie used an African American woman as a model for this androgynous image. McKenzie said she "wanted to incorporate women who have been so neglected and left out." McKenzie's picture also includes the "yin yang symbol, representing perfect harmony and respect for Eastern spirituality," and a feather, "paying homage to Native American spirituality."

The "Faces of Jesus" collection includes passion images that challenge cultural prejudices. In Becky Harrelson's "The Crucifixion of Christ," the plaque on the cross above Christ's head reads "faggot" in capital letters. Harrelson explains in the caption: "Today gays are socially acceptable and religiously justifiable targets for hate. And just like gays, Jesus was made a hate target in his time because he dared to be different, to tell the truth even though his words and his position subverted the religious establishment." Paul comments on this picture: "The artist is not saying that Jesus was gay. One could substitute other words that condemn and express violence toward others. Homophobia is the last acceptable prejudice, widespread in our culture and bolstered by a heretical distortion of Christianity. We must see rejection of gays for what it is—violence toward that which God has created and called 'good.'" Also, in the collection is a photograph of Edwina Sandys' 1975 bronze statue "Christa," depicting a woman on the cross. When this statue was first exhibited, Deborah Sokolove[1] commented: "Some visitors to the exhibition called 'Christa' an abomination, at once a challenge to the immutable truth that Jesus was a man and a pornographic invitation towards the further abuse of women. Still others found in it great beauty, truth, and even comfort as they considered that Jesus' self-giving was not about his gender, but rather his humanity. For these viewers, the 'Christa' seemed to say that wherever women are being abused, there Christ is still being crucified." Another female crucifixion image, by an unknown artist, is titled "After El Greco." The artist has replaced the male Christ figure on the cross in El Greco's painting with a female Christ figure. Paul comments: "Christ on the cross identifies with all the persecuted of the world. Women are the largest group on earth who have been and today are consistently persecuted and denied opportunity to be all that they are meant to be. Ironically, it is often religion itself that supports this oppression."

Near the end of the "Faces of Jesus" tour, Paul smiles as he points out two luminous images of Sophia. Pamela Matthews' "Sophia" holds the world in a gentle embrace, arms blending into the long swirls of her hair. Bathed in golden pink light, She closes Her eyes and rests Her head on one arm. This inscription accompanies the painting:

"Matthews pictures Christ as a loving woman. Early Christian teachers spoke of Christ as 'our Mother.' Clement of Alexandria in the second century said, 'The Word, Christ, is both father and mother.' Anselm in the eleventh century stated, 'But you also, Jesus are you not also Mother? Are you not Mother, who as a hen gathers her own chicks under her wings? Truly, you also are Mother.' Julian of Norwich in the fourteenth century wrote, 'but our Mother, Jesus alone—carries us with endless loving.'" Alex Grey's "Sophia" in glowing hues of purple, pink, and gold is depicted as the "Mother-Light—the living, guiding presence of wisdom." The inscription continues: "She is the Goddess as a vessel of rebirth and spiritual transformation. Sophia is revealed here as guide for the times of crisis humanity is now facing, having embraced the entire world in her spirit-nourishing heart. Her halo symbolizes wisdom beyond rational understanding. In Sophia, infinite vision and wisdom are united as one level of being. Male and female were torn apart in the story of Eden and have yet to come together again. The Christian church has continued the war on women by eviscerating the feminine in the name of God while it divinized the masculine. It is vitally important to the healing of the world to restore a fully feminine image of the Divine Spirit so male and female can be united once again."

Paul points out pictures of Martin Luther King Jr., Dorothy Day, Gandhi, Hildegard of Bingen, and Mother Theresa, saying that they also are "Faces of Jesus." Voice rising with excitement, Paul talks about his belief that we all are divine. "We all are the light of the world," he explains. "Jesus not only said, 'I am the light of the world,'[2] but 'You are the light of the world.'"[3] To emphasize this truth, Paul has placed a framed mirror as the final piece in the "Faces of Jesus" exhibit.

Paul Smith's story begins at Water Tower Baptist Church in St. Louis, Missouri. "I was enrolled in the Baptist church before I was born," Paul says. "I'm Baptist born, Baptist bred. I grew up in a Baptist church and loved it. It was a lifesaver." Paul was an only child of parents he describes as "dysfunctional." Because of his parents' constant arguing, he felt that church was the only sane and safe place he could go. He says he'll always appreciate Water Tower Baptist Church because it "saved" his life. When he was only eleven or twelve, Paul began asking questions like, "How come they do this in the Bible, and we don't do this now? How does this fit?" He didn't get many answers.

When Paul was eighteen, he became the youth minister at Fourth Baptist Church, a large inner city church in St. Louis. He inherited a camp for disadvantaged youth. This camp was Paul's first experience of bringing change to the church. When he realized that he could do anything he wanted with this camp, he thought, "How would it be to dispense with all the Bible studies and just get up early in the morning and play music out on the hills and have quiet time for fifteen minutes? Then we could have some interesting subjects to talk about, have small groups where everybody shared and prayed for each other, and then have a campfire at night where we just sat and watched the fire and then sang a few songs." For fifteen years Paul led this St. Louis citywide youth camp. For a month in the summer, thousands of teenagers attended camp during the week, and college students came on the weekends. "It was my chance to try church out, what I thought might work," Paul says. "It was incredible, connecting with God in a real way and connecting with one another."

At Washington University in St. Louis, Paul majored in chemical engineering. "I was there on a full academic scholarship, the only way I could afford to go," Paul recalls. "My second year at the university, I was climbing around at the top of a big chemical tank at Mallinckrodt Chemical Company with my chemical engineering class and thought, 'What in the world am I doing up here? This is terrible!' I was a straight-A student in high school, and back then all the guys who were straight-A students became engineers. So that's what I was going to do. Then one day driving to school, I heard Earl Nightingale[4] on the radio say, 'What do you love to do most? If you can make your living at it, do it.' I thought, 'What I love to do most is see people find spiritual renewal, spiritual connections in life through Jesus. That's what I love. Well, I guess I ought to be a preacher.'" Paul told his pastor, who said, "Oh, that's really fine." Paul has worked for the church all his life, except for one summer when he was a teenager and had a job at Singer Sewing Machine Company.

After graduating from Washington University with a BA degree in psychology, Paul Smith went to Midwestern Baptist Theological Seminary in Kansas City. Panic attacks that he thinks he'd had all his life became worse his first year in seminary. "We didn't know about agoraphobia[5] then, but I was having lots of panic attacks," Paul says. "Lofton Hudson had just opened his counseling center, the first

Christian counseling center in Kansas City. I found the help I needed through counseling with him." Some churches in St. Louis wanted him to come on staff, so he dropped out of his first year in seminary and returned to St. Louis, where he served as associate pastor at Fourth Baptist and then as associate pastor at Webster Groves Baptist.

A businessman and deacon at Compton Heights Baptist Church in St. Louis, Clyde Montgomery, adopted Paul as his "spiritual son" and began to introduce him to the neo-Pentecostal renewal healing ministry, the Order of St. Luke.[6] Clyde paid Paul's way to Pittsburgh for a healing service at an evangelical reformed church.

Paul said to Clyde, "All these people you're with are charismatics."

"What's that?" Clyde asked.

"They all pray in tongues."

"What's that?"

Clyde was appreciating the spiritual experience without having labels for it. He helped connect Paul with Tommy Tyson, a charismatic Methodist minister, and Francis McNutt, a Catholic priest who was a leader in the Catholic charismatic renewal movement. "They helped shape me because they were very enthusiastic about their experience with the Spirit," Paul says. "I found something a little bit more like the Book of Acts, experiencing the Spirit. There was a move from my head to a little more experience. I've always led with my head because I'd shut down my emotions to survive at home."

After three years in St. Louis, Paul returned to Midwestern Baptist Seminary to finish his last two years. Back in Kansas City, he planned to visit many churches before he decided which one to join. The second church he visited was Broadway Baptist, because he knew the pastor, Cloyce Davis, who had worked in the seminary library. Broadway's music minister had just left. Since Paul had served as music director at Compton Heights Baptist Church in St. Louis while attending Washington University, playing piano and organ all through college, he took the offer to become the music minister of Broadway. When he finished seminary in 1963, the church hired him as associate pastor. In 1966, Rev. Cloyce Davis left, and Broadway called Rev. Paul Smith as pastor. He's been the pastor of the church ever since then.

From the time he was a youth minister, Paul has wanted to reform the church. Paul believes this drive comes from his personality type on the Enneagram,[7] which he calls "the most powerful psychospiritual tool around." Paul is an Enneagram One, a Reformer. Paul further describes this type: "We look at something and think how it could be better. That's the way I've looked at the church. Enneagram Ones are perfectionists; we need to be perfect for ourselves, not because of what other people think. We have a problem with anger; we can't be angry, but we are angry. We're obsessive and have a lot of anxiety. The redeeming part is that we're reformers. We're willing to be leaders and do whatever is necessary to make things better. We have this drive to change the world! Nothing less will do. All along I've wanted to reform the church." Beginning with reforming the youth camp in St. Louis when he was eighteen, Paul moved on to make changes at Broadway Baptist Church.

The first change Rev. Paul Smith made was to establish small groups in the church. Enthusiastic response followed. People delighted in the opportunity to share their lives and be prayed for in small groups. After that, nobody wanted to go to traditional Bible and doctrine classes with only the first five minutes given to connecting with one another. So Sunday school and Training Union[8] died, but Broadway had 400 people in small groups. Broadway became the "in" church in Kansas City, voted the best church in the city by some of the local magazines. The church grew from 100 people in Sunday morning worship to 400 or 500 in three services. The budget doubled and tripled and then quadrupled. "We were enormously successful—had a big band and orchestra," Paul says. "For me that was a combination eco trip and genuinely wanting to see things improve."

The next change Paul made at Broadway Baptist Church was to move from hierarchical to team leadership. He wanted to change what he calls the "star system of pastoring, the rent-a-shepherd system." He believes this system kills churches by making the pastor the star. So Paul built a pastoral leadership team that consisted of all men at first. Then the Spirit began saying to him, "What about the women?" Two years of intensive biblical study convinced him that he had been wrong in his belief that men should be in charge at home and at church. Paul looked around and saw Marcia Fleischman serving as a leader on the Panel of American Women in the community and working with the children at the church. He thought, "She must be a good speaker, and she's so sharp." Marcia pushed for equality of women in the church, and Paul began adding women, including Marcia, to the leadership team.

After Paul came to believe in the equality of women in the church and home, he planned a special occasion for his wife, Karen. He tells this story in one of his books: "I moved the trestle table over in front of our large New England fireplace, cooked the steaks, and served them. Then at the appropriate grand moment I said, 'Karen, I want to tell you that I have changed my mind about husbands being in charge and wives obeying. I have decided we should be partners in our marriage and both be in charge. We should each offer our different gifts and make all decisions mutually.' I raised my glass in a toast while she stared at me, bewildered. I thought I had just freed the slaves, and she didn't know what in the world I was talking about. In her mind we had always made decisions together anyway, so what was the big deal. But it was a big deal for me—and for Broadway."[9]

In 1985, Broadway Baptist Church, which had been ordaining women as deacons for some time, now began ordaining women as pastors. At this time, a year after the Southern Baptist Convention adopted a resolution opposing the ordination of women, few Southern Baptist churches ordained women, and to this day the majority of Southern Baptist churches refuse to ordain women.[10] So the ordination of women caused controversy at Broadway, and some people left the church.

Even though Paul encouraged Broadway to ordain women, he came to believe that ordination of anyone is not good for the church. "It's the worst thing that ever happened to how the church calls forth everyone's gifts," Paul says. "Ordination is the way we exalt certain spiritual gifts and deflate other gifts. It's great for the person who's ordained, but everybody else is sitting there thinking, 'What am I?' If they think they've got gifts, nobody recognizes them or gives them a label. So I went on a campaign. I had my name taken off the sign in front of the church and off the bulletin. The pulpit chairs came down, and I sat in the congregation like everybody else. I dressed like everybody else, no coat and tie. The church bought into the ministry of all believers. We had team teaching; other people would teach besides me. We call it 'teaching,' not 'preaching,' because who wants to be preached at?"

After the worship service one Sunday morning a woman who had been visiting Broadway Baptist for a little while had this exchange with a church member sitting next to her:

The visitor began, "I'd like to talk to the minister. Could you show me the minister?"

"Well, I'm one of the ministers," the Broadway member answered.

Bewildered, especially since the church member she was talking with was a woman, the visitor continued, "Well, like a pastor?"

"Which one? We have five pastors." The member saw that the visitor was frustrated, so she said, "Why don't you go talk to Paul over there?"

The visitor stomped up to Paul and said, "What are you trying to do in this church, play 'find the pastor?'"

"We're all ministers; we all believe that," Paul said. "How can I help you?"

It turned out that the visitor needed someone to talk with and to pray for her. The church member she'd been sitting by was on the church's healing prayer team and was just the person she needed. Paul brought them back together, and they talked and prayed. Paul says that the visitor got "exactly what she needed from the real minister."

Because of his strong belief that all members of the church have ministry gifts, Paul had earlier initiated a spiritual gifts workshop. He had developed a series of ten sermons on spiritual gifts and then realized that people needed some way to discover their gifts. The spiritual gifts workshop helped people to think about their gifts and to get feedback through questionnaires sent to people who could help identify their gifts. "People would come out of the workshop exhilarated that they had spiritual gifts and that they were in the ministry," Paul says. "Then we had a bank of people who knew what their spiritual gifts were. If somebody wanted something done in the church, we'd ask, 'Who's got this ministry gift?'" Missionaries translated the spiritual gifts workshop into German, Portuguese, and Spanish. People on staff at Midwestern Baptist Theological Seminary wanted to use the workshop, but found that it had every gift mentioned in the New Testament, including speaking in tongues, prophecy, and healing the sick. They said, "We can't do that." So Paul developed a non-charismatic version of the gifts workshop. Then he taught the workshop at a Unity ministerial school, and developed a "more expansive" Unity[11] version. The latest revision, Paul says, has progressed to be "much more integral."[12]

The spiritual gifts workshop taught that women have all the gifts that men have, so Broadway Baptist decided to call women as pastors. When the church moved to women pastors, one of the male leaders said, "I can't come to this church anymore; I don't want women running things." Several men with this attitude left the church with their families. Paul admits that working with women pastors was "not natural" for him because of his experiences with his mother and his wife. "My mom had frequent schizophrenic episodes while I was growing up," Paul recalls. "I would come home and find her in the closet, laughing. I would have to be the one to call the doctor because Dad was off having an affair. My wife and I had to spend much time in counseling, working on issues we both brought to the marriage. I knew that somehow I wasn't very romantic, but I didn't know why. So I was not at home with women. But Jesus was comfortable with women. And Marcia was wonderful. I could be comfortable working with her."

As Paul was becoming more comfortable with women, he began to think, "If we're all in the image of God, why do we always call God 'He' and never 'She'?" Paul did a thorough theological exploration, as he had done with other changes he had initiated in the church: small groups, team leadership, all members as ministers according to their spiritual gifts, and ordination of women. As he researched and read, it became clear to him that the church also needed to reform worship language. Paul began teaching classes on the biblical basis for including female divine images. A two-year discussion and debate ensued. Groups of people from outside the church came also to express their views for or against inclusive language. "It shook up a lot of people," Paul recalls.

Broadway Baptist eventually voted officially to begin using gender-inclusive language; the church voted that it was okay to call God "Mother" and "She" in worship services. "That's the Baptist way, to vote on things," Paul says, "When we voted for gender-inclusive language, we lost some members. We taped all my teachings. I remember listening to myself and whenever I would call God 'Mother' or 'She,' I noticed I would start breathing heavy because I'd be nervous about it. It wasn't natural for me. My most powerful name for God is 'Abba,' or

'Daddy.'" Paul acknowledges that it's an ongoing challenge for him to use the Divine Feminine. Even after teaching, advocating, and writing the book *Is It Okay to Call God "Mother"?: Considering the Feminine Face of God*,[13] Paul says that it's still not natural for him to use feminine divine names: "When I wrote that book, I knew it was right and it was a justice issue. I was following truth rather than what appealed to me."

Andy Cullen, a Presbyterian pastor, and Paul have been best friends for twenty years. After Paul talked with him about gender-inclusive language, Rev. Cullen tried to teach female images of God in his Presbyterian church. He didn't find church members too receptive, but his daughters and some other people listened to his teaching. "You know, I think about my daughters," Andy said to Paul. "I don't want them to grow up thinking God's a man, because like you say, 'If God's male, then they're not very godly. They're not in the image of God.'" Paul believes that the Divine Feminine is the most powerful channel to get people to begin expanding beyond traditional Christianity and to see that the church needs to change. "It's more and more apparent to people that women are equal and that the image of God has to be both male and female," Paul explains. "Both men and women are saying, 'I go to work on Monday morning, and there's equality, but I've just come out of church on Sunday morning, and there's not equality at all. There's something wrong with that.'" Because Paul saw this need for reforming the church, he wrote his book to give biblical support for calling God "Mother."

After Broadway Baptist voted for gender-inclusive language, the church started calling God "She," "Mother," or "Mother-Father." Paul says, "We tried 'Father-Mother,' but I like 'Mother-Father' because we need to start with 'Mother,' and it just sounds better." Visitors still come to Paul after worship services and ask, "Why do you call God 'She'?" He tells them that God both includes and transcends male and female and that using only masculine terms for God discounts the Divine in all of us. Paul says that the Baptist democratic system also helped the church accept this language change: "You know Baptists. Once we vote on something, people may not agree with the vote, but we did vote on it. The majority spoke." Paul believes that when we begin to question our image of God, we begin to open up, and that once we begin to open up, "then the possibilities are endless."

About five years after Broadway Baptist began including feminine divine language in worship services, some of the gay church members said to Paul: "You've changed your mind about women ministers and so many issues. Why don't you go back and read the Bible again and change your mind about gays?" Paul had thought the Bible taught that homosexuality was wrong, and Broadway had been "benignly anti-gay," telling the church organist that he shouldn't go to gay bars. Paul knew that some church members struggled with homosexuality. One church member had gone to counseling intended to change his sexual orientation, and the church had prayed for him. But it became clear that he was gay, and nothing was going to change him. Paul's wife, Karen, was the first one to say to this church member, "You know, maybe you're okay just like you are." Paul finally decided to study what the Bible says about homosexuality and to do thorough theological research on this issue just as he had on other controversial issues. "I realized I had been totally, absolutely, incredibly, 100 percent wrong," he says. "I began to teach some classes and to write about my discovery.[14] This issue was really tough for the congregation, and tension grew around it. One of our associate pastors, whose wife was anti-gay, opposed the whole thing."

Broadway Baptist Church invited guest speakers with varying viewpoints to address the issue of homosexuality. Prominent pro-gay speakers, like Peggy Campolo[15] and Paul Simpson Duke,[16] spoke and led discussions. The church discussed and debated the issue for two years. When the church was about ready to vote on whether or not to become gay affirming, a group of people decided that they didn't want any more changes because every change had resulted in the loss of church members. This group met with Paul to tell him they didn't want him to say anything controversial anymore. "They told me I'd have to check my sermons out with them," Paul recalls. "They had gotten people on the bandwagon for their cause. They weren't particularly anti-gay, but they thought the issue wasn't important enough to lose any of their friends over. Half of the church leaders sided with them. They recommended that Marcia and I be fired." The church voted to keep Marcia and Paul as copastors, but the vote was close. The opposing group, close to half the church, left to start another church. "The pain was excruciating, the fact that these people I'd met with and loved and worked with wanted to get rid of me after thirty years here," Paul says. "That really hurt. It was also really hard on Marcia, who at the time was getting ready for a lung transplant. It was just awful." After the opposing group left, Broadway immediately voted to become gay affirming.

Kansas City Baptist Association had been threatening to oust Broadway Baptist Church for about twenty years. The Association tried to get rid of the church upon learning that Paul didn't believe in eternal hell,[17] then again when Broadway ordained women pastors. At that point the Association also accused the church of being charismatic. "The local Kansas City Baptist Association would then affect the state convention, and then it's the state that removes you from the Southern Baptist Convention (SBC)," Paul explains. "Finally when we became gay affirming and started doing holy unions, and that made the newspapers, then the Missouri Baptist Convention voted to remove us from the SBC. That made the news. We were on TV—heresy, local Baptist church removed from the SBC! I just loved it! We were hoping that we could wait long enough to be thrown out and make the news. Then the word would get out that they're some Baptists who think it's okay to be gay." After being removed from the SBC in 2004, Broadway Baptist Church became Broadway Church. Paul began to feel a new freedom: "I no longer think about looking over my shoulder. Now I can say and teach whatever I'm learning."

Soon after Broadway Church became welcoming and affirming, Paul began to wonder about his own sexual orientation. "I run everything through my brain, so I can't have feelings unless it's theologically okay to have them," he says. "Changing my mind about gays freed up something in my head to question why I was so unromantic. I had just figured that's the way I was with my wife and with women in general. Then I began to realize that it was more than that. I gradually got in touch with those feelings, and I came out to myself. When I told my wife, Karen, that I'd decided I'm gay, her response was, 'What a relief!' She knew there was something missing. I was contributing to our difficulties because I wasn't able to love her like she needed to be loved." Paul and copastor Marcia Fleischman visited the long-term members of the church in their homes to tell them that Paul was gay. They all said, "You're the same person we've always known; there's nothing different about that." Some of the older people said, "Well, we don't understand any of that, but we've always loved you, and you're the same person." Then Paul met with all the church members and came out to them. No one left the church or was even upset by Paul's coming to realize he was gay. Karen and Paul had already announced that they were separated.

Paul and Karen, who had been married for thirty-three years, remain friends. Paul's children and grandchildren have also been affirming of his coming out. His son, Monte, named for his spiritual mentor Clyde Montgomery, told Paul that he was proud of him. His daughter, Beth, said that she had wondered all along if he were gay, but she didn't ever say anything. Paul says that when he came out, "Beth loved it!" In 2007, Paul went through the tragic loss of Beth, who died of colon cancer when she was only forty-one. "We were very close," he says. "Beth was a single mom with one daughter who was recently legally adopted by Beth's best friends. My granddaughter, Dahlby, now age twelve, spends every Saturday with me and my partner, Ivan. She and her new family know Ivan and I are gay and are great with it."

When Paul came out to Andy Cullen, his Presbyterian pastor friend, Andy was shocked. Paul and Andy had been meeting every week for lunch for years and had gone through many things together. "When I told Andy I was gay, he shut down and didn't say much," Paul says. "I found out later that he hyperventilated and felt sick for the entire week. It was such a shock. He didn't know what to do. It took him a whole year to work through it, but now he's the poster boy for Presbyterian pastors. He is so pro-gay that he goes around and speaks on the pro-gay circuit." Paul believes that what changes people most is knowing someone who is gay.

Paul describes the changes in his spiritual life after he came out: "It moved from my head to my heart. My experiences with God began to deepen. I had been hanging around charismatics who were very heartfelt, but I just couldn't get it because I was denying so much of myself." About this time Paul began to explore integral philosophy, especially that developed by Ken Wilber.[18] This philosophy gave him a new framework for prayer. "I had practiced listening to God for forty years," Paul says. "I would ask God about situations and then journal. I would hear some things that were amazingly prophetic and gave me guidance and encouragement. But I didn't know anything about meditation. Now that came alive for me, and I began to practice what

I call 'connecting prayer' and 'being prayer.' I don't think prayer is saying things to God. Prayer is connecting with spiritual realities."

The theological center of the Gospels is the transfiguration[19] of Jesus, not the crucifixion and the resurrection, Paul believes. "The transfiguration was the central spiritual event of Jesus' life. It's the center of all the Gospels. Jesus took his disciples Peter, James, and John up a mountain to pray. Jesus got away; he evidently had been doing this for a long time. Jesus' spiritual energy systems became so radiant that they were visible to the disciples as 'his face shone like the sun, and his clothes became dazzling white.'[20] Then Jesus talked to Moses and Elijah, who had been dead for hundreds of years and who were his spiritual guides. Jesus had just told the disciples that they were going to see what the kingdom of God looks like. Then we have the transfiguration with Jesus becoming so numinous that he glowed and talked with spiritual guides. He needed guidance and encouragement to face his upcoming death, consequence of his attacking the oppressive religious, political, and social power structures of the day. The commentaries address theological ideas present in the account of the transfiguration, such as Moses representing the law and Elijah representing the prophets. But they don't talk about Jesus having a conversation with his spiritual guides. I have spiritual guides, what I call the 'intimate dimension' of experiencing the Spirit through other spiritual beings. I've found that an amazing number of people have guides they don't ever talk about, because they don't think it's okay. If it's good enough for Jesus, it's good enough for me." As I listen to Paul talk about the centrality of the transfiguration, I recall the prominence of the glowing transfiguration images in the "Faces of Jesus" exhibit in one of the main entrances to Broadway Church.

Recently Paul has published a book entitled *Integral Christianity: The Spirit's Call to Evolve*,[21] and has finished a year of teaching each chapter in the book. Paul comments on this experience: "People have responded in various ways. What's lacking is a way to lead them into this personally. A half-hour on Sunday morning isn't going to do it. When I retire, I think I'll start small groups and connect with people to help them get in touch with their guides—not just talk about God, but to experience male and female divinity. I think prayer is becoming conscious of Divine presence. The deepest form of prayer is what I call 'being prayer' or 'abiding prayer.' Mystics in the Eastern traditions and

Christian mystics, such as Meister Eckhart[22] and St. Teresa of Avila,[23] teach us about contemplative states. In the deepest state we experience God as pure consciousness, that divine consciousness that was in Jesus and is also in us. Jesus said that we are all gods.[24] The goal is to live in that consciousness and then manifest it, like Jesus did, to change the world."

Rev. Paul Smith has been changing the world by changing the church for many years. Paul's prophetic work came to my attention through his book *Is It Okay to Call God "Mother"?: Considering the Feminine Face of God*. This was the first book I'd read by a male theologian who gave biblical support for feminine divine language in the church. I was deeply impressed by the strong case Paul made, and wrote an endorsement for his book in which I stated how encouraging it was "to hear an evangelical male voice affirm the necessity of feminine images of God." In this book Paul makes the connection between violence against women and male-dominated church leadership and language: "The war on women is the longest running, most destructive, and most pervasive war on earth. Many Christians are so oblivious to the war on women that they do not see how they participate in it—for many, every time the church meets. We are so accustomed to our church habits and have them so religiously justified we do not see the male domination in our church leadership and religious language."[25]

In *Is It Okay to Call God "Mother"?: Considering the Feminine Face of God,* Paul makes clear the importance of including female divine names and images in public worship. "Churches have been making God exclusively masculine in public for a long time, and changing in private will not reverse the damage," he states. "This is a decidedly public issue. Nothing will change business as usual in our churches unless those of us who are convicted by the Holy Spirit first change our own behavior and then work towards change in the church."[26] Paul goes on to give a sequence of steps for changing worship language: stop using gender-exclusive words for people, stop using masculine pronouns for God, start calling God "Mother" in personal prayer life, experiment with using feminine pronouns and metaphors for God with others, ask others to study this issue, encourage worship leaders to change language about persons, promote the adoption of a church service policy of gender-neutral language for God, encourage incorporation of feminine divine metaphors and pronouns into worship services.

At the conclusion of his book, Paul quotes Teilhard de Chardin, "Faith has need of the whole truth." Then Paul makes his final call to action: "Now is the moment in history for the church to see more of this truth in the awesome light of God's revelation of herself as recorded in Scripture. Is it okay to call God 'Mother'? It is not only okay but it is just and holy, righteous and necessary. Now is the time to break the conspiracy of silence about the feminine face of God. God's Word is rousing itself again, wrestling itself free from the grip of patriarchy and sexism."[27]

When I began research for this book on stories of ministers who are changing the church, I remembered Paul and found his website. I discovered that Paul's voice for the Divine Feminine has grown even stronger through the years. One of his recent "teachings" is titled "The Cover-up of the Divine Feminine: Is it Okay to Call God, 'Goddess'?"[28] Paul refers to Dan Brown's popular book *The Da Vinci Code*,[29] saying that its premise is true: there has been a cover-up of the Divine Feminine. In this "teaching," Paul further states: "The feminine has been demonized and called unclean for thousands of years. As long as the worst thing you can call a boy or man is 'sissy' or 'gay,' the war on the feminine is still going on. The most sexist hour of the American week is on Sunday morning. An observer going into most church services would notice that they have only men as priests, pastors, and deacons. As long as God is male, then male is God. Using exclusively masculine words to the exclusion of feminine words such as 'Goddess' says something that Jesus never intended, that God is more like a man than a woman. As long as we refuse to challenge the male-only divine images deeply imbedded in our psyche, women will not be seen or treated as equals with men. 'God' has become a male word. If you don't think 'God' is a male word, just use the word 'Goddess' and see the reaction. If the word 'God' included both male and female, there would not be that reaction. So the answer to my beginning question today—Is it okay to call God 'Goddess'?—is yes, of course. This is an exciting time for all of us as the Spirit of Goddess is calling us to continue the revolution that began in the early church and was stopped and covered up. It's a great time for women, for gays, for all of us to grow in our understanding of our Creator and Her creation."

In my interview with Rev. Paul Smith at Broadway Church, he kept repeating that we have to let the Divine "out of the male prison," that locking the Divine in "a male prison as the big guy upstairs blocks transformation." Paul elaborates on including the Divine Feminine to support social justice and to expand spirituality: "It's the first opening to include feminine as well as masculine divine images. Exclusively masculine symbols have been so degrading for women. Including feminine divine images is connected to other justice issues. Valuing the feminine will value all people, wherever they are on the scale from homosexual to heterosexual. Now I see the Divine Feminine connected to expanding the whole image of the Divine to include the infinite, intimate, and inner dimensions. We need to get rid of the image of 'the big man in the sky,' and making Jesus the only divine being totally robs us of our divinity."

Changing both language and visual symbols to include the Divine Feminine will help people expand their experiences of the Divine, Paul says. "It's very important to have the words 'She,' 'Mother,' and other feminine references. Many Catholics relate to God as Mary. They found a way when the church said 'no' to the Divine Feminine. They found a way—good for them. Others find the way through 'Sophia' or 'Mary Magdalene.' Like words, visual images are powerful. It seems to me that today we are more in a period similar to that of the medieval church where the only Bible people had was in the form of statues and images at church because few people could read. Today everybody can read, but they don't. So it's more about images. The reason I have the 'Faces of Jesus' exhibit is that people are going to remember these images. That's why my teachings are filled with PowerPoint images, and our worship services are filled with visual images. That's the way to sneak under our cognitive defenses and move to our spirit. I don't know why forty years ago I started collecting pictures of Jesus. I'm a head person. But these pictures just speak to my heart. I don't look at them; they look at me. Whatever consciousness the artist had in painting the picture, that connects with me. It didn't used to, but now it does. Now I know what I'm doing." Paul mentions one picture in the "Faces of Jesus" collection that people either love or hate: "Virtuous Giving," by Michael Floyd, a former member of Broadway Church and graduate of Midwestern Baptist Seminary. Paul comments on this picture: "Jesus is seen as a pregnant woman on a birthing table ready to give birth. Meister Eckhart said, 'What does God do all day long? God gives birth.'"

Paul believes that experience is a key to people's including the feminine in their images of the Divine. "One good experience would take care of it all," he says. "The medieval Christian mystics can refer to Jesus as feminine because of their experience. You can go only so far with the cognitive, and the other has to be experienced and practiced. I think Jesus really did experience God as a Daddy and a Mama. And we all experience and feel our divinity more when we hear 'She' and 'He' in church."

Bringing change to the church has cost Paul the loss of some friends and church members. Also, Paul's physical health has suffered. In the middle of the church conflict over homosexuality, his heart stopped. The paramedics had to use the defibrillation paddles six times to get it going again. A defibrillator was permanently implanted in his chest. But Paul has not considered leaving the church because he believes in using the structure we have. "You've got to end up with a religious organization," he says. "The minute two spiritual people get together, then you have a religious structure. So why invent the wheel all over again? Many spiritual teachers are now saying that it's not enough to have just personal enlightenment; we need collective enlightenment. We need a community; we need to get together and talk. Christians have already got that. Let's just use the structure we've got. If Broadway had not allowed me to grow, I would have had to leave this church. I'm not willing to sacrifice my spiritual growth for the church, because my spiritual growth is all I have to offer the church. It would be stupid to be here as the minister and not give what I have to offer. Most pastors have to change churches in order to grow spiritually. You grow a little bit where you are, and then the church says 'no.' It's like the crawdad syndrome. Crawdads are always pulling at the crawdad that's trying to get out, to pull it back down. But Broadway Church has allowed me to grow."

The church should encourage everyone to grow, Paul believes. "The Christian life is about evolving. God is an evolutionist. Pure Consciousness before the Big Bang said, 'It's time to manifest something. Let's have a Big Bang and start the world, and let's keep it evolving.' Here we are after fourteen billion years, and the world is still evolving. Spiritually we're evolving to new levels. Gregory of Nyssa,[30] in the fourth century, talked about the eternal progress of the soul. He believed that God was infinite, and that the soul progresses infinitely. The soul never arrives. Evolution has been unconscious or instinctual, but now we're at the level of consciousness where we can decide to evolve, because that's what the Christian life is. The Christian life is not about being saved. We're all saved. The Christian life is about realizing and manifesting our divinity. Jesus was our model, and we're supposed to do life like Jesus did it. We're still learning and growing, and then have a drive to make that manifest by changing the world."

Paul continues to make his spiritual growth manifest in the world. One way is by picketing at a large Baptist church in Kansas City. When this church invites people from Focus on the Family[31] to hold an anti-gay meeting, Rev. Paul Smith and Rev. Marcia Fleischman stand in front of the church holding big signs that read, "Gay is good. God loves gays." The last time they picketed, the Associated Press reporter interviewed them. When the reporter showed his anti-gay bias, Paul said, "Well, I'm gay." This statement got on the Associated Press newsline. Fred Phelps leads his anti-gay protestors to picket Broadway Baptist regularly. When someone wrote "sodomites" on the sign in front of the church, the first response Broadway got was from the Jewish Federation, offering to help pay for a new sign.

Although the Jewish Federation supported Broadway Church's prophetic stand, most religious institutions resist change, Paul says. "What institutions do best is defend themselves against change. Churches do it particularly well because they think they are defending God. Pastors, priests, bishops, denominational personnel, and seminary professors are hired to preserve the religious institution, not change it. They are hired to stop trouble, not make it. Once you have entered the professional ministry, you usually don't get to change your beliefs or practices without leaving. Change can only come from current church leaders if they are brave, sufficiently outraged, and, at times, willing to lose their jobs. The most difficult challenge is that they must be willing to do their own inner work so that when they press for change, they are not just being obnoxious."

Like many pastors, Paul has had to wrestle with what he calls "terminal niceness." He says that pastors have the psychological makeup to get along with people and take care of them. "We have been taught that leaders are to be servants and not troublemakers. But those two are not exclusive of each other. We are to serve God and not our selfish ambitions, and sometimes serving God means making trouble. There is a time to be kind and a time to be harsh. Slavery is wrong and its remnants continue to oppress African Americans. Patriarchy is wrong and oppresses women. Heterosexism is wrong and oppresses gays. I would certainly not appear on a panel to discuss slavery where a representative of the Ku Klux Klan was also on the panel to defend the idea of racism. I am no longer willing to be on a panel to discuss gay issues where there is someone present to represent the anti-gay side. That question is settled, and I will not lend legitimacy to any discussion of it that pretends it is still open for debate."

The original vision of all religious traditions, Paul believes, is to lead in changing the world for the better, to be a step ahead of the culture. "That has actually happened in the past when the great religious traditions were first founded," Paul says. "But the traditional religions of the world, including Christianity, have now been around for a long time and yet have not continued to evolve. Most often, they have de-evolved. They now act as a brake on spiritual growth instead of an encouragement to it! If most religion is at a traditional stage in a modern/postmodern society, then it is a dysfunctional presence. It not only hinders the society's evolution, but it distorts the message of its founder. In the act of preserving Jesus' message and passing it down, the church departed from what Jesus taught. He taught us to keep listening, to continue learning, to keep evolving. We have refused. So we have not ended up with the religion *of* Jesus. We have ended up with a religion *about* Jesus. We have ended up with an often dead religion that uses some of Jesus' words in claiming to be the religion of Jesus. Jesus demonstrated that God is love and only love. Only that which leads to more compassion, more liberating justice, more understanding, more respect, and more love is that which leads to God."

On the Broadway Church website is the mission statement officially adopted by the congregation in 2001, articulating this theology of the preeminence of Love:

> Broadway is an inclusive, theologically progressive, healing community focused on the spiritual transformation that comes from following Jesus Christ. Because we follow the life, teachings, and person of Jesus Christ we have come to the following:

- We experience God as love and reject all punishing, vengeful, and violent images of God.
- We follow Jesus' example as he embraced, ignored, and rejected parts of the Scripture of his day.
- We are convinced that hell is a human construct and not a punishment by our Creator.
- We believe that God communicates directly with every person.
- We see each person, as Jesus did, as a divine being on a human journey.
- We accept God's promise that every person without exception will awaken to the light of divine love.
- We cherish the healing, transforming power of the Spirit of God within each person.
- We address God as Mother and Father while agreeing that God includes and transcends all human metaphors and is Ultimate Mystery.
- We have found that the self best evolves with the support of others.
- We learn, grow, and risk as a community committed to spiritual transformation.
- We practice justice, welcoming and affirming diversity.
- We respect other traditions and spiritual paths.
- We embrace the Spirit breaking through the barriers that keep people from unconditional love.

With passion Rev. Paul Smith talks about spiritual transformation as the purpose of the church. "The only measure of a church is transformation in ever more inclusive love," he states. It is clear that Paul means spiritual transformation of individuals within the church, resulting in transformation of the church community and in transformation of the world. In forty-seven years of pastoring Broadway Church, Paul has led numerous significant changes, about one every three or four years. These changes have resulted in loss of members, but also in spiritual growth of many. The changes have contributed to social justice reforms in the wider culture. Instead of resting on his laurels, Paul continues to advocate and encourage growth. He could have done what some church members during a time of controversy advised: "Paul, don't do anything new anymore. Become an elder statesman; move back. Just be an encourager, no more of what the Spirit is saying now. We don't want any more changes." But Paul believes so strongly in continuing to grow and be part of the Spirit's ongoing creative work in the world that he cannot stop. He feels that he would die if he stopped growing.

Even when he dies, Paul believes he will continue growing. "We're going to keep growing and learning," he says. "I believe in individual immortality. At the transfiguration, there were Moses and Elijah; they knew who they were, and Jesus knew who they were. They had been in heaven, that spiritual realm, a long time. Many modern and postmodern philosophers left out the spiritual, the eternal. But all the mystics and transcendentalists—all the way from Plato—believed in the eternal. The core of all spiritual traditions is that we are spirit beings who are connected to the Divine, and we're eternal. We'll live forever. I consider my daily meditations as preparation for dying, as rehearsal for dying because that's what happens when we die. We let go of the body, which we're not. We let go of our emotions, which we're not. We let go of all forms which are not us. That which is really us continues on to the spiritual realm and continues evolving and deciding what forms we will take. Maybe we'll take another form in some other or some parallel universe. We'll keep growing. There's this bigger thing that we'll be part of forever."

While Paul talks about his meditation experiences as preparation for immortality, his face glows. I recall the striking Alex Grey painting "Spiritual Energy System," in the transfiguration section of the "Faces of Jesus" exhibit. This painting is of a large androgynous figure, radiant with soft pink and blue beams of light flowing through and around the figure. Paul comments on this picture: "Here is an image of you, Jesus, and everyone experiencing heightened divine awareness. The body becomes a permeable channel for the circulation of the subtle and causal energies of spiritual consciousness that are ever present and interpenetrate the self and surroundings. Parallel lines of universal divine force stream through the body extending out of the crown of the head and curling back around to the feet, creating a flow of spiritual energy. This work is best viewed facing it, with palms open outward, mirroring the image. Think of it as looking in an actual mirror and seeing yourself as the spiritual being that you are, but may not normally be aware of. Intense prayer, praise, worship, devotion, deep meditation, moments of great insight, feeling one with the Divine, transcendent awareness, an overflowing of Divine presence, and/or experiencing your own divinity, all produce this energy flow in and around you."

For Rev. Paul Smith, including the Divine Feminine in the church is crucial to spiritual transformation. This transformation, Paul says, is the reason for the existence of the church. "Then we need to turn spiritually transformed people loose in the world."

10

Rev. Judith Liro

Priest

St. Hildegard's Community,
St. George's Episcopal Church, Austin, Texas

Seated in a large circle with members of St. Hildegard's Community on July 11, 2010, Rev. Judith Liro leads this Collect she has created:

> *Ancient Love, Vibrant Life-giver,*
> *Stir compassion in us,*
> *Longings in our heart and action:*
> *for our own bodies and for all bodies,*
> *for the Earth fallen prey to robbers,*
> *for Half-the-sky passed by. Amen.*

Rev. Liro and several lay members of the community, wearing albs[1] covered with flowing lime green chasubles,[2] lead the liturgy from within the circle. Mary Ermey, former choir director of St. George's Episcopal Church, plays guitar accompaniment for the music throughout the service. We begin by singing a lovely original composition by Mary, "I Will Kindle My Fire," with the flame symbolizing "pure love" for everyone. A little later we sing "This Ancient Love,"[3] including these words: "Long before She laid her arm of colors 'cross the sky, there was a love, this ancient love was born." The offertory hymn, "O Beautiful Gaia,"[4] images the Divine as "Ancient Sophia." After the Eucharist, we sing a version of the "Prayer of Jesus," entitled

"Ground of All Being,"[5] which balances the images of "Mother of life" and "Father of the universe."

In her sermon, based on Jesus' parable of the Good Samaritan,[6] Rev. Liro picks up the image of "Half-the-sky" from her Collect. Alluding to the title of a book by Nicholas Kristof and Sheryl WuDunn,[7] Rev. Liro uses "Half-the-sky" as a symbol for the women of the world. According to a Chinese Proverb, "women hold up half the sky." In Rev. Liro's creative interpretation of the Good Samaritan parable the injured one represents the women of the world, as well as the earth and our own bodies. "What if the injured one, beaten and left for dead, is *Half-the-sky*?" she asks. Rev. Liro illustrates both the "worldwide oppression and empowerment of women" from the book by Kristof and WuDunn. "My three examples—our bodies, the earth, and women of the world—are connected," she says. "It is patriarchal ordering and values that have demeaned them all, setting them up for exploitation. Jesus didn't know the word 'patriarchy,' but his parable shows that he was well aware of the brokenness to the human family when artificial lines of value, domination, and exclusion are drawn. He calls us to kinship and friendship and community with ourselves and with each other, with Divine Love and the web of Life."

Hildegard of Bingen, for whom St. Hildegard's Community is named, used the word *Viriditas*[8] to designate the "green growing power" that the Holy Spirit brings "to all of life, transforming dried-up and shriveled lives and institutions into a New Creation."[9] As I worship with St. Hildegard's Community, I experience the reality of this "green growing power." Not only are the hymns and sermon empowering, but the physical setting nourishes my spirit. Susan LeVieux, one of the community members, has created a beautiful canopy and banners of forest green and teal and lime green silk cloth. The canopy drapes from a Celtic knot in the center of the ceiling above the circle of worshipers. At the front and back of the room hang banners in the varied shades of green, several featuring circular Celtic symbols. "Celtic Season"[10] is one of the mini-seasons St. Hildegard's Community offers during the "Ordinary Time"[11] of the liturgical year.

Later Judith tells me that she and others in the community read *Half-the-Sky* in the book group, "Vision Begins to Happen," and that she has tried to bring the power of the book into conversation with Scripture in a way that addresses the deadly imbalance in our world.

"This particular liturgy addressed patriarchy directly—singling out women, the earth, and our human bodies," she says. "If you came here regularly, the experience would be more subtle. For me feminism is about a healthy balance of feminine and masculine and is not anti-male. It encourages both men and women to embrace their wholeness. Our hope is for all of us to know full humanity that comes from living in deep connection with God's wholeness. Liberating God from narrow metaphors opens up new possibilities for divine-human relationship. I believe that "half-the-sky passed by" applies to our naming of the Divine as well. God is the injured One imprisoned in the narrowness of our naming and understanding. Often St. Hildegard's uses diverse divine images that are gender-neutral. At other times we intentionally pray with feminine names such as 'Sophia' to balance the male images that most of us carry around already. We experience tremendous vitality brought by this wholeness."

For many years Judith Liro has been transforming the symbols and language of the church. This reserved, soft-spoken minister does not like the conflict this has caused. "I'm aware of some people who are cut out to be prophets; they enjoy stirring up trouble," she says. "I'm not like that." But beginning when she was at Episcopal Theological Seminary of the Southwest,[12] Judith caused a stir by suggesting that the seminary do an inclusive language liturgy that she had experienced at the denomination's General Convention. "It created this huge uproar from women as well as men," she recalls. "My suggestion was for a one-time liturgy with something under consideration in our own church. A woman who had been one of my closest friends never spoke to me again after that. One of my best-loved professors was also strangely opposed. I discovered that there were Prayer Book[13] fundamentalists. I understood the need for approving final texts, but I couldn't understand why you wouldn't be open to a process to change words that were getting in the way of the meaning." In her homiletics class in the seminary's Christ Chapel, Judith had preached a sermon on the importance of inclusive language in which she included these statements: "Some say that the issue of language is trivial, even cosmetic. I would heartily disagree. It is about as inconsequential as the air we breathe because it shapes who we are and affects how we think. . . . If the words we use to pray and worship exclude persons even when we have no desire to be exclusive . . . then I believe we are faced with a fundamental danger . . . If you would tell me of the great difficulties involved in changing language and conclude that nothing can be done, I would counter that the difficulties run as deep as human sin and that our restoration is dependent upon God."

Born in San Antonio, Texas, Judith Reagan Liro grew up there with a younger sister, Jyl, in a family she describes as "loving and close-knit" and "matriarchal in a way." Her mother, who had a master's degree, taught school for many years, and Judith had a number of aunts who were also schoolteachers and "very strong women." Her mother's three sisters and their families and her maternal grandparents were an important part of Judith's extended family. Judith's father owned a small business. Her parents modeled respect for each other and a partnership marriage. Another strong influence in her childhood was an African American housekeeper, Irene Neece, called "Mamie," who worked for her family two days a week. "She was like a second mother to me," Judith says. "Through loving and being loved by Mamie I understood the common humanity of different races even though I grew up in a racist segregated society. She was a very true believer, and a mother in the faith to me."

Along with the warmth and safety of her family, Judith experienced the fear of growing up in the midst of World War II and the Cold War. "I grew up with 'duck and cover' drills at school along with Dick and Jane readers," she says. "Surreal parallel universes—one where everything is cozy and the other a picture of complete destruction. After the War everyone went to church, but we didn't. My parents weren't atheists but weren't religious either."

Even though she seldom went to church as a young child, Judith remembers having a "sense of the Holy." When she was four, she went to a Methodist church Communion service where she experienced a "sense of Mystery." When she was five and her sister, Jyl, was born, she wrote a letter for her dad to take to the hospital to give to the stork to take to God. "I had a contemplative streak and liked to climb up our fig tree and sit on the garage roof," Judith recalls. "I didn't think of it as prayer, but I loved being in the silence."

Beginning when Judith was in third grade, she went with her cousins to the Church of Christ. "I loved the Bible stories and the singing," she says. "I wanted to be baptized, but my mother didn't want me to, because she didn't approve of the Church of Christ's viewpoint that they were the only ones going to heaven. I think that was formative for me in that my mother was critical in a good sense, not just going along with everything." When she was twelve, Judith initiated worship at home with her family. "Every Sunday morning I would sit the four of us down, and we would read the Bible, and we would send money to CARE,[14]" she recalls.

In her high school years Judith and her family became involved in Oak Hills Presbyterian Church, in a new part of San Antonio. Judith, Jyl, and her father were baptized on the same morning in a YMCA upstairs room, where this new church was then meeting. "I was very active in the church, president of the youth, preaching on Youth Sunday," Judith says. "By the time I was about to graduate, I was wanting to go to seminary in Christian education. It didn't occur to me about wanting to be ordained. I was still firmly in my role, what was permitted as female. I'm sure that the way I thought about God was male. But I feel that the Presbyterian Church gave me a sense of social justice. From the Church of Christ I received the interest in the Bible and an awakening to some sense of sexism. They had women teach Sunday school to small children, but as soon as you got to fifth or sixth grade, you had to have a male teacher. That struck me as very odd."

When she was in high school, the civil rights movement also became important to Judith. "Because of Jesus' teachings, I was beginning to have different ideas about civil rights than my family of origin," she says. "Desegregation was being implemented in San Antonio schools. My father and I argued the issue almost every day when he drove me to school. It was good-humored and a way to articulate my convictions. My heart thrilled with the courage of civil rights activists. I felt set free to love beyond my own family and to experience a caring that could stretch out to the world."

Judith chose to go to Colorado College in Colorado Springs with Donna, her soul friend from high school. "I was drawn to the mountains and the physical beauty of Colorado as well as to the small liberal arts environment," Judith says. "The first year I went through a stage of losing my faith and stopping going to church. I became a scientific materialist, and the spiritual dropped out of the picture. I decided to major in behavioral psychology, and liked it for a while because it pared things down to what could be measured and controlled. At some level I wanted life to be that way."

At Colorado College Judith dated Joe, an Air Force Academy cadet who had grown up in a Roman Catholic Polish American family, and she fell "passionately in love" with him. "Trying to have everything measurable didn't seem feasible anymore," she says. In 1964, the same week they both graduated from Colorado College, Judith and Joe became the first cadet couple to be married in the newly completed Air Force Academy Catholic chapel.

Stationed in Okinawa, Joe and Judith went to All Souls' Episcopal Church, where she was confirmed and he was received. "I didn't have my faith back like it was before, but I was really nourished by the liturgy," Judith says. "It wasn't a matter of being able to think myself back, but in the liturgy I was connecting to what is sacred. During this time we were expecting our first baby, and it was a time of wonder." In 1968, Christopher was born in a military hospital, full of the wounded from the Vietnam War. "Being an Air Force wife wasn't as narrow as one might think," Judith recalls. "I taught school with the wife of the man who led the Okinawan resistance. When we returned to Colorado, the anti-war movement was in full swing, and I participated. We were both eager for Joe to be out of the Air Force, and he left as soon as he completed the required six years."

In 1969, Judith and Joe experienced the tragedy of a stillborn son. "He died because the cord was wrapped around his neck," Judith says. "It was a very heart-breaking experience. At that time Christopher was twenty-one months old, so I had so much to do. Later while Joe finished a Master of Public Administration degree in Boulder, Colorado, I was librarian for two elementary schools in Colorado Springs. In 1971, he took a job with the city of Austin so we could be closer to my parents. In 1973, our daughter, Kate, was born after an anxiety-filled pregnancy, and I enjoyed those precious years of her infancy. Pregnancy, birth, and mothering were deeply spiritual experiences for me."

Several years after the birth of Kate, Judith became depressed because of unresolved grief over the stillborn child. "It was a spiritual struggle because I was angry at God," Judith says. "I was very angry that the world was made this way that babies died. It was a 'dark night of the soul' experience. The church grew in importance to me at this time. We were going to All Saints' Episcopal Church, and the rector, Armistead Powell, walked me through that time. I experienced coming out of the depression as a resurrection experience. I seem to live liturgically. When I first went to Armistead for pastoral counseling, it was the beginning of Lent, and we continued to meet each week. On Maundy Thursday I sobbed quietly in church, and then on Good Friday I had a mystical experience of Jesus being present with me in compassion. On Easter I experienced resurrection as I found myself in a place of new beginnings. Betsy Aylin Baldwin, director of Christian education, and others in the All Saints' community also helped me in healing grief and in reclaiming my full spiritual nature that had been packed away in college."

Judith says she "really enjoyed parish life" as she became much more active at All Saints' Episcopal Church. "I started teaching Sunday school, and was on the vestry.[15] Joe and I both were youth group leaders and helped with camps. I designed adult education and invited professors from the University of Texas and the seminaries to present lecture series."

Her work with the church youth group led Judith to take a class on youth ministry at Austin Presbyterian Theological Seminary. The next year she took Old Testament, which she also relished. In 1980, she began studying at Episcopal Theological Seminary of the Southwest. "I didn't at that point have a sense of call to ordination," she says. "It was a call to study theology. After a year in seminary I had a mystical experience at a Christian education conference at Camp Allen.[16] In working with youth I had gotten into clowning. During a day of silence at camp I started doing this clown thing that was part mime and part dance. Moving in silence was a way of being open to the Spirit, following what was bubbling up. Through that movement experience with a few friends I knew that I was being called to be ordained." Judith acknowledges these Diocese of Texas conferences as a major influence. A grant brought nationally recognized speakers: John Westerhoff, Tom Groome, and Maria Harris. "Their ideas as well as the creative nature of the conferences took root in me," she says. "One line I heard there—'A priest is one who sings and dances and leads the way'—was like a seed planted in my heart."

When Judith went to Rev. Powell to get the support she needed for the ordination process, he would not give it. "He had known me in my most vulnerable, depressed times, and he couldn't see me in this role," Judith recalls. "He also thought it would be too hard for Joe. I was devastated, and after much grieving, I prepared to move on to another parish where I could find support." Later when Judith was telling Rev. Powell about her experience of baptizing a stillborn baby while she was doing clinical ministry at St. David's Hospital as part of her seminary training, he suddenly said, "I think you should be ordained." At first Judith didn't realize what he was saying. But he repeated, "I think you should be ordained." Judith was thrilled that the parish where she had experienced rebirth could sponsor her. Yet she realized that Rev. Powell's not supporting her initially strengthened her commitment: "I had come to a place of deeper confidence in my call that I would need on this journey."

When she was in seminary, Judith also awakened to the importance of inclusive language. In a book group at All Saints' Episcopal Church, Judith heard Bea Ann Smith talk about experiencing frustration in traditional worship services. "She felt that the masculine language kept her from worshiping, and I had never thought of such a thing," Judith says. "She was in so much pain about it, and it really touched me." Judith was also moved by the grief of Susan Bock, who came to the seminary from Detroit, where she had experienced inclusive language in Messiah Episcopal Church. "Susan was sobbing because there was no inclusive language at seminary," Judith recalls. "Those two women affected me very deeply. The whole wall that I had grown up with was broken down. " Soon after, Judith preached the sermon on inclusive language in her seminary homiletics class. "In the sermon I talk about becoming a 'nerve of the Body of Christ,'" she says. "I carried that pain because then I would hear the exclusive language, and I couldn't go back into places without being grieved. There were times when I had to leave because I was very emotional."

Judith reflects that seminary was "an important time of formation" for her "intellectually and through transformative relationships" with faculty and students. "It has been the solid grounding that has helped me to evaluate and understand newer theologies and interpret Scripture in the years to come. Liturgics professor Bill Adams included the importance of inclusive language as a justice issue." Although Judith had no courses in feminist theology, the seminary did host a lecture series sponsored by Southwestern Network for Women's Ministry. The

Network brought to the seminary feminist theologians, like Rosemary Radford Ruether, and women priests, like Alison Cheek, one of the "Philadelphia Eleven."[17] "That was a time when women in some dioceses were not being ordained, and would come to the Network to find support," Judith says. "We had theologically exciting lectures and then a time called 'Sarah's Circle' for the outpouring of the pain and the joy of ministry. Relationships with ordained women and lay leaders through the Network nourished and supported me."

Ordination in the Episcopal Church is a long process that involves approval of the rector, meeting with a parish discernment group, being approved by the vestry, writing a spiritual autobiography, personal interviews, meeting with the bishop, and then having an interview with the whole Commission on Ministry, composed of about twenty-five clergy and laypersons in the diocese. Later the ordination candidate goes through psychological exams and interviews with a psychiatrist. At the time Judith was going through the process, some people on the Commission did not believe in the ordination of women. "I was scared about the ordination process," Judith says. "It was very hard to be approved. Two male classmates decided that there should be a woman president of the seminary student body. I would never have thought to run because I'm an introvert. But with their encouragement I ran and was elected. As president I was a representative to the board of trustees, where the bishop of Texas and I became acquainted. So after making it through the various hoops, I was made a postulant.[18] I think that was the Spirit's opening a way."

In 1984, Judith graduated from seminary. But she was one of the only graduates who did not have a ministry position. Bishop Maurice Benitez came up with a plan for Judith to work half-time as a chaplain at St. George's Court, a retirement center for low-income seniors and people with disabilities, and half-time in the parish of St. George's Episcopal Church. "I was excited about coming here to St. George's," Judith says. "Rector John Price was very supportive, and Mary Ermey, church secretary at the time, was great. The half-time salary that was to come from the parish never materialized above a quarter-time salary. But I was full of enthusiasm, so I was working probably more than half-time. I was also giving a lot of attention and energy to the retirement center. Harriett Hogle, the new director of St. George's Court, and I enjoyed working together as partners in ministry. But my heart was really in the parish. I loved the full range of parish work."

In November of 1984, Judith was ordained deacon at All Saints' Episcopal Church, and in June of 1985, she was ordained priest at St. George's. She was the first woman ordained an Episcopal priest in Austin. "The first years it felt like it was sufficient just to be a woman standing at the altar or a woman preaching," Rev. Liro says. "The people in the parish were warm and welcoming, although there were a few who wouldn't come if I were presiding at the Eucharist or would cross to the other side so they wouldn't have to take Communion from my hand. I was asked if I would stay away once a month for the sake of those who were uncomfortable, but I refused." In addition to liturgy, Rev. Liro loved teaching and pastoral care at St. George's. She also developed parish retreats and new adult education opportunities, including Education for Ministry (EFM). She comments that EFM gave laity a wonderful opportunity "to grow into the fullness of their own baptismal ministries," and provided her a place where she was "free to share new ideas and know the intimacy of a supportive community that met weekly." EFM laid a foundation that later grew into the Servant Leadership School and St. Hildegard's Community.

During her first years as a priest Rev. Liro also collaborated with Sarah Bentley, a United Church of Christ pastor, and Maryrose Hightower-Coyle, a member of St. George's, in starting "Round the Well," an ecumenical women's group that met monthly for feminist liturgy. "Sarah had graduated from Union Theological Seminary and had studied with some of the great feminist theologians," Judith recalls. "The three of us had already been meeting regularly to read feminist books such as Elizabeth Schüssler Fiorenza's *In Memory of Her*[19] and Rosemary Radford Ruether's *Women-Church*.[20] 'Round the Well' met in the large parish hall at All Saints' Episcopal Church, and we started doing informal, non-Eucharistic liturgies. The first service we did was 'Remembrance of the Holocaust of Women'[21] from *Women-Church*. I had read in history about the witch trials, but they had no emotional connection for me. I had been deeply moved by what we call the 'Holocaust' with the Jews and others. When we did the 'Holocaust of Women' ritual, it got through to me that I was part of a group who had experienced a holocaust, but it was not called that. It was called the witch trials, and it wasn't like these were real people who were being murdered, like it was with the Jews. These were 'witches,' and I had only Halloween imagery for witches; I didn't have an understanding of who witches really were. But when we did that ritual, I experienced that real women were killed. That was an awakening experience not only about women but about the transformative power of ritual."

After Rev. Liro had been at St. George's for four years, the rector moved, and she served as the priest-in-charge as the church went through the search for a new rector. Rev. Jim Williams, who had recently been ordained, worked as a volunteer assistant to Rev. Liro so that she could continue her part-time chaplain ministry at St. George's Court. Early in the process the bishop met with the vestry to say that the church could call Jim as the rector, but not Judith, because of a rule that those who had been on the staff of a church couldn't be called as the rector. Since Jim had been a volunteer, he could be called. "That meant that basically Jim and I would change positions," Judith says. "Jim turned them down." In 1989, the church called Rev. David Hoster as the new rector; David and Judith had led summer camps together at Camp Allen.

During the time she was priest-in-charge, Rev. Liro read Elizabeth O'Connor's book *Cry Pain, Cry Hope*[22] about the Church of the Saviour in Washington, DC, and chose it for a group to read in a Sunday morning class. "I started reading some of O'Connor's earlier books and wanting to go to the Church of the Saviour," Judith says. "I had a history of liking to learn, and I had done continuing education routinely. This time I found others wanting to go along." As interest grew, Rev. Liro influenced Rev. Hoster to join with those going to the Church of the Saviour's Wellspring Retreat Center. In August of 1990, David Hoster, Kathleen Burnside, Harriett Hogle, Mary Ermey, Judy Sessions, and Judith went on retreat. "I found the contemplative-active-community model that was presented very transformative," Judith says. "I felt like I had come home; there was something about that pattern that was life-saving for me. It was a balance, a way to guide my ministry. I recognized that it was a very ancient pattern of contemplation, community, and ministry, a basic pattern found in Jesus' life as well as in monastic communities that had renewed the church. The Wellspring retreat was four days, with silence from Thursday evening till Friday afternoon. I had been making silent retreats for some time with friends and on my own; now I had a longing for more silence.

At All Saints' I had been introduced to silent retreats led by Father Whiston, an Episcopal priest who had been a missionary in China. Now I learned that he had also been responsible for introducing silent retreats to the Church of the Saviour."

In the fall of 1990 at St. George's Episcopal Church, Rev. Liro preached an updated version of the sermon on inclusive language that she had preached in her class at seminary. "All hell broke loose," Judith recalls. Rector David Hoster told her that one reason he thought people were so upset was that they thought she was going behind his back because he was gone that Sunday. But Judith had showed him the sermon before she preached it, and he didn't see a problem with it. "I think people were angry because the sermon touches on what holds patriarchy in place," Judith says. "It's attempting to uncover it and identify the core of this whole system that is basically evil and that we all participate in and don't even know that it's there. I think that's why it's so hard to get people to even be aware of the need for inclusive language. It's so tied into everything. Without patriarchy, we couldn't keep wars going. The world would grind to a halt. The economy would be changed. Language is the sacrament, the visible part. And if we start messing with that, it might make everything else unravel. I think that people are not conscious of it, but I think there's the sense that we can't go there."

In addition to setting off a furor at St. George's by the inclusive language sermon, Rev. Liro had written a column for the church newsletter that had stirred controversy. When the new rector came, the church planned to buy a rectory. "I wrote an article suggesting that the parish buy a house that took healing racism into consideration, buying in a mixed neighborhood rather than farther away," Judith says. "I wrote about how this could be an opportunity for the church to model something new. Some in the parish took it that I was accusing them of being racist when I was writing about the patterns that impact all of us who grow up in this country."

Around this time a few things happened in her diocese that also troubled Rev. Liro. One was a poster for Bring-a-Friend-to-Church month that showed George Bush Sr. bringing Margaret Thatcher to a big, wealthy Houston church. In the same month Bishop Benitez, a former fighter pilot, gave an address at Diocesan Council that was supportive of the Persian Gulf War, and there was a Courtesy Resolution for the delegates to accept his address. "I felt trapped, like I couldn't vote against it," Judith recalls. "But voting for it was like voting that I supported the war. I was horrified by it. I felt like this was not my church. Where was Jesus in the war, political power, and wealth? And then all this was going on at St. George's with inclusive language and racism. Overwhelmed, I started thinking of leaving—the Episcopal Church, the priesthood, everything."

Eventually Rev. Liro felt called to recreate, rather than to leave, the church. "This has meant going into the unknown, responding to the Spirit's leading and wisdom, cocreating the Body of Christ for a new century as a part of the Episcopal Church," she says. In November of 1990, she went back to the Church of the Saviour for a retreat called "Recreating the Church." Then in the spring of 1991, she spent three months on sabbatical at the Church of the Saviour. The sabbatical included a month-long silent retreat, classes at the Servant Leadership School, and a class on Authentic Movement in an Episcopal church in the center of Washington, DC. "It was an amazing time of transformation," Judith says. "I took a class with Gordon Cosby on call, and a class with Mary Cosby[23] on prayer. The second month at Dayspring Retreat Center, I walked around Dayspring and was healed by the land, more than two hundred acres in suburban Maryland intensely alive with the miracle of spring. I was healed in this combination of classes and people and the beauty of nature. I processed my grief and anger about my trouble in the parish and my disillusionment with the diocese. In the Authentic Movement class, we were not supposed to move from our minds but be moved internally. The first time, I had a profound experience of starting out moving and then coming to a grinding halt and being unable to move. We were supposed to draw after that, and I drew a dead tree stump. I thought, 'This is me. I'm a dead tree stump.' To me those experiences that are non-verbal, that have to do with art and movement, are part of the Sacred Feminine. During this sabbatical I experienced enough healing that I could pray with openness, wanting wisdom on how my call would evolve."

The day before Judith left her sabbatical, she experienced what she calls her "third ordination." Her husband, Joe, had come to DC to drive back with her to Austin, and they decided to go to the National Cathedral. When they arrived, they learned that an annual celebration of social justice was about to begin. "We sat in the transept[24] because there was a choir singing, and we were trying to be considerate," Judith recalls. "The Eucharist started, and after a while most of the people in the transept left. Joe and I were there with just a couple of people sitting apart from the congregation. I felt that the Holy Spirit was acting out this story in what happened. Here was the part of the Episcopal Church that was committed to social justice and was open. Back in Austin I felt isolated like being in the transept, but still part of this whole church that I felt deeply connected to. The service was great; all the hymns were ones that I would have picked out for my ordination. Verna Dozier, an African American laywoman and one of my heroes, preached a stirring sermon. I got to know her when she came to speak at Southwestern Network for Women's Ministry. She did a lot of Bible teaching and wrote books about the laity,[25] and a book called *The Dream of God*.[26] I knew that her path to the Episcopal Church had been through Church of the Saviour. On my sabbatical I had visited with her, sharing my doubts and confusion. I was stunned that she was here preaching!"

Midway through the service at the Cathedral a young African American woman came and sat beside Judith. "She was a hospice chaplain who had been driving by and felt this urge to come into the Cathedral," Judith says. "There in the almost deserted transept the three of us belted out 'Lift Every Voice and Sing.' She said, 'You have a beautiful voice.' I don't really have a beautiful voice, but I came to understand that as a word from God, who delighted in my offering my voice as I went back to recreate the church. I told the young woman that I had been on sabbatical and that we were leaving the next day. She said, 'Then I should lay my hands on you and bless you.' That was like another ordination. It was such a gift to go back feeling that the Holy Spirit had created this send-off and that Joe had been part of it."

After returning from her sabbatical, Rev. Liro felt renewed energy for her ministry. "It was another resurrection experience," she says. "That experience in the Cathedral felt like a divine confirmation of what I had already discerned: my call was to the Episcopal Church. Although I had experienced disillusionment, I deeply loved my church and knew I was a vital part of the church, even when I experienced isolation. I began a practice of centering prayer on the sabbatical, and that has continued to sustain me and open me to God's healing and leading into the present. For a number of years I continued to have spiritual direction with Don Russell from Wellspring, who helped me be true to myself in a more complete way."

The laypeople at St. George's who had gone on retreat to Church of the Saviour also felt energized to implement some of the models they had learned. Kathleen Burnside felt called to start a School of Christian Living, later called the Servant Leadership School. "As I helped her articulate her call, I began to hear a call to join her," Judith says. "This would be a significant way to recreate the church. Education for Ministry (EFM) provided excellent spiritual formation, but we hoped the School would go further in empowering action in the world." Two others from St. George's, Linda Herbert and Vera Shirley, joined Judith and Kathleen to begin the School in the fall of 1992. As a part of the School, Maryrose Hightower-Coyle and Judith offered "Vision Begins to Happen: A Feminist Book Group." One of the first books the group read was Elizabeth Johnson's *She Who Is*,[27] which later inspired liturgy at St. Hildegard's. "We also started having Journey Inward, Journey Outward retreats," Judith recalls. "Thanks to generous contributions from Gretchen Lara Shartle, we brought Don Russell from Wellspring to help lead these retreats that were on that threefold path. There would be talks about the inner journey, about call, and about community. Each retreat began with silence. By 1995 there were about forty people in the Austin area who had gone either to the Journey Inward, Journey Outward retreats we had here, or they had gone back to the Church of the Saviour. And there were also many who had been in the School. All this going on at St. George's was creating some tension. We tried to offer an energizing newness to the parish without causing a rupture. There was a need for new wineskins."[28]

Also stirring tension in the parish was Rev. Liro's preaching on nonviolence. "I was converted to nonviolence through reading Walter Wink's *Engaging the Powers*,[29]" Judith says. "I realized that I had yearned deeply to believe in nonviolence, but I kept thinking that it was impossible, that nonviolence couldn't be effective because that wasn't the way the world was made. Walter's book helped me see that the 'principalities and powers' had cast their spell on all of us, had us in a trance thinking that the only thing that would work was violence. It helped my mind catch up with my heart." Judith had gotten to know Walter Wink and June Keener-Wink through her friendship with Gretchen. Judith had also gone with Gretchen to a conference called

"Spirituality and Sexuality" at San Francisco Theological Seminary, where Gretchen's husband, Jorge Lara-Braud, taught theology and culture. "It was one of the most amazing conferences that I ever attended," Judith says. "We had movement that June Kenner-Wink led, and Bible study led by Walter and June. Studying sexuality was one important element, and the overall experience was transforming. The Divine Masculine and the Divine Feminine danced together!" Judith studied with Walter Wink and June Kenner-Wink at a number of other conferences. "They brought art and movement into my experience so that I included it in EFM and later in our Servant Leadership School," Judith says.

Another "conversion experience" that Rev. Liro identifies during these years was in her understanding of sexuality. "St. George's was a parish open to gay and lesbian people, and they came out to me in personal conversations," she says. "As I experienced the authenticity of their lives and after I had studied both Scripture and science at the 'Spirituality and Sexuality' conference, I could no longer consider sexual orientation as sinful. I came to believe that there is a tremendous responsibility to be loving, responsible, and authentic whatever our orientation. Since then my ministry has included working to bring a renewed understanding of human sexuality to the church."

The tension at St. George's came to a head after a worship service on August 6, 1995, commemorating the fiftieth anniversary of Hiroshima. "David Hoster and Kathleen Burnside crafted the liturgy, and I preached," Judith recalls. "It was a service that tore the parish apart. I was really careful to express nonviolence in a way that wasn't polarizing. I tried to connect nonviolence to the kind of sacrifices that had been made in World War II, that were important in the lives of some of the parishioners. But I didn't succeed, at least not with everybody. It wasn't just the sermon, but the prayers and the whole service. It was like an earthquake that changed the landscape, and my journey turned dramatically in a particular direction."

That same month the Servant Leadership School offered a retreat on the discernment of call. "We had classes at St. George's ahead of time, and then we went to Moye Retreat Center in Castroville for silence from Thursday until Friday afternoon and then did small group work around call," Judith says. "I went as one of the leaders, not expecting any major revelation to emerge in my own journey. In the middle of one night, I woke up and experienced a call to begin a community within St. George's. It was very powerful. I wrote about it in my journal, trying to express what it was. It came from my own yearning for worship that was tied to community and also expressed my love of the Anglican liturgy, which I see as full of mystery and color and drama. I felt that I was expressing a call that was not just mine, but something that was welling up in St. George's, especially in the community of people who had been in the School."

A few weeks later at a parish retreat, church members found the task of writing a new mission statement almost impossible. The following week Rev. David Hoster and Rev. Liro met. "David said he had learned from the retreat that we had two ways of being church that were incompatible," Judith recalls. "He sensed that we would all go under if we couldn't find a fruitful way to deal with the parish differences. He thought that we needed to separate and to free each one to be 'church' in a way that was authentic for them and that I should lead the emerging one, and he should lead the other, the traditional one. I could hear the truth of his words, but I was also very upset. I didn't want to separate. I had been in the parish for eleven years, and I had great affection for all the people including many who were upset with me. I prayed following our meeting and had another mystical moment. I felt God turning my head from the internal conflict and pointing my eyes outward to Austin. The message that I received was, 'I'm sending you to these people who aren't in the church and who are spiritually thirsting and starving.' So I went back to David and said that I felt he was right about finding a way out of the impasse and that I wanted to focus on creating something that would reach out. People who had become committed leaders in the Servant Leadership School began to meet on Sunday afternoons in my office for worship. We also worshiped on Sunday mornings at St. George's. We had conversations with the vestry, and there were a number of vestry members who were supportive. We started talking about St. George's birthing this new community."

Rev. Liro and Rev. Hoster sought ways to support the two communities within St. George's. "The parish did a pledge drive for people to say where they wanted their money to go," Judith says. "We didn't know how many people would want to go with the new community and how many people would want to stay with the traditional. Most of the people felt drawn to stay with the traditional. David wanted to make the new venture work, so for two years he worked twenty hours a week at a drug treatment center. I can't imagine another rector who wouldn't have just said that this is too divisive or the money's not there, so you need to go find another job. He believed the new community came from the Holy Spirit, and he sacrificed personally. The funding pledged for the new community was about $20,000, including what was paid to the pension fund. So my actual take-home pay was about $14,000. The Church of the Saviour had given me the model of being willing to work at a lower wage in order to do what you believe in. I felt some conflict, like I was letting down women's right to have full and equal pay. But I felt that I had to honor my call to recreate the church."

St. Hildegard's Community officially began on Epiphany, January 6, 1996, with a creative service blessing both the new community and the traditional community of St. George's Episcopal Church. The service began in St. George's sanctuary and continued with a procession to Kleberg, the parish hall, where St. Hildegard's had chosen to meet. "This was our opportunity to go in peace, blessing each other," Judith says. "It was beautiful. I still feel much gratitude for those who contributed monetarily to both communities. There were also a few who left. And there was grief. For some it meant that St. George's had lost the beauty of David and me both at the altar, the male and the female voices. Once when I was out of town and David came to St. Hildegard's Community to preside at the Eucharist, a little girl who had grown up in St. Hildegard's expressed to her mother that she didn't know that men could be priests. It's part of the incompleteness that happened when we separated; the people from each community missed out on something that had been there before."

The new community chose to take the name of St. Hildegard, the twelfth-century mystic, because of her creativity and commitment to justice. The worship setting also flowed from the vision statement the community had crafted. "We wanted to sit in a circle, so we settled on Kleberg, the parish hall," Judith says. "We wished we could have been in the church with the beauty of high ceilings, limestone, oak, and stained glass, but we chose a humbler place because we thought it was really important to worship in a circle. We wanted a place without pews, and that wasn't possible except in Kleberg. We wanted the freedom to dance and to move. I had been influenced by St. Gregory of

Nyssa Episcopal Church in San Francisco and the way they incorporated pre-Constantinian customs within an Episcopal service. Besides the importance of dance, they modeled giving the sermon seated as a teaching presence and included a response time that welcomed additional voices. They sat in one place for the Service of the Word and danced in procession to stand together around the altar table. St. Hildegard's decided also to keep vestments to tie into Anglican worship with the solemnity and the colors. Having people vested helped to make the circle more of an intentionally sacred space. I liked having not just the priest vested, but other people vested as was the case in a traditional service. When we started in Epiphany, we had navy blue banners that Kathleen and James Burnside made that looked celestial. They had painted stars, shining light coming forth from the banners hanging way up in the space above the center of the circle."

Commitment to inclusive language proved to be the most challenging for St. Hildegard's Community in relationship to the institutional church. In an article in the newsletter of Evangelical and Ecumenical Women's Caucus, Rev. Liro writes about this commitment: "In the years leading up to the birth of our community, we had become more convinced that the dominance of male imagery in the language of the liturgy was undermining the possibilities for women to experience ourselves as beloved, gifted, and responsible beings. With the sacred feminine devalued, the shadow side of the masculine supported violence and dehumanization. What sense did it make for some of us to counsel women who were survivors of domestic abuse and rape and fail to see the church's role in weaving the subtle underpinnings of this culture? How could those of us who worked to prevent war or heal its wounded, fail to see the way words in our worship unconsciously played a supporting role in its justification? St. Hildegard's longed to be a place where the wholeness of God and humanity could be experienced as much as possible. When we chose to be a Eucharistic community, we entered into a carefully guarded domain—the sacred core identity of the Anglican tradition. In order to incarnate these transforming changes, we had to find a way to compromise with integrity. I believe that Sophia showed us the way."[30]

When Rev. Liro asked the bishop to allow St. Hildegard's Community to use the inclusive language texts that had been authorized by General Convention,[31] he said no. So the community chose to use the texts in the Book of Common Prayer with the informal name of "Rite III." St. George's had already been using Rite III for annual Epiphany services and parish retreats. "Rite III empowers the creation of your own words that would be part of the total Eucharistic prayer, and it doesn't require the permission of the bishop," Judith explains. "That first year at St. Hildegard's was exhilarating with a flurry of creativity around liturgy. We had many people wanting to try different things." In January of 1997, Bishop Payne called for a meeting with Rev. Liro and Rev. Hoster.

"Are you using the Book of Common Prayer?" he asked her.

"It's Rite III, so it's in the Prayer Book," she replied. "It's authorized by the Prayer Book."

"Well, send me what you're doing."

A group of people in St. Hildegard's Community worked for a while with Judith to put together a packet to send to the bishop, including sample liturgies and statements from people about why St. Hildegard's was meaningful to them. Judith received a letter from him on Good Friday, stating that they needed to meet when he came to Austin because he felt they had gone too far.

At the meeting on May 8, Bishop Payne asked Rev. Liro to consider resigning Holy Orders so that St. Hildegard's could leave the Episcopal Church and continue as a faith community outside the Episcopal Church. "He was soft-spoken and very kind," Judith recalls. "I started crying. It was embarrassing to fall apart and be in tears."

During this difficult time Rev. Liro received vital support from Rev. David Hoster as well as from St. Hildegard's Community and from some women priests in the Episcopal Church. "This was a time of deep discernment for the community and for me personally," Judith recalls. "I had to struggle with my internalized patriarchy to find voice in these challenges." Rev. Dena Harrison, whom Rev. Liro had mentored and who now worked closely with the bishop and later became a bishop herself, was an advocate. Another resource for Judith was Virginia Marie Rincon, who had been a member of St. George's and was now graduating from Episcopal Divinity School in Cambridge, Massachusetts. Virginia Marie arranged a meeting for Judith with Rev. Dr. Sue Hiatt, who had been on the faculty there for many years and who was considered the "architect" of women's ordination in the Episcopal Church. Judith recounts their conversation:

"Have you committed a terrible moral offense?" Sue asked Judith.

"No, I haven't committed any terrible moral offense," Judith replied. "I did promise something in my ordination vows to be faithful to the worship of the Episcopal Church, and I think I'm pushing the limits on that."

"Bishops only ask their priests to resign when there is a terrible moral offense. So if you were asked to resign, that is wrong."

"Well, I can see that. I'll have to think about it some more."

"You need to find out where you are and what you want and not just automatically assume that what the bishop is asking for is what you're called to do."

Following Virginia Marie's graduation, Judith attended a conference where Dr. Dorothee Soelle,[32] Rev. Dr. Carter Heywood,[33] and Dr. Beverly Harrison[34] spoke. Then Judith went to Greenfire Retreat Center,[35] where she met with Rev. Alison Cheek and several other women priests. "I was immersed in the strength of women who had prophetic ministries," Judith says. "All this encouragement was like the Spirit blowing the breath back into me."

When Rev. Liro returned to Austin, she wrote Bishop Payne, saying that she wasn't called to resign Holy Orders and that she hoped the Holy Spirit would lead them to a place of agreement. She received a letter back from him, telling her he was delighted that she wanted to stay. The bishop asked Rev. Liro, Rev. Hoster, and Rev. Robbie Vickery, the Dean of the Austin Convocation, to meet to discuss an agreement for St. Hildegard's. "I told the bishop that I wanted to use the inclusive language texts that are approved by General Convention," Judith recalls. "He was willing to let us use inclusive language for half the year, but the other half the year we were supposed to use the regular Prayer Book. I said, 'I really feel called to be a part of the church, but to me that's like saying to Rosa Parks that she could ride anywhere on the bus for half a year, and the other half of the year she would have to sit in the back. I can't agree to that.' I felt this great calm and peace, which I attributed to all the people praying for me. I felt like I had voice. I wasn't caught up in fear. The final agreement was for Rite III for the whole year, including the authorized inclusive language texts for half the year. There had been a breakthrough. Bishop Payne told me that he believed inclusive language was coming to the church. He had given a whole lot, and I had stood my ground but also compromised. It was hard for the community, and some left. Also, Bishop Payne decided there should be no publicity about St. Hildegard's. It was something we accepted, but it affected us at a soul level."

Rev. Liro expresses gratitude for Rev. Robbie Vickery, whom she felt was an advocate for her and for St. Hildegard's Community. She shared with him a parable she had written to emphasize the "indifference of the Church toward the pervasive masculine language in our liturgies by showing how offensive and unacceptable a comparable racial marker would be":

> Once there was a major religion whose Holy Scriptures having been formed in racist cultures contained explicit markers of a racial nature upon the Divine Name. In the Bible, the Book of Common Prayer, and The Hymnal 1982 God's name was often preceded by the adjective "white" that was usually capitalized. In the Beatitudes Jesus proclaimed, "Blessed are the pure in heart, for they shall see White God." One of the most beloved Psalms frequently read aloud in the Burial Office said, "White God makes me lie down in green pastures and leads me beside still waters." The Collect for ordinations began "O White God of unchangeable power and eternal light" and the first line of Hymn 680 rejoiced "White God our help in ages past." And God-of-all colors-and-no-color, being grieved at this diminishment and seeing how creation perceived through this misshapen lens was likewise diminished, sent prophets to awaken and liberate the faithful people. And most people said it really wasn't a problem. Everyone knew that God wasn't really white.[36]

St. Hildegard's Community has continued to flourish with Rev. Liro's prophetic, creative leadership and the gifts of members. "We've been blessed with this immensely creative community, rich with gifts," Judith says. "There's been an outpouring of energy by everyone who's been a part of St. Hildegard's, whether it's been for a short time or for many years. Creating a community grounded in everyone's gifts has been part of being non-hierarchical. There's a sense of honoring and celebrating that each person brings something essential." St. Hildegard's members have also worked together to write a statement of commitments to the community. "Not everybody does all of them, but they are an expression of what we believe in order to live faithful lives," Judith explains. "There's a commitment to have a daily quiet time; a commitment about mindfulness, to be aware of our actions and try to live with love; a commitment about call, that we take love into the world in different ways; a commitment about accountability, that we'll meet in small groups or one-on-one to be more open about our lives and what we're struggling with and what's fruitful; a commitment about community, being faithful in worship and giving and sharing the work."

Although Rev. Liro never has drawn a large salary, she celebrates the financial resources that have come to St. Hildegard's Community. "I feel like we've been sustained financially," she says. "It's amazing to have had any salary for me as well as what we've had for the life of the community. There's been the generosity of the community, a core of faithful members who have given faithfully over all these years. There's been an anonymous donor who gave to St. George's when St. Hildegard's was beginning, and David shared a portion of this donation each year. Resources have come to us in surprising ways: the gift of a yellow Volkswagen Bug from my neighbor, the tithe on an inheritance, and the Trinity Grant[37] of about $86,000 to develop the Viriditas Project.[38] As the grant money was coming to an end, we were getting to another time of stress without money, as well as to that point of wanting to reach out with what we had created. With Rev. Hoster's help, we prepared a proposal for a diocesan strategic mission grant and received one for developing a website as well as strategies that will allow us to reach out."

St. Hildegard's Community brings love and justice into the world in a variety of ways. "The Community itself is a healing place," Rev. Liro says. "It is a place to learn to be gentle with ourselves and others, to embrace our humanity. It is shaped by our limitations and weaknesses as well as strengths and gifts. Weaving intimacy and caring, sharing joys and struggles, eating and playing together require a core group who tends the community. Shared leadership takes place in our work groups—Liturgy, Financial, Community Gatherings, Pastoral, Vision and Commitments, and the Servant Leadership School (SLS) are the main ones. It's as if every committee is also a prayer group and support group. The classes in the SLS are this way as well. For me this has meant close personal relationships happen naturally, and I am spiritually nourished in the course of working. This foundational community life offers healing to those who come to the classes or liturgies. Doing work 'in community' takes longer but it creates something unique, using the wisdom of the whole. For example, almost everyone in the community was involved in ways large and small in developing the Viriditas Curriculum, and we will soon have nine graduates. I like to describe our liturgies as 'Singing Justice.' I have been personally transformed by our liturgies. The love and mercy of God has been sung and danced into my soul over these years. Although I don't know how the Spirit will recreate the church, I feel that one dimension will be community—intimacy, relationship, and mutual support in seeking authenticity. I've been sustained by the caring, honest, genuine love of the community, the significant relationships, and the challenges community presents. I wish there was time to call each person by name who has been a gift to me. I imagine that every priest is transformed in his/her ministry, and my transformation has been deeply impacted by this special calling."

St. Hildegard's Community and Rev. Liro also reach out into the wider community with their justice actions. "Reaching out beyond our circle happens organically," she says. "Each member follows a call of doing their loving in the world. The community helps sustain those who are bringing healing into the world in their jobs as therapists, teachers, nurses, or working with elderly or special needs. One example of 'call' that also involves the community is *Austin Tan Cerca de la Frontera*.[39] Judith Rosenberg and Josefina Castillo do solidarity work with women in collectives in Mexico. They lead delegations to the border; they have a Women and Fair Trade event every November. Ten community members have gone on delegations, and some members volunteer and shop at the Fair Trade event. Other members are called to work with conscientious objectors, to work to end the death penalty, to build bridges of understanding to Muslims, to help refugees, to care for creation."

At a Women's Conference in Minsk, Belarus, where Joe was working at the time, and in a recent presentation to the women's group of St. David's Episcopal Church in Austin, Rev. Liro used a powerful metaphor to advocate for inclusion of female divine images in the language of liturgy to support justice and healing: "Patriarchy is helped to stay in place by words and symbols that shape our expectations and make us deaf to alternatives. . . . I like the useful metaphor of several factories that are built on a river and pollute the water of a village downstream. A hospital is built to treat the illnesses that result, but there is still a need to track down the source of the pollution and to clean up the water itself. Many organizations including the Church do the important work of the hospital. Yet I have also come to realize that the Church is one of the factories that contributes to the problem. Our liturgical language with its current, heavily masculine content supports a patriarchal hierarchical ordering. It often contradicts the life of our parishes that are more balanced. Having ordained women serving has helped make us more whole. A woman Presiding Bishop bringing loving wisdom—a couple of years ago it seemed unthinkable. . . . And yet the language hasn't caught up. Most are simply unaware of the power of language. The status quo that includes the exploitation of the earth, poverty, racism, sexism, heterosexism, militarism . . . is held in place by a deep symbolic imbalance, and we are unwitting participants in it." Rev. Liro says that she is grateful for those working in the Episcopal Church to write and officially adopt expansive language resources and hopes that St. Hildegard's creations can contribute to these resources for wider use.

Several years ago Judith and Joe went on a pilgrimage to the island of Iona. "I felt led to be more nurtured myself by the Sacred Feminine through the Celtic teaching and experience," Judith says. "At the Bay of New Beginnings one of the leaders of the pilgrimage, John Philip Newell,[40] asked people to pick up a rock that might stand for an intention they were making. "Out of thousands of rocks, I picked up one that had on it a symbol of the Feminine," Judith says. "John Philip said he'd never known anyone else to pick one like it. These are supposed to be some of the most ancient rocks on earth. To have this symbol gave me a sense that something bigger than I could wrap my mind around was happening. Somehow I was being communicated with that the Sacred Feminine is emerging, that somehow I'm a part of that. I'm hoping that what I'm doing in a small way will begin to come in a larger way." Judith's vision for the future of the Sacred Feminine includes an interfaith dimension so that people look beyond differences for "commonality" and "appreciation of diversity."

Judith describes the importance of her family throughout her journey. "My family has been like this deep river flowing in my life where I've given and received," Judith says. "My marriage to Joe has been both anchor and adventure. I've felt the Sacred Feminine not only in those early years of pregnancy, birth, breast feeding, and then the loss of our baby, but also in the years of parenting. I was always living in the tension of giving to my children and not wanting my passion for my ministry to take away from what I gave to them. They have grown into wonderful adults. My grandchildren bring so much joy, and I have to see them as often as possible. My daughter, Kate, and her husband, Tony, and their daughters, Reagan and Hayden, live east of Houston. My son, Chris, and his wife, Risa, and their sons, Will and Theo, live in Chicago. The love of family helps me to love more in my work as well."

Rev. Judith Liro continues to affirm Sophia's hand in her call to recreate the church: "St. Hildegard's Community has come about through Sophia's grace. Sophia-Spirit is creating a welcoming, healing, justice-nurturing place as She dances with us and weaves our lives together. Our life is in God's hands, and we live sustained by Her breath and energy."[41] The liberating ministry of Rev. Liro and St. Hildegard's Community inspires hope for the future of the church as a part of New Creation in the world.

11

Rev. Dr. Rebecca L. Kiser

Pastor
First Presbyterian Church, West Plains, Missouri

"Our Bible contains lots more images and metaphors for God than the official, orthodox Trinitarian formula," Rev. Dr. Rebecca Kiser proclaims in a powerful sermon on Holy Wisdom. "God is indefinable in human thought and language, so we end up using many names to try and capture the hugeness, the awesome enormity, the variety of experiences that make up our story with God. In the text we read from Proverbs on the figure of Wisdom, you'll notice in your Bibles that the 'W' is capitalized as a name, and Wisdom is pictured as a woman calling out to people to come to her and find Wisdom. We call several books of the Protestant Old Testament the 'Wisdom books'—Job, Psalms, Proverbs. And in the Catholic Bible there is also a book called the Wisdom of Solomon. People who study world religions often talk about the 'wisdom traditions' within various religious traditions. The figure of Woman Wisdom, or Lady Wisdom—or in Greek, *Sophia*—is a part of this. Several folks who have studied Holy Wisdom in both Proverbs and the Wisdom of Solomon, where there are more chapters about her, have noticed a great correlation between what is said of her and what is said of Christ, especially in the book of John. Much of what is said in John's prologue about the Word was taken from what is said in other places about Holy Wisdom. It's neat to read about Holy Wisdom on Trinity Sunday, because this name emphasizes that God can't be captured by any one definition, one experience, one perspective, one interpretation. Rather, God comes to each of us in the way we need in order to hear, to respond."

Members of First Presbyterian Church in West Plains, Missouri, tell me how delighted they are to have Rev. Kiser as pastor. One young woman expresses her pride that Rev. Kiser is not only the first woman pastor of this church but also the first woman pastor in the city of West Plains. Another member says he is impressed with her sermons and organizational skills, and another appreciates the creativity and continuity in the worship services she leads. The 125th anniversary of First Presbyterian of West Plains comes in 2011, and the church plans a big celebration. In a Sunday school class I attend, Rev. Kiser challenges people to think of a creative year-long community mission project to include in this celebration. With a uniquely painted sanctuary First Presbyterian also blends the new with tradition. The walls and arched ceiling in muted tones of rose, green, and gray catch my eye. Otherwise, the sanctuary resembles that of many traditional Protestant churches with two long rows of dark oak pews with red velvet cushions, wood floors except for red carpet down the middle aisle and in the pulpit area, tall luminous stained glass windows with geometric designs, and pipe organ. This church also follows tradition in using hymnals instead of screens with song lyrics projected on them. "Every other church in town projects words on a screen," Rev. Kiser comments. "We don't even have a screen."

Rebecca Kiser's story begins in a Washington, DC, independent fundamentalist church: Boulevard Heights Baptist. "Sometimes I've described myself as growing up pasting cotton balls on David's sheep and using up all the Crayolas on Joseph's coat of many colors," she says. "I grew up in Sunday school. The Baptist church turned out to be helpful because it gave me a really good knowledge of Scripture, a lot of memorization from the King James Version. There have been things in the theology I've had to unlearn, but I got a good grounding in Scripture and a good community experience in this medium-sized church of about 200 members. We were all connected. I didn't have any living grandparents, but I had a lot of grandparents at church. The church had a strong family-community-type feel, and I was happy there. We were three blocks from church, so we could walk. My dog followed me everywhere; she got a perfect attendance award at Vacation Bible School one year from a teacher with a good sense of humor. Right across the street from our house was my friend Joannie, and we played together all the time. The only trouble was that Joannie and her family were Catholics, and we were Baptists. Never mind that we spent all this time together almost daily for the years of my young life; on Sunday mornings, we went our separate ways. My church taught me that the Catholics were these awful people who prayed to Mary and saints, not real Christians like us, so I invited her to every revival meeting we had, and we had two per year. Of course, her church was teaching her that we Protestants were not real Christians, and forbade her to enter our buildings. So there was this impasse on Sunday, although the rest of the week we were fine."

Rebecca's mom, Ruth Kiser, worked for the government during World War II, and then taught high school math and later fifth grade. Her dad, Howard Kiser, served in the U.S. Navy and then used his training in mapmaking as he worked for the Naval Hydrographic Office, now called Naval Oceanographic Office. Rebecca, called "Becky," also grew up with a sister, Melissa, twenty months younger.

When Becky was seven years old, another younger sister, Susie, died from a genetic disease. "Susie lived for only two years; she died when I was in first grade," Becky recounts. "She died in March, and that summer I had my experience of going forward in the Baptist church, 'being saved,' in Baptist talk. I think there's some sort of correlation with my sister's dying, with the trauma of that. I don't know, but these experiences are only a few months apart, so I think there is some significance."

Missionaries who came to speak at her Baptist church also influenced Becky. "I wanted God to use me to do something like that," she recalls. "I seemed to have known really early on that I wanted to give my life to God. I thought I would serve God somehow; only I didn't think it would be as a preacher because, of course, there were no women preachers. But there were women missionaries and women choir directors. My mom had me in piano lessons, so some way or another I was going to serve church and serve God. I never thought about doing anything else too much except teaching. I thought about being a teacher for a while because that's what my mom was."

When Becky was in high school, Boulevard Heights Baptist Church went through turmoil because the founding minister, who had been there about twenty years, retired but didn't leave the church.

The next few ministers stayed only a short time. Becky had connected with Marie Chapman, the wife of one of these ministers. "I was upset when they left because those were some of my angst teenage years, and Marie had been really important to me, so I hated to lose her," Becky says. "I used this as an occasion to start looking at other churches and seeing how other churches did things. Also, I got into the 'Jesus people' stuff: the coffee houses, the long hair and jeans, carrying your Bible to school, and stickers all over your car."

After graduating from high school, Becky entered Philadelphia College of Bible. She acknowledges the "big influence" of a "really neat" piano teacher, Dr. Ron Boud. After several years at the Bible college, Becky traveled with a gospel band for a year. "I did keyboard for a Jesus band," she recalls. "We all lived together, and worked with Youth for Christ.[1] We did clubs during the week, and concerts and tours other times. I got disillusioned with the idea of the Spirit living in community, because that didn't work very well. About the time we got offered a record contract, we couldn't stand to stay together any longer."

Becky left the band and went to Wheaton College to finish her degree. "My dad died between my two years at Wheaton," Becky recounts. "That became the time when I began to rethink everything. I'd had some other experiences that put cracks in things, but after Daddy died, I had to rethink my faith. Fundamentalism cracked up and fell away. Then I didn't have anything in its place except that I still believed in God; I just didn't believe all the trappings that I'd been taught anymore. I had to put things back together, looking with a more open mind than I had before, instead of all the certainty of the fundamentalists. I began to explore a bit."

Other strong influences in her time at Wheaton were "Doc" Bill Phemister, her piano teacher; Dr. Rex Hicks, the choral director; and the book *All We're Meant to Be*.[2] "While I was at Wheaton, I read *All We're Meant to Be*, which Letha Dawson Scanzoni and Nancy Hardesty wrote," Becky says. "In that book, they wrote about the feminist ideas of women's value and women's rights, yet from within the world of evangelical language and style of biblical scholarship, quoting Scripture and doing striking exegetical work. They and other women within evangelical churches became the start of the biblical feminist movement, beginning an organization called the Evangelical

Women's Caucus, now the Evangelical & Ecumenical Women's Caucus (EEWC),[3] still going strong. *All We're Meant to Be* was such an eye-opener of a book that I never forgot the authors' names." Twenty years later Becky was "tickled" when one of her friends mentioned Letha:

"You'd probably get along with my friend Letha."

"Letha Dawson Scanzoni," Becky replied.

"How do you know her?"

"I remember her book from when I was like nineteen or twenty."

Letha and Becky became friends and colleagues in EEWC. "Letha became a mentor to me," Becky says.

In 1978, Becky graduated from Wheaton College with a Bachelor of Music in Piano Performance degree. Then she took a position, which she called "youth director, etc.," at Allentown Baptist Church in Camp Springs, Maryland. This church was dually aligned with the Southern Baptist Convention and the American Baptist Churches USA. Dick Delleney, the pastor, helped Becky expand her theological perspective. "He was probably more in line with the American Baptists, so things were widening a bit for me," she says. "He loved to preach from the Gospels because those were Jesus' words." Rev. Delleney encouraged Becky to broaden her view of what women could do in ministry, suggesting that she consider going to Louisville Presbyterian Theological Seminary, where women were finding openness to all their ministry gifts. She had interviewed at Southern Baptist Theological Seminary in Louisville, where an "older gentleman" told her "youth and music were good places for women in the church." The Presbyterian seminary greeted her with the enthusiastic response that she could do anything in ministry: "We are looking for women like you." Rev. Delleney and some of his friends wrote a letter to Southern Seminary expressing their displeasure over the limiting message Becky received there: "Why are you saying these kinds of things to women who come to interview and ask about seminary?" The people who had "different attitudes" from those who tried to restrict women in ministry gave Becky the "outer affirmation" she needed to pursue her call.

In 1979, Becky enrolled in Louisville Presbyterian Theological Seminary to work on a Master of Divinity degree. "It was like coming home," she recalls. "It was absolutely wonderful. There were a bunch of women. The women who came before me really did a lot of door opening. They had walked out of class when professors wouldn't use inclusive language. We had a women's caucus, very political sounding. Coming from where I was, the women sounded liberal and strident to me. I realized that the young women who came in every year after me went through the same transition as I had. We used to call it 'having your consciousness raised.' There was a split in the seminary women's group. Some wanted to pound the pulpit and say, 'We demand this.' And others were like, 'Wait a minute; I don't know.' I fell somewhere in the middle, with neither of the groups. Most of the women who were coming into the seminary were used to saying 'God-He' and weren't having any trouble with that, and yet were walking through all these doors that had been opened by women who had had a rougher time. Once I started hearing the arguments for inclusive language and hearing all the biblical support that came from what Letha and Nancy had written in *All We're Meant to Be*, I was like, 'Oh! Oh! Well, yes! Why wouldn't anybody who heard this and had it explained, why wouldn't they welcome it? It's a biblical understanding being unfolded.' So I fully expected to go out of seminary and teach inclusive language and leadership, and people would have the same reaction, like, 'Wow! It is in the Bible. Look at that. Wow! How wonderful!' Then, of course, that was not the reaction of the church at all. For me that was such an eye-opener."

At seminary Becky worked on a task force that published an inclusive language worship resource for use in the chapel. "We edited all of our hymnals," she says. "Inclusive language about people was a given by that time, but inclusive language about God was the cutting edge. At one point I got into a really big discussion with a systematic theology professor about language for God. We were trying to say 'Creator, Redeemer, Sustainer,' and he just went ballistic. He let loose his anger that had been going on for several years. He got really red-faced and said that if you weren't baptized in the name of the 'Father, Son, and Holy Spirit,' those exact words, it was not a Christian baptism and didn't count. There was some real resistance to the language change. Some people were really invested in the maleness aspect of the language. Words have power."

While at the Louisville seminary, Becky also worked with youth groups, and then her senior year served as the intern pastor of a church. "I had a supervisor, but I was preaching every week," she recounts. "The seminary emphasized field education. My senior year I had a little congregation. I discovered I really loved preaching. Everything was affirming that this was my call."

When she was in seminary, Becky married Will Lowrance, who was also studying to be a pastor. "We were a clergy couple with hyphenated names, 'Kiser-Lowrance,'" she says. "We were going to go out and work together and be equal. But we got different treatment in the job search. He had some interviews and offers, and I was getting calls from people who wanted only a one-third-time pastor. How can you move for that? At that point my husband was really supportive, and we made a covenant that we would not move until we both had calls. We did try to get one church that was calling him; I worked hard to present the idea of being called as an evangelist to the Committee on Ministry (COM) there. The COM went so far as to have me come down and make a presentation, and then they vetoed it. I thought they were open and interested, but they were just trying to get my husband to come. They said to me, 'Well, if you really had faith, you would come with your husband, since he has a call, and have faith that God would find you work here.' I said, 'We've prayed about it, and we have faith that God's going to call us both.' My husband was supportive of that and told the church he couldn't come."

Becky and her husband, Will, decided to look for a larger parish where they could be copastors. In 1983, soon after Becky graduated from seminary, they went to the Presbyterian General Assembly in Atlanta. This was also the year that the northern and southern Presbyterian churches voted to reunite.[4] "They came together and had a big festive march," she recalls. "Will and I worked the vocation agency booth—stood there and shook hands and met executives and handed out our dossiers. That's how we got our call. An executive we met there was looking for a clergy couple to come up to Wisconsin to work with a five-church parish."

In August of 1983, Becky and Will became copastors of Maplewood Presbyterian Parish in Cornell, Wisconsin. In September of that year Becky was ordained as a Minister of Word and Sacrament. When they arrived at the Wisconsin parish, one of the members said to Becky: "You know the presbytery[5] told us we couldn't ask for pictures, and we didn't know if you were black or white. But we listened to your tape and we said, 'At least you're not shrill!'" Rev. Kiser says that the "only real issue" where she encountered opposition because of her gender came when she moderated the trustees during a building campaign. "Will and I had split up all the groups, and it was my turn to moderate the trustees," she recalls. "They were having leak problems with a flat roof on a fellowship hall, so they decided to do a capital campaign and put a pitched roof on it. The trustees could not get their minds around me as a leader in the building campaign. I just could not get through to them when I talked about getting a ballpark cost for the roof. In frustration, I took Will with me to a meeting. A few minutes into the meeting he, as we had agreed, began repeating exactly what I had just said that had raised arguments. The committee responded to him, 'That's exactly right, pastor!' After the meeting I said to Will, 'Okay, you get to moderate the trustees, because they can't hear me about money and about building.' The way our skills worked together was that he hated that kind of work, and I was good at it. But the trustees couldn't see past my gender."

Overall, the people in this rural Wisconsin parish supported both the Revs. Kiser-Lowrance. "That was really affirming being there," Becky says. "I felt like I had found my place. We were the first pastors of this new parish that included five small churches, so we got lots of experience. We had five sessions[6] between us and a parish council and five women's groups—lots of bazaars, lots of picnics, lots of everything. Altogether in the churches there were 300 members. This was in upstate Wisconsin—very rural, marginal farming, dairy, snow driving in the winter. It was a neat adventure with wonderful people. The women's groups sent us to a regional conference to educate us about their mission and let us know it was more than bake sales. It really opened my eyes to the work of the Presbyterian Women. The women had been doing their own growth work and their own explorations from a different direction than ordained ministry. Their theology and mission activity and statements on the worth of women were really progressive."

While in Wisconsin, Becky and Will had their first two children, Grady and Casey. "When we had a second child, Will went through this big panic," she recalls. "He was like, 'Our churches are all going to fold, and we're going to be living in the snow under a freeway or something!' It always looked like our churches were barely making it, like there was hardly enough in the budget, even though people gave enough to cover basic expenses. Will put his dossier out, looking for another parish. I decided that I wanted to be home with kids for a few years; the idea of trying to balance everything felt overwhelming. So I gave him permission to look for a call in a place that was big enough that there would be possibilities for me too."

Rev. Kiser moved with her husband to Virginia Beach when he received a call to Bayside Presbyterian Church. "It was quite the adjustment to be a mom and homemaker," she says. "I didn't expect it to be such an adjustment. It really did feel like a loss of part of myself, and I wondered a good bit if I'd made the right decision. One place it was hard was in money. That was his money; I wasn't earning any. Somehow or another my sense of worth had been tied up with that. It was hard to think about it as our money. I had my name out for what they call 'random supply,' when you fill in for other preachers. So I was doing some preaching here and there."

Also, when she lived in Virginia Beach, Rev. Kiser taught short courses at Dolphin Tales, a Christian bookstore that carried books on the women's movement and the men's movement. There she taught a four-week course called "Worshipping with God as Mother," drawing from Miriam Therese Winter's book *WomanPrayer, WomanSong*.[7] Also, she team-taught groups in a sixteen-week study of *Women Who Run with the Wolves*.[8] "Those groups got a great response for a long time," she recalls.

In 1989, Becky and Will had a third child, Emma, born in a terminal condition. Emma lived only six weeks. "That turned out to be a huge trauma in my own life, and in all our lives," Becky says. "Will and I lasted about another six years married, but he moved out on Emma's birthday. I think her death was where the split came. We'd gone on and had Joe after that though, so I have three living children and one I lost. After my dad died and after Emma died were times of major theological rethinking for me, inner reworking of everything."

In an article entitled "God of the Casserole" in *Update: Newsletter of the Evangelical & Ecumenical Women's Caucus*, Rev. Kiser relates the transformation that took place in her divine images after Emma's death. "As I began sorting out and dealing with my anger and grief, two images of God in the feminine arose in my prayer and became agents of healing and restoration," she writes. "This was surprising to me because, at the time, I was not comfortable using feminine pronouns or imaging God in the feminine. . . . The first image of God in feminine form came when I was in depression, having trouble getting up and getting dressed. . . . As I wept one night at the kitchen table, dryer buzzing and dishes stacked in the sink, thinking no one had ever suffered as I did, I looked over and saw a little woman there doing my dishes. She was in a shapeless robe and disreputable slippers, and her hair was up in those pink rollers I remember from childhood. She turned around, took the cigarette from the corner of her mouth, and said these un-counselor-like words: 'Honey, things happen to everybody.' Then she disappeared. I began to giggle, then laugh, then absolutely hoot. Where were the graceful angels with light surrounding them? Where was the majesty and exalted imagery? Where were choirs of heavenly comfort? My vision probably sang off-key and with a twang! Yet with one deftly-inserted and well-timed line of reality, she put my feet back on earth and reminded me that I stood in a long tradition of women who grieved their lost children of many colors, and put me in touch with the strength of women through many generations."[9]

As she continued to work through her anger at God for not healing her baby, another image of the Divine Feminine came to Becky. "I had talked of seeing God in the people who came to be with us, bringing dinners and fruit baskets and desserts as well as their love and care," she writes. "Yet I had difficulty accepting this image of God or feeling any comfort from it. . . . Suddenly, I remembered that old picture from my Sunday school days, where Jesus is standing at the heart's door and knocking—only when I pictured it now, Jesus was carrying a covered casserole. Again I laughed, with an edge of anger. What do I do with a God bearing casseroles? All the same, the image captured me and wouldn't go away, so I decided to sculpt it and see what happened. The form that emerged from under my hands was once again a woman, like so many of the people who had come to my door. She carried a 9x13 pan of either lasagna or chicken and rice; I couldn't decide. She became a focal point of all my ambivalent feelings, for I felt gratitude and comfort from her presence at the same time that I experienced a raging anger that she didn't do more, that she wasn't more powerful. I raged at her again and again, and still she stayed, her face concerned, her gift in her hand. She was not put off by my anger; she didn't take her gifts and go home. Nor did she become defensive or abusive in the face of my outburst. I came finally to realize that she is who she is, and the anger was mine, the expectations were mine, the desires for protection and security were mine, the disappointment that came from a false image of God was mine. She is who she has always been: compassionate, strong, present, passionate, truth, connected from the womb, unafraid, encompassing, mysterious."[10]

In this article, written six years after losing Emma, Rev. Kiser also describes how these two experiences of the Divine Feminine have helped her move from simply avoiding the exclusive use of masculine pronouns for God to the inclusion of feminine names and images. "Even though I had broadened the imagery I used in speaking of God, my gender-avoiding language meant that I experienced God as a genderless, generic friend," she writes. "God was beyond gender, I told myself and others. So these two new experiences of God in the feminine were initially disconcerting and awkward.... In these encounters, God was deeply a woman, not genderless. I am still working to integrate these experiences of God as the archetype of Great Mother into my own life and dialogue with both the Bible and tradition around them.... Encountering God this way has made me reevaluate the notion of God as beyond gender and see God as encompassing both genders—gender-*full* rather than genderless. I have also had to deal more deeply with my own feelings about being a woman and have come to value the feminine anew.... I look on the growth of spirit and creativity I have experienced as gifts from my daughter Emma and think it is somehow appropriate that it was she who, through her brief time on earth, introduced me to the Great Mother in God."[11]

In Virginia Beach Becky also found support in a Presbyterian Women's circle. "That's when I was at home and raising kids," she recalls. "When I didn't have a call myself, I attended a daytime circle of moms with kids, and that was fun. We did the *Horizons* Bible lessons, published by the denomination.[12] They were thought-provoking women's studies."

In 1993, Rev. Kiser attended the first Re-Imagining Conference in Minneapolis.[13] "I was attracted by the literature and knew a couple of the speakers," she says. "I figured I'd see some of my seminary friends. I like going to conferences, and it looked like a neat one. And, of course, it was very, very neat! It turned into a giant high point for me. I went up a day early to the preconference event, a tour of artists' studios. One of the artists had done a series of paintings of women who had had mastectomies. She did women in the classical poses, like with the turn of the trunk and the head over the shoulder. But they didn't have breasts anymore or had only one breast. They were so beautiful. That was worth the whole conference right there, just to see that feminine beauty, even with the surgery. And then the language throughout the whole conference was inclusive. We could sing without changing words under our breath, and they called Christ 'Sophia.' They used the name 'Christ-Sophia,' and they called God 'She' for the whole three days. It was delightful! I just opened up and entered into the whole thing."

In an *EEWC Update* review of Mary Jo Cartledgehayes' book *Grace*,[14] Rev. Kiser also recounts her transforming experience of the Re-Imagining Conference. "The deciding factor for me to send in my registration was that the planners intentionally called the schedule the 'Time Flow,' even re-imagining how to hold a conference!" she writes. "Like Cartledgehayes and many others who attended, Re-Imagining was a formative conference for me. . . . For the first time, I heard God addressed in female pronouns for three days straight, in worship and in sermon and by folks on the podium. I moved through my initial awkwardness and discomfort, to discover the power of celebrating my gender as in the image of the Divine. It was a turning point in my own appreciation of the feminine, as well as a turning point in claiming my own point of view as I returned to a presbytery holding hearings and town meetings about a conference they considered heresy and even blasphemy."[15]

The controversy that occasioned the town meetings began shortly after the conclusion of the conference when *The Layman*[16] denounced it. "When I got home, *The Layman* was published, and then all the brouhaha started," she recalls. "One of the guys from our presbytery who was on General Assembly Council and I had to sit on a panel and let people ask us why in the world we ever considered going to the conference. I hadn't gone to be deliberately provocative or anything. I thought it was going to be one of those conferences that you go to and have fun, and nobody ever cares. But people did care. A couple of the churches really became reactionary. People were sitting on the front row with tape recorders, intimidating as hell. There was a woman from another presbytery who was going to come up and be moral support for me, and she got so freaked out by her own presbytery that she was afraid to come. We were there to answer questions and let people yell at us, in the name of having a town meeting for people's concerns. But it really was not nice. It took something that had really been an important experience for me and tried to vilify it, so that was very difficult. A couple of women accosted me in the restrooms with their anger. I guess that's when I began to realize how much people were invested in the maleness of the tradition."

For many years Rev. Kiser felt repercussions from the Re-Imagining Conference. "One church that was in my neighborhood needed a part-time pastor, and I interviewed," she recalls. "One of the guys in the interview got right in my face and said, 'You will have this pulpit over my dead body, because you tried to neuter God.' God was really male to him. Otherwise, how could you neuter God? He also said, 'Well, God has to be male or otherwise He couldn't have made Mary pregnant.' I'm thinking, 'How literal do we want to be here? Come on. This is almost in the realm of silly.' But that's where he was. God could obviously impregnate women, so He must be male. That's such a bizarre thought."

In spite of all the criticism, Rev. Kiser continued to affirm the Re-Imagining Conference as "liberating and forward-looking." The conference inspired her to write a few poems that were published in the *Re-Imagining* quarterly. "That was one of my first attempts to put something out there," she recalls. "One poem is about birthing a daughter. I didn't have a good relationship with my mother, and I was scared of having a girl baby. But it made me deal with issues on the inner level about being a girl and what I was going to teach her and how I was going to be with her. I had to work on negative things that I had internalized about being female because I didn't want to give them to my daughter. Of course, she got enough from the culture." The last line of Rev. Kiser's poem, "Birth Prayer," is this: "I vow that the world will not do to her as it has to me."[17] Now Becky describes her relationship with her adult daughter, Casey, as a "delightful experience." She says, "I've been challenged to be more feminist and to not give up the feminine side."

Rev. Kiser tells a story to illustrate the difference that a feminist perspective and inclusive language can make. When Casey was around nine, she and her mother had this exchange:

"Mom, God must be a man because all the hymns say, 'He.' And they always say 'He' in church."

"Well, your mother doesn't say 'He' in church. God had to make men and women to show God's image."

"Well, I don't know."

Then Casey went with her mother to Good Samaritan Episcopal Church in Virginia Beach, where Rev. Kiser played the keyboard for the services. One Sunday the church sang "Washerwoman God," by Martha Ann Kirk and Colleen Fulmer.[18] After the service, Casey said to her mother, "Well, that song had God as a woman, so, Mom, you might be right." Rev. Kiser comments on the power of this Divine Feminine name in the song: "Even just one hymn, even hearing God as woman affirmed one time by the whole church led Casey to say that I might be right, which is a big thing coming from your own kid!"

For a while Rev. Kiser held other part-time ministry positions in the Virginia Beach area. She served as part-time interim pastor of Bow Creek Presbyterian Church and then part-time temporary pastor of Grace Covenant Presbyterian Church of Princess Anne. When she became a single parent, she held the two part-time positions of Hunger Action Enabler and Resource Center Director with the Presbytery of Eastern Virginia. "I had to buy a house for the first time in my life because we'd always lived in what Presbyterians call the 'manse,'"[19] she says. "I also had to learn to juggle being a single parent and going back to work full-time."

At Grace Covenant Presbyterian, a new church development, where Rev. Kiser preached for eighteen months, she met resistance to her use of inclusive language. After she had been there a year, the woman who typed the Sunday bulletins noticed that Rev. Kiser avoided the traditional male pronoun references to God. "It took her about a year of typing my bulletins before it hit her that I wasn't using pronouns," Rev. Kiser recalls. "She went ballistic, and said that I had stolen her grandfather from her. She couldn't get past this strong identification of God with her grandfather."

When Rev. Kiser worked for the presbytery, she also experienced some opposition. "The Re-Imagining Conference stayed in people's memory about me as I was working with churches," she says. "Out of sixty-something churches, I was in forty-five of them. But there were some who wouldn't invite me even to work in hunger action or anything, because of what they remembered about me."

In the Presbytery of Eastern Virginia, Rev. Kiser also worked as Education and Resource Facilitator and then as Acting Coordinator of Campus Ministries. In the latter position she spent 60 percent of her time as campus minister at Old Dominion University in Norfolk, and 40 percent interpreting all campus ministries to 65 churches in the presbytery. Among her services as campus minister Rev. Kiser organized ongoing programs, planned campus outreach through special events like a Labyrinth Prayer Walk, led the presbytery in purchasing a physical plant that was named the Student Faith Center, participated in interfaith events through the University Chaplains Association, and worked with the Women's Center on the Women in Leadership Development program and on the closing ceremony of Sexual Assault Awareness Week. After three years in campus ministry, the funding for the full-time position ran out, so she took the position of interim pastor of Ocean View Presbyterian Church in Norfolk. "It became really important to me when the kids were teenagers to keep them near their dad, and help them not lose that relationship," she says. "So I took whatever needed to be done in the Norfolk area."

After the interim position ended, Rev. Kiser became an assistant manager with Ten Thousand Villages, a fair trade organization associated with the Mennonite church.[20] Although she saw this job as ministry, she really wanted to work in the church, so she interviewed for a pastorate. She was one of the top two candidates with four different churches, but she was not the person called. "The 'second call' was where I ran into the wall, as many women have found when they have temporarily left a predictable career path in other fields as well," she writes. "While the church folk were outwardly affirming of my choice to be home with my young children, getting another call has been difficult."[21]

Rev. Kiser did not let obstacles deter her from growing as a minister. Through these years while she was serving in a variety of positions, she completed training in spiritual direction and in interim ministry. She calls herself a "lifetime learner." Encouraged by Letha Dawson Scanzoni, Becky became active in Evangelical & Ecumenical Women's Caucus and a frequent contributor to the EEWC newsletter and other publications. And she took the challenge of going back to school to get a Doctor of Ministry degree. "When I started studying about spiritual direction, we read some books by Matthew Fox,"[22] she says. "I was looking for a DMin program. First, I called all the Presbyterian seminaries to see if they offered a program in spirituality. At that time none of the Presbyterian seminaries offered a DMin in spirituality. I kept looking. I picked up my *Creation Spirituality* magazine, and one of those annoying little cards fluttered out; it announced the opening of Matthew Fox's University of Creation Spirituality in Oakland, California, offering a new Doctor of Ministry program. So I said, 'This is cool! All right let's look into that.' I taped the card on the wall by my desk, so I wouldn't lose it." In an article entitled "Lessons from a Fearful Venturer," Becky writes this dialogue with herself as she struggles with the decision to pursue this degree:

> "These people are too radical, you'll never be able to put it on your dossier. It will not help you get a church in this denomination. You'll have to leave the children. What will the church people think?
>
> It will be adventurous; you'll get exposed to some new ideas; you liked the books; it will be good for you to do it; you'll get to see California.
>
> It will damage my children. We'll have to spend lots of money on child care, and it will cost money for the degree, too. And you've never even heard Matthew Fox speak!
>
> I really am excited to go; the courses sound like things I'd go to conferences for—they interest me.
>
> You'll be going outside the denomination again—aren't you just a little tired of being marginalized already? Don't you really want to do something right and mainstream?
>
> No, I'm realizing it's not necessarily my path to do everything mainstream; lots of other people already do that. If it's too weird, I can come home."[23]

In June of 2001, Becky completed her Doctor of Ministry degree. With enthusiasm she recalls her experience with teachers and classmates who stretched her mind and spirit. "I knew it would be a treat to meet Matthew Fox and learn from him," she says. "I liked Matthew Fox's idea of original blessing and the way he talked about the prophet and the mystic being two sides of the same call. When he was accused of being 'new agey' or something, he said, 'No, this is actually very Christian and very ancient Christian. I think *The Coming of the Cosmic Christ*[24] is his best work. And the other teachers were writing intriguing books. They were people doing things related to creation spirituality or explorations in spirituality that can be brought back into Christianity, and that have been there. I had a class with Brian Swimme,[25] who wrote *The Hidden Heart of the Cosmos*.[26] I took fascinating classes that Clarissa Pinkola Estés[27] and Andrew Harvey[28] team-taught with Matthew Fox, and a class that Hal Taussig[29] taught on the Divine Feminine, including Sophia. Also, I took a class with Sister Jose Hobday,[30] a Native American Catholic sister. I did two classes with Jeremy Taylor,[31] who wrote books on dreams, and a class with David Abram, who wrote *Spell of the Sensuous*.[32]" The doctoral program included "Art as Meditation," using art and dreams as a part of "inner processing and spiritual work." Bruce Silverman[33] led a drumming group, and David Abram[34] led walking meditation. "We went walking in the headland hills outside of San Francisco, and I joked that there were twelve of us in the class following our teacher around, learning the mysteries of life," Becky laughs.

Her DMin project and dissertation is entitled "The Other Day in the Garden." Working with the local civic league, city council, and area businesses in Norfolk, Virginia, she started an organic, communal community garden. In her dissertation she includes events, problems, lessons, pictures, results, and creative reflections about this experience. "The assignment was to do something that challenged ourselves in our own personal growth and to work into that *Transformativa*,[35] into something that would bring a change to society," Becky says. "I'd been gardening since seminary, and the eco-theology spoke to me strongly, creation spirituality's awe and love of creation. So I decided to design a community garden that would be organic or natural and would incorporate a central commons area, a place that would invite the public in. It would have free-form beds and not straight paths because I was reading about curving paths inviting more meditation and thinking. The challenge was to bring this garden into being in the world, because I'm good at the theoretical and at theology, and I know how to work in church, but I didn't know how to work in the civic sphere outside of church. The best thing was going through our civic league, which was active. The civic league was behind me. People came out of the woodwork to help—people who were organic hippies, a woman who was a biological researcher at the university, young couples who thought it was really cool. We got this whole mix of people." Becky met the challenges of finding the property for the garden, getting insurance coverage, and obtaining permission from the city council. After the first year, the city government gave Becky and her team an award for environmental responsibility. Also, the community garden became one of the "art spots" on the annual art walk. "It became just what I wanted," she says. "It became a community spot and a real garden experience. It turned into a neat project, and it's ongoing."

In a sermon on Hildegard of Bingen, preached in 2004 at a Presbyterian Women's gathering, Rev. Dr. Kiser expresses her ongoing passion for gardening and creation spirituality. "Now I am a gardener, and I love spring," she says. "I love cool mornings when the ground can be worked, and I can just wear myself out digging and playing in the dirt, and go home tired, with the smell of soil still on my hands. I love green. My soul soars when the garden is lush, and flowers are blooming, the bean plants are up, the tomato cages full of leafy plants, rows of red radishes, purple eggplants, dark burgundy hollyhocks, sunflowers—I love all of them. I hadn't made the connection to incarnation until I read Hildegard. I thought incarnation just referred to Jesus, which of course it does. But you see, Hildegard makes that mystical leap that sees Jesus, wholly God and wholly human, as teaching us a deeply incarnational truth of reality—that God is here with us, Immanuel, that the material, the human flesh, the 'matter' of life, is interpenetrated with God. Spirit and matter are not separate things. God is here. Spirit moves around, among, and within us. We have not looked at this creation that God calls 'good' in the very first chapters of our book of faith and seen God, and therefore we have not cared for it, been stewards of it, but rather have been users and exploiters of its gifts. We've made religion and salvation matters of the inner life and a future, non-earthly heaven—and here we sit when the world God made, and the world God sent the Christ to save is at the brink of ecological suicide. Perhaps it is to us that the vision of Hildegard, of that greening power of the One who is life itself, that all is interpenetrated with God, of that deep view of incarnation—perhaps her words, rediscovered in this day and age, are those words we need to hear and live for the world to be literally saved."

In West Plains, Missouri, Rev. Kiser also participates in a community garden. "The county offices here were already planning to do a community garden, but I jumped in with them," she says. "Environmental issues have been on my mind and heart since I started doing the work for the community garden in Norfolk. I read a lot about eco-spirituality or 'ecofeminism,' as some were calling it. That's a big issue for me." During my visit to West Plains Becky drives me to the garden and talks with excitement about her vision of expanding the garden and involving more people. She has used one plot to grow produce for a local food pantry, and the Community Garden Committee is challenging groups to take a plot for hunger relief. First Presbyterian Church accepted this challenge.

At a conference in Atlanta Rev. Kiser had learned of the opening at the West Plains church. Rev. Mary Newbern-Williams,[36] who had been the associate executive in the presbytery in Virginia where Becky served, and was now the General Presbyter of John Calvin Presbytery in Missouri, told her about the church, and she expressed her interest. She interviewed, and in October of 2009, Rev. Dr. Kiser became pastor of First Presbyterian Church of West Plains, Missouri. "This is what I really love doing," she affirms.

As the first woman pastor of a mainline church in West Plains, Rev. Kiser believes her very presence invites change. "I think it challenges people's mindsets just to see a woman up front," she says. "And I think of it as giving little girls more options. If they've only seen male pastors, suddenly they're seeing a female pastor, and say, 'Oh, yeah, I could be one of those!' Professional women are conscious of these issues too. I hate it that the church is often the last to see something that seems to me so obviously a Christian expression. We're the last ones to get on the bandwagon. And then people call us 'politically correct,' like it's not really a theological issue. It was hard at first to give my experience of discrimination as a woman the same kind of credence I'd been giving the experience of African Americans in our country. That was an obvious issue to me in the country and the world, but to apply that to women was hard. Once I got past that and began to see the women's issue as a similar thing, suddenly all these other groups demanded my empathy as well—LGBT persons, other minorities, battered women, disabled people. It opened up a sensitivity to all kinds of minority positions. I think the ability to take another person's point of view is good for the church and the culture. I think that's what the Christian Gospel is about. I'd like the church to be proactive on some justice issue. I wish we'd taken the lead on the gay and lesbian issue. Our churches are really a part of our culture, and we don't stand apart and criticize it really well or speak God's word to it. Learning to talk feminist or womanist theology opens up a lot of doors."

The other ministers in West Plains have welcomed Rev. Kiser into the ministerial fellowship. "The mainline denominations have women clergy, so I don't think I was the first one that any of them had seen," she says. "They invited me, as the newbie in town, to preach for the community Ash Wednesday service, so I got some exposure there. I haven't felt any discomfort with me as a minister here."

Rev. Kiser sees her sermon on Holy Wisdom as indicative of her approach to expanding people's theology through biblical preaching and teaching. "My style is to be like a bridge, to go out and explore things and then find ways to bring them back in and bridge them," she says. "That comes through in my sermons and in my attitudes. I consciously move between illustrations with men and women. I read Psalms that are more like prayers and say, 'You,' instead of 'He.' I use some of the neat hymns that have many names of God. We have to have words to shape our thinking. It's important to put out the varied imagery to give people different categories for their thoughts. I think the assumption that God is male and you always call God 'He' is an unquestioned, unconscious thing for many people. And the first time somebody makes them think outside that, it's almost devastating. It feels like you've really blown up their religion until their faith expands to take that in and they realize, 'Oh, I've been living in this part, but look, there's all this part.'"

At a workshop, Rev. Kiser heard Rev. Susan Cole[37] describe a waking dream. "The waking dream was that Sophia (Divine Wisdom) called to her, and she came outside a door to meet Sophia," Becky recounts. "And Susan looked back and saw a beautiful church. She thought, 'Oh, I've had to leave the church to follow the Divine Sophia.' But then Susan looked and there was a bigger church, a bigger world, and her view enlarged. There was a bigger experience that she could be a part of. I thought, 'Wow! What a cool image that is!' It's really stuck with me. But it does feel scary at first. Your faith has to grow to take that in."

Rev. Dr. Kiser loves the church and delights in her ministry within the church. The only time she ever thought about leaving the church was after the Re-Imagining Conference. "I got into a negative spot about the church," she recalls. "Some people became mean-spirited after the conference. I've come to see that people bring power issues and whatever our issues are into the church. We can't help it. We're just a bunch of human beings. We act out our issues on whatever stage we have. What saved me at that point was becoming involved with the hunger action people and the peacemaking and social justice element in the church. I went to some regional and national conferences with the hunger action and peacemaking people, and they were delightful. The church attracts people at all levels of faith and spirituality. I wanted everybody to jump into the Scripture with both feet and to read *All We're Meant to Be* and see the truth in that. And not everybody does, and not everybody will. That was kind of disillusioning. But I came to a point where I said, 'Well, they'll have to kick me out. I'm going to stay. If those naysayers can send out their letters with things underlined in red and arrows pointing to what disturbs them, my voice needs to be heard too. They'll have to kick me out, because I won't leave.' You can't really change anything from the outside, but you can stay inside and quietly start to form things from a different direction, like in that book *Defecting in Place*.[38]"

In bringing change to the church, Rev. Kiser recognizes the power of language inclusive in race and gender. "I think the church has not realized where it's an oppressor and how it's contributed to oppression because we've been in the majority that benefits," she comments. "It's easier to do handouts than to take somebody's point of view. But that's an important move as people grow in faith. Your ears change. For a silly example, I had an African American boss, David Greene,[39] who really liked the song 'White Christmas.' My ears hear 'white' and 'black' differently now, like if you say, 'Oh, I'm having some dark thoughts,' I say, 'Don't use that language.' So when he said he liked 'White Christmas,' I just hooted. But he got it. I hear things now that I hadn't heard. It's a real consciousness-type thing. Some people in the Virginia Presbytery are teaching that God's name is 'Father,' that it's not a metaphor, that language is not metaphorical, and that it is only correct to call God 'Father.' They're not getting this from Presbyterian seminaries. 'Father' is one of the metaphors used in Scripture; I think the mistake is using it exclusively. In some of my pastoral prayers I've used 'Mother' imagery and have preached on passages with this imagery. I've thought of doing a sermon series on the Lord's Prayer and talking about the 'Our Father' image from the 'Abba' name Jesus used that means 'Daddy' or 'Father-Mother.'"

In a presentation to the Theophilus Club, an interfaith clergy group in Norfolk, Rev. Dr. Kiser describes the evolution that took place in her understanding of the power of language. "I arrived at seminary with a feeling of call and a love of the church, very comfortable with calling God 'Father' exclusively, and just beginning to learn about the formative power of language about people," she says. "As my eyes were opened and my consciousness raised, it seemed to me natural and obvious that inclusive language about people was simply a given, and that all people of thought realized that 'Father' was one name among many for God; although it was an important metaphor, it was not the only one. I thought I was among the last ones learning this in my wonderful, newly chosen denomination of Presbyterianism whose slogan was 'Reformed and Always Reforming' and now believed in ordaining women. I thought that all people of good will, and surely that meant all Christians, simply needed to have this explained to them, and they would certainly want to do all they could to embrace inclusive language and a variety of images, names, and metaphors for God so that women could be fully included. Well, I have since learned how totally naïve I was, even about religious leadership. I was totally surprised that the church didn't take to these liberating insights, but rather rose up in fierce backlash, especially against the 1993 conference Re-Imagining, which was probably the most forward-looking conference on Christian theology to that date, and will probably go down in history as a watershed event in the lives of all the attendees. I know it was that for me."

Rev. Kiser's theology continued to expand many years after she had graduated from seminary when she read Sallie McFague's book *Metaphorical Theology*.[40] "In this book, McFague gives form and language to the long-standing spiritual intuition that God is so beyond any human name as to make any one name false as soon as it is spoken," Becky says. "McFague gave words to the feminist critique of the Christian church for focusing so much on the one metaphor of God as 'Father' that it has become idolatrous, making true Mary Daly's insight that if God is male, then male is God. Realizing the status of women as a minority, and outside of the structure, McFague writes as one whose perspective as an 'outsider' has helped her to see the mythos we church folks have been immersed in so much so as to be unconscious of its effect on us. She draws from liberation theology's insights about dominant power structures' blindness to the very structures that oppress, as they are the beneficiaries of the system that exists, and the realization that the voice from the margins, that sees the injustices, can be the prophetic voice of God leading to the salvation of the whole."

In a review of Carolyn Bohler's book *God the What?: What Our Metaphors for God Reveal about Our Beliefs*,[41] Rev. Kiser also comments on the value of expanded theology. "We of EEWC especially appreciate a broader use of feminine metaphors for God, recognizing the way an unreflective use of solely masculine metaphors for God has resulted in a virtual identification of God with the masculine, to an unfortunate and idolatrous end," she writes. "In this book, Bohler invites us to open up our imaginations and play with those metaphors from Scripture and classic writing and those that arise in our own faith journeys."[42]

When talking about the future of the church, Rev. Dr. Kiser tells the story of going to the final service of First Presbyterian Church in Newport News, Virginia. "They had gotten down to a size where they realized they could not continue," she recounts. "I wasn't preaching every Sunday then, so I decided I would go to the closing service of the church and support the pastor on his last Sunday. It was one of those old First churches with beautiful stained glass windows and a pipe organ and wood and wainscoting, chair rails down the hallways, wooden banister, parlor—just a beautiful church in the 1950s model. I remember walking through the church and running my hand down the chair railing and getting the feeling that it wasn't just that church that was closing, but more like that era of church was closing, like the way we've been doing church is closing. Something's changing. My feeling is that we're in a transitional phase of some kind. There are things I'd love to see happen in the church."

One of Rev. Kiser's visions for the church is more opportunity for women ministers. In a sermon entitled "Gifts from the Other Side," Rev. Kiser comments on how long it took the Presbyterian Church to approve women's ordination. "It took us a while—overtures came to the General Assembly and were defeated for fifty years before we finally approved it, and Margaret Towner was ordained in 1956," she says. "The Spirit of God is still working in humanity to open our eyes to God's truth, even though it takes a long while sometimes to break through our cultural norms and our insecurities. Just think about it—for so long, the church of Jesus Christ operated without the benefit of leadership from half its membership!" Rev. Kiser laments that women still have more difficulty than men in finding churches beyond the entry level.

In 2006, for the fiftieth anniversary of women's ordination in the Presbyterian Church, Rev. Kiser organized a celebration. She contacted all the women of her presbytery to find out when they were ordained and where they had served. "We published that and read it at the celebration," she recalls. "We had the ones who were there to stand up. As we went down the list of names, it became obvious how many had gone into social work, how many had become counselors, how many were members at large, how many were interims. There were only four or five who had church positions. People came up afterwards and said they had no idea we had that many women in our presbytery and that so many of them couldn't find church jobs. For example, my friend Rev. Susan Haugh went into social work because she couldn't get a second call. So she retrained and did her ministry with people in another way. When Susan retired, she asked me to speak at the presbytery meeting about her ministry. I spent some time interviewing her, getting the details about her life and some of her insights and wisdom. She was one of the first 100 Presbyterian Church (USA) clergywomen. She led the way, and has been a real encouragement and mentor to me and others. After I spoke about Susan at the presbytery meeting, she was invited to comment. At the same meeting we took two young women under care to go to seminary and to become pastors. Susan said, 'I hope you all hear out of all this that when you make these promises to these young women, you need to be ready for their gifts.'"

Rev. Dr. Kiser continues to elaborate her vision for the future of the church. "It would be a widely inclusive group of people who have learned to be together, despite all kinds of dissimilarities, that ideal of unity in the midst of diversity," she says. "The worship at our General Assemblies is always wonderful and very diverse! They include people from many countries and rousing sermons. I love to see people do creative worship and bring all kinds of gifts into it, all kinds of people and all kinds of imagery. When we can welcome those different from ourselves, we discover more about the fullness of humanity and the fullness of God. It means we've moved beyond living in fear, and are learning to live in a bigger picture where we trust a God who is all in all. It means we've entered the welcome of the table, where God says that people will come from north and south and east and west and sit together at table. I have this ideal, and I would like to work toward it."

Through her prophetic preaching, writing, leadership, and gardening, Rev. Dr. Becky Kiser does indeed work to make this ideal vision a reality. Overcoming opposition and obstacles, she has been changing church and society for many years.

12

Rev. Dr. Nancy Petty

Pastor
Pullen Memorial Baptist Church,
Raleigh, North Carolina

On Pentecost Sunday, May 23, 2010, Rev. Dr. Nancy Petty stands before the congregation of Pullen Memorial Baptist Church and delivers a powerful sermon entitled "What Does This Mean?" The Pullen sanctuary looks like that of a large traditional church with double rows of wooden pews stretching to the back of the long rectangular room, stained glass windows, balcony, chancel with choir loft and pipe organ and two pulpits. But anyone can quickly tell that Pullen is more than a traditional church: a woman stands preaching from the large pulpit, and her sermon consists more of questions than answers. With strong, energetic voice, Rev. Petty asks, "How is this Pentecost story happening at Pullen? What does this mean to be a Spirit-filled people? How do we find the Spirit within ourselves? How can we be transformed by the message of love and hope and justice and peace and compassion? How do we continue to turn the world upside down? How do we live into the oneness of the Spirit in spite of our differences?" She preaches about "the fire of transformation and the fire of reformation" that came on the day of Pentecost recorded in the Book of Acts,[1] not erasing but transforming differences. Rev. Petty concludes with the challenging question, "Why not be totally changed by fire?"

In this worship service the readings, hymns, and even the announcements reveal that the Pullen church is on this journey of transformation. In the Call to Worship we pray for open minds and "truth to set us free." Then we sing "Like the Murmur of the Dove's Song," which images the Holy Spirit as a female dove, as well as flame and wind.[2] Lay worship leaders present the Acts passage in a unique way to illustrate what the people gathered on that day of Pentecost might have experienced. Standing in various places in the sanctuary, the worship leaders read the Scripture passage in four different languages at the same time. We experience differences being transformed, not erased, before we hear Rev. Petty preach this point. Before and after the sermon we sing "I'm Coming to Gather All Peoples of Earth," which includes the phrases "holy diversity" and "Divinity shining in each human face."[3] Near the end of the service we sing "Be Still and Know," beginning with the lines: "Be still and know that Ruah dwells within; Spirit of Power, She lives in us each day."[4] The "Pullen Update," inserted into the worship guide, promotes an environmentally focused Vacation Bible School (VBS): "ReNew: The Green VBS." This VBS is designed to inspire children "to grow in faith, have fun, and learn to change the world."

Pullen Memorial Baptist Church practices as well as teaches the changing of the world through stewardship of creation. Rebecca Askew, chair of the building committee, explained to me the care taken in the recent addition of a chapel and the renovation of classrooms, including the installation of an environment-friendly geothermal heating and cooling system.[5] Pastor Nancy Petty told me about a Care of Creation group in the church, focusing on ecology and featuring such programs as "Creating a Just and Sustainable Community."

Nancy Petty grew up hearing her father tell her, "You can do anything you want to do." Nancy lived with an older sister and her parents in the small town of Shelby, North Carolina, and went to a small Southern Baptist church. Her father owned an apartment complex, and her mother was a nurse. Her sister, Allyson, two years older than Nancy, also became a nurse. "Allyson and I have been close all our lives," Nancy says. "My dad was one of the more active laypeople in our church, Sandy Plains Baptist. Dad and I spent most of our time at church together. This little church bought a bus, and Dad and I did a bus ministry together, and always planned Vacation Bible School together from the time I was really young. My world in that small community centered on my church. That was our social life. We had church on Sunday morning, Sunday night, and Wednesday night. Every Sunday night after church my parents would invite people from the church to our home and cook breakfast for them—biscuits and gravy and country ham. So it was like that church community then moved to our home after each Sunday night service. That was what I grew up in, so I really didn't know anything different than church."

At Sandy Plains Baptist Church when she was in fifth grade, Nancy professed her faith. Her parents are still members of this church, which Nancy calls "conservative but not fundamentalist." All the pastors of the church when Nancy was growing up were seminary educated and "very thoughtful in their sermon preparation and delivery, open, though conservative theologically." Nancy says she grew up "with very traditional faith teachings and values."

When Nancy was in high school, she felt called to be a missionary. "I knew that my love for church was deep, and that I'd spent most of my life in the church with Dad, but I'd never seen anyone other than a man in the role of pastor or in any other leadership role in the church," Nancy says. "I went to kindergarten at the church, and my kindergarten teacher was a woman, and all my Sunday school teachers were women. But growing up I never saw a woman in a ministerial role. When I got to high school and was so invested in church and leadership in my youth program, I had this sense of connection to church and what happened in church. I did what many other young girls who feel that nudge and that calling probably did; I said I wanted to be a missionary. That was fine at that time in my life. My calling continued as a process, more of just living into it, and being open to it. I have never experienced anything in my life more real than my calling."

After graduating from high school, Nancy enrolled in Gardner-Webb, a Baptist college near her home. Her dad wanted to make sure she would stay in college so he asked her to try out some summer school classes. "I took an Old Testament class that summer, and loved it—just fell in love with it!" Nancy recalls. "I convinced Dad that I did want to go to college, and that I was committed to doing the work. But I didn't know what I was going to major in. That first year I took some religion classes and realized that was my passion. Those were the classes that really sparked my interest. In my second year I decided to major in religion. While I was in college, I became president of the Baptist Student Union, and I was also very active in Fellowship of Christian Athletes and student government."

In 1985, Nancy graduated from Gardner-Webb College with a religion major. "I didn't know what came next," she says. "What do you do with a religion major? No one had explained that to me." Dr. Craven Williams, president of Gardner-Webb at the time, called Nancy into his office to talk about her future.

"What are you doing after graduation?" he asked her.

"Oh, I don't have a clue," she responded.

"My sister is part of a mission of First Baptist Church of Raleigh. They're starting a mission church in Raleigh, and they need a youth minister for the summer. I think you should go do that."

"Okay, I'll do that."

At Gardner-Webb Nancy had lived on campus, but her family was just ten miles away. When she moved to Raleigh, she felt that this was the first time she had been away from home. She served as the minister of youth at Greystone Baptist Church, a mission of the Raleigh Baptist Association in collaboration with First Baptist Church. "That was an amazing summer for me because it affirmed everything about how I felt and where my gifts were and what I had to offer," Nancy recalls. At the end of that summer the pastor of the church, Rev. Alan Sasser, drove her to Southeastern Baptist Theological Seminary.

"What are we doing here?" Nancy asked.

"We're here to enroll you in seminary," he said.

"Really? Okay, that sounds good to me. I don't have any other plans."

"And the church would like to keep you on as youth minister while you do your seminary work."

During the three years Nancy studied at Southeastern Seminary, she continued as part-time youth minister at Greystone Baptist Church. "In seminary this whole new world opened up for me," Nancy says. "I had been taught the biblical stories from a very traditional perspective, and that gave me a good foundation. I'm grateful for what I learned both in that small community church where I grew up and at Gardner-Webb. At Southeastern I realized that there was a different way to look at the biblical text and to think about it and read it and understand it. It was the most exciting time for me. This was an amazing time because of my discoveries at seminary, along with finding my place in the local church and feeling that this is where I belong."

At Southeastern Seminary, Nancy for the first time experienced a woman teaching theology. "When I think about the people who influenced me and my spiritual journey and my ministry, I would say my dad first, and then Dr. Elizabeth Barnes[6] at seminary," Nancy says. "She was the first woman I ever experienced teaching theology and biblical materials. I was amazed. I tried to take every class she taught, because it was different hearing theology from her. I don't know how to explain it, except that she spoke with an authenticity and from an experience that I connected to. Also, Dr. Barnes was the first person I came out to in seminary. It was on a final take-home exam, and I was weaving in my story on a question concerning narrative theology. I decided I would tell my story and come out, because I was not out in seminary. For the longest time, Dr. Barnes was the only person who knew of my sexual orientation. When my first relationship ended and I was devastated, she was the first person I called. I was living in Charlotte at the time. She said to me, 'Nancy, I can be there in three hours.' I said, 'No, you don't need to. Just knowing that you're there and that you would come means a lot to me.' When we talk about how the Divine Feminine and women are changing the church, and the impact of women not only in the church but in theological education, it's her face that I put on that. In a profound way she reflected God to me by the grace and compassion and unconditional love she extended me. Having this woman who embodied all of that for me, and who was teaching me how to think about systematic theology and Christian principles, opened me to see that women have a place in theology that I had never understood before. And if she had a place as a woman, then I could have a place as a woman."

Also significant to Nancy at Southeastern Seminary were Dr. Bob Poerschke,[7] professor of Christian education, and Dr. Alan Neely,[8] missions and liberation theology professor. "Bob took me under his wing that first year of seminary," Nancy says. "I remember one of our first assignments was to write our theological presuppositions. I poured myself into my paper. When I got the paper back, I flipped through and couldn't find a mark on it until I got to the last page where he had written in red, 'Who is this zapping God you serve?

Please come see me, and let me introduce you to a God of compassion and grace.' That was all that was on my paper. I wasn't sure what he was talking about, but I went in, and we had a conversation about it. Bob talked to me about how to experience and image God in a way other than that judgmental God I had grown up hearing about. That was a formative moment in my life. I became Dr. Poerschke's teaching assistant and grader for my last year and a half of seminary. Dr. Alan Neely also helped shape my ministry. He taught liberation theology and the problem of evil. Those were things that were not offered where I had grown up and in the college I went to. I'd never heard of liberation theology. I sought out these people—Elizabeth, Bob, and Alan—because I wanted to understand a different way of hearing and reading the biblical story. How fortunate I am to have had these three professors at Southeastern who took an interest in me and who not only cared about my theological education but about my ministry and my personhood."

In May of 1988, Nancy Petty graduated with an MDiv degree from Southeastern Seminary, and in August of 1988, Greystone Baptist Church ordained her. But this church, where she had been part-time youth minister during her seminary years, was still trying to get established and could not give her the full-time job she needed. Another church in Raleigh, St. John's Baptist, called her as full-time minister of Christian education and youth. "It was a small Southern Baptist congregation," Nancy says. "They had never had a woman minister, and they thought they were ready for a woman to be on staff. But there were men in that church who would stand in the vestibules until I finished my part in worship, and then they would come in to church." Toward the end of her first year at St. John's Baptist, Rev. Petty went to talk with her trusted seminary professor, Dr. Alan Neely, about her frustrations.

"I can't do this anymore. I can't be in a place where I have to deal with that kind of resistance in my face so clearly every week. I'm quitting," she told Neely.

"You can't quit! You'll never get another job if you quit one job before you get another. Everybody knows you don't do that," he exclaimed.

"I don't care if I never get another job. I'm quitting. I'm not staying in a church where the men stand out front until I finish my part and then come in. I can't do it."

Rev. Petty resigned from her ministry position at St. John's Baptist Church in September of 1989, a little more than a year after she had begun. She then interviewed with Wake Forest Baptist Church in Winston-Salem, North Carolina, and St. John's Baptist in Charlotte. Both churches extended a call to her. "I was drawn to the people at Wake Forest Baptist; I had this incredible interview with them," Nancy recalls. "But they worshiped in the huge chapel on the university campus. That chapel held about 800 people, and there were only about 200 people in this church. I go a lot on feeling, and I didn't feel that I could go there. So I went to St. John's as minister to youth and young adults. St. John's was a very progressive, open church in Charlotte, and Tom Graves, who had taught ethics at Southeastern, had gone there as pastor. I knew him, and he was good friends with Alan Neely, who told me I would have great opportunities there. St. John's had this large youth program with about ninety kids. I served there for three and half years."

When Rev. Tom Graves left St. John's Baptist and the church called another pastor, Rev. Petty knew she could not stay. "Within the first three months in about every sermon this new pastor preached, he told some story in which he would include a 'little old lady' in his former church, and it went all over me!" Nancy says. "I started getting his sermons, and I would highlight all those places where he would devalue and demean women, and then put the sermons back in his box. That didn't go over well. So it became obvious to me that we were not going to be able to work together. They had just hired him as senior pastor, and I was the full-time youth minister. But if somebody was going to leave, it wasn't going to be the pastor who had just gotten there."

Rev. Petty learned of an open position at Pullen Memorial Baptist Church in Raleigh. Rev. Mahan Siler, pastor of Pullen at that time, told her she should apply for this position of minister of education. In February of 1992, the church had voted to be a welcoming and affirming congregation. "I was interviewing with them the month after they had taken that vote," Nancy recalls. "They were reeling from all of this. It was in the paper every day. So I get to my interview and think to myself, 'I'm not going to another church and be in the closet. I can't do it that way. Surely they're going to ask me what my position is and if I'm aware of the vote they've just taken and where I fit in all this.' And I was going to tell them. But it never came up. I was floored! They never once said anything about what they had just been through. It must have been because they were so exhausted with it. They had been ousted from the Raleigh Baptist Association and the Southern Baptist Convention. Everybody had thrown them out the month before I interviewed with them. But they did not ask me once what I thought about what they'd just done. So I was thinking, 'This is crazy. Should I say something? What do I do?' I didn't know what to do. I didn't think I was going to get the job because I was young, just twenty-seven years old, and this is a predominant church in the South. So at that time I didn't say anything about my sexual orientation."

In June of 1992, Rev. Petty became minister of education at Pullen. On her last Sunday at St. John's in Charlotte, she preached, and the church gave her a going-away party. "I didn't know there was a reporter there that day," she says. "And he came up and started talking, and didn't identify himself as a reporter. He was asking what had drawn me to Pullen and those kinds of things. Here I am—single, not out, and I'm coming to this church that has just made this decision about being a welcoming and affirming church. The next morning I wake up, and my picture in color is on the front page of *The Charlotte Observer* with the headline, 'Trailblazing Woman Goes to Church Ousted for Accepting Homosexuals.' It was this article about me and about my coming to Pullen. The reporter never said anything inappropriate, but there was just enough to raise suspicion. My parents live about an hour from Charlotte, and that's the paper they read. My mother's a nurse, and she went to work that day and the phones kept ringing. It got so that she had to go home because her friends kept calling, asking, 'Is your daughter gay?' I was not out to my parents. The next day ABC and NBC and CBS were calling, wanting to do interviews with me, and I panicked. I didn't talk to any of them. The secretaries were freaking out, going wild, and I was locked in my office. My mother was calling, crying, so I called her back and told her I would come home to talk to her and Dad. They said, 'People are asking, and we don't know what to tell them.' They never asked me, 'Are you gay?' They just asked, 'Why do you want to go to this church?' I told them why I wanted to come to Pullen; it had nothing to do with my being gay. So that settled them down."

Not long after Rev. Petty began her ministry at Pullen, she felt compelled to talk to the pastor, Rev. Mahan Siler, about her sexual orientation. "I just couldn't shake it, that I had done exactly what I'd said I wasn't going to do: go to another church and not be out," Nancy says. Late one Friday night she called Rev. Siler and asked him to meet her for breakfast the next morning.

"There's something I need to tell you, because I can't live like this any longer," she began. "I'm a lesbian. And if that's going to be a problem, let's do something now, because I've only been here three months."

He reached across the table and took her hand and said, "Nancy, that issue has been settled at Pullen, and it's not an issue."

At this time Rev. Petty was not in a relationship and wasn't planning to be "sounding a trumpet." She told Rev. Siler that she preferred to get to know the people at Pullen before they learned about her sexual orientation.

"I'm not going to hide it, and if I get asked, I will tell the truth, but I don't want to lead with that," she said.

"Okay. What if someone asks me?"

"Then I want you to tell them the truth or tell them to come talk to me."

Even at a church as open and accepting as Pullen, Rev. Petty at times found she still had to struggle for equality as a woman minister. "I don't know if I could have articulated what was going on with me internally around how the church viewed women, valued women, how they included them in leadership positions," Nancy says. "But I could recognize sexism when I saw it, and I would try my best to call it out the only way I knew how. When I had the opportunity to preach, sometimes I would get the feedback, 'You sound like an angry woman.' So I was trying to figure out how to address these issues, because they are real. I knew them in my own experience in church and working in a church and in my own life. But how do you get other people to understand what you're trying to say? Mahan Siler was sensitive to the issues, but he also participated in ways. He is the most incredible person when it comes to advocating for women and gays and lesbians in the church. But even he sometimes had trouble being able to see where there was the rub. When I came to Pullen, there were only two full-time ministers, Mahan and I. I was minister of education, but I was functioning as an associate. When he would go on sabbatical, I was the only one left. I would go to all the meetings that he was supposed to be going to. So he came back from this sabbatical and walked into a committee meeting. I'd been working with this committee all summer long while he was gone. He walked into the room and said one thing, and everybody turned to him and listened to him. At that moment they were willing to scrap every piece of work we'd done all summer, because he said something else."

It was late when Nancy got home after the committee meeting. She couldn't sleep. "It must have been 10:30 or 11:00 p.m.," she says. "I called and told him, 'I don't know if you're in bed or not, but you need to get up. We have to talk.' I went to his office and said, 'Look, don't ever do that to me again. I've been here all summer, holding this together, working with this committee, and you walk into the room. I don't think you get what you do when you walk into a room. Your voice is always going to carry that kind of weight and power because (a) you're a man, and because (b) you're the pastor. And if you want to have a colleague you work with and partner with in ministry, you're going to have to rethink how you do some of that.' We had a serious talk, and I think maybe he understood. It wasn't that I wanted to be pastor. I made a very good associate. I was willing to do the grunt work. But I wanted to be treated as an equal. And I wasn't being treated as an equal, and that didn't feel good to me. I knew from my experience in my previous churches that it had to do with the fact that I was a woman, not just that I was the associate and not because I was younger, but because I was a woman."

Rev. Petty discovered that it's harder to confront sexism in a church like Pullen, known for justice stands. When she tried to tell church members of the unequal treatment she experienced as a woman minister, they were incredulous. "They almost fell over," Nancy says. "They couldn't believe I was accusing them. What I said in a sermon that got me in some trouble was that it's a lot more difficult to deal with subtlety than it is if people are just blatant. It's the same thing that Martin Luther King said in his 'Letter from Birmingham Jail,' that it's not the Ku Klux Klan that is a threat to justice and equality, but the white moderate.[9] It's true because of the subtleties with the white moderates. When you call the injustice out, they say, 'Oh, you're just angry. You're just too sensitive.' That is so not what this is about. Yeah, I may be sensitive and I may feel anger, but there's a reason why. I've always felt that when people say those things, they're trying to take the focus off the real issue. It's a diversion. If they can say, 'Well, she's just an angry woman' or 'This is her defense' or 'She's just too sensitive,' they take the focus off what we should be talking about. But those are hurtful comments. I wish people could understand that it feels like an attack when they say those things. It would feel much better if people would come talk to me, so that we can try to understand one another."

In 1994, two years after beginning her ministry at Pullen, Rev. Petty entered the Doctor of Ministry program at McCormick Theological Seminary. She juggled her full-time ministry at Pullen with commuting to the Chicago seminary for course work. In June of 1997, she received her DMin degree.

When Rev. Mahan Siler retired in 1998, Pullen hired a part-time interim pastor, Rev. Linda McFadden, mainly to lead worship each Sunday. Rev. Dr. Petty performed all other pastoral functions. "I was basically the pastor of the church in that interim time, a little over a year," she recalls. "As I was literally pastoring the church, I would call Mahan and ask, 'How did you do this?'"

Based on these conversations, Mahan Siler wrote a book called *Letters to Nancy*.[10] "In the book there is a letter in which he talked about the issue of women in ministry," Nancy says. "He quoted my saying, 'You just don't get it.' He said to me in that letter, 'In any situation you were always geared toward the relationship. I was always oriented toward dealing with the idea and the question of what the institution needs.' I think that was helpful for him to name for us. In the eighteen years I've been here at Pullen my focus has been on building relationships, so that I have that entry into being people's pastor when they really need their pastor, and to build that relationship such that when we disagree, there's a relationship to hold us together in our disagreement. I wondered about that difference Mahan named in how we ministered. I think just to categorize would not be accurate. But I do wonder about how women approach this role differently than men. I think typically we equate gender with certain roles. The belief that women are more relational has been symbolized in the roles women have played in the church, like the children's minister. Men have taken on the more academic and theological roles. But what was so powerful to me about Elizabeth Barnes was that she was a professor, a PhD, who was in that place that had been reserved for men. For whatever the reason, the church continues to assign positions and roles based on gender, even in a church like Pullen, who would like to think of themselves as not doing that. I think the GLBT community is changing that, because those roles are just not as clear."

In 2000, Pullen Memorial Baptist Church called Rev. Jack McKinney as pastor. After eighteen months at Pullen he asked Rev. Nancy Petty if she would consider being copastor. "I'd never thought of that," she says. "I loved doing what I was doing. I told him I needed some time to think about that. So I took the summer to think about where I felt God was calling me. I told the congregation, 'This feels like a really important conversation to have. I can be happy doing what I'm doing now, or I can be happy doing the copastorate. I'm willing to have the conversation, but I want you to know that this isn't an all or nothing.' But then I realized at some point that I was invested and that the copastorate was important to me. I think the shift came when I heard people say, 'Nancy's already been doing this work. She should get the title.' And I thought, 'They're right.' I thought that when the copastorate conversation started that my sexual orientation might be an issue. And it was for some people, but not many. I said, not from the pulpit but in groups, that it's one thing to have a lesbian on your staff, and it's a different thing emotionally for your pastor to be a gay person. I knew this from listening to people and watching people. I don't know what that's about for some people, if they're embarrassed by it. But some people raised that question. It's hard for people at Pullen to even raise that question because it looks like they're not being supportive. But I thought it was good to have the conversation up front rather than have this underlying current that you can't really talk about."

After six months of deliberation, in April of 2002, the church voted for Nancy to be copastor. "The copastorate in theory was totally equal," she says. "We did all the pieces of the job together. We didn't divide out and say, 'you take these pieces of the job, and I'll take these pieces.' We made the exact same amount of money. We split the preaching fifty-fifty, and for the first several years we went to all the committees together. Eventually we stopped that, but in those early years it felt important so that people would start thinking differently.

It's interesting that Jack stayed in the office which has traditionally been the pastor's study, and I stayed in the office I had been in. I'm learning now that there's symbolic stuff in that. So I think that separated us somewhat. I think there were some people who were okay that there was a woman pastor because there was a man pastor too. The copastor vote had to pass by two-thirds. I don't remember the exact numbers, but I think it passed by about five votes."

The months of scrutiny before the copastor vote took their toll on Nancy. "Some people said awful things," she recalls. "I'd been here ten years, and the people knew me well. For six months the whole congregation got to evaluate me and my ministry. There were some significant disappointments in that a couple of older women, who were important to me, really fought it. It was very difficult for me. When the vote was actually over, and the copastorate went through, I got depressed. That first year of the copastorate I could barely function. I was functioning; I was doing my job. But I about came unglued. I thought I was going to have to go to the hospital, because of the grief and sadness of what people said in ways that were not compassionate. But somewhere along the way, after that first year, I started healing from all of that, and made it through."

Although Rev. Petty and Rev. McKinney functioned as equal pastors, the church at times still responded to them according to traditional gender roles. "Around relationship issues in the church and pastoral issues, I was the authority," Nancy says. "Around vision, big picture, direction of the church, Jack was the authority. We tried our best to work on that together. And he did a lot of intentional backing out of leadership so that I would be in those leadership places. But I think as long as there was a man who carried the title of leader, pastor, copastor of this church, a woman wasn't going to have that full authority. And my experience in working in this church with two male pastors, Mahan and Jack, is that the laypeople will come and say things to a woman minister they would never say to a male minister. When people would get upset with Mahan or Jack, they wouldn't tell him. They would come and tell me. I would say, 'You need to go tell him.' And they'd say, 'I can't go tell him.' But if people were upset with me, they didn't have any trouble coming into my office and telling me. I think that's a gender issue; it's that mother-father thing."

Rev. Petty believes that one of the greatest values of the copastorate was the model presented of female and male in this leadership role. "We modeled that both genders can be in this role. Particularly for our children and youth, I think that's really significant for them to see that both women and men can be pastors. Some of the girls in the youth group have said to me, 'I've never had a woman pastor before you. And now I know that if I want to be a pastor, I can do that.'"

Although the Baptist tradition does not connect the gender of the Divine and of ministers as closely as does the Catholic tradition, Rev. Petty often speaks of women ministers and women in general as synonymous with the Divine Feminine. Beginning in seminary, Nancy saw Dr. Elizabeth Barnes as the face of the Divine Feminine. "I go back to how significant it was in my own experience to have that encounter with Dr. Barnes, to see a woman and hear a woman's voice and hear how women's stories intersect with the biblical stories," Nancy says. "That's why I think telling the stories of women in the Bible is so important, because it gives visibility to the fact that not all the disciples were men. As we talk about how to image the Divine Feminine, representing the feminine is really important to me because I know how much that meant to me and how it changed the way I see myself as a theologian and as a pastor. And a number of women have said to me, 'You don't know what your presence means. You don't have to say anything. It's not about what you say. It's who you are standing up there, and that I can look up there and see myself there.' Over the years I've continually listened to women tell me what a difference it makes to have a woman in the pulpit, that it in some way symbolizes their story, their experience." Thus Nancy has come to see that women ministers make a powerful statement of the sacredness of women's stories and of women as equal images of the Divine.

The women's group that Nancy started at Pullen also reflects this close connection she sees between the divine and human feminine. The group carries the feminine divine name, *Ruah*,[11] and began with a focus on the stories of biblical women. "The purpose of the group at the beginning was to look at the stories of women in the Bible," Nancy says. "It's important to connect with the biblical stories. To do that, women have got to be able to see ourselves in these stories. That's where I think the church has failed our daughters and our mothers. We are in those stories, but the church hasn't told those stories and taught those stories. So we feel alienated from the biblical texts. As we look to the present and future about how to bring in the Divine Feminine, we really need to rethink how we're teaching the biblical texts. The *Ruah* group spent about a month rewriting the creation story from a feminist perspective. That was such a liberating experience. We were finding ourselves in a different way in that story. We researched other creation stories and read other creation stories and tried to understand how different faiths have interpreted the creation story. It opened up for us a whole different way to approach the Bible. It was amazing. The *Ruah* group then moved from looking at biblical stories to telling our own stories."

The *Ruah* group also initiated a committee to expand the visual imagery in the sanctuary of Pullen Memorial Baptist Church. Cheryl Stallings, who had helped start the *Ruah* group; Gretchen Staebler, Financial and Publications Secretary at Pullen; and many others in the *Ruah* group became members of a visual imagery group. "It was the vision of the women in the *Ruah* group to bring more feminine divine imagery into our sanctuary," Nancy explains. "We talked about how difficult it was to come into the sanctuary for worship every Sunday and look at five men in the stained glass windows when this church proclaims an inclusive, open, welcoming theology. Most of our imagery in the sanctuary is masculine: Christ the King, up there in one window, and then Peter, Paul, Moses, and Elijah on either side of him. There's this beautiful creation window, but it's all the way over on the side where people can't see it. Men and women serve on the visual imagery committee. There are men in the church who also feel strongly that our sanctuary needs to be more representative."

Some members of the visual imagery group wanted to take out the stained glass windows with masculine imagery, but this proved an impractical solution because the windows are valued at about 1.5 million dollars. To explore alternative ways of expanding the imagery the committee brought in Catherine Kapikian, a liturgical artist with the Center for the Arts and Religion at Wesley Theological Seminary in Washington, DC. She recommended the addition of inclusive imagery, especially feminine imagery, on the two large blank walls on both sides of the sanctuary and in the paraments on the Communion table, the pulpit, and the lectern. "It's important for our images to be in alignment with who we say we are as a church and what our theology is," Nancy explains. "We say that here all people are equal, that women are just as important in the church as men, that women's stories are important. And yet none of our imagery in this church tells that story. And it's not just women that we need to represent in the imagery, but children and creation. Our church has a Care of Creation mission group. Nothing in our imagery speaks to that value as part of our theology. There's nothing in our church that persons with disabilities would visually see that makes them feel welcome. I don't know that the person who is privileged in our world understands how significant that is for other people to see themselves represented in worship so that they feel they belong. The visual imagery group set out to include the Divine Feminine as the top priority, and then to move to make the imagery inclusive of children and creation. Also, two women together and two men together would represent a large part of our story as a church. It's important for us to model in a visual way and with our words what we say we believe, as opposed to saying one thing and then walking into a sanctuary where everything is about men."

Some members of the church have opposed any changes in the sanctuary imagery, and Rev. Petty's negotiating skills and patience have proved valuable. "We have people in this church who don't want anything in the sanctuary to change," Nancy says. "They feel that the worship space is beautiful and to add anything is going to make it look awful. Many people feel strongly about that. It's hard to know if it's because they don't want the feminine imagery in there, or if they truly feel that this space was designed for the purpose and they don't want it to change. My guess is that it's both. Some people ask, 'Why do we have to bring feminine imagery in? We have a woman pastor, and we know what we believe. Why is it important to put stuff on the walls?' I keep saying, 'Because it's theologically the right thing to do.' There's one woman in the church, who's a very open woman, but when it comes to this issue, she struggles. Over time I've had conversations with her about why this is important. And it's not just laying out this well-practiced theological argument. I have to go and engage her on a level of where she's emotionally connected, and what all of this represents to her. Her husband was the architect for the sanctuary, and she was the one who raised most of the money for those stained glass windows. So when we talked about changes in the sanctuary, she panicked. Over about eight years, before this visual imagery committee got started, I was in conversation with her. When the committee formed, she was upset. So I asked her to be on the committee. Hearing other people's stories and their hearing her story opened space for conversation. She started out not wanting anything to change in the sanctuary, and now she sees that it would be great to add inclusive imagery on the blank walls. I never dreamed we'd get there! She's eighty-something years old."

Rev. Petty works hard to balance her roles as pastor and as prophet. "Change takes time, but my preference is to move forward when I see something that needs to be done and there's a reason to do it," she says. "I go back to King's 'Letter from Birmingham Jail,' which is a significant piece of writing for me and how I see my ministry. King writes about being 'disturbers of the peace and outside agitators.' That's what the church is called to do, and that's what we as ministers are called to do. So when I come to this issue of Divine Feminine imagery and language, I know I need to agitate people about this, that it's not about trying to comfort people. At the same time it's important to meet people where they are and to try to understand what it is within them that's resistant. That delicate balance of being pastor and prophet is a constant challenge. How do I play both of those roles? Sometimes I can't. That's the reality. Sometimes I have to choose whether it's my prophetic voice or my pastoral voice that's needed. With the Divine Feminine and women's issues in the church, I've tried to know when it's time for the prophetic voice and when it's time for the pastoral. In this church I have an advantage that many ministers don't have. Because of the tradition of this church, I'm expected to be an agitator. But it's important to decide what issues are important. If Divine Feminine imagery and language are important enough to me, I make that decision to follow my conscience and take whatever heat I get. I get my strength and my courage from that internal conviction and commitment. When it's a true conviction, then I find the way to lead. It has to be a theological conviction to see it through and not get discouraged."

A deep conviction for Rev. Petty is instilling a theology of openness and inclusion in children, and she believes that inclusive language and symbolism are vital to this process. "What I hear children say lets me know how important language and symbolism are," Nancy explains. "I have two children, Jasmine, who's seventeen, and Nora, who's twelve. They've grown up with two moms in a church that for the most part has used inclusive language, and yet they still call God 'He.' I don't know whether that's because we haven't been consistent enough or we've not been clear enough. The children in this church have seen women in the pulpit, not as much as men, but they've seen women. My younger daughter, Nora, in a social setting or at church will say, 'My momma's the pastor of the church.' And yet she calls God 'He.' I think it's hard for Pullen children to go out in society where all of their friends are calling God 'He' and to try to articulate why they might call God 'She.' That voice outside the church, how our culture talks about God, carries more weight than what they hear in church. And I don't know that we give them the confidence to explain their beliefs. It was the same thing we saw with our youth when the church began to do Holy Unions. Their friends would rag them about going to that 'gay' church. Parents wanted the church to give the young people some handles to talk with their friends and to explain what they think the Scripture says. It's hard for them to move beyond this church and feel safe out in the world, trying to articulate a different way of talking about God, when it's not understood in the culture."

In addition to these constant cultural messages, Rev. Petty believes that the biblical texts and visual imagery continue to influence children's naming of the Divine. "We still have children coming out of Pullen calling God 'He,' though they rarely hear that in worship," Nancy says. "When we read the Bible in worship, we make sure we use inclusive language. But if they're reading the Bible at home, they find 'Father, Father, Father.' They have to make that shift for themselves. But it's a difficult task. And then they see all these masculine images in the sanctuary. In this church there's been more resistance to feminine visual imagery than to inclusive language. In theory people can talk about something all day long and feel comfortable with it, but when it comes to actually putting it into practice, it's harder. Maybe that's why there's still a struggle even in a church like Pullen. And maybe we've gotten complacent. We think we've arrived. And that can be dangerous. We can talk about inclusive imagery all day long, but when it comes to implementation, that's where the resistance comes."

Nancy gives credit to Larry Schultz, minister of music, for helping the church implement language and imagery inclusive of the Divine Feminine. "Credit goes to Larry for including feminine divine names," Nancy says. "We sing about God as Mother Eagle, as Mother, as Spirit, *Ruah*. Also, Larry has helped us to use images that celebrate the feminine and masculine within each of us and to use non-gender images; God is like a rock and like the sky—all of those rich biblical images. I can't overstate how significant Larry has been in helping us make some of these shifts particularly in worship language, but also visually with movement, how he has led the choir to embody for the congregation the words of hymns and anthems. That's been a passion of his. And he's done it in very gentle ways, but he's also been very firm and unapologetic. It makes a big difference to have someone on a church staff other than the pastor who's carrying some of that message and vision, because people get tired of hearing it from the pulpit. If it's being supported in other ways, you can talk less about it and practice it more. And coming from a man makes a huge difference, because they can't accuse Larry of being an 'angry woman.'"

Inclusive language, leadership, and theology can liberate men as well as women, Nancy believes. "I don't think it's just women who've been oppressed by our patriarchal culture and church," she explains. "Men have been oppressed too, because they've had to carry this load and power all by themselves and have been cut out of being able to nurture and care and connect on a different level. As more women move into roles that traditionally men have held, what does that mean for men moving into roles that women have traditionally held? How could that be freeing, and how could that change the church in redemptive and reconciling ways? Over the years a number of men in this church have worked with our children and youth in significant ways. When we talk about changing church, I wonder what it would mean for the church not to think of roles and gender together, but to think of who's best suited in various places."

Being a welcoming and affirming church, Nancy says, helps to change traditional gender roles. Recently a group of Pullen laypeople volunteered to provide labor for the renovation of youth classrooms. "We had many GLBT people show up for those work days, so the roles began to shift," Nancy continues. "Typically, you think of renovation, and that kind of moving walls, building walls, as a man's job. Well, we have these lesbians in the church who just die to build a wall, who had all that kind of energy inside of them. Then we have some men who say, 'I don't know a thing about building, but I can sweep and paint, and I'll fix lunch.' We saw that we didn't have to put people in boxes. I try not to shy away from either where I feel my feminine side coming out or my masculine side, because I think both are important. Maybe our work is to integrate those. I believe we're all created in the image of God, and God is both male and female. God is all of that. So if we're created in that image, then we're all of that too."

Toward the end of 2009, Rev. Jack McKinney resigned as copastor of the Pullen church, and the deacons asked Rev. Petty what she wanted to do. "It was another one of those moments when I had to do my discernment and ask where God wanted me now, if it was to be solo pastor of Pullen church. I got clear that it was time for me to take this step. It was about me, and it wasn't about me. It was about me in that I felt I was ready, that I'd been doing the job, that I could do the job. But it also felt like God was calling me to this time for a larger purpose that was outside of me. My fear and anxiety came in when I thought about whether I could make it through this process. I knew I could do the job. Jack had been gone for three months, and I'd been doing the job by myself. It was never about can I do the job; am I called to do the job? It was about can I survive another process of people talking about me? When I stated clearly that I wanted to be pastor, the church decided to have a vote. I didn't think I could do that again. The last time I almost ended up in a psychiatric hospital. The church would have never put a man through that. If I had been the one to leave, the church would have never done that. I don't know that a man would have put up with that. But on my way to the Y to exercise one day, I stopped in the chapel to ask for something to get me through. The clear message came, 'I will give you what you need.' And all through that process, in my prayer time I'd ask if I had discerned right. And there was this constant 'yes' that was so outside of me."

On May 2, 2010, Pullen Memorial Baptist voted 200 to 26 to affirm Rev. Nancy Petty as solo pastor. One of the members who voted not to affirm her had been speaking against her for several months. People asked her why he was so opposed, so she called him to meet with her, and they had this exchange:

"Well, there's this feminist movement sweeping through the church and taking over the church," he said. "And it's got to be stopped. Women are taking over the church, and it's not right. And I don't like this feminist movement."

"Women have always run the church," Nancy responded. "Men have had the leadership roles, but it's the women who have kept the church alive. So that isn't anything new. My being in the pastor role is new. But there's not this feminist movement all of a sudden sweeping through the church. I understand that there's grief in this for some people, because when women move into roles that traditionally men have had, then men may go through a time of trying to figure out where their place is. I understand that there's loss in this for you, but I'll be your pastor."

As pastor of a congregation known across the country for activism, Rev. Petty realizes people expect her to speak out on social justice issues. "Because I came to this pulpit, I have a position and I have some power, and I need to be accountable to that," she says. "But I try not to go looking for issues because that doesn't seem real to me. When there's something that I feel that is calling me to speak out on, then that's the place I need to be. For one of the former pastors, Bill Finlator, it was opposing the Vietnam War. For Mahan Siler, it was advocating for the full acceptance and welcoming of gays and lesbians into the church. For me at this time the issue of diversity in our schools is what I'm willing to spend extra time and energy fighting for."

About five months before the vote to affirm Nancy as pastor, she wrote a point-of-view article for Raleigh's *News & Observer*, opposing the Wake County school board's plan to dismantle the district's policy designed to promote school diversity and to move to a community-based system of student assignment.[12] "We must not fool ourselves by thinking that the issues at hand are not issues of race, economic status, privilege and power," she wrote. "If we allow our elected leaders to return us to a place of segregation and intolerance within our schools—a place where the gap between the haves and have-nots is widened rather than closed—it is ultimately our children who will suffer."[13] From the positive experience of her own children attending diverse schools, Nancy knew this was an important issue for her to speak out on. "The majority of school board members were now very conservative and doing away with our socioeconomic diversity policy, which was a nationally recognized school system model," she says. "I see the value in my children going to school with people not like them, and what they've learned and who they've become because of that."

Nancy's newspaper article stirred quite a bit of response from the community. Late one night when she was already in bed, she received a phone call and recounts this conversation:

"Rev. Petty, this is the Rev. William Barber, president of the NAACP of North Carolina and pastor of Greenleaf Christian Church. I just read your point-of-view article in the *News & Observer*, and I'd like to talk with you about it. I was shocked that there was a white minister in Raleigh who would write something like that. I want to meet with you."

"Well, I'd love that," Nancy said.

"The NAACP is very interested in this issue. We're going to be a voice in it. And I'd like to partner with you."

One of the first events that Rev. Petty and Rev. Barber partnered on was the fourth annual Historic Thousands on Jones Street rally.[14] "I made this speech that got people riled up," Nancy says. "I can cut loose in a setting like that and connect." After the rally, Rev. Barber called Nancy and said, "I've had all these black people coming up to me saying, 'Barber, where did you find that white woman? We've got to keep that white woman!'" Since then William Barber has preached at Pullen, and he and Nancy have been together in the newspapers, on TV, and all over the city advocating for school diversity. "We have teamed up to bring power to this issue," she says. "William Barber is this man everybody in North Carolina knows. He's articulate, passionate, and very large. He is a massive presence. So here's this large African American man, who's the president of the NAACP and a pastor, and this smaller white lesbian pastor of this predominantly liberal church in the South, and these two people come together. You couldn't plan that! That's only God, and She is just laughing Her head off! Now every time he comes to Raleigh, we're together, and people know our connection. He's gotten criticism from some of his people who say, 'You know what church she's pastor of, and she's a lesbian.' In the black community that's tough. So he's had to stand up for me, and I've had to stand up for him. I've gotten criticism because some people worry that I might get in trouble. People at Pullen want their pastor to be visible, but they don't want me in jail. There's never been a pastor here who's gone to jail."

While the church was in conversation about affirming Nancy as pastor, the school board held a meeting to vote on banning the district's diversity policy. "Barber called that we had to go and we'd probably get arrested," Nancy says. "That was two or three months before the vote to call me. I was thinking, 'I'm going to get arrested in the middle of this. Some people in this church are not going to appreciate that. They're going to say I'm trying to stir trouble, and there are different ways to fight the school board other than creating a scene and getting arrested.' I didn't know what to do. For a whole weekend my stomach was torn up. In the end I realized that if speaking my conscience on this issue is the reason that I would not be affirmed as the pastor of this church, then I needed to know that. I couldn't let whether or not I get a job dictate my following my conscience. So I went to the school board meeting. Barber was planning to speak, and I was going to stand with him. And then when he finished, we were going to refuse to move."

Before Rev. Barber rose to speak, high school students out in the hallway started protesting, screaming and banging on the floor to come in to the meeting. "I jumped up, and Barber got up, and we went for the doors," Nancy says. "The police had closed the doors and weren't allowing anyone to leave. I said to one of the officers, 'You can have a scene in here and out there, or you can let the two of us out there.' He opened the door, and Barber and I went out in the hallway. I sat down in the middle of the floor with the students and started to chant. The student who was leading the protest got more vocal, and a police officer handcuffed him. Things went ballistic. Barber and I finally got the kids calmed down, and told them, 'If you're going to do civil disobedience, you have to go by the rules. Everybody stand up. We're going out with the police now.' So the police officer said, 'Everybody who doesn't want to be arrested, go that way right now. If you do, come down this hallway and go down those steps.' A good portion of the students went down the steps, and Barber and I went down with them. There were about forty of us, and the police officers said, 'We can't arrest all of you.' So they arrested only the student they had handcuffed. As we were leaving, Barber said to me, 'Well, damn, we can't even get arrested!'"

On June 15, 2010, Rev. Petty and Rev. Barber and two other activists did get arrested at a protest at a school board meeting. This meeting focused on implementing the vote the board had taken on March 23 to end the diversity policy, and board members were now moving toward assigning students to schools closest to their neighborhoods.

"Who does benefit from your recent decisions?" Petty asked the board. "Our entire community? Or selected communities where the wealthiest live?"[15] Nancy and the other protestors were arrested for second-degree trespassing after they interrupted the school board's meeting, staged a sit-in, and then stood together with joined hands and sang "We Shall Overcome."

In taking stands for justice, Nancy sees the importance of women and men in partnership. "Women need to be willing to partner with men because they do have power," she says. "And if we want to share that power, then it's important to nurture those relationships and be in partnership with them. On the school board issue, Barber reached out to me, and I reached back out to him. Together we've been able to tap into a power that's much greater than either one of us alone."

Rev. Petty has also found that she makes a prophetic statement by just being who she is. Before a wedding where she was officiating, a little girl spotted her in her robe, and they had this exchange:

"So you're the priest!" the little girl hollered out.

"Yes, I'm the minister here, and I'm going to marry Jessica and Ronnie today," Nancy said.

"I've been watching you since you got here. When I saw that robe, I knew you were the priest."

A little while later, while they were still waiting for the ceremony to begin, the girl began running around Nancy in a circle, saying, "You're the priest! You're the priest! You're the priest!" Nancy says she doesn't know the girl's background: "If she goes to the Catholic Church, she probably has never seen a woman priest, and she was paying close attention to who's in this role."

In Nancy's expansive vision for the future of the church, this little girl and everyone will have equal value and opportunity. "As I think about my vision for the future of the Divine Feminine and how we talk about our faith, it's my hope that the church can represent all people as equal," she says. "I want both our girls and our boys to know that when we say we are made in the Divine image, that means all of us. It doesn't matter what gender you are, what your sexual orientation is, what color you are, how well you're educated or not educated. Everyone has gifts to offer. If there's one vision that points me in my ministry, it's that we are all equal. My vision is for the church to live into that and believe it in a way that's counter to our culture. I don't think our culture will ever really understand that, because there are systems in our culture that require that hierarchy of leadership. Instead of the church reflecting the culture, it's my hope and vision that we can represent something different and be a different voice in the world. And then we take that message out, and when we are in places of leadership in our community and in our culture, we bring a different perspective."

Nancy's vision recalls the words of Mary in the Magnificat about bringing "down the powerful" and lifting "up the lowly."[16] Sitting with Nancy in her office, I notice a picture of a pregnant African American Mary. Nancy tells me that this striking black Madonna image was enlarged to fifteen feet tall and hung in the Pullen sanctuary during Advent. I think about the challenging questions Nancy raised the day before in her Pentecost sermon: "How do we turn the world upside down? What does this mean to be a Spirit-filled people? How can we be transformed by the message of love and hope and justice and peace and compassion?" The questions continue to echo through the prophetic ministry of Rev. Nancy Petty and Pullen Memorial Baptist Church.

Conclusion

> *I learned not only how to write stories, but to love them, to revere them even. I discovered the power of honest, personal, revelatory writing. Humans, I discovered, need stories the way we need air.*
> —Sue Monk Kidd[1]

In writing this book I discovered anew the power of stories as I felt my mind expand and my spirit soar. It is my prayer that you too have felt inspired and empowered by these stories. The discoveries I made in writing these stories of liberating ministers exceeded my expectations. As I traveled around the country interviewing ministers who are changing church and society through the inclusion of female divine names and images in worship, I learned much more than I had imagined. These ministers also increased my confidence that life-giving changes are occurring through the inclusion of the Divine Feminine in the church. Common themes emerge in these stories, revealing wisdom for transformation.

Love of Church and Desire for Reform

The stories in this book reveal that these liberating ministers have had a deep love for the church since they were children. Ever since she can remember, Stacy Boorn "really loved being at church, loved being part of the worship service." As a little girl, Isabel Docampo "loved Sunday school" and delighted in reading her Spanish Sunday school book. When she was young, Bridget Mary Meehan felt drawn to the Eucharist, and she made her first Communion when she was seven years old. At the age of twelve, Susan Newman became the superintendent of her church's Sunday school, because she knew more about the

Bible than most of the adults at the church. Marcia Fleischman says that she has been "looking for God" all her life and that she felt the "presence of the Spirit" at the age of twelve when she taught a lesson in a communicants' class at her church. Larry Schultz became involved in music ministry when he was only thirteen, and he was ordained at age sixteen. Paul Smith grew up in church and "loved it," becoming a youth minister when he was eighteen. From the time she was "really young," Nancy Petty helped her dad with the church's bus ministry and in planning Vacation Bible School. Virginia Marie Rincon has "always been drawn to the altar and the sacrament." No matter how much criticism the ministers in this book have endured from their efforts to change the church, their love for the church continues.

Their stories show that they stay in the church also to reform it and for the spiritual power they receive from a faith community. Bishop Bridget Mary Meehan says of the Roman Catholic Women Priests movement, "We are not leaving the church; we are leading the church into a new era of justice and equality." Even though a church official suggested that Rev. Judith Liro resign her Episcopal ordination because of the liturgical changes she was bringing to St. Hildegard's Community, she has not left this denomination but continues to work within it for reform. Rev. Susan Newman has never considered leaving the church because she believes that the church needs her to bring change. "The church needs somebody running around with a sharp pen busting all these sexist and racist and classist balloons that the church has," she says. Citing the book *Defecting in Place*,[2] Rev. Rebecca Kiser believes that she can change the church better from the inside than the outside. As we read in their stories, these ministers also see the church as a powerful instrument for social reform. Rev. Virginia Marie Rincon says that she stays in the church because she wants to use her priesthood "to make a difference." When Rev. Monica Coleman developed the Dinah Project to assist churches with healing responses to sexual violence, she also used her role as a clergyperson. "Black people still respect the clergy more, so it makes a big difference if something comes from clergy," she says. Rev. Paul Smith has not considered leaving the church because he believes in using the structures we have to change society. He says that we need community and that "Christians have already got that."

Balancing Prophetic and Pastoral Ministries

In order to work within the church these ministers have found creative ways to balance their prophetic and pastoral work. Rev. Nancy Petty, for example, has advocated for expanding the visual imagery in the sanctuary of her church while listening to the feelings of people who opposed the changes. "So when I come to this issue of Divine Feminine imagery and language, I know I need to agitate people about this," she says. "At the same time it's important to meet people where they are and to try to understand what it is within them that's resistant. That delicate balance of being pastor and prophet is a constant challenge." Working with first-generation immigrants from a Roman Catholic background, Rev. Virginia Marie Rincon includes the familiar image of the Virgin of Guadalupe but expands beyond the submissive Virgin to a "strong woman of action." Rev. Rebecca Kiser sees herself as "like a bridge," as she brings female divine imagery to her congregation while maintaining some traditional liturgy. Rev. Monica Coleman says that while "it's a little easier to pull off gender-neutral than female images in the black church," in her writing she can portray black women as Saviors.

Often these ministers struggle with their call to change the church while keeping doors open so they have opportunities to do so. Rev. Larry Schultz feels the conflict between his commitment to writing music with imagery that balances female and male divine imagery and the realities of the publishing world. "There's a sense of having to get my name out there for publishers to look at me, so I need to do enough that's going to be pleasing to them and that they're going to publish; then they'll have some confidence to take my music with more expansive imagery," he says. In order for St. Hildegard's to be a prophetic Eucharistic community within the Episcopal Church, Rev. Judith Liro found "a way to compromise with integrity" by using "the texts in the Book of Common Prayer with the informal name of 'Rite III'" and expanding the sacred imagery.

Affirming the Power of Worship Language and Imagery

In the interviews for this book, I asked the ministers why they believe language and symbolism are important enough to go to all the effort to change two thousand years of church tradition. The ministers spoke with passion about their deep belief in the power of worship language to contribute to justice and equality in church and society. In changing worship to include female divine names and images, they have risked the censure of church officials as well as loss of job opportunities and promotions. But they believe that working for change is worth the risks because worship language is inseparable from social justice and partnership in relationships.

"Words make a lot of difference," Rev. Isabel Docampo states. "Women who never hear God as female unconsciously integrate that they are not totally created in God's image, limiting their sense of worth and power. Men who never hear God as female unconsciously integrate that they have greater knowledge and worth because they always hear their male gender equated with ultimate power and wisdom." Likewise Rev. Susan Newman affirms the power of language. "Words are powerful because our world is shaped by our language," she says. "The way we communicate and bring images to people through our language, through the words we choose, and through our images—that is powerful; that is what creates our mindset. I think it's important to recognize that some women have suffered negative relationships with their fathers, so God cannot be Father to them, but God could be Mother." Rev. Judith Liro says that the dominance of male imagery in traditional liturgy undermines "the possibilities for women to experience ourselves as beloved, gifted, and responsible beings." Rev. Paul Smith asserts that "God both includes and transcends male and female and that using only masculine terms for God discounts the Divine in all of us." Bishop Bridget Mary Meehan believes that including female divine images in worship "will enrich our spiritual growth and help us to transform political, social, and economic systems that oppress us." Because of the "prevalence of patriarchy," Rev. Monica Coleman says we need to include female divine names and images in worship, and "the fact that people rail so much against female language for God shows how important it is." In a church publication Rev. Larry Schultz and Rev. Nancy Petty state that since "language instills truths of equality and justice in human relationships," they use "a variety of feminine, masculine, and non-gender images in referring to God and humanity" in their worship services.

Overcoming Resistance and Developing Resilience

Changing Church also reveals that there continues to be strong resistance to including the Divine Feminine in worship, but that doing so may be easier than some people think. These stories show a surprising similarity among denominations in the forms that the resistance takes and the comments people make, like this one we see in Rev. Stacy Boorn's story: "How dare you change the nature of God! You're leading your congregation astray." Whatever the denomination, people in the pews and church officials fear the institutional changes that will come from changing traditional worship language. The intense resistance to including female divine names and images and the repercussions that many ministers have experienced from using this expansive language in worship prove the importance of our language for Deity, though some continue to argue that it is a peripheral issue. Either at a conscious or subconscious level, many people understand that patriarchal theological language provides the foundation for the status quo that they do not want changed. As Rev. Judith Liro asserts in her story, our language for divinity "holds patriarchy in place" and "if we start messing with that, it might make everything else unravel." Rev. Monica Coleman agrees: "It's just amazing to me how much people are attached to God's being a man." After experiencing backlash from a Re-Imagining Conference that featured female divine imagery, Rev. Rebecca Kiser realized "how much people were invested in the maleness of the tradition." Letha Dawson Scanzoni, one of the founders of Evangelical & Ecumenical Women's Caucus, offers a word of hope that strong resistance itself can indicate that change is happening: "A stepped-up backlash is a sign of the impact of the catalyzing change stage."[3]

As we have seen in some of these stories, like those of Rev. Larry Schultz and Rev. Nancy Petty, church members may be open and even longing to include female divine visual imagery and names in worship. Rev. Stacy Boorn has found that many people who have felt alienated from the Christian tradition have experienced a "whole new sense of church and communion, coming through and beginning with images of the Divine Feminine." In the stories of Rev. Marcia Fleischman and Rev. Paul Smith, we read that some people left the church over the inclusion of the Divine Feminine, but that this change came more easily than becoming a GLBT affirming and welcoming church.

The stories in this book demonstrate that the ministers have developed resilience through overcoming obstacles to fulfill their calling. Some of these ministers have faced challenges even to their right to be ordained ministers. Rev. Isabel Docampo had to stand up to several Baptist pastors who demanded that she rescind her ordination because they believed it was unbiblical for women to be ordained. In Rev. Marcia Fleishman's story we read about Kansas City Baptist Association's putting her and several other women on "trial" because they were ordained. Bishop Bridget Mary Meehan continues to defend her ordination to Roman Catholic authorities, who continue to deny that she is a legitimately ordained priest and to excommunicate her. As we have seen in these stories, often challenges come from church members. Three women walked out on Rev. Stacy Boorn's first sermon, and in one church Rev. Nancy Petty served, some men stood in the vestibule and refused to come into the sanctuary until she had finished her part of the worship service. Rev. Paul Smith got flak from some church members and denominational organizations when he led his church to move from hierarchical to team leadership, to ordain women, and to become a welcoming and affirming congregation. Some of these ministers have overcome obstacles of both racism and sexism to pursue their calling. "It's very difficult as a black woman to get called to a church," Rev. Susan Newman says. "There are churches that don't mind your being the assistant, but they're still not ready for you to be senior pastor." Rev. Virginia Marie Rincon says that it takes courage to use her "voice as a woman and especially as a Latina woman," but that the "calling of the Divine Feminine, like the *Virgen de Guadalupe*," gives her strength. We see in all these stories that the ministers have experience in handling opposition, giving them strength and savvy as they advocate for including the Divine Feminine in church. Bridget Mary Meehan views controversy as positive because the increased publicity helps the Roman Catholic Women Priests movement grow: "Opposition has always proved a blessing to us."

Overcoming obstacles has given the ministers in this book the tenacity and skill needed to change centuries of male-dominated liturgy and leadership in the church. Even congregations like Broadway Church and Pullen Memorial Baptist, who have voted for inclusive imagery, have found that implementing this change can be messy and conflictual. Rev. Nancy Petty says that "even in a church like Pullen," people can talk about inclusive visual imagery "all day long," but resist the implementation of it. And the preponderance of masculine divine symbols in the culture work against churches who try to include the Divine Feminine. Rev. Petty expresses consternation that although Pullen has inclusive language guidelines and strives toward gender balance in worship language and leadership, some of the children in the church, including her own, still call God "He." She says that they hear all their friends calling God "He," and that the way our culture talks about God often "carries more weight than what they hear in church." In addition, she believes that the biblical texts often contribute to this exclusive language because people read a variety of translations at home and don't take care to use inclusive versions as the church does in worship services. Undaunted by these challenges, Rev. Petty and the other liberating ministers in this book redouble their efforts to find creative ways to include female divine names and images in church. Because of the predominance of male divine language and imagery in the culture, some of these ministers believe in giving precedence to the Divine Feminine in church.

Various Approaches to Liberating Worship Language and Imagery

The stories in this book reveal a variety of approaches to liberating worship language and imagery. The ministers use various terms and definitions of terms for the language they use in worship. Among these terms are "inclusive," "expansive," "gender-balanced," and "gender-neutral." Some use the word "inclusive" to mean avoidance of gender-specific references, while others use it to mean balancing female and male divine images. Liturgical scholar Deborah Sokolove observes that "any attempt to move away from patriarchal language is generally called 'inclusive' regardless of whether it simply calls God a rock" or expands vocabulary for God to include female and male.[4] Rev. Judith Liro and Rev. Larry Schultz use the word "expansive" to mean including a variety of female, male, and non-gender references to Deity. Some of the ministers in this book consider "God" and "Christ" to be "gender-neutral," while others believe these names to be exclusively masculine. Rev. Stacy Boorn believes in using "God/dess" and "Christ-Sophia" in liturgies to be inclusive of female and male. For this book I sought ministers who include female divine names in worship, but I had no rigid formula or quota for these references. I discovered that ministers in some cultural contexts find it especially difficult to introduce female divine images. Rev. Monica Coleman comments: "Trying to get inclusive language into a black church is like pulling teeth. There's resistance to inclusive language in white churches also. But I think there are more conservative black churches, even though there are some progressive ones." As the first woman pastor in the town of West Plains, Missouri, Rev. Rebecca Kiser has found that she has to move slowly in bringing additional changes to her church.

Some of the ministers in this book see their main mission as giving precedence to the Divine Feminine or as including female divine names and images in worship. Rev. Stacy Boorn leads Ebenezer/herchurch Lutheran in a kind of "affirmative action" for the Divine Feminine as an "attempt to balance the predominantly androcentric and hierarchical images of God that abound in our biblical tradition." Others try to achieve an equal balance of female and male divine names and images in worship. Rev. Larry Schultz, as we read in his story, has difficulty in finding music with this balanced imagery, so he alters lyrics or creates new music. "It's very important for me to balance images, to help interpret the feminine that was lost when patriarchy took over," he says. "It gives me purpose and meaning to have discovered the Divine Feminine and other theologies of inclusion. This is the Good News message for me now." Rev. Judith Liro leads St. Hildegard's also in the mission of transforming community and liturgy through the balance of female and male divine names and images.

The ministers in these stories also express their desire to find more expansive non-gender divine language and imagery, as well as language and imagery that represent the full continuum of gender so as to be more inclusive of LGBTQ persons. Rev. Nancy Petty, for example, advocates for visual imagery in her church that includes not only women, but children, persons with disabilities, homosexual persons, and nature. Raising possibilities for expanding divine imagery, Rev. Larry Schultz comments: "The Divine Feminine opens up so much more in our imaging Mystery. There are ways of singing about the Divine that we haven't explored, like with transgendered images. And what are the divine images on other planets? What are their expressions of Mystery? Perhaps there's a third gender out there, or four or five genders." Rev. Marcia Fleischman also sees the Divine Feminine as a "doorway" to other expansive visions. All of the ministers in this book recognize the metaphorical nature of our naming of Divine Mystery, beyond all our language.

Some of the women ministers in this book equate ordained women and the Divine Feminine. They see their very presence as pastors or priests as bringing the Divine Feminine into worship. Rev. Susan Newman affirms the importance of women of various races in the pulpit so that people can "see themselves, that we're all created in the image of God and that God is male and female, and that God is black, brown, yellow." While they include female divine names in their worship services, Bishop Bridget Mary Meehan and Rev. Nancy Petty also believe they represent the Divine Feminine. Rev. Rebecca Kiser agrees that her presence in the pulpit invites change. "I think it challenges people's mindsets just to see a woman up front," she says. Professor of Liturgy Marjorie Procter-Smith comments that the presence of clergywomen "challenges the centuries-long tradition that has marginalized women as religious leaders," but that "their presence may also be read as affirmation by women of the very historical structures and practices that have kept women out of religious leadership and continue to make women's exercise of religious leadership difficult."[5] Rev. Isabel Docampo also cautions about assuming that the inclusion of women clergy will necessarily bring change to the church. She expresses sadness that many women, even when they are pastors or bishops, have not felt "free to change things," that often they have felt they had to conform instead of transform the church.

Working for Justice in Church and Society

The ministers in this book, women and men, have used their positions as ordained clergy to change the church. These stories demonstrate that ministers who include female divine names and images also take prophetic stands on race, class, sexual orientation, ecology, and other social justice issues. These ministers do what Professor Marjorie Procter-Smith calls "emancipatory" work that contributes to the "freedom of *all* people, recognizing the intersection and interrelationship of these multiple forms of oppression."[6] These liberating ministers understand the power of worship language to shape social reality, to provide a foundation for justice and freedom for all people. Rev. Isabel Docampo states, "The names which we use to address the Divine in prayer and song, Sunday after Sunday, affect not only our relationship with the Divine, but also our relationship with all of humanity, and how we see and understand ourselves." Rev. Judith Liro comments, "Our liturgical language with its current, heavily masculine content supports a patriarchal hierarchical ordering. Most are simply unaware of the power of language. The status quo that includes the exploitation of the earth, poverty, racism, sexism, heterosexism, and militarism is held in place by a deep symbolic imbalance, and we are unwitting participants in it."

These stories reveal that the liberating ministers understand the necessity of including the Divine Feminine for justice in church and society. Realizing the connection between gender equality and divine images, Rev. Paul Smith began including female divine images in his church and wrote a book giving biblical support for calling God "Mother." He says, "Nothing will change business as usual in our churches unless those of us who are convicted by the Holy Spirit first change our own behavior and then work towards change in the church." Rev. Virginia Marie Rincon also sees the Divine Feminine as vital to equality for women in the church, saying that since men are still dominant, "it's important to put those Divine Feminine images in front of people in our liturgies and in our meetings." Bishop Bridget Mary Meehan works for justice in the church through the ordination of Roman Catholic women priests. She comments: "Women priests remind us that women are equal symbols of the Holy. Women and men are created in God's image, and both may represent Christ as priests. The Divine has a female face because all of us, male and female, are created in the divine image." Rev. Stacy Boorn leads Ebenezer Lutheran in the mission of being a "prophetic voice within the patriarchal church." She believes that the church must change in order for there to be justice in the world. "I don't see how the world is going to change until the religious institutions change because they are so much a part of who the world is," she says. "The more we can provide church in a different way, the more we can hope things change."

In addition to working for change in the church, the ministers in this book also participate in justice initiatives in the culture outside the church. They demonstrate the close connection between inclusion of the Divine Feminine in worship and social justice in the church and in the wider culture. They work for justice not only for women but for racial minorities, LGBTQ persons, the economically disadvantaged, the earth. For example, Rev. Virginia Marie Rincon founded TengoVoz "to give voice" to Latinas, leads rallies for immigrant rights, works to prevent domestic violence, and helps people find jobs. Rev. Susan Newman helped get the Marriage Equality Law passed in Washington, DC, works in HIV/AIDS education, and advocates for children and families especially through her book *With Heart and Hand: The Black Church Working to Save Black Children*. Rev. Isabel Docampo says she has probably been preaching the same "justice sermon" all her life. From her story it is obvious that she has preached this sermon not only through her words in church, but through her actions in various communities as she has worked in such areas as urban missions, workers' rights, domestic violence, nuclear disarmament, literacy, and interfaith dialogue. Rev. Monica Coleman served as a community organizer with low-income neighborhoods, advocates against domestic violence, and works on mental health and environmental issues. Among the justice issues Rev. Marcia Fleischman has championed are LGBTQ rights and overcoming racial and religious discrimination. Rev. Rebecca Kiser's ministry has included hunger relief, peacemaking, and environmental issues.

Deepening Spiritual Experience through the Divine Feminine

Another discovery through the stories in this book is the importance of the Divine Feminine to the deepening of spiritual experience. These ministers enrich their personal spiritual lives as they fulfill their prophetic mission of bringing liberating change to church and society. These stories reveal that including female divine images expands experience of Divine Mystery. Rev. Isabel Docampo, after suffering discrimination as an ordained woman, discovered the personal importance of the Divine Feminine. She says that the first time she heard female divine names she felt that her "soul had been touched in a new and profound way" and that she "was being affirmed for the first time as truly created in the image of the great Divine with the full blessing of the Divine." As Rev. Monica Coleman identifies with female divine images from various faith traditions, she also experiences affirmation and awe. Rev. Virginia Marie Rincon finds deep spiritual meaning in the Virgin of San Juan and the Virgin of Guadalupe. Her grandmother used to go to the shrine of the Virgin of San Juan and pray for Virginia Marie to fulfill her call, and she relates to the Virgin of Guadalupe because she sees her as a *mujerista* like herself.

Some of the stories in this book reveal further mystical possibilities opened through the Divine Feminine. Rev. Marcia Fleischman, for example, tells of a mystical experience that helped her heal from her dad's and boyfriend's negative messages about women. When she was questioning whether or not she was made in the divine image, she heard God say to her, "Just as your daughter looks like you, you look like me." Mystical experiences of the Divine Feminine helped Rev. Rebecca Kiser to heal from the loss of her six-week-old daughter and to see "God as gender-*full* rather than genderless." Teaching and writing on the divinity within each person, Rev. Paul Smith believes that including the Divine Feminine opens mystical experience. "We all feel our divinity more when we hear 'She' and 'He' in church," he says. Rev. Susan Newman also teaches that female divine images help us all to claim our "divinity and walk in it every day."

Moving from Hierarchical to Egalitarian Church Structure

Another theme in these stories is the movement from a hierarchical to an egalitarian church. These liberating ministers strive to break down the separation between clergy and laity while they use their ordained status to give them power to bring change. Bishop Bridget Mary Meehan, for example, says that in order to have credibility in the Roman Catholic Church, women have to be ordained as priests: "In order to bring change we have to fit within the structure, to be ordained as priests with apostolic succession." However, she believes in using her power as an ordained priest to transform the hierarchical model of the church into a "discipleship of equals." She views the ordination of women priests as necessary in the meantime to bring justice for women in the church, to remind people that women have equal value. Likewise Rev. Virginia Marie Rincon believes in using her role as clergy when it supports her justice work. She doesn't always wear her priest collar because she doesn't believe in separating herself from the laypeople with whom she ministers, but she will put the collar on when she needs it to give her power for her ministry. "Putting the collar on gives you power to some people," she says. Rev. Stacy Boorn believes, "inclusion of the Divine Feminine will change the whole structure of the church" and "eventually the clergy structure will be dismantled." She explains how "egalitarian language for the Holy Other supports egalitarian communities; inclusion of the Sacred Feminine empowers women and men to look at alternative structures, to change power structures that leave people out or belittle them or give a person power over others."

In one church featured in this book we see that moving to an egalitarian church structure led to inclusion of women as pastors and of the Divine Feminine. At Broadway Church, Paul Smith established small groups and team leadership, and then began adding women, including Marcia Fleischman, to the leadership team. Later they led the church to include female divine language in worship. Paul gradually came to believe that "ordination of anyone is not good for the church," because it exalts "certain spiritual gifts and deflates other gifts." He took his name off the church sign, dressed like the laypeople in the church, and encouraged laypeople to lead worship.

As Rev. Marcia Fleischman's story shows, women ministers may experience the downside of a diminished clergy role more than their male counterparts. Because Broadway Church was downplaying the distinction between clergy and laity when Marcia was ordained, there was no ordination ceremony for her. "It was hard enough for me to own my position as it was, struggling for equality as a woman minister," she says. Some of the other ministers in this book also see the importance of clergy status for women until there is full equality for women in church and society.

Visions for the Future

The liberating ministers in *Changing Church* articulate expansive visions for the power of the Divine Feminine to change the church and the world. They envision communities inclusive in gender, race, sexual orientation, class, ability, and religion. A prominent theme in these visions is interfaith cooperation in working toward peace and justice. Rev. Isabel Docampo describes a dialogue group of Jewish, Muslim, and Christian women as her vision of the Divine Feminine, bringing people into "relationship with the Great Other and with the 'other,' whoever that may be—women, poor people, different races." In her vision "women would no longer be expendable and disposable anywhere on this planet." As we "stay connected" to a diversity of people, she says, and the "stories are told and received, every person is transformed." Rev. Susan Newman's vision also includes everyone in all faith traditions, putting aside differences and finding common ground "to do justice and work to uplift suffering humanity." Likewise Rev. Rebecca Kiser envisions "a widely inclusive group of people who have learned to be together, despite all kinds of dissimilarities, that ideal of unity in the midst of diversity." She loves to see "all kinds of people" engaged in "creative worship," bringing "all kinds of gifts" and "all kinds of imagery." Rev. Monica Coleman's "vision for the Divine Feminine" looks like "feminist" churches such as "Ebenezer/herchurch in San Francisco" and "Circle of Grace in Atlanta." She explains that in addition to having female and other diverse images, so that all people "can see themselves in worship," these churches are "very welcoming" to people of all faiths. Rev. Coleman's vision includes "a national organization of people doing feminist church" with a website that helps people to find these churches.

In this book we read stories of other ministers who share this passion for spreading the Good News of the Divine Feminine. Rev. Larry Schultz, for example, envisions the spread of expansive theology throughout the church and the world. "For me the Gospel to share is the Divine Feminine and expanding imagery and theology because of all the benefits for women and men and children," he says. "I want to provide music resources that include female and male divine images so that both girls and boys grow up to know they're valued." On a pilgrimage to the island of Iona, Rev. Judith Liro had a mystical experience of being part of the continued emergence of the Sacred Feminine. She expresses her hope that what she is "doing in a small way will begin to come in a larger way." Rev. Marcia Fleischman envisions the Divine Feminine reaching from the church to encompass the whole world. She sees a black Madonna, surrounded by rays of light, embracing the earth, empowering abused women and girls and bringing justice and peace to all people around the world.

An Invitation

As I write this book, I am teaching a community college course called "How to Write and Publish Your Story." Seeking to inspire students to believe in the sacred power of stories, I quote various authors, such as Ursula K. LeGuin: "The story is one of the basic tools invented by the human mind, for the purpose of gaining understanding"[7]; and Dorothy Allison: "Two or three things I know for sure, and one of them is that to go on living I have to tell stories, that stories are the one sure way I know to touch the heart and change the world."[8] It is my hope that the stories in this book have increased your understanding of the vital contribution of the Divine Feminine to justice and peace, and that these stories have touched your heart to join in changing the world through the inclusion of female divine names and images in faith communities. This book comes to you with the invitation to join these liberating ministers in changing the church and the world. And I invite you to write your story!

Notes

Introduction

1. "About.com.Women's History, Toni Morrison Quotes, speech." Online: http://womenshistory.about.com/od/quotes/a/toni_morrison.htm.

2. Letha Scanzoni and Nancy Hardesty, *All We're Meant to Be: A Biblical Approach to Women's Liberation* (Waco, TX: Word, 1974). This book is now in its third edition: Letha Dawson Scanzoni and Nancy A. Hardesty, *All We're Meant to Be: Biblical Feminism for Today* (Grand Rapids: Eerdmans, 1992).

3. Sharon Neufer Emswiler and Thomas Neufer Emswiler, *Women & Worship: A Guide to Nonsexist Hymns, Prayer, and Liturgies* (New York: Harper & Row, 1974; revised and expanded edition, 1984).

4. Virginia Ramey Mollenkott, *The Divine Feminine: The Biblical Imagery of God as Female* (New York: Crossroad, 1986). Dr. Virginia Ramey Mollenkott is Professor Emeritus of English Language and Literature at the William Paterson University of New Jersey. Among her other numerous publications are *Women, Men, and the Bible* and *Is the Homosexual My Neighbor: A Positive Christian Response* (with Letha Dawson Scanzoni).

5. Jean Shinoda Bolen, *Goddesses in Everywoman: A New Psychology of Women* (New York: Harper Perennial, 1984). The most recent edition of this book is *Goddesses in Everywoman: Powerful Archetypes in Women's Lives* (New York: Harper Paperbacks, 2004). Dr. Jean Shinoda Bolen is a psychiatrist, Jungian analyst, and internationally known speaker. Among her other numerous books are *Crossing to Avalon: A Woman's Midlife Quest for the Sacred Feminine* and *Urgent Message from Mother: Gather the Women, Save the World*.

6. Rosemary Radford Ruether, *Sexism and God-Talk: Toward a Feminist Theology* (Boston: Beacon, 1993). Dr. Rosemary Radford Ruether is the Carpenter Emerita Professor of Feminist Theology at Pacific School of Religion and the Graduate Theological Union. Among her other numerous publications is *Integrating Ecofeminism, Globalization, and World Religions*.

7. Elisabeth Schüssler Fiorenza, *In Memory of Her: A Feminist Theological Reconstruction of Christian Origins* (New York: Crossroad, 1989). Dr. Elisabeth Schüssler Fiorenza is currently the Krister Stendahl Professor of Divinity at Harvard

Divinity School. Among her other numerous publications is *Discipleship of Equals: A Critical Feminist Ekklesialogy Of Liberation*; and *Jesus: Miriam's Child, Sophia's Prophet: Critical Issues in Feminist Christology*.

8. Miriam Therese Winter, *WomanPrayer, WomanSong: Resources for Ritual* (Oak Park, IL: Meyer Stone, 1987). The most recent edition of this book is *WomanPrayer WomanSong: Resources for Ritual* (Eugene, OR: Wipf & Stock, 2008). Dr. Miriam Therese Winter, Roman Catholic Medical Mission Sister and theologian, is professor of Liturgy, Worship, Spirituality, Feminist Studies at Hartford Seminary, Hartford, Connecticut. Among her other numerous publications is *The Singer and the Song: An Autobiography of the Spirit*.

9. *Sophia* is the Greek word for "Wisdom," linked to Christ in the Christian Scriptures.

10. Mary Kathleen Speegle Schmitt, *Seasons of the Feminine Divine: Christian Feminist Prayers for the Liturgical Cycle*, Cycle C (New York: Crossroad, 1994) 18–19.

11. Miriam Therese Winter, Adair Lummis, and Allison Stokes, *Defecting in Place: Women Taking Responsibility for Their Own Spiritual Lives* (New York: Crossroad, 1995).

12. Carol Schaefer, *Grandmothers Counsel the World: Women Elders Offer Their Vision for Our Planet* (Boston: Trumpeter, 2006) 212.

13. Paul Smith, *Is It Okay to Call God "Mother"?: Considering the Feminine Face of God* (Peabody, MA: Hendrickson, 1993.)

14. Rev. Marcia C. Fleischman, *Wild Woman Theology: In the Arms of Loving Mother God* (Bloomington, IN: AuthorHouse, 2009).

15. Bridget Mary Meehan, *Exploring the Feminine Face of God* (Kansas City, MO: Sheed & Ward, 1991); and *Delighting in the Feminine Divine* (Kansas City, MO: Sheed & Ward, 1994).

16. *Hokmah* is the word for "Wisdom" in the Hebrew Scriptures.

17. *Ruah* is the Hebrew word for "Spirit" in the book of Genesis and elsewhere in the Hebrew Scriptures.

18. See my book *In Whose Image?: God and Gender* (New York: Crossroad, 2001) for a detailed account of female divine names and images in the Hebrew and Christian Scriptures and in Christian history.

19. Amnesty International, "Broken Bodies, Shattered Minds: Torture and Ill Treatment of Women"(2001).

20. United Nations General Assembly, "In-Depth Study on All Forms of Violence against Women: Report of the Secretary General, 2006," A/61/122/Add.1.6 (July 2006).

21. The United Nations Population Fund, The State of World Population 2000 report, "Lives Together, Worlds Apart: Men and Women in a Time of Change" (2000).

22. Nicholas D. Kristof and Sheryl WuDunn, *Half the Sky: Turning Oppression into Opportunity for Women Worldwide* (New York: Knopf, 2009) xvii.

23. Louise Arbour, United Nations High Commissioner for Human Rights, "International Women's Day: Laws and 'Low Intensity' Discrimination against Women" (March 8, 2008).

24. Sister Joan Chittister OSB, Founder and Executive Director of Benetvision, Chair of Global Peace Initiative for Women, comments on the Asia Pacific Breakthrough: The Women, Faith and Development Summit to End Global Poverty, Melbourne, Australia, December 2–3, 2009. Online: http://ncronline.org/blogs/where-i-stand/travel-diary-%E2%80%93-part-one.

25. Sister Joan Chittister comments on the Parliament of the World's Religions, December 3–9, 2009, Melbourne, Australia. Online: http://ncronline.org/blogs/where-i-stand/parliament-worlds-religions.

26. *Children's Letters to God*, compiled by Eric Marshall and Stuart Hample (New York: Simon and Schuster, 1966) n.p.

Chapter 1

1. Shiloh Sophia McCloud's art focuses mainly on Divine Feminine images. Shiloh's work is "dedicated to bringing images and acts of healing to the world." (http://www.wisdomhousecatalog.com/homeforshilohsophia.html)

2. "We Eat the Bread of Teaching," Omer Westendorf (1916–1997).

3. An alb is a full-length white linen ecclesiastical vestment with long sleeves that is gathered at the waist with a cincture, a cord, or sash of cloth.

4. Seminex is the abbreviation for Concordia Seminary in Exile (later Christ Seminary-Seminex). Seminex was formed in 1974 after a walkout by faculty and students of Concordia Seminary in St. Louis, an institution of the Lutheran Church—Missouri Synod.

5. See Introduction, n. 6.

6. Dr. Mary Daly, pioneering feminist theologian and philosopher, taught at Boston College for thirty-three years. Her best-known book is *Beyond God the Father: Toward a Philosophy of Women's Liberation*. Her other publications include *Gyn/Ecology: The Metaethics of Radical Feminism* and *The Church and the Second Sex*.

7. The Association of Evangelical Lutheran Churches (AELC) was a U.S. church body that existed from 1976 through the end of 1987. The AELC formed when approximately 250 congregations withdrew from the Lutheran Church—Missouri Synod (LCMS) in 1976. The AELC ceased to be an independent body when it became part of the new Evangelical Lutheran Church in America (ELCA) on January 1, 1988.

8. Rosemary Radford Ruether, *Sexism and God-Talk* (Boston: Beacon, 1983).

9. *Shekhinah* is a feminine Hebrew word translated "dwelling" or "settling," and is used in the book of Exodus to denote the dwelling presence of God and/or the glory of God.

10. Luke 13:20–21.

11. BPA is short for bisphenol A, a controversial compound found in polycarbonate plastics. Some studies have shown that it can cause medical ills in lab rats.

12. A synod is a regional or national organization of Lutheran congregations.

13. After the vote to lift the ban on LGBT clergy in committed relationships, Harry Knox, director for the Human Rights Campaign Religion and Faith Program stated, "The ELCA has studied, prayed and listened to the witness of its LGBT sisters and brothers, and has come to consensus in community. This decision reflects the best of Lutheran tradition."

14. Rev. Stacy Boorn has published two books of splendid photographs: *Natural Colors: "California"* and *Alaska: Wet and Wild* (www.blurb.com). Also, her works are on exhibit in "A Woman's Eye Gallery"(www.awegallery.com) and at stacy.awegallery.com.

15. Lana Dalberg, MA in theology and MFA in writing, and a mother, dedicated this poem to her mother, Anabelle Dalberg, on Mother's Day, 2004.

16. Mark 12:38–44.

Chapter 2

1. The Reverend Dr. Susan Newman, *Your Inner Eve: Discovering God's Woman Within* (New York: Random House, 2005) 94.

2. Ibid., 84, 93, 94, 102.

3. Mark 2:1–5, 11, 12.

4. Ruth 1:6–18.

5. The words "a soul can find a home" are paraphrased from the first stanza of Maya Angelou's poem "Alone," which Rev. Dr. Newman quotes at the beginning of her sermon. "Alone," *The Complete Collected Poems* by Maya Angelou (New York: Random House, 1994) 74–75.

6. Matthew 11:28, KJV

7. Luke 18:16, KJV.

8. Matthew 5:48.

9. Gospel Music Workshop of America (GMWA), an international music convention, was founded in 1967 by Rev. James Cleveland and Albertina Walker.

10. Ephesians 2:8–9, KJV.

11. Ephesians 5:16–17, KJV.

12. The Reverend Dr. Susan Newman, *Oh God! A Black Woman's Guide to Sex and Spirituality* (New York: Ballantine, 2002) 141.

13. The two main African American Baptist denominations are the National Baptist Convention, USA (NBCUSA) and the Progressive National Baptist Convention (PNBC). In 1961 the Progressive National Baptist Convention (PNBC) focusing on civil rights and social justice, separated from the NBCUSA and formed in Cincinnati, Ohio.

14. In 1969 Rev. H. Wesley Wiley became the first African American pastor to lead Covenant Baptist Church, a predominantly white congregation at the time. He also served as Director of Cooperative Ministries with the Home Mission Board of the Southern Baptist Convention. He oversaw the gradual transition of Covenant to a predominantly black congregation, and led the church to grow and to establish an early childhood school and a gospel choir.

15. Rev. Dr. Samuel DeWitt Proctor was known nationally as a distinguished preacher, educator, and author. He taught in the graduate school of Rutgers University from 1969 to 1984. He served as pastor of the Abyssinian Baptist Church in New York, and as an associate director of the Peace Corps under Presidents John Kennedy and Lyndon Johnson. Among his numerous publications is *The Substance of Things Hoped For: A Memoir of African American Faith*.

16. Rev. Dr. Boykin Sanders is currently Professor of New Testament & Greek at the Samuel DeWitt Proctor School of Theology, Virginia Union University. Among the churches he has pastored are the Dexter Avenue King Memorial Baptist Church in Montgomery, Alabama, and Pleasant Hill Baptist Church in Boston, Massachusetts. Among his published works is *Blowing the Trumpet in Open Court: Prophetic Judgment and Liberation*.

17. Dr. Lawrence Neale Jones was dean of the chapel at Fisk University in the early 1960s and then held several top positions at Union Theological Seminary before serving as dean of Howard University School of Divinity from 1975 to 1991. Dr. Jones, a minister in the United Church of Christ, also served as pastor of churches in Ohio, New York City, and Washington, DC. Among his published works is *From Consciousness to Conscience: Blacks and the United Church of Christ*.

18. The Ecumenical Institute of the World Council of Churches, founded in 1946, brings together people from diverse churches, cultures, and backgrounds for ecumenical learning, academic study, and personal exchange.

19. Bishop Ernest W. Newman, the United Methodist Church's first African American bishop in the Southeastern Jurisdiction, served as bishop over the Nashville area from 1984 until his retirement in 1992, and on the boards of trustees of many United Methodist-related schools of higher education.

20. Rev. Dr. Isaiah DeQuincy Newman was a leading figure in the civil rights movement in South Carolina, one of the lieutenants working with Dr. Martin

Luther King Jr. He helped organize the Orangeburg branch of the NAACP in 1943, helped found the Progressive Democratic Party, and served the South Carolina NAACP as executive secretary from 1960 to 1969. In 1983, at age seventy-two, he was elected to the South Carolina Senate, becoming the first African American to serve in that body since Reconstruction. For about forty years, he served United Methodist churches in Georgia and South Carolina and held key positions with the UMC's South Carolina Conference and its General Conference. As a member of the UMC Merger Committee in the 1970s, he played a major role in bringing an end to segregated congregations.

21. Rev. Dr. Omega Newman, a distinguished United Methodist pastor, was one of the founders of Black Methodists for Church Renewal.

22. Andrew Young has served as Mayor of Atlanta, as United States Ambassador to the United Nations, as a member of the U.S. House of Representatives, and as President of the National Council of Churches USA. He was active during the 1960s civil rights movement and was a friend of Dr. Martin Luther King Jr.

23. Rev. Dr. Henry Mitchell served congregations in New York and California before being named in 1966 as the first Martin Luther King Jr. Professor of Black Church Studies at Colgate Rochester Divinity School. He subsequently served as dean and professor of history and homiletics at the School of Theology at Virginia Union University. He and his wife, the Rev. Dr. Ella Pearson Mitchell, team-taught as visiting professors of homiletics at the Interdenominational Theological Center, and taught together as mentors in the Doctor of Ministry program at the United Theological Seminary. Among his published books is *Celebration and Experience in Preaching*.

24. Rev. Dr. Edward L. Wheeler, president of Christian Theological Seminary in Indianapolis since 1997, has also served as professor of church history at United Theological Seminary, dean of the chapel and professor of religion and society at Tuskegee University, pastor of Zion Baptist Church in Cincinnati, Ohio, associate director of the Department of Black Church Relations at the Home Mission Board of the Southern Baptist Convention. Dr. Wheeler's published works include *Uplifting the Race: Black Ministerial Leadership in the New South, 1865–1902*.

25. Rev. Dr. E. K. Bailey, founder of the Concord Missionary Baptist Church in Dallas, began E. K. Bailey Ministries, Inc. in 1989 to provide principles and practices of church growth to African American pastors and lay leaders.

26. Rev. Dr. Cynthia Hale, founding and senior pastor of Ray of Hope Christian Church in Atlanta, Georgia, gave the opening invocation at the 2008 Democratic National Convention and the Scripture reading at the National Prayer Service for the Presidential Inauguration of Barack Obama. She has contributed to *The African American Pulpit Journal* and to *Power in the Pulpit II: How America's Most Effective Black Preachers Prepare Their Sermons*.

27. Rev. Dr. Carolyn Ann Knight has served as assistant professor of homiletics at the Interdenominational Theological Center in Atlanta, Georgia, as adjunct professor at LaGuardia Community College and New York Theological Seminary, and

as the permanent part-time professor of preaching at Union Theological Seminary. She was named one of America's Fifteen Greatest African American Women Preachers by *Ebony* magazine in 1997.

28. Rev. Dr. Gregory Ingram was elected the 118th bishop of the African Methodist Episcopal Church in the year 2000. He has pastored Oak Grove African Methodist Episcopal Church in Detroit, Michigan, and other AME churches.

29. Rev. Dr. Alvin O'Neal Jackson, pastor of Park Avenue Christian Church in New York City, has also served as pastor of Mississippi Boulevard Christian Church of Memphis and as pastor of National City Christian Church and president of the National City Christian Church Foundation of Washington, DC.

30. Rev. Dr. Frank Thomas, pastor of Mississippi Boulevard Christian Church, previously pastored New Faith Baptist Church, Matteson, Illinois. He teaches preaching on the adjunct faculty at McCormick Theological Seminary in Chicago, and serves as co-executive editor of *The African American Pulpit*. Among his published books is *They Like to Never Quit Praisin' God: The Role of Celebration in Preaching*.

31. The Children's Defense Fund (CDF), founded in 1973 by Marian Wright Edelman, is a non-profit child advocacy and research organization. CDF promotes policies and programs that lift children out of poverty, protect them from abuse and neglect, ensure their access to health care and quality education, and give them a moral and spiritual foundation.

32. The Children's Defense Fund sponsors the Children's Sabbath with the assistance of a multifaith advisory committee and the endorsement of hundreds of denominations and religious organizations. This annual celebration, held every third weekend in October, provides the opportunity for communities of faith to strengthen existing efforts for children and discover new opportunities. Every year, CDF compiles a multifaith resource manual that guides the Children's Sabbaths celebrations.

33. Romans 12:1-2.

34. "Still I Rise," *The Complete Collected Poems* by Maya Angelou (New York: Random House, 1994) 163.

35. Coretta Scott King was an activist, author, and civil rights leader. The widow of Martin Luther King Jr., Coretta Scott King helped lead the 1960s civil rights movement. She was also active in the movements for women's rights and LGBT rights. Among her published works is her memoir, *My Life with Martin Luther King, Jr.*

36. Jeanne Moutoussamy-Ashe, photographer and author, published a book, *Daddy and Me: A Photo Story of Arthur Ashe and His Daughter Camera*, detailing her husband tennis pro Arthur Ashe's last year, using their daughter's experiences as a point of view.

37. Karen Lowery is a gospel singer and daughter of Rev. Joseph Lowery, a minister in the United Methodist church and leader in the civil rights movement.

38. Bernice Johnson Reagon founded the internationally renowned African American women's a cappella ensemble Sweet Honey in the Rock. She is also a composer, scholar, and social activist who participated in the 1960s civil rights movement as a member of The Freedom Singers.

39. Susan D. Newman, *With Heart and Hand: The Black Church Working to Save Black Children* (Valley Forge, PA: Judson, 1994).

40. Newman, *Oh God!*

41. Newman, *Your Inner Eve*.

42. The Balm in Gilead, Inc. is a not-for-profit, non-governmental organization with a mission of engaging faith institutions in preventing diseases and improving the health status of people of the African Diaspora.

43. The Religious Coalition for Reproductive Choice (RCRC) brings the moral power of religious communities to ensure reproductive choice of underserved populations through education and advocacy.

44. Prior to the Civil War, slavery was legal in the District of Columbia. Although the majority of the members of the early All Souls Church in DC, called First Unitarian at that time, were sympathetic with the Southern attitude on slavery, many of the church's ministers made statements against slavery as early as 1824.

45. The "beloved community" was a dream of Dr. Martin Luther King Jr. to create a world in which all persons in the nation and the world live in peace and harmony.

46. John 4:24.

47. Newman, *Oh God!* 17–18.

48. Luke 15:3–32.

49. Newman, *Oh God!* 143–145.

50. Habitat for Humanity, founded by Millard and Linda Fuller with a mission of eliminating poverty housing, brings people of all backgrounds, races, and religions together to build houses in partnership with families in need.

51. Oxfam is an international confederation of 14 organizations working together in 100 countries and with partners and allies around the world to find lasting solutions to poverty and injustice.

52. Crop Walks are community-wide events sponsored by Church World Service and organized by local congregations to raise funds to end hunger at home and around the world.

Chapter 3

1. Bridget Mary Meehan was ordained a Roman Catholic priest in July of 2006 and a bishop in April of 2009. A Roman Catholic male bishop in Europe, who is in full apostolic succession, ordained three women as bishops who have ordained

other women bishops, including Bridget Mary, who now can validly ordain women priests. Because of her belief in an egalitarian Christian community, Bridget Mary prefers not to be called "Reverend," "Mother," or "Bishop," telling parishioners to call her simply "Bridget Mary." But because she sees the church as currently in a transition from a hierarchical to an egalitarian model, she believes that women priests are important to bring justice for women as equal images of the Divine; thus she will allow the use of the title "Bishop" in reference to her.

2. Excerpt of liturgy from Mary Magdalene Apostle Catholic Community in San Diego.

3. Sisters for Christian Community (SFCC), formed in 1970 in response to Vatican II, is an egalitarian and ecumenical religious order outside the structure of the Catholic Church.

4. St. Brigit of Kildare, one of Ireland's patron saints along with St. Patrick and St. Columba, is believed to have been a nun, abbess, and founder of several monasteries, and to have been inadvertently consecrated as a bishop by Bishop Mel. The mythology, religious traditions, and symbols originally associated with the Goddess Brigit later came to be ascribed to this Christian saint.

5. Bridget Mary Meehan and Regina Madonna Oliver, *Affirmations from the Heart of God* (Liguori, MO: Liguori, 1998) 16.

6. Ibid., 13–14.

7. Founded in 1845, Congregation of the Sisters, Servants of the Immaculate Heart of Mary (IHM) is a Catholic teaching order.

8. The desert mothers and fathers were Christian women and men in the third through fifth centuries CE who developed a reputation for holiness and wisdom by practicing solitude in the deserts of Egypt and the Holy Land.

9. The Society of Sisters for the Church (SSC) was founded in 1976 by Sister Eileen Kelly, Vicar for Religious of the Diocese of Paterson, New Jersey.

10. Fort Myer Memorial Chapel, adjacent to Arlington National Cemetery, serves the military community at Fort Myer, Virginia, and has been the setting of many funerals of those buried in the Cemetery.

11. GS (General Schedule) is the designation for the pay scale within the U.S. civil service that includes the majority of white-collar personnel positions.

12. Rosemary Radford Ruether, Elisabeth Schüssler Fiorenza, and Elizabeth Johnson are leading Christian feminist theologians and scholars. See Introduction, nn. 6–7. Among Elizabeth Johnson's groundbreaking books is *She Who Is: The Mystery of God in Feminist Theological Discourse*.

13. Bridget Mary Meehan, *Exploring the Feminine Face of God* (Kansas City, MO: Sheed & Ward, 1991).

14. Ibid., 78–79.

15. Bridget Mary Meehan, *Delighting in the Feminine Divine* (Kansas City, MO: Sheed & Ward, 1994) xi.

16. Bridget Mary Meehan and Regina Madonna Oliver, *Heart Talks with Mother God*, illustrated by Betsy Bowen, Barbara Knutson, and Susan Sawyer (Collegeville, Minnesota: The Liturgical Press, 1995) 8.

17. Ibid., 18–19.

18. Bridget Mary Meehan, *Praying with Women of the Bible* (Liguori, MO: Liguori, 1998).

19. Bridget Mary Meehan, *The Healing Power of Prayer* (Liguori, MO: Liguori, 1988).

20. Sheed & Ward and The Liturgical Press, which published others of Bridget Mary's books, are also Catholic presses.

21. The Confraternity of Christian Doctrine is commonly referred to by its abbreviation, CCD, or simply as "Catechism"; it provides religious education to Catholic children attending secular schools.

22. In 1980 Mother Mary Angelica founded the Eternal Word Television Network as a voice for American conservative and traditional Catholics; she hosted shows until 2001.

23. Bridget Mary Meehan and Regina Madonna Oliver, *Praying with a Passionate Heart* (Liguori, MO: Liguori, 1999) 31.

24. Bridget Mary's blog (http://bridgetmarys.blogspot.com/) communicates developments in the Women Priests movement.

25. Google Videos and YouTube are free video-sharing Internet sites at which users can upload, share, and view videos.

26. *Democracy Now!* is a progressive, daily, independent, award-winning news program, hosted by Amy Goodman and Juan Gonzalez, and aired by more than 900 radio, television, satellite, and cable TV networks in North America.

27. Elsie Hainz McGrath, Bridget Mary Meehan, and Ida Raming, *Women Find a Way: The Movement and Stories of Roman Catholic Womenpriests* (College Station, TX: Virtualbookworm.com) 91–92.

28. *Anam Cara* are Gaelic words meaning "soul friend."

29. Susan L. Rife, "Woman Called to Priesthood," *Sarasota Herald-Tribune* (April 15, 2007).

30. "Clandestine Ordinations," *California Catholic Daily* (April 23, 2009) 1.

31. Mother Theodore Guerin (1798–1856), founder of the Sisters of Providence of Saint Mary-of-the-Woods, was excommunicated by her local bishop when she refused to give him control over her congregation. In 2006, Pope Benedict canonized her, designating her as St. Theodora.

32. Mother Mary MacKillop (1842–1909), founder of the Australian-based Sisters of St. Joseph of the Sacred Heart, was, in 1871, officially excommunicated by her local bishop, on the grounds that "she had incited the sisters to disobedience and defiance." Pope Benedict canonized her in 2010.

33. "Declaration on the Question of the Admission of Women to the Ministerial Priesthood," *Vatican Council II: More Postconciliar Documents*, ed. Austin Flannery (Collegeville, MN: Liturgical, 1982) 339.

34. The U.S. Conference of Catholic Bishops (USCCB) on January 6, 2010, announced steps to promote the enactment of immigration reform legislation.

35. Sarasota United for Responsibility and Equity (SURE) is an interfaith justice ministry to foster community-wide action on such issues as poverty, crime, health care, housing, education, and the environment.

36. Mother Mary Clare Millea, the superior general of the Apostles of the Sacred Heart of Jesus, in 2009 became the visitor for the Vatican to investigate American nuns.

37. These comments were quoted in two Irish newspapers, *Laois Nationalist* (August 24, 2010) and *Mayo News* (August 24, 2010).

38. *Exploring the Feminine Face of God*, xi.

39. *Heart Talks with Mother God*, 10.

40. Mary Beben and Bridget Mary Meehan, *Walking the Prophetic Journey* (Boulder, CO: WovenWord, 1998) 82.

41. Bridget Mary's Blog (March 11, 2010).

42. *Delighting in the Feminine Divine*, 136.

Chapter 4

1. New Wineskins Community, in Dallas, explores news ways of seeing divinity and interpreting Scripture so that the spiritual gifts of everyone are equally valued and nurtured. The name "New Wineskins," coming from the metaphor in Matthew 9:17, describes the search for new language and symbols to proclaim the Gospel of liberation and shalom. This Community's rituals include female and male divine names and images to symbolize shared power and responsibility.

2. Bobby McFerrin, "The 23rd Psalm" (ProbNoblem Music, 1990).

3. Fulgencio Batista y Zaldívar was a U.S.-backed Cuban military leader, president, and dictator. He was the leader of Cuba from 1933 to 1944 and from 1952 to 1959, before being overthrown as a result of the Cuban Revolution, led by Fidel Castro.

4. In Spanish *tu* is the singular informal word and *usted* is the singular formal word translated "you" in English.

5. Univision is a Spanish-language television network in the United States.

6. Training Union, a teaching program on Sunday evenings that was popular in Southern Baptist churches in the 1950s through 1970s, emphasized doctrine, Christian ethics, mission history, and current outreaches.

7. From 1914 to 1970, Girls' Auxiliary was a popular Southern Baptist missions organization for girls 6–12. Girls earned badges and moved up the ranks, called "forward steps," by memorizing Scripture and information about Southern Baptist denominational leaders and missionaries, and by participating in service projects. The highest rank was Queen Regent. In 1970, the organization became Girls in Action.

8. Esther 4:14.

9. In 1984, the Southern Baptist Convention passed a resolution that clearly opposed women as pastors.

10. Feeding America, until 2008 named America's Second Harvest, is the nation's leading domestic hunger-relief charity with the mission of feeding America's hungry through a nationwide network of member food banks.

11. During the 1980s, SANE/FREEZE expanded its work to oppose U.S. military intervention in El Salvador and to end U.S. military aid to the Contras in Nicaragua.

12. The *Baptist Message* is the news journal for Louisiana Baptists.

13. Elsa Tamez's *Bible of the Oppressed* (Maryknoll, NY: Orbis, 1997) is an excellent example of Latin American liberation theology and liberationist hermenutics.

14. Robert McAfee Brown, *Saying Yes and Saying No: On Rendering to God and Caesar* (Louisville, KY: Westminster John Knox, 1986).

15. The Church of the Savior in Washington, DC is a network of nine ecumenical Christian faith communities, including Potter's House and Seekers Church, and over forty ministries that have grown out of the original Church of the Savior community founded in the mid-1940s as an alternative approach to traditional church structures.

16. The Baptist Peace Fellowship of North America (BPFNA), founded in 1984 and headquartered in Charlotte, North Carolina, is a nonprofit organization of various Baptist denominations with a mission of gathering, equipping, and mobilizing Baptists to build a culture of peace rooted in justice.

17. The Alliance of Baptists is a progressive organization formed in 1987 by individuals and congregations who separated from the Southern Baptist Convention as a result of the fundamentalist takeover controversy. Since 1995, Alliance congregations and individuals have come from various traditions including the American Baptist Churches USA, the United Church of Christ, and the Christian Church (Disciples of Christ). The Alliance partners with the Cuban *La Fraternidad de Bautistas*.

18. The Hartford Institute for Religion Research, at Hartford Seminary, has

developed an academic discipline called Congregational Studies, focusing on local congregations for the purpose of better understanding the life and dynamics of the lived reality of faith communities.

19. Sallie McFague, *Metaphorical Theology: Models of God in Religious Language* (Philadelphia: Fortress, 1982).

20. *Sábado Gigante* ("Giant Saturday"), a Spanish-language television show, is Univision's longest-running program and the longest-running variety TV show in the world. *Sábado Gigante* is hosted by Chilean journalist Mario Kreutzberger, using the name "Don Francisco."

21. SCUPE (Seminary Consortium for Urban Pastoral Education) offers experiential learning in academic courses that prepare individuals to become effective agents of transformation in our urban world. SCUPE collaborates with seminaries, universities, denominations, churches, organizations, community groups, and individuals.

22. IAF (Industrial Areas Foundation), is a national community organizing network founded in 1940. In 1972, IAF began to shift toward the congregation-based community organization developed in San Antonio, Texas, by Ernesto Cortes Jr., called Communities Organized for Public Service.

23. This video series comes from the FaithTrust Institute, a national, multifaith, multicultural training and education organization, working to end sexual and domestic violence. Founded in 1977 by Rev. Dr. Marie M. Fortune, the FaithTrust Institute offers a wide range of services and resources for addressing the religious and cultural issues related to abuse.

24. In *Waking the World: Classic Tales of Women and The Heroic Feminine* (New York: Putnam, 1996), Jungian psychiatrist Allan B. Chinen has gathered twelve fairy tales from around the world that are united by one common thread: a woman overcomes adversity and betrayal to transform her situation and the world.

Chapter 5

1. Acts 2:2–3.

2. Larry E. Schultz and Jann Aldredge-Clanton, "Sister Spirit, Brother Spirit," *Inclusive Hymns for Liberating Christians* (Austin: Eakin, 2006) 1.

3. Larry E. Schultz and Jann Aldredge-Clanton, *Imagine God!: A Children's Musical Exploring and Expressing Images of God* (Dallas: Choristers Guild, 2004).

4. The Orff approach to teaching music education to children, named for German composer Carl Orff, includes instruments such as miniature xylophones, marimbas, glockenspiels, and metallophones, all of which have removable bars and resonating columns to project the sound.

5. Larry E. Schultz and Jann Aldredge-Clanton, *Imagine God!*

6. Royal Ambassadors (RAs), a Southern Baptist mission education organization for boys in grades 1–6, uses activities that are designed to help boys learn about missions and get them personally involved in practical missions experiences.

7. Oral Roberts University, founded in 1963 by evangelist Oral Roberts, is a charismatic Christian university in Tulsa, Oklahoma.

8. Ted Haggard, founder and former pastor of New Life Church in Colorado Springs, led the National Association of Evangelicals from 2003 until 2006, when he resigned from all of his leadership positions after he admitted his sexual infidelity and methamphetamine use.

9. James M. Pendleton, *Baptist Church Manual* (Nashville: B&H, 1966).

10. In Baptist tradition, ministers are ordained by local, autonomous Baptist churches. An Ordination Council, usually composed of ordained deacons and pastors from the ordaining church, asks persons being ordained to briefly tell of their conversion experience and their call to the ministry, and may question them about biblical theology, doctrine, ethics, and personal beliefs.

11. NASB, New American Standard Bible; TLB, The Living Bible; and NIV, New International Version.

12. Falls Creek, a Baptist conference center and youth camp in the Arbuckle Mountains of Oklahoma, is the largest youth camp in the United States.

13. "Tenderly Comes Our Shepherd God," *Imagine God!*, 27–31.

14. Dr. Norman Vincent Peale, one of New York City's most famous preachers, was pastor of Marble Collegiate Church in Manhattan for fifty-two years and author of numerous books including *The Power of Positive Thinking*.

15. Chevis F. Horne, "The Language of the Bible: Literal or Symbolic?" *The Baptist Program* (February 1977) 5–6.

16. In 1976 Southern Baptists launched a twenty-five-year evangelistic plan, that in 1979 was titled "Bold Mission Thrust," to take the gospel of Christ to every person on earth by the turn of the century.

17. Beginning in the 1960s and continuing into the 1990s, a theological/political campaign struggled for control of the resources and ideological direction of the Southern Baptist Convention. The fundamentalist takeover was achieved by the systematic election, beginning in 1979, of fundamentalists to lead the Southern Baptist Convention. Leaders they labeled theologically "moderate" or "liberal" were voted out of office. Fundamentalist leaders fired all "moderate" or "liberal" presidents, professors, and department heads of Southern Baptist seminaries, mission groups, and other convention-owned institutions and replaced them with fundamentalists. The fundamentalist takeover opposed the ordination of women and the equal leadership of women in church and home.

18. Rev. Dr. Molly Marshall, the first woman to teach theology at Southern Baptist Theological Seminary, was forced to resign in 1994. When she went to

Southern in 1984, she was also pastor of Jordan Baptist Church in Eagle Station, Kentucky. Fundamentalists in the Southern Baptist Convention criticized her and the seminary because she was an ordained woman and pastor, and scrutinized her writings, addresses, and lectures. Although she was granted tenure in 1988, a new fundamentalist president, Albert Mohler, came in 1993, and forced her to resign the next year. She is now president of Central Baptist Theological Seminary in Shawnee, Kansas, affiliated with the American Baptist Churches U.S.A. and the Cooperative Baptist Fellowship.

19. Albert Schweitzer, *The Quest of the Historical Jesus* (London: A. & C. Black, 1926).

20. Brian Wren (words) and Carlton R. Young (music), "Bring Many Names" (Carol Stream, IL: Hope, 1987).

21. Brian Wren, *What Language Shall I Borrow? God-Talk in Worship: A Male Response to Feminist Theology* (New York: Crossroad, 1990).

22. The Cooperative Baptist Fellowship (CBF), theologically moderate, withdrew in 1991 from the Southern Baptist Convention (SBC) over philosophical and theological differences, such as the SBC prohibition of women serving as pastors.

23. Galatians 3:28.

24. On April 20, 2001, at the annual Alliance of Baptists Convocation, held at Oakhurst Baptist Church, in Decatur, Georgia, I gave one of the covenant addresses, entitled "A Still More Excellent Way in Worship."

25. At the Convocation these two hymns were sung to traditional hymn tunes. Later, Larry wrote beautiful new tunes for each: "Sister Spirit, Brother Spirit," *Inclusive Hymns*, 1; "O Spirit of Power," *Inclusive Hymns*, 18.

26. The hymn version of "Are You Good and Are You Strong?" is published in *Inclusive Hymns*, 61, and the anthem version is published by Alfred Publishing Company (Los Angeles, CA, 2008).

27. "Gloria Patri"(Latin for "Glory Be to the Father") is a short hymn of praise used frequently in Christian liturgies. The traditional lyrics are "Glory be to the Father, and to the Son, and to the Holy Ghost. As it was in the beginning, is now and ever shall be, world without end."

28. Isaac Watts (1674 –1748) is called the "Father of English Hymnody," because he was the first prolific and popular English hymn writer, credited with about 750 hymns.

29. Brian Wren, *Praying Twice: The Music and Words of Congregational Song* (Louisville, KY: Westminster John Knox, 2000).

30. The musical setting is by Joseph M. Martin, *Song of Wisdom from "Old Turtle"* (Nashville: Shawnee, 2000.) The book is by Douglas Wood, with illustrations by Cheng-Khee Chee, *Old Turtle* (New York: Scholastic, 2007).

31. Rev. Dr. Carl Daw, an Episcopal priest and adjunct professor of hymnology at

Boston University School of Theology, was executive director of the Hymn Society in the United States and Canada from 1996 to 2009. See ch. 5, n. 18 above for an identification of Rev. Dr. Molly Marshall. Rev. Dr. Michael Hawn, professor of church music at Perkins School of Divinity, was president of the board of directors of Choristers Guild from 1990–92, 2001–3, and elected fellow of the Hymn Society in 2008.

32. "Mother God Goes to Children's Church," *SBC Life* (August 2004) 12.

33. Larry E. Schultz, "Whoever Welcomes You Welcomes Me" (Dallas: Choristers Guild, 2006).

34. Matthew 10:40.

35. Exodus 3:14.

36. Larry E. Schultz and Jann Aldredge-Clanton, *Sing and Dance and Play with Joy!: Inclusive Songs for Young Children* (Raleigh, NC: Lulu, 2009).

37. Larry E. Schultz, "Sing a Festive Song" (Dallas: Choristers Guild, 2003).

38. String theory is a developing theory in particle physics that attempts to reconcile quantum mechanics and general relativity. String theory proposes that the electrons and quarks within an atom are one-dimensional oscillating lines ("strings"). The theory proposes that these strings can vibrate. String theories also require the existence of several extra, unobservable dimensions to the universe, in addition to the usual three spatial dimensions. (Online: http://theory.tifr.res.in/~mukhi/Physics/string2.html; http://superstringtheory.com/basics/basic4.html)

39. Larry E. Schultz, "Composer of All the Music We Hear," *Inclusive Hymns for Liberation, Peace, and Justice* (Waco: Eakin, 2011) 42.

Chapter 6

1. Monica A. Coleman, *Making a Way Out of No Way: A Womanist Theology* (Minneapolis: Fortress, 2008) 170.

2. Octavia E. Butler, *Parable of the Sower* (New York: Four Walls Eight Windows, 1993).

3. Coleman, *Making a Way Out of No Way*, 142–43.

4. Ibid., 163.

5. Nancy H. McLaughlin, "Bennett Professor in Elite Group," *News & Record*, Greensboro, North Carolina (May 31, 2005) A4.

6. The Gold Award is the highest achievement within the Girl Scouts of the USA. Senior Girl Scouts aged 14–18 are eligible to earn this award. One of the requirements for the award is to plan and implement an action project that provides a lasting benefit to the girl's larger community.

7. *Lectio Divina*, a Latin term for "divine reading" or "holy reading," is a

traditional Christian practice of prayer and scripture reading intended to promote communion with the Divine and to increase knowledge of the Bible.

8. National Black Women's Health Project (NBWHP), founded in 1983 in Atlanta, Georgia, addresses health and reproductive rights of African American women. In 2002 the name was changed to the Black Women's Health Imperative.

9. Dr. Angela Yvonne Davis is a political activist, educator, and author, who worked in the civil rights movement and the Black Panther Party. She is the former director of the Feminist Studies Department of the University of California, Santa Cruz. Among her many published books is *Women, Race, & Class*.

10. Rev. Dr. Renita Weems, former professor at Vanderbilt University and visiting professor at Spelman College, has been celebrated by *Ebony Magazine* as one of America's top fifteen preachers, and is also widely acclaimed as a speaker and author. Among her many published books is *Just a Sister Away: Understanding the Timeless Connection between Women of Today and Women in the Bible*.

11. Dr. Evelyn Brooks Higginbotham, the Victor S. Thomas Professor of History and of African and African American Studies at Harvard University, has held the position of chair of the Department of African and African American Studies since 2006. Among her many publications is *Righteous Discontent: The Women's Movement in the Black Baptist Church: 1880–1920*.

12. Dr. Henry Louis Gates Jr., Alphonse Fletcher University Professor and Director of the W. E. B. Du Bois Institute for African and African American Research at Harvard University, is a noted literary critic, educator, scholar, and writer. Among his many publications is *Colored People: A Memoir*.

13. Dr. J. Lorand Matory, chair of the Department of African and African American Studies at Duke University, was formerly professor of anthropology and African and African American studies at Harvard University. Among his published books is *Black Atlantic Religion: Tradition, Transnationalism and Matriarchy in the Afro-Brazilian Candomblé*.

14. Rev. Dr. James Hale Cone, Charles Augustus Briggs Distinguished Professor of Systematic Theology at Union Theological Seminary in New York City, is an acclaimed proponent of Black liberation theology. Dr. Cone is best known for his groundbreaking works, *Black Theology & Black Power* and *A Black Theology of Liberation*.

15. Rev. Dr. Delores S. Williams, Paul Tillich Professor of Feminist Theology at Union Theological Seminary, is a prominent womanist theologian. Formerly an assistant professor of theology and culture at Drew University Divinity School, Dr. Williams presents a sociohistorical approach to womanist theology. Among her publications is *Sisters in the Wilderness: The Challenge of Womanist God-Talk*.

16. Dr. Victor Anderson, Oberlin Alumni Professor of Christian Ethics at Vanderbilt Divinity School, is also Professor of African American and Diaspora Studies and Religious Studies in the College of Arts and Sciences. Among his

publications is *Creative Exchange: A Constructive Theology of African American Religious Experience*.

17. Dr. Sallie McFague, Distinguished Theologian in Residence at Vancouver School of Theology and formerly Carpenter Professor of Theology at Vanderbilt Divinity School, is a feminist theologian, best known for her analysis of metaphor as central to the ways we speak about God. Among her many published books is *Models of God: Theology for an Ecological, Nuclear Age*.

18. Dr. Howard Harrod taught ethics and sociology of religion at Vanderbilt Divinity School and the Department of Religious Studies from 1968 until 2002. Among his many publications is *The Animals Came Dancing: Native American Sacred Ecology and Animal Kinship*.

19. Dr. Fernando Segovia, Oberlin Graduate Professor of New Testament and Early Christianity at Vanderbilt Divinity School, has served on the editorial boards of a variety of academic journals, has worked as consultant for foundations and publishing houses, and has lectured widely both nationally and internationally. Among his published works is *Decolonizing Biblical Studies: A View from the Margins*.

20. Monica A. Coleman, *The Dinah Project: A Handbook for Congregational Response to Sexual Violence* (Eugene, OR: Wipf & Stock, 2010; originally Cleveland, Ohio: Pilgrim, 2004) ix–x.

21. Ibid., x.

22. Ibid., xi.

23. Genesis 34 details the rape of Dinah, the only daughter of Leah and Jacob. Shechem raped Dinah and negotiated for a bride price. But Dinah's brothers, Simeon and Levi, in revenge killed Shechem, his father Hamor, and other males in the city.

24. Coleman, *The Dinah Project*, 8–9.

25. Process theology, influenced by the metaphysical process philosophy of Alfred North Whitehead and further developed by Charles Hartshorne, claims that God is changing, as is the universe. Process theology has been especially helpful in Rev. Dr. Coleman's work with survivors of violence because it is a religious perspective that affirms God's compassion in every event, believing that what we do and what creation does make a difference to God.

26. Circle of Grace Community Church in Atlanta, Georgia, is an inclusive Christian feminist worshipping community.

27. Nancy H. McLaughlin, "Bennett Professor in Elite Group," A5.

28. Ibid.

29. *Imago Dei* is a Latin term meaning "image of God."

30. The Woodhull Institute, a nonprofit organization that provides professional development and leadership training for women, teaches ethical conduct and the compassionate use of power.

31. Civic Frame is a nonprofit organization that uses art and intellectual work to encourage civic participation, media literacy, and critical thinking.

32. Beautiful Mind Blog: http://www.beautifulmindblog.com

33. Dr. David Ray Griffin is Professor of Philosophy of Religion and Theology, Emeritus, Claremont School of Theology and Claremont Graduate University, and codirector of the Center for Process Studies. His published books include *God, Power, and Evil: A Process Theology*.

34. Coleman, *Making a Way Out of No Way*, 167, 169–70.

Chapter 7

1. Marcia C. Fleischman, *Wild Woman Theology: In the Arms of Loving Mother God* (Bloomington, IN: AuthorHouse, 2009) iv.

2. Ibid., 125.

3. Prednisone is a corticosteroid immunosuppressive medicine that helps prevent organ rejection.

4. *Abba* is the word for "Father" or "Daddy," and *Amma* is the word for "Mother" in the Aramaic language Jesus spoke.

5. Campus Crusade for Christ, started in 1951 by Bill and Vonette Bright on the UCLA campus, developed a simple plan called the "Four Spiritual Laws" for use in Christian evangelism.

6. Broadway Church was "Broadway Baptist Church" until voted out of the Southern Baptist Convention in 2004. Broadway Church maintains ties to the Alliance of Baptists, progressive in theology and social stances.

7. Some people in charismatic traditions refer to this prayer language as "speaking in tongues."

8. From the 1930s to the 1960s, hundreds of towns across America had "sundown rules," preventing African Americans and other minorities from remaining in town past sundown. Such laws excluded them from living in the communities where they worked. Since the civil rights movement of the 1960s there have been laws against sundown towns and counties, but some, like Advance, Missouri, persisted after that time.

9. In Baptist tradition, ministers are ordained by local, autonomous Baptist churches. According to Baptist polity, any local Baptist church can vote to license and ordain a person to be a minister.

10. James 1:2.

11. ENFJ (Extraversion, iNtuition, Feeling, Judgment), an abbreviation used in the publications of the Myers-Briggs Type Indicator (MBTI), refers to one of sixteen personality types. The MBTI assessment was developed from the work of psychiatrist Carl G. Jung in his book *Psychological Types*. The ENFJ profile includes being

people-focused and believing in the possibilities of people. People with this profile have charisma and are focused on understanding, supporting, and encouraging others.

12. Marcia C. Fleischman, *Angels Everywhere* (Bloomington, IN: AuthorHouse, 2008) 26–28.

13. In Sue Monk Kidd's novel *The Secret Life of Bees* (New York: Penguin, 2002), the black Madonna is a powerful symbol of freedom and comfort for the three main characters—May, June, and August—and for their women friends who come to their home to worship Her.

14. Dennis Linn, Sheila Fabricant Linn, and Matthew Linn, *Good Goats: Healing Our Image of God* (Mahwah, NJ: Paulist, 1993).

15. Fred Phelps founded Westboro Baptist Church, an independent Baptist church based in Topeka, Kansas, which is notorious for anti-gay protests at churches, military funerals, gay pride gatherings, and political gatherings.

16. "The Girl Effect" affirms the ability of adolescent girls in developing countries to bring social and economic change to their families, communities, and countries. There are 600 million adolescent girls living in poverty in the developing world. "The Girl Effect" happens when these girls have safe places to meet, education, legal protection, health care, and job skills training. Then they thrive, and everyone around them benefits.

17. Greg Mortensen, *Three Cups of Tea: One Man's Mission to Promote Peace. . . . One School at a Time* (New York: Penguin, 2007).

18. Fleischman, *Wild Woman Theology: In the Arms of Loving Mother God*, 1–2.

Chapter 8

1. In 1999 in Portland, Maine, Rev. Virginia Marie Rincon founded *TengoVoz* ("I have voice") to advocate for Latina women and children and to facilitate women's groups. *TengoVoz* also presents lectures on the prevention of domestic violence; provides crisis intervention; organizes and collaborates in rallies and peace vigils related to immigrant rights, domestic violence issues, and racial profiling; translates and interprets documents; provides life skills coaching; and organizes cultural events, such as *Dia de Los Muertos*.

2. The *Virgen de Guadalupe* ("Virgin of Guadalupe"), also known as *Nuestra Señora de Guadalupe* ("Our Lady of Guadalupe"), is the most popular religious and cultural image in Mexico and is growing in popularity in the United States. According to tradition, Juan Diego, an indigenous peasant, saw a vision of a young woman near Mexico City on December 9, 1531. He told the local bishop, who asked for some proof. Three days later, the image of the brown-skinned Mary appeared miraculously on his cloak when he was showing it to the bishop. The *Virgen de Guadalupe* continues to be a mixture of the Aztec and other cultures that blended

to form Mexico. Some anthropologists believe that Our Lady of Guadalupe is a Christianized "Tonantzin," a general title for female deities in Aztec culture, used to convert the Aztecs to Christianity. (Online: http://www.mexconnect.com/articles/2614-our-lady-of-guadalupe-tonantzin-or-the-virgin-mary)

3. The *Virgen de San Juan* ("Virgin of San Juan") has shrines in San Juan de los Lagos in the state of Jalisco in central Mexico, and in San Juan, Texas. The shrine in San Juan de los Lagos is one of the most popular pilgrimage shrines in Mexico, and the shrine in Texas is one of the most visited in the United States. Devotion to the *Virgen de San Juan* began after the Spanish conquest of Mexico, when Spanish missionaries placed a small image of the immaculate conception in the church of San Juan de los Lagos. In 1623, a family of traveling acrobats stopped in this town to give a performance. While practicing their act, the youngest daughter lost her balance and was killed. A woman who was the caretaker of the church placed the image of the Virgin Mary over the girl's body and prayed for the Virgin's intercession. The child came back to life. As word spread of the miracle, devotion to the *Virgen de San Juan* grew. (Online: http://www.olsjbasilica.org/web/static/history)

4. A *mujerista* is a person who works for equal economic, social, political, and religious opportunities for Latina women. The work of Dr. Ada María Isasi-Díaz established the field of study that she named "*mujerista* theology." In her book entitled *Mujerista Theology: A Theology for the Twenty-First Century* (Maryknoll, NY: Orbis, 1996) she states: "The goals of *mujerista* theology have always been these: to provide a platform for the voices of Latina grassroots women; to develop a theological method that takes seriously the religious understandings and practices of Latinas as a source for theology; to challenge theological understandings, church teaching, and religious practices that oppress Latina women, that are not life-giving, and, therefore, cannot be theologically correct" (1).

5. A *curandera*, literally translated "healer," is a traditional folk healer or shaman in Latino/a culture, who is dedicated to curing physical or spiritual illnesses. Many curanderos/as use Catholic elements, such as holy water and saints' pictures, along with other cultural religious elements. They are respected as deeply religious and spiritual members of the community.

6. *Curandismo*, traditional Latino/a medicine used to supplement conventional medicine, is a mind-body-spirit healing approach steeped in ceremony.

7. José Doroteo Arango Arámbula, better known as Pancho Villa, was one of the most prominent Mexican generals during the revolution from 1910 to roughly 1920.

8. The Denver Developmental Screening Test (DDST), commonly known as the Denver Scale, is widely used for screening cognitive and behavioral problems in preschool children; it is administered by a health or social service professional.

9. *Cursillos de Cristiandad* (short course of Christianity), a ministry of the Roman Catholic Church, was started in 1944 by a group of laypeople in Spain. It has since been used by other Christian denominations, some of which have modified its

methods and name. The three-day-weekend courses, led by priests and laypeople, focus on personal spiritual development and show laypeople how to become effective leaders.

10. Seminary of the Southwest, formerly known as Episcopal Theological Seminary of the Southwest, is located in Austin, Texas.

11. Rev. Alison Cheek, who served as director of the feminist liberation theology program at Episcopal Divinity School, was one of the first eleven women (and the first Australian woman) to be ordained priest in the Episcopal Church.

12. On July 29, 1974, the first eleven women were ordained to the Episcopal priesthood in Philadelphia. This ordination, performed by bishops who had retired or resigned, was denounced as "irregular," and these women became known as the "Philadelphia Eleven": Merrill Bittner, Alison Cheek, Alla Bozarth, Emily C Hewitt, Carter Heyward, Suzanne R. Hiatt, Marie Moorefield, Jeanette Piccard, Betty Bone Schiess, Katrina Welles Swanson, and Nancy Hatch Witting. In September 1976, the General Convention of the Episcopal Church approved the ordination of women to the priesthood.

13. Dr. Joanna Dewey, currently the Harvey H. Guthrie, Jr. Professor Emerita of Biblical Studies at Episcopal Divinity School, is a specialist in the Gospel of Mark and in feminist approaches to the New Testament. Her publications include *Mark as Story* (with David Rhoads).

14. Dr. Kwok Pui-lan, William F. Cole Professor of Christian Theology and Spirituality at Episcopal Divinity School, is an internationally known scholar and pioneer in Asian feminist theology and postcolonial theology. Among her many published works is *Postcolonial Imagination and Feminist Theology*.

15. The third eye, also known as the inner eye, is a mystical concept in some spiritual traditions. It is also referred to as the gate that leads to inner realms and higher consciousness.

16. Gustavo Gutiérrez, *A Theology of Liberation: History, Politics, and Salvation*, (Maryknoll, NY: Orbis, 1988).

17. Rev. Dr. Harvey Cox, who served as Hollis Research Professor of Divinity at Harvard Divinity School, became widely known as a theologian with the publication of *The Secular City* in 1965.

18. The Rt. Rev. M. Thomas Shaw was consecrated a bishop in 1994 and became the fifteenth bishop of Massachusetts in 1995.

19. The North American Free Trade Agreement (NAFTA), signed by the governments of Canada, Mexico, and the United States, was implemented in 1994 to create a trilateral trade bloc in North America.

20. Greenfire Retreat Center in Tenants Harbor, Maine, from 1991 to 2008 offered a place for renewal and inspiration for women from any faith tradition.

21. Rev. Dr. Carter Heyward has served as professor of theology at Episcopal

Divinity School and liturgical coordinator of the Mountain Mission of St. Clare: An Episcopal Chapel of Peace. Among her many publications is *Touching Our Strength: The Erotic as Power and the Love of God.*

22. Martin Luther King Jr., "Letter from Birmingham Jail (April 16, 1963)," in *Why We Can't Wait* (New York: Penguin Books, 1964).

23. Mount Holyoke College in South Hadley, Massachusetts, a research liberal arts college, is renowned for educating women leaders.

24. The term "postulant" is most common in the Roman Catholic and Anglican churches to describe the ecclesiastical status of a person who has discerned a call to the priesthood and received parish and diocesan endorsement. The candidate retains postulant status until ordination to the transitional diaconate.

25. The vestry is an administrative body in an Episcopal parish composed of the rector and a group of elected parishioners.

26. In the Episcopal Church, the canon to the ordinary functions in support of the bishop in his or her oversight in the diocese and the wider church. The canon is like a chief of staff.

27. Rev. Virginia Marie Rincon, "The Human Face of Immigration," Church World Service Immigration and Refugee Program Blog (July 12, 2010) 3. Online: http://supportimmigrationreform.org/blog/the-human-face-of-immigration/.

28. Rev. Virginia Marie Rincon, "TengoVoz: The Power of Voice," *Maine Women's Journal* (Summer 2005) 52.

29. Rt. Rev. Barbara Clementine Harris, ordained Suffragan Bishop of the Episcopal Diocese of Massachusetts on February 11, 1989, was the first woman bishop in the Worldwide Anglican Communion.

30. The Rt. Rev. Chilton R. Knudsen was elected Bishop of Maine in November 1997, the only woman among a slate of five nominees.

31. Kristen Muszynski, "Rev. Virginia Marie Rincon Looks to Foster Latino Connection," *Biddeford Journal Tribune* (September 24, 2005) C4.

32. Episcopal Migration Ministry (EMM) is one of nine national agencies working in partnership with the U.S. Department of State, local faith groups, and community organizations to assist refugees.

33. Savae and San Antonio Vocal Arts Ensemble, "Guadalupe: Virgen de los Indios," Audio CD (San Antonio: Talking Taco/Iago, 1999).

34. Nahuatl, a Uto-Aztecan language, is spoken by an estimated 1.5 million people who live mainly in Central Mexico. Since about the seventh century CE, it was the language of the Aztecs. With the introduction of the Latin alphabet, Nahuatl also became a literary language. Online: http://www.omniglot.com/writing/nahuatl.htm.

35. Savae Vocal Ensemble and San Antonio Vocal Arts Ensemble, "Native

Angels: Musical Miracles from the New World," Audio CD (San Antonio: Iago Records, 1996).

36. Justin Ellis, "Children Replay Miracle," *Portland Press Herald* (December 13, 2006) B1.

37. Dennis Hoey, "Latino Community Rallies as Man Faces Deportation," *Portland Press Herald* (May 27, 2010).

38. Rincon, "The Human Face of Immigration," 1–2.

39. Arizona Senate Bill 1070 (the Support Our Law Enforcement and Safe Neighborhoods Act), the nation's toughest bill on illegal immigration, aims to identify, prosecute, and deport illegal immigrants. The bill, signed by Arizona governor, Jan Brewer, on April 23, 2010, brought immediate protests and reignited the divisive battle over immigration reform nationally. SB 1070 goes beyond federal law to make it a state misdemeanor crime for an immigrant to be in Arizona without carrying the required documents.

40. The Rev. Canon Mary Moreno Richardson, Coordinator for Hispanic Ministry at St. Paul's Cathedral and the first Latina priest ordained in the Diocese of San Diego, is the creator and director of the Guadalupe Art Program, a spiritual empowerment program for Latina youth using art, dance, and music.

Chapter 9

1. Deborah Sokolove is the director of the Henry Luce III Center for the Arts and Religion at Wesley Theological Seminary, where she also teaches courses in art and worship.

2. John 8:12.

3. Matthew 5:14.

4. Earl Nightingale was a well-known motivational speaker, author, and radio host. His radio program, "Our Changing World," became highly popular in the United States and in many other countries.

5. Agoraphobia is an anxiety disorder, traditionally thought to involve a fear of open or public places; however, it is now believed that agoraphobia develops as a complication of panic attacks.

6. The International Order of St. Luke the Physician is a worldwide interdenominational body of Christians who believe that the healing of the body, mind, and spirit is a vital part of the total ministry of Jesus Christ.

7. Enneagram, a psychospiritual model of personality types, is an application of the nine-pointed enneagram geometric figure in relation to personality. Each of the nine Enneagram personality types expresses a distinctive and habitual pattern of thinking and feeling.

8. See ch. 4, n. 6.

9. Paul Smith, *The Church with Something to Offend Almost Everyone: Reflections on Twenty-Five Years of Renewal at Broadway* (Kansas City: Paul R. Smith, 1992) 70.

10. Unlike some denominations, Baptists don't consider ordination a sacrament of the church. According to Baptist polity, each local church is autonomous and can choose whether or not to ordain women. The first Southern Baptist church to ordain a woman as pastor was Watts Street Baptist Church in Durham, North Carolina, ordaining Rev. Addie Davis in 1964. In 1965, the American Baptist Convention adopted a resolution advocating the ordination of women. In 1984, the Southern Baptist Convention adopted a resolution opposing the ordination of women. Since resolutions are not binding on churches within these Baptist conventions, the practice of ordination varies.

11. Unity, a worldwide Christian organization, also known as the Unity School of Christianity and informally as Unity Church, was founded in Kansas City, MO, in 1889 by Charles and Myrtle Fillmore.

12. In his book *Integral Christianity: The Spirit's Call to Evolve* (St. Paul, MN: Paragon, 2011), Paul Smith elaborates a mystical spirituality, applying integral philosophy to Christian faith and practice.

13. Paul R. Smith, *Is It Okay to Call God "Mother"?: Considering the Feminine Face of God* (Peabody, MA: Hendrickson, 1993).

14. In 1998, Broadway Baptist Church published a Bible study book by Paul Smith, entitled *The Bible and Homosexuality: Affirming All Sexual Orientations as Gifts from God*.

15. Peggy Campolo, a progressive reformer of evangelical Christianity, supports full equality for LGBT persons within church and society, including marriage rights for homosexual couples.

16. Rev. Dr. Paul Simpson Duke and Rev. Stacey Simpson Duke are copastors of First Baptist Church, Ann Arbor, Michigan, and campus ministers for the American Baptist Campus Foundation at the University of Michigan.

17. In 2007, Broadway Church published a Bible study book by Paul Smith, entitled *Hell? No!: A Bible Study on Why No One Will Be Left Behind*.

18. Kenneth Earl Wilber II developed what he called "Integral Theory" and in 1998 founded the Integral Institute for teaching and applying this theory. His work integrates knowledge from psychology, business, politics, science, and spirituality.

19. The transfiguration of Jesus is recorded in Matthew 17:1–13; Mark 9:1–13; and Luke 9:27–36.

20. Matthew 17:2.

21. Paul Smith, *Integral Christianity*.

22. Meister Eckhart (Eckhart von Hochheim) was an influential fourteenth-century German philosopher, theologian, and mystic, writing on spiritual psychology and metaphysics. His work is noted for mythic, metaphorical content.

Notes to Chapter 10

23. St. Theresa of Ávila was a prominent sixteenth-century Spanish mystic, reformer, Carmelite nun, writer of the Counter-Reformation, and theologian of contemplative prayer.

24. John 10:34 records Jesus' answer to those who accused him of blasphemy for claiming to be God's Son: "Is it not written in your law, 'I said, you are gods'?" Jesus here refers to Psalm 82:6: "I say, 'You are gods, children of the Most High, all of you.'"

25. Smith, *Is It Okay to Call God "Mother"?*, 104–5.

26. Ibid., 256, 261.

27. Ibid., 273.

28. Paul R. Smith, "The Cover-up of the Divine Feminine: Is It Okay to Call God, 'Goddess'?" Address, Broadway Church, Kansas City, MO, June 18, 2006. Online: http://www.revpaulsmith.com/ ("Teachings"); http://www.feniva.com/prs/teachings/DaVinciCode3.PDF.

29. Dan Brown, *The Da Vinci Code* (New York: Bantam Dell, 2003).

30. St. Gregory of Nyssa, a fourth-century Catholic bishop, contributed to the doctrine of the Trinity and to the theology of God as infinite. Gregory and his brothers, Basil of Caesarea and Gregory of Nazianzus, are known as the Cappadocian Fathers.

31. Focus on the Family, an evangelical organization founded in 1977 by James Dobson, is based in Colorado Springs, Colorado. This organization promotes social conservative public policy, strongly opposing LGBT rights and same-sex marriage.

Chapter 10

1. See ch.1, n.3.

2. A chasuble is the outer liturgical vestment worn over the alb by clergy for the celebration of the Eucharist in churches that use full vestments, primarily in Roman Catholic, Anglican, and Lutheran churches.

3. Carolyn McDade, "This Ancient Love," *As We So Love* (Blue Jaye, 1996).

4. Carolyn McDade, "O Beautiful Gaia," *Love Songs to Earth* (Carolyn McDade, 2003).

5. J. Philip Newell, *Ground of All Being: The Prayer of Jesus in Color* (San Antonio: New Beginnings, 2008).

6. Luke 10:30–37.

7. Nicholas D. Kristof and Sheryl WuDunn, *Half the Sky: Turning Oppression into Opportunity for Women Worldwide* (New York: Knopf, 2009).

8. *Viriditas*, a Latin word that literally means "greenness," was one of Hildegard's guiding images.

9. From a brochure on "The Viriditas Project" of St. Hildegard's Community, funded by a grant from Trinity Episcopal Church of New York

10. Celtic Christianity is a strand of the Christian tradition that developed in Ireland and Britain during the Early Middle Ages. Current reconstruction of Celtic theology includes God's goodness in all creation, humanity made in the divine image, God's constant presence, and seeking authentic holy community (http://www.celticchristianitytoday.org/Home_Page.php).

11. Ordinary Time, a season of the liturgical calendar, comprises the period following Epiphany (January 6) and the period following Pentecost (seven weeks after Easter) which do not fall under the special seasons of Advent, Christmas, Lent, or Easter. The liturgical color usually assigned to Ordinary Time is green.

12. See ch. 8, n. 10.

13. The Book of Common Prayer (BCP) is the title of a number of prayer books of the Church of England and of other Anglican churches; these prayer books contain the words of structured liturgical services of worship. The current BCP of the U.S. Episcopal Church was adopted in 1979, and the supplemental Enriching Our Worship, in 1998.

14. CARE, a humanitarian organization fighting global poverty, places special focus on working alongside poor women because of the belief that women have the power to help whole families and entire communities escape poverty.

15. See ch. 8, n. 25.

16. The Camp Allen Conference and Retreat Center is an institution of the Episcopal Diocese of Texas.

17. See ch. 8, n. 12.

18. See ch. 8, n. 24.

19. Elisabeth Schüssler Fiorenza, *In Memory of Her: A Feminist Theological Reconstruction of Christian Origins* (New York: Crossroad, 1989).

20. Rosemary Radford Ruether, *Women-Church: Theology & Practice* (San Francisco: Harper & Row, 1986).

21. Ibid., 223–28.

22. Elizabeth O'Connor, *Cry Pain, Cry Hope: Thresholds to Purpose* (Waco, TX: Word, 1987).

23. Gordon and Mary Cosby founded Church of the Savior, which includes the Servant Leadership School, Dayspring Retreat Center, Wellspring Retreat Center, a coffeehouse, and many other ministries.

24. The transept is the area set crosswise to the main body of the church in a cruciform building in Romanesque and Gothic church architecture.

25. Verna J. Dozier, *The Authority of the Laity* (Washington, DC: Alban Institute, 1984); *The Calling of the Laity* (Alban Institute, 1988).

26. Verna J. Dozier, *The Dream of God: A Call to Return* (Cambridge, MA: Cowley, 1991).

27. Elizabeth A. Johnson, *She Who Is: The Mystery of God in Feminist Theological Discourse* (New York: Crossroad, 1992).

28. Matthew 9:17.

29. Walter Wink, *Engaging the Powers: Discernment and Resistance in a World of Domination* (Minneapolis: Fortress, 1992).

30. Judith Liro, "Community, Creativity, Contemplation, and Call as a Feminist Spiritual Path," *EEWC Update* 29, no. 1 (Spring 2005) 13–14.

31. The General Convention, the Episcopal Church's governing body that meets every three years, includes the House of Deputies and the House of Bishops. The work at Convention is carried out by deputies, who are elected from their dioceses and include both clergy and laypeople, and by bishops, representing each diocese.

32. Dr. Dorothee Soelle, a liberation theologian who was a professor of systematic theology at Union Theological Seminary in New York City, wrote numerous books, including *The Strength of the Weak: Toward a Christian Feminist Identity*.

33. See ch. 8, nn. 12 and 21.

34. Dr. Beverly Wildung Harrison, professor of ethics at Union Theological Seminary for thirty-four years, authored books including *Justice in the Making: Feminist Social Ethics*.

35. See ch. 8, n. 20.

36. A shortened form of this parable was later published in an article about a lecture Dr. Marjorie Procter-Smith gave at Episcopal Theological Seminary of the Southwest. Rev. Judith Liro, "Christian, Feminist & Emancipatory," *Ratherview* 29, no. 1 (Fall 2006) 10.

37. The Trinity Grant is one of the primary, most prestigious grants for the Episcopal Church. The Trinity Grants Program, part of Trinity Episcopal Church in New York City, is one of America's oldest philanthropies.

38. The Viriditas Project is a curriculum created by St. Hildegard's Community to form spiritual leaders to serve their faith communities and to work for justice and healing for the world. The curriculum offers six ten-week core classes in spring and fall over three years, and two four-day summer retreats.

39. *Austin Tan Cerca de la Frontera* (ATCF: "Austin So Close to the Border") began in 1999 as an activist project of American Friends Service Committee (AFSC), a Quaker organization that includes people of various faiths who are committed to social justice, peace, and humanitarian service. In 2010, AFSC closed the Austin office, and ATCF is now an independent non-profit organization, sending delegations to border cities to meet with workers.

40. John Philip Newell, a poet and teacher who formerly served with his wife

Alison as co-warden of Iona Abbey in the Western Isles of Scotland, is internationally acclaimed for his work in the field of Celtic spirituality.

41. Liro, "Community, Creativity, Contemplation, and Call as a Feminist Spiritual Path," 14.

Chapter 11

1. Youth for Christ is an evangelical Protestant organization working with young people around the globe.

2. See Introduction, n. 2.

3. The Evangelical & Ecumenical Women's Caucus (EEWC) is a nonprofit organization of Christian feminists: women and men who believe that the Bible supports the equality of the sexes. It was originally named the Evangelical Women's Caucus (EWC) because it began in 1973 as a caucus within Evangelicals for Social Action. In 1990, "Ecumenical" was added to the organization's name to make it clear that members from all faiths are welcome. The organization's quarterly publication, *EEWC Update*, edited by Letha Dawson Scanzoni, changed its name to *Christian Feminism Today* in 2006.

4. In 1861, Presbyterians in the South split from the original PCUSA, forming the Presbyterian Church in the Confederate States of America, which became the Presbyterian Church in the United States (PCUS) after the Civil War. In 1983, the PCUS, whose churches were located in the Southern and border states, merged with the United Presbyterian Church in the United States of America (UPCUSA) to form the Presbyterian Church (USA).

5. Groups of local Presbyterian churches are united in accountability to a regional body called a "presbytery." Presbyteries are made up of a minister and an elder from each parish, as well as other clergy such as college theology professors, chaplains, and retired ministers.

6. The session, the governing body in each local Presbyterian church, is composed of the pastor and elected elders.

7. Miriam Therese Winter, illustrated by Meinrad Craighead, *WomanPrayer, WomanSong: Resources for Ritual* (Oak Park, IL: Meyer Stone, 1987; reprinted, Eugene, OR: Wipf & Stock, 2008).

8. Clarissa Pinkola Estés, *Women Who Run with the Wolves: Myths and Stories of the Wild Woman Archetype* (New York: Ballantine, 1992, 1996).

9. Rebecca L. Kiser-Lowrance, "God of the Casserole," *Update: Newsletter of the Evangelical & Ecumenical Women's Caucus* 19, no. 2 (Summer 1995) 2.

10. Ibid., 3.

11. Ibid., 2–3.

12. *Horizons: The Magazine for Presbyterian Women* provides information,

inspiration, and education on current issues dealing with family life, the mission of the church, and the challenges of culture. The magazine also includes a Bible study, written by leading theologians and pastors in the Reformed tradition.

13. In response to the World Council of Churches Ecumenical Decade: Churches in Solidarity with Women, three Minnesota councils of churches hosted in 1993 an international theological conference called "Re-Imagining." The conference brought together female theologians, clergy, and laypeople to examine ideas about God and the church born out of women's experience. Approximately two thousand people attended, from forty-nine states and twenty-seven countries and forty denominations. The conference sparked controversy and became national news. It was identified by *The Christian Century* as one of the top religion stories of the year. The conference led to the creation of the Re-Imagining Community, which held several more conferences and published a quarterly journal.

14. Mary Jo Cartledgehayes, *Grace: A Memoir* (New York: Crown, 2003).

15. Rebecca L. Kiser, "Interacting with *Grace*," *EEWC Update: Newsletter of the Evangelical & Ecumenical Women's Caucus* 26, no. 4 (Winter 2003) 4–5.

16. In 1968, the Presbyterian Lay Committee, an advocacy group supporting conservative positions within the denomination, began the publication of *The Layman*. Today this journal is mailed to 100,000 Presbyterian households worldwide, but the Presbyterian Lay Committee has lost its official connection to the denomination.

17. Rebecca L. Kiser, "Birth Prayer," *Re-Imagining: Quarterly Newsletter of the Re-Imagining Community* 15 (May 1998) 11.

18. Martha Ann Kirk wrote the lyrics, and Colleen Fulmer composed the music for "Washerwoman God." Dr. Martha Ann Kirk, a member of the Sisters of Charity of the Incarnate Word, is a professor of religious studies at the University of the Incarnate Word in San Antonio, Texas, where she also directs an outreach program with story, drama, and dance focusing on issues of justice and peace. Among her publications is *Women of Bible Lands: A Pilgrimage to Compassion and Wisdom*. Colleen Fulmer is a singer, composer, liturgist, retreat director, and Methodist minister. Her collections of songs, which develop themes of justice and peace, include *Dancing Sophia's Circle: We Bring Who We Are*.

19. "Manse" is a term Presbyterians use for a house provided for a minister; some denominations call this house a "parsonage."

20. Founded in 1946, Ten Thousand Villages, one of the world's largest fair trade organizations and a founding member of the World Fair Trade Organization, is a nonprofit program of the Mennonite Central Committee and strives to improve the lives of thousands of disadvantaged artisans in thirty-eight countries.

21. Kiser, "Interacting with *Grace*," 6.

22. Rev. Dr. Matthew Fox, formerly in the Roman Catholic Dominican order, was an early and influential exponent of creation spirituality. In 1993, Catholic

authorities ordered his expulsion from the Dominican order on charges that he was a "feminist theologian," called God "Mother," preferred the concept of "original blessing" over original sin, worked too closely with Native American spiritual practices, and didn't condemn homosexuality. In 1994, Fox was ordained an Episcopal priest, and in 1996, he founded the University of Creation Spirituality in Oakland.

23. Becky Kiser-Lowrance, "Lessons from a Fearful Venturer," *Update: Newsletter of the Evangelical & Ecumenical Women's Caucus* 20, no. 4 (Winter 1996–97) 1.

24. Matthew Fox, *The Coming of the Cosmic Christ: The Healing of Mother Earth and the Birth of a Global Renaissance* (San Francisco: Harper & Row, 1988).

25. Dr. Brian Swimme, director of the Center for the Story of the Universe at the California Institute of Integral Studies, has authored books on cosmology, evolution, and religion and was featured in the television series "Soul of the Universe."

26. Brian Swimme, *The Hidden Heart of the Cosmos: Humanity and the New Story* (Maryknoll, NY: Orbis, 1999).

27. Dr. Clarissa Pinkola Estés, poet and psychoanalyst, is Managing Editor for TheModeratevoice.com, a news and political blog, and a columnist on issues of social justice, spirituality, and culture for the *National Catholic Reporter*. Among her numerous publications is *Women Who Run with the Wolves: Myths and Stories about the Wild Woman Archetype*.

28. Dr. Andrew Harvey, religious scholar and teacher of mystic traditions, is the founder of the Sacred Activism movement, serves as the director of the Institute of Sacred Activism, and is the author of numerous books, including *The Return of the Mother*.

29. Rev. Dr. Hal Taussig, visiting professor of New Testament at Union Theological Seminary and copastor of the Chestnut Hill United Methodist Church in Philadelphia, is a founding member of the Jesus Seminar, and the cochair of a national seminar of the Society of Biblical Literature. His numerous books include *A New Spiritual Home: Progressive Christianity at the Grass Roots* and *Wisdom's Feast: Sophia in Study and Celebration* (with Susan Cole and Marian Ronan).

30. Sister José Hobday, a Seneca elder and sister of the Franciscan order, was one of America's most popular speakers on prayer and spirituality. Her publications include *Simple Living: The Path to Joy and Freedom*.

31. Rev. Dr. Jeremy Taylor, founding member and past president of the Association for the Study of Dreams, has written books integrating dream symbolism, mythology, and archetypal energy, including *The Wisdom of Your Dreams: Using Dreams to Tap into Your Unconscious and Transform Your Life*.

32. David Abram, *The Spell of the Sensuous: Perception and Language in a More-Than-Human World* (New York: Vintage Books, 1997).

33. Bruce Silverman is a drummer, teacher, counselor, music therapist, workshop leader, and ritual maker who founded and has directed the Sons and Daughters of Orpheus, a community of artist-healers.

34. Dr. David Abram, founder and creative director of the Alliance for Wild Ethics, is a cultural ecologist, philosopher, and performance artist. Among his many publications is *Becoming Animal: An Earthly Cosmology.*

35. Matthew Fox proposes that the spiritual life develops along these four paths: *Via Postiva* (wonder) and *Via Negativa* (emptying), resulting in *Via Creativa* (newness) and *Via Transformativa* (justice).

36. Rev. Mary Newbern-Williams, General Presbyter of John Calvin Presbytery, had served as the Associate General Presbyter of the Presbytery of Eastern Virginia. The General Presbyter, often called the Executive Presbyter, performs the administrative duties of the presbytery, often with the additional role of a pastor to the pastors.

37. Rev. Susan Cady Cole has served as pastor of Arch Street United Methodist Church in Philadelphia and in other churches. Among her publications are *Sophia: The Future of Feminist Spirituality* (with Hal Taussig and Marian Ronan) and *Wisdom's Feast: Sophia in Study and Celebration* (with Hal Taussig and Marian Ronan).

38. Miriam Therese Winter, Adair Lummis, and Allison Stokes, *Defecting in Place: Women Claiming Responsibility for Their Own Spiritual Lives* (New York: Crossroad, 1994). This study, based on a survey of more than 7,000 women, reveals some of the pervasiveness of women's feelings of alienation from patriarchal religion, their response in revisioning divine imagery and church, their seeking nurturing in ecumenical women's groups, and their continued involvement in their own denominations.

39. Rev. David Greene was Associate General Presbyter in the Presbytery of Eastern Virginia, when Rev. Kiser served there.

40. Sallie McFague, *Metaphorical Theology: Models of God in Religious Language* (Philadelphia: Fortress, 1982).

41. Carolyn Jane Bohler, *God the What?: What Our Metaphors for God Reveal about Our Beliefs in God* (Woodstock, VT: Skylight Paths, 2008).

42. *Christian Feminism Today* (formerly *EEWC Update*) 33, no. 3 (fall 2009) 4.

Chapter 12

1. Acts 2:1–21.

2. Carl P. Daw, "Like the Murmur of the Dove's Song" (Carol Stream, IL: Hope Publishing Company, 1982). The Pullen congregation sang the hymn from *Chalice Hymnal* (St. Louis: Chalice, 1995) 245.

3. Larry E. Schultz, "I'm Coming to Gather All Peoples of Earth," *Celebrating Grace Hymnal* (Macon, GA: Celebrating Grace, 2010) 696.

4. Jann Aldredge-Clanton, "Be Still and Know," *Inclusive Hymns for Liberating*

Christians (Austin: Eakin) 56.

5. Geothermal power is extracted from heat stored in the earth. This geothermal energy comes from the original formation of the planet, from radioactive decay of minerals, and from volcanic activity. Geothermal power is cost effective, sustainable, and environmentally friendly. (Online: http://www.geothermal-energy.org/) For the Pullen church buildings, wells were drilled about 100 feet deep. Geothermal pumps heat and cool the buildings. In the winter, the geothermal pump removes heat from a heat exchanger and pumps it into the indoor air delivery system. In the summer, the process is reversed.

6. Dr. Elizabeth Barnes, the only female theologian on the faculty of Southeastern Baptist Theological Seminary for many years, became one of the targets of the fundamentalists in the 1980s. She later taught at Baptist Theological Seminary at Richmond.

7. Dr. Robert Ernst "Bob" Poerschke, spent over two decades as a professor of Christian education at Southeastern Baptist Theological Seminary.

8. Dr. Alan Neely served as a professor of missions at Southeastern Baptist Theological Seminary from 1976 to 1988, and then joined the faculty of Princeton Theological Seminary. Among his publications is *A New Call to Mission: Help for Perplexed Churches*.

9. Martin Luther King Jr., "Letter from Birmingham Jail (April 16, 1963)," in *Why We Can't Wait* (New York: Penguin, 1964).

10. Mahan Siler, *Letters to Nancy: Reflections on Pastoral Ministry* (Eugene, OR: Wipf & Stock, 2001).

11. See Introduction, n. 17.

12. In the fall of 2009, newly elected Wake County school board members began plans to end thirty years of policy designed to promote school diversity. They proposed to eliminate references to diversity in the student assignment policy and move the state's largest district toward neighborhood schools. Critics immediately saw this change as leading to racial resegregation.

13. Nancy Petty, "Backsliding in the Wake County Schools," Raleigh *News & Observer* (January 29, 2010).

14. Historic Thousands on Jones Street (HK on J) is a movement spearheaded by the North Carolina NAACP that unites more than 100 progressive organizations from across the state that are active in a number of different issues, including workers' rights, the environment, and civil rights. Each year, thousands of people from across the state gather in Raleigh to march to the State Legislature on Jones Street and to rally in support of a fourteen-point People's Agenda for social justice. Over the past four years since it began, the HK on J movement has helped to win many progressive reforms in North Carolina.

15. Thomas Goldsmith and T. Keung Hui, "School Board Sit-in Ends with Arrests," Raleigh *News & Observer* (June 16, 2010).

16. Luke 1:52.

Conclusion

1. Sue Monk Kidd, *Firstlight: The Early Inspirational Writings of Sue Monk Kidd* (New York: Guideposts, 2006) 8.

2. Winter, Lummis, and Stokes, *Defecting in Place*.

3. Letha Dawson Scanzoni, "Why We Need Evangelical Feminists," in *New Feminist Christianity: Many Voices, Many Views*, eds. Mary E. Hunt and Diann L. Neu (Woodstock, VT: Skylight Paths, 2010) 73.

4. Deborah Sokolove, "More Than Words," in *New Feminist Christianity*, 186.

5. Marjorie Procter-Smith, *Praying with Our Eyes Open: Engendering Feminist Liturgical Prayer* (Nashville: Abington, 1995) 37.

6. Marjorie Procter-Smith, *The Church in Her House: A Feminist Emancipatory Prayer Book for Christian Communities* (Cleveland: Pilgrim, 2008) x.

7. Ursula K. LeGuin, quoted in Christina Baldwin's *Storycatcher* (Novato, CA: New World Library, 2005) 44.

8. Dorothy Allison, *Two or Three Things I Know for Sure* (New York: Plume, 1996) 72.

www.ingramcontent.com/pod-product-compliance
Lightning Source LLC
Chambersburg PA
CBHW020605300426
44113CB00007B/518